Immigrants and Minorities, Politics and Policy

For further volumes:
http://www.springer.com/series/8832

David L. Leal · Stephen J. Trejo
Editors

Latinos and the Economy

Integration and Impact in Schools, Labor
Markets, and Beyond

 Springer

Editors
David L. Leal
Department of Government
University of Texas at Austin
1 University Station A1800
Austin, TX 78712-0119, USA
dleal@austin.utexas.edu

Stephen J. Trejo
Department of Economics
University of Texas at Austin
1 University Station C3100
Austin, TX 78712-0301, USA
trejo@austin.utexas.edu

ISBN 978-1-4419-6681-0   e-ISBN 978-1-4419-6682-7
DOI 10.1007/978-1-4419-6682-7
Springer New York Dordrecht Heidelberg London

Printed on acid-free paper

Springer is part of Springer Science+Business Media (www.springer.com)

This is the volume to read for anyone interested in current American immigration issues or the role of Hispanics in the US economy.

Daniel S. Hamermesh
Killam Professor of Economics
University of Texas, Austin, TX, USA

The future of America is closely intertwined with the successful integration—economically, politically, and socially—of the Latino population. Latinos now comprise one of every seven workers and almost one of every five students in the United States. The research reported in this volume describes the challenges faced by Latinos in schools, the labor market, and in communities and explains their prospects for upward mobility. These studies suggest that a significant investment in expanding educational opportunities may be the single most important policy lever to incorporate Latinos into the American mainstream.

Charles Hirschman
Professor of Public Affairs and Boeing International
Professor of Sociology
University of Washington, Seattle, WA, USA

Acknowledgments

This volume is primarily based on papers presented at two panels of the Inter-University Program for Latino Research (IUPLR) conference "SIGLO XXI: Economies of Class, Economies of Culture" held at the University of Texas at Austin on April 14, 2007. Thanks to all who attended the panels and commented on the papers. The panels were made possible by the support of the Irma Rangel Public Policy Institute at the University of Texas at Austin. We also acknowledge the excellent work of Institute staff in preparing the papers for publication, particularly Dr. Jill Strube and Stuart Tendler, Project Coordinators, as well as Jennifer Lamm, B.J. Lee, and Shinya Wakao. In addition, we would like to thank the staff of the Center for Mexican-American Studies (CMAS) at the University of Texas at Austin for their efforts in hosting and organizing the conference. Lastly, thanks to Jon Gurstelle and Barbara Fess for their support of this volume.

Contents

Contributors

Mevlude Akbulut-Yuksel Dalhousie University, Halifax, Nova Scotia, Canada, mevlude@dal.ca

Catalina Amuedo-Dorantes San Diego State University, San Diego, CA, USA; IZA – Institute for the Study of Labor, Bonn, Germany, catalina.amuedo.dorantes@gmail.com

Hoyt Bleakley University of Chicago, Chicago, IL, USA, hoyt.bleakley@chicagobooth.edu

Aimee Chin University of Houston, Houston, TX, USA; National Bureau of Economic Research (NBER), Cambridge, MA, USA, achin@uh.edu

Alberto Dávila University of Texas – Pan American, Edinburg, TX, USA, adavila@utpa.edu

Brian Duncan University of Colorado, Denver, CO, USA, brian.duncan@ucdenver.edu

Richard Fry Pew Hispanic Center, Washington, DC, USA, rfry@pewhispanic.org

Arturo Gonzalez Office of the Comptroller of the Currency, Washington, DC 20219, USA, arturo.gonzalez@occ.treas.gov

Chinhui Juhn University of Houston, Houston, TX, USA; National Bureau of Economic Research (NBER), Cambridge, MA, USA, cjuhn@uh.edu

Adriana Kugler Georgetown University, Washington, DC, USA; National Bureau of Economic Research (NBER), Cambridge, MA, USA, ak659@georgetown.edu

David L. Leal University of Texas at Austin, Austin, TX, USA, dleal@austin.utexas.edu

Francesca Mazzolari Centro Studi Confindustria, Rome, Italy, francesca.mazzolari@gmail.com

Marie T. Mora University of Texas – Pan American, Edinburg, TX, USA, mtmora@utpa.edu

Max Neiman Public Policy Institute of California, San Francisco, CA, USA, neiman@ppic.org

Curt Nichols Baylor University, Waco, TX, USA, Curt_Nichols@baylor.edu

Pia M. Orrenius Federal Reserve Bank of Dallas, Dallas, TX, USA, pia.orrenius@dal.frb.org

Belinda I. Reyes San Francisco State University, San Francisco, CA, USA, reyesb@sfsu.edu

Albert Saiz University of Pennsylvania, Philadelphia, PA, USA, saiz@wharton.upenn.edu

Jeremy M. Teigen Ramapo College, Mahwah, NJ, USA, jteigen@ramapo.edu

Stephen J. Trejo University of Texas at Austin, Austin, TX, USA, trejo@austin.utexas.edu

Mutlu Yuksel IZA – Institute for the Study of Labor, Bonn, Germany, yuksel@iza.org

Madeline Zavodny Agnes Scott College, Decatur, GA, USA; IZA – Institute for the Study of Labor, Bonn, Germany, mzavodny@agnesscott.edu

Chapter 1
Introduction

David L. Leal and Stephen J. Trejo

Latinos and the Economic Future

The chapters in this volume provide the unique insights of economists on a wide range of issues of central importance for assessing the economic incorporation, progress, and impact of Latinos[1] in the United States. The contributors primarily write in the labor economics tradition of investigating the individual-level factors relevant to economic participation. Labor economists and public policy scholars are centrally concerned with the issues addressed in this volume—education, immigration, employment, and earnings. The chapters provide a comprehensive perspective on the key factors that determine whether Latinos will be able to achieve their economic potential, which has substantial individual, national, and even international implications.

At 15.1% of the US population in 2007, Latinos are the nation's largest minority group. They are a growing presence in all sectors of the economy, play an increasingly important role in government and politics, and are influential across a wide range of cultural domains. According to the Pew Hispanic Center (1, p. 5), even in the midst of the current recession, "Hispanics are still the principal source of change in the US working-age population and labor force." During a recent 1-year period (the first quarter of 2007 to the first quarter of 2008), the Latino working age population grew by 3.5% while the overall US growth figure was 1.1%. Of the 2.6 million new potential workers, Latinos constituted 1.1 million. In addition, Latino labor force participation rates remain several points higher than those of non-Latinos (1, p. 5). More generally, one out of every two people added to the US population is Hispanic (2). Any discussion of the American economic future needs to include a careful understanding of Latinos.

However, just as Latino population growth is no guarantee of Latino political and policy influence (3), neither does a growing labor force necessarily entail improvements in income, skills, or occupational status. Despite the growing attention

D.L. Leal (✉)
University of Texas at Austin, Austin, TX, USA
e-mail: dleal@austin.utexas.edu

D.L. Leal, S.J. Trejo (eds.), *Latinos and the Economy*, Immigrants and Minorities, Politics and Policy, DOI 10.1007/978-1-4419-6682-7_1,
© Springer Science+Business Media, LLC 2011

paid to Latinos in recent years, this population is characterized by relatively low socio-economic status. Whether the discussion involves education, income, savings, occupations, or job skills, Latinos rank behind the majority Anglo (non-Hispanic white) population and often behind other minority groups.

For example, according to Bureau of Labor Statistics (BLS) data for 2008,[2] half of Asian-American men, 34% of Anglo men, 23% of African-American men, and 15% of Latino men held jobs classified as management and professional. Furthermore, Latinos are significantly overrepresented in a number of lower-skill job categories, such as construction (44%), maids and home cleaners (41%), and grounds maintenance workers (41%). As noted by Catanzarite and Trimble (4, p.149), "Latinos constitute a large and growing share of the United States' labor force. Hence, they are—and will increasingly be—critical to the productivity of the US economy. Yet, Latinos experience a number of significant labor market disadvantages, including high unemployment rates, low wages, overrepresentation in low-level occupations, and limited mobility."

As the Latino population expands in terms of both numbers and percentage (see discussion below), it is increasingly clear that its future is inextricably linked with that of the US economy. With Latinos taking on a growing number of economic roles—from workers to consumers to entrepreneurs—this century's labor force will increasingly rely upon Latino workers. According to the BLS,[3] Latinos in 2008 comprised 14% of all workers, African Americans were 11%, and Asian Americans 5%. In 1999, the BLS estimated that the respective figures in 2008 would be 12.7%, 12.4%, and 5.7%.[4] These data therefore underestimated future Latino labor force representation as well as overestimated that of other groups. Such underestimations of Latino demographic change are not rare, and they suggest that many current predictions may also fall short of the mark. Furthermore, as the baby boomer generation retires, the economy will increasingly rely on Latino and immigrant labor (5).

In addition, Latino population growth is fueled not just by continued immigration from Spanish-speaking countries, but also by the youth of the US Hispanic population and its above-average fertility rate. Over the past couple of decades, immigration was more important than US births in driving Hispanic population growth. Passel (2008) projects that this will reverse in the near future, however, so that births will increasingly drive Hispanic population growth in the coming decades. These demographic forces have produced a burgeoning second generation of young, US-born (and US-educated) Hispanics. The median age of second-generation Hispanics is thirteen, so most have not yet finished school. As emphasized in a recent report from the National Academy of Sciences (6), the fact that this large cohort of second-generation Hispanics will come of age and enter the labor market over the next two decades presents both an opportunity and a challenge. Will these Americans have the education and labor market skills to realize their potential as well as help to support retirees from the baby boom generation?

Stakeholders are increasingly aware that the US cannot maintain its global position without an educated and skilled workforce. According to Octavio A. Hinojosa Mier, Executive Director of the Congressional Hispanic Leadership Institute, "due to our demographic and economic growth, Hispanics will play a greater role and have an increasing impact in all sectors of our domestic economy, as well as the global economy."[5] The chapters in this volume address the numerous topics that will be critical to deciding whether the US develops such human capital—or allows a significant and growing share of the population to fall short of its promise.

Lastly, immigrants are an important part of such developments: "Immigrants constitute the majority of the Latino working-age population and labor force. Not surprisingly, they are a key source of growth in the Latino labor force...The Latino immigrant working-age population increased 462,000 in 2007 and 430,000 in 2006" (1, p. 7). Any research on Latinos and the economy must, therefore, take into account the crucial dynamic of immigration, which several chapters in this volume directly address.

The Chapters

Probably the largest obstacle to the socioeconomic achievement of Hispanics is their relatively low level of educational attainment (US-born Cubans are an exception, however). Failure to complete high school is unfortunately common among Latinos, even among those who were born and raised in the United States, and even among those in the third generation and beyond.[6] Inevitably, college attendance and completion rates are also much lower for Latinos. Hispanic educational attainment is low not only in comparison with advantaged groups in American society such as Anglos, but also in comparison with disadvantaged minority groups such as African Americans (7). The schooling deficit of US Latinos largely explains their below-average earnings, so finding a way to eliminate this deficit would go a long way toward bridging the economic divide that remains between Hispanics and most other Americans (8). Educational attainment also has implications for a wide variety of other personal, civic, and community outcomes, and education plays a role in almost all stages of an individual's lifecycle.

Because education is such a crucial policy issue for Latinos, four chapters in the volume focus explicitly on this topic. Each of these chapters addresses important new facets of the topic that have received relatively little attention in the voluminous academic literature on Latino schooling. The first two chapters analyze issues relevant for public primary and secondary schools, and the following two chapters consider factors that can influence whether Latinos pursue higher education.

In recent years, Latino immigrants have increasingly settled in new regions of the United States (e.g., Georgia, North Carolina, and Utah) where formerly they had little or no presence (9, 13). Richard Fry's chapter provides one of the first analyses of how this "Hispanic diaspora" has changed the characteristics and quality of the public schools that educate Latino children. The picture that emerges is complex. On the one hand, schools attended by Latinos in these new settlement regions tend to have favorable learning environments (e.g., more suburban, lower poverty, smaller class sizes) compared to the schools attended by

Latinos in the traditional settlement areas (e.g., California, Florida, New York, and Texas). On the other hand, within new settlement regions, the particular schools that experienced rapid growth of Latino enrollments are changing, including increased poverty and declining enrollments of Anglo students as overall enrollments soar. Going forward, it will be important to monitor the net effect of these changes on the educational success and achievement of Latino students in the new versus traditional settlement regions and scholars will also want to follow educational outcomes over time as schools in the new settlement regions have a chance to accommodate the shifting characteristics of their student populations (e.g., the presence of large numbers of students for whom English is a second language).

The chapter by Belinda Reyes and Max Neiman explores the question of whether the voting system used to elect local school boards affects Latino representation on these boards. Using data from school districts in Central California, they show that voting systems do matter. Holding other relevant factors constant, Latinos are much more likely to win school board elections when districts are partitioned geographically into "wards" and the residents of each ward elect a single board member to represent them, as opposed to an "at-large" system in which the votes cast by all residents of a district are used to select the entire slate of board members. Moreover, Latino representation on school boards seems to influence district policies that matter for Latino students, such as the prevalence of Latino teachers and of teachers with training in bilingual education. For the school districts in their sample, the authors also conducted a survey eliciting the views of board members, superintendents, and principals. The results of this survey provide insight into how and why Latino representation on school boards and in administrative positions might matter for district and school policies.

Turning to higher education, the chapter by Aimee Chin and Chinhui Juhn considers the impact of state laws that permit eligible unauthorized immigrants to enroll in public colleges and universities as state residents and thereby qualify for in-state tuition. California and Texas passed the first such laws in 2001, and by 2006 a total of ten states had passed similar measures with the potential to substantially lower the cost of college for unauthorized students. This chapter provides a comprehensive framework for assessing whether these laws raise high school completion and college attendance for the affected groups. So far, the evidence indicates that the short-run responses have not been large, but there are reasons to expect bigger responses over the longer term. This detailed analysis lays the groundwork for evaluating long-run effects of the state laws enacted to date and also for studying the more extensive "Dream Act" legislation being considered at the federal level.

The chapter by Arturo Gonzalez highlights a significant obstacle faced by Hispanic college students that deserves further investigation: almost two-thirds are so-called "first-generation" college students in that neither of their parents has any experience with postsecondary schooling. By contrast, only half of African-American college students and about a third of Anglo and Asian-American college students are first-generation. Compared to their peers with better-educated parents, first-generation college students are much less likely to start out directly in a 4-year institution (rather than in a community college or other type of institution), and they ultimately are much less likely to earn a 4-year degree. As a result, Hispanic college students face unique challenges that require additional research and perhaps policies and programs specifically designed to address these challenges.

The next two chapters study key aspects of the adjustment process that immigrants from Latin America undergo as their focus and primary attachment gradually shifts from their home nation to the United States. Catalina Amuedo-Dorantes and Francesca Mazzolari show that the amnesty provisions of the 1986 Immigration Reform and Control Act (IRCA) had a significant effect on the amount of money remitted to the home country by the initially unauthorized immigrants from Latin America who were granted permanent legal resident status. In particular, legalization reduced total remittances from affected Mexican immigrants by about 40%. The corresponding reduction by affected immigrants from other countries in Latin America was smaller but still potentially significant. In the following chapter, Mazzolari analyzes the decisions made by several Central and South American countries in the first half of the 1990s to begin to recognize dual citizenship. As a result, immigrants from these countries acquired US citizenship during the 1990s at a much higher rate than did comparable immigrants from Latin American countries that did not expand nationality rights. Each of these chapters illustrates how specific policy changes, such as legalization or the recognition of dual citizenship, can encourage the social, economic, and political incorporation of US immigrants.

Economic issues often dominate policy debates surrounding Latino immigration, and the remaining chapters in this volume address several of the most prominent such issues. In the Earnings section, the first chapter (by Marie Mora and Alberto Davila) provides provocative evidence that the earnings penalty suffered by Latino men with limited English skills has shrunk in recent years, most dramatically during the 1980s, and especially among those with relatively little schooling. Over this period, immigration increased the supply of Latino workers with limited English skills, but other factors point to even stronger growth in the demand for these workers.

In the next chapter, Pia Orrenius and Madeline Zavodny document another instance of labor market resilience by Latino workers. Given their low levels of human capital and the prevalence of immigrants, Latinos constitute a disproportionate share of the low-wage work force, and this suggests that they would be heavily impacted by changes in federal and state minimum wages. As expected, hikes in the statutory minimum wage significantly increase the hourly earnings of Latino teenagers and low-education adults, but the corresponding declines in employment are either modest (for teenagers) or absent (for adults). Among teenagers, the disemployment effects of the minimum wage are smaller for foreign-born Latinos than for US-born Latinos or for African Americans.

Continuing the examination of Latino income, David Leal, Curt Nichols, and Jeremy Teigen use recent Current Population Survey (CPS) data to test whether serving in the military results in an income boost or penalty. Since the military's shift away from what Moskos termed an "institutional" to an "occupational" orientation

(10–12), the armed forces have, to one degree or another, advertised themselves as a "great place to start." Implicit in such recruiting pitches is the idea that military service provides young recruits with training and life skills that will be valuable to them later in life. Their chapter finds that while military service provides no income change for African Americans and Anglos, it has a positive effect on the subsequent earning potential of male Latinos.

The next section—Economic Impacts of Latinos—contains two chapters that study the effect of Latinos on wages and housing markets. A persistent and fundamental economic concern about large-scale immigration from Latin America is that it depresses the wages and employment opportunities of less-skilled native workers. Even among economists, this topic generates considerable controversy (e.g., see the competing views of Borjas (14) and Card (15)). The chapter by Adriana Kugler and Mutlu Yuksel revisits this issue with a couple of intriguing innovations. First, they estimate the labor market impact of recent Latin American immigrants on previous Latin American immigrants and on US-born Latinos. In terms of human capital and labor market skills, recent Latino immigrants are more similar to previous Latino immigrants and to US-born Latinos than they are to the typical native worker, and so these estimates should provide an upper bound on the overall detrimental effects of immigration from Latin America. Second, the authors exploit Hurricane Mitch as an exogenous source of migration from Central America to US border states. This analysis suggests that recent immigration from Latin America has not created adverse labor market consequences for previous immigrants or for US natives.

Albert Saiz's chapter provides a comprehensive treatment of an understudied question: how have immigration, in general, and the population growth associated with Latino immigration, in particular, influenced US housing markets? He demonstrates that Latinos tend to live in metropolitan areas with more expensive housing, and that metropolitan areas with more rapid growth in their Latino populations also experience larger increases in housing prices and rents. Within metropolitan areas, however, neighborhoods that become more heavily Latino experience slower growth in housing prices and rents. These findings suggest that a large influx of Latino immigrants into a city drives up overall housing demand and average house prices and rents, but at the same time, ethnic segregation intensifies—with Latino neighborhoods viewed by most residents as less desirable places to live.

In the last section—Inter-Generational Incorporation and Economic Outcomes—two chapters consider longer term issues of economic and social integration for Latino immigrants and their descendants. The chapter by Mevlude Akbulut-Yuksel, Hoyt Bleakley, and Aimee Chin reports results from a clever and compelling approach for assessing the causal effects of English proficiency on a wide range of immigrant outcomes. The authors' approach exploits the fact that younger children learn languages more easily than do older children and adults, and, therefore, immigrant children from non-English-speaking countries who arrive in the United States before age ten or so learn English more quickly and completely than do comparable children who immigrate at slightly older ages. The nonlinear and discontinuous relationship between age-at-arrival and English proficiency explains why a similar pattern of age-at-arrival effects emerges for immigrant outcomes that depend on English proficiency. These associations imply that not only is English proficiency an important determinant of educational attainment and lifetime earnings, but it also affects the likelihood that an immigrant marries, who they marry, how many children they have, and the type of neighborhood in which they live. The relationship between arriving at a young age and English proficiency is much stronger (i.e., more positive) for Latinos than it is for other immigrants from non-English-speaking countries, but the ultimate impact of English proficiency on most outcomes is somewhat smaller for Latinos.

The chapter by Brian Duncan and Stephen Trejo explores how intermarriage by Mexican Americans influences the ethnic identification of the children produced by these marriages. Not surprisingly, virtually all children with two Mexican-origin parents are identified as Mexican in US Census data, but about 30% of the children of intermarried Mexican Americans are not identified as Mexican. As this dynamic plays out across generations, it is likely that an increasingly small fraction of the descendants of Mexican immigrants continue to identify themselves as Mexican. Moreover, this process of ethnic leakage is highly selective, because Mexican Americans who intermarry tend to have much higher education and earnings than Mexican Americans who do not intermarry. Consequently, available data for third- and higher-generation Mexicans, who usually can only be identified by their subjective responses to questions about Hispanic ethnicity, probably understate the socioeconomic attainment of this population. In effect, through the selective nature of intermarriage and ethnic identification, some of the most successful descendants of Mexican immigrants assimilate to such an extent that they fade from empirical observation. Unfortunately, although the direction of this measurement bias seems clear, we do not yet have a good idea of its magnitude.

Latino Population Growth: Facts, Trends, and History

In order to better understand the place of Latinos in America's economy (as well as society and politics), it is important to understand the demographic and historical background of Latino population growth. While interest in Latino populations is growing across the social sciences, it is often accompanied by a lack of specific information about the historical place of Latinos in the United States, the key events that have influenced migration patterns, the complexities of Latino communities, and basic facts about the size and growth of Latino populations in the 20th century and the first decade of the 21st.

Across the last few decades, the most important demographic change in the United States is the growing Latino population. In 1970, the US Census found that Latinos constituted 9.6 million individuals, or 4.7% of the overall population. These figures increased to 14.6 million and 6.4% in 1980, to 22.4 million and 9% in 1990, and to 35.3 million and 12.5% in 2000. This population, therefore, grew by 52% from 1970 to 1980, 53% from 1980 to 1990, and 58% from 1990 to 2000. The Census estimates that by 2050, Latinos could number over 100 million and constitute almost a quarter of the US population.

In the first 6 years of the current decade, Latino populations grew by almost nine million people. The most recent Census data (2007) indicate that Latinos now constitute 15.1% of the US population, while Anglos are 66% and African Americans are 13.5%. In the most recent year for which data are available—July 1, 2006 to July 1, 2007—the Latino population grew by 3.3%, the Asian population increased by 2.9%, and Anglos grew by 0.3%. As a result of such transformations, four states now have "majority-minority" populations (California, Hawaii, New Mexico, and Texas), and in three states the combined minority population is 42% (Georgia, Maryland, and Nevada).[7]

In the 2000s, Hispanics have accounted for over half of all US population growth, compared to just under 40% in the 1990s (16). These increases reflect both net migration and what demographers call natural increase (births minus deaths). Of this Latino growth in the 2000s, about 40% is due to migration and 60% from natural increase. Latino populations are also relatively young, which portends considerable future growth. In 2007, the median age was 27.6 for Latinos and 36.6 for the overall population.[8] Furthermore, 22% of the nation's children are Latino, a figure projected to rise to 29% by 2050.

The fact of Latino population growth is increasingly recognized in America. In a nation where salsa outsells catsup, it is clear that Latinos are influencing all aspects of economic, political, and cultural life—to the consternation of some. In possible reaction to such transformations, recent years have seen grassroots agitation about "illegal immigration" that some observers believe is rooted in worries about Latinos more broadly. Nevertheless, the reality is that Latinos are irreversibly intertwined with the fabric of everyday America. While Latinos are often misunderstood, it is increasingly clear that the economic vibrancy of the United States is directly related to the condition of its Latino populations.

These trends are closely related to another dynamic—the growing immigrant population. The United States is now in the midst of a fourth "great wave" of migration, although the foreign born population share in 2000 (10.4%) is still lower than the figures from 1860 to 1930. Nevertheless, this is a substantial increase from the low in 1970 (4.7%), and subsequent decades have seen steady increases (6.2% in 1980 and 7.9% in 1990).[9]

The number of both authorized and unauthorized immigrants has increased considerably over the last four decades, and just over half of the foreign-born population originated in Latin America. By comparison, the Latin American share was 9.4% in 1960, 19.4% in 1970, 33.1% in 1980, and 44.3% in 2000.[10]

According to the Department of Homeland Security (DHS), in this post-1965 Immigration Act period (see below), 46.6% of all individuals obtaining legal permanent resident status are from the Americas.[11] These data do not include the large flow of unauthorized immigrants. Data from the DHS indicate that 11.8 million unauthorized immigrants live in the United States. The large majority (seven million, or 59%) is from Mexico, and six of the top ten senders of unauthorized immigrants are from the Americas (Mexico, El Salvador, Guatemala, Honduras, Brazil, and Ecuador). An additional 1.7 million unauthorized immigrants are from the top nine non-Mexican Latin American sending nations.

The Pew Hispanic Center estimates that the US saw 800,000 unauthorized entrants per year from 2000 to 2004 and 500,000 from 2005 to 2008 (17). Today, in the midst of a recession that has adversely affected economic sectors that employed many migrants, there is no increase in the return of unauthorized immigrants, although crossings along the US–Mexico border are down by about a quarter. In response to public worries about unauthorized migration, the US government is engaged in a far reaching deportation effort that removes about 400,000 individuals per year. Some local law enforcement agencies are cooperating with immigration enforcement efforts through the "287g" program, and some states and localities are passing laws aimed at discouraging the presence of unauthorized immigrants. Immigration reform is currently stalled. The future could include increased enforcement, some form of regularization for the unauthorized, or both.

Despite such political concerns about immigration, Latino populations are long-standing, clearly rooted in many parts of the US, and unlikely to decline in number. There are many historical events that set the stage for the growing population of Latin American-ancestry people in the United States, particularly the mid-19th century Mexican–American War and the Treaty of Guadalupe Hidalgo, whereby Mexico's northernmost territory became the American southwest. In addition, the Spanish-American War led to the formal incorporation of Puerto Rico and informal US influence in Cuba. The Texas Revolution, largely led by American immigrants, set Texas on a path that ultimately led to incorporation in the United States. The United States also has a long history of political and economic involvement in Latin American and Caribbean nations, thereby creating links that encourage migration.

There were also several "push" factors in the Americas that prompted millions of people to move north. These include the land policies of the Mexican President Porfirio Diaz in the late 19th century, the Mexican Revolution and the Cristero Revolt in the early 20th century, and an authoritarian Mexican political system throughout the 20th. The Cuban Revolution in 1959 spurred a migration that would change the politics of Florida and the United States, and the civil wars in Central America in the 1980s resulted in new migrant streams to the United States.

As a result, while Mexican Americans are the majority of Hispanics, the population diversified considerably in the 20th century. According to the 2000 Census, Mexican Americans constituted about 60% of Latinos, Puerto Ricans were 9.6%, Cuban Americans were 3.5%, Central Americans were 4.8%, South Americans 3.8%, Dominicans 2.2%, and about 17% did not identify their national origin.[13]

In addition to the above-noted push factors, US economic growth has long proved a "pull" for people across the globe. In addition to the demand for labor generated during periods of economic expansion, the two world wars led to the increased recruitment of American hemisphere workers, and four million Mexicans worked in the United States through the Bracero Program.

Furthermore, changes in US law after World War II relaxed many immigration restrictions, diversified the flow of immigrants, created new opportunities for legal migration, and regularized millions of unauthorized immigrants. These include the Displaced Persons Act (1948), the 1965 Immigration and Nationality Act (INA), and the 1986 IRCA.

To be sure, some dynamics serve to discourage migration, but they were generally episodic. For instance, many immigrants were repatriated to Mexico during the Great Depression, deported during Operation Wetback in 1954, and removed in the more recent post 9/11 environment. Nevertheless, the economic logic of migration tends to mitigate enforcement efforts over the long term, and the cross-cutting partisan dynamics of the issue will likely continue past patterns of formal and informal support for immigration—regardless of public opinion. This indicates that Latinos will undoubtedly remain a large, growing, and increasingly important segment of the US population. Economists and policymakers must accordingly pay more attention to Latinos and better understand the many factors relevant to their economic and political integration, successes and failures, and effects on others and the nation.

Notes

1. We use the words Latino and Hispanic interchangeably, as they are largely equivalent, although some individuals and organizations have a preference for one or the other.
2. Labor Force Statistics from the Current Population Survey, Labor Force Characteristics by Race and Ethnicity, 2008. December 4, 2009. http://www.bls.gov/cps/race_ethnicity_2008_occ_ind.htm
3. Labor Force Statistics from the Current Population Survey, Labor Force Characteristics by Race and Ethnicity, 2008. December 4, 2009. http://www.bls.gov/cps/race_ethnicity_2008_occ_ind.htm
4. TED: The Editor's Desk. December 14, 1999. "The labor force in 2008: race and Hispanic origin." http://www.bls.gov/opub/ted/1999/Dec/wk2/art02.htm
5. Hinojosa Mier, Octavio A. 2009. "Prepared Remarks by Octavio A. Hinojosa Mier, Executive Director, Congressional Hispanic Leadership Institute, Wednesday, October 28, 2009, Northrop Grumman Professional Development Summit, Washington, DC." http://www.chli.org/news/32258/Remarks-STEM-How-the-U.S.-Hispanic-Community-will-define-the-Future-of U.S.-Global-Competitiveness.htm
6. That is, even for the U.S.-born grandchildren and later descendants of Latino immigrants.
7. Census Bureau News. May 1, 2008. "U.S. Hispanic Population Surpasses 45 Million, Now 15 Percent of Total." Washington, DC: U.S. Department of Commerce. http://www.census.gov/Press-Release/www/releases/archives/population/011910.html
8. Census Bureau News. May 1, 2008. "U.S. Hispanic Population Surpasses 45 Million, Now 15 Percent of Total." Washington, DC: U.S. Department of Commerce. http://www.census.gov/Press-Release/www/releases/archives/population/011910.html
9. U.S. Census Bureau. December, 2001. "Profile of the Foreign-Born Population in the United States: 2000." Washington, DC: U.S. Department of Commerce. http://www.census.gov/prod/2002pubs/p23-206.pdf
10. U.S. Census Bureau. December, 2001. "Profile of the Foreign-Born Population in the United States: 2000." Washington, DC: U.S. Department of Commerce. http://www.census.gov/prod/2002pubs/p23-206.pdf
11. Less than 3% are from Canada and Newfoundland.
12. The US Department of Homeland Security uses the term "unauthorized," which seems the most neutral. "Illegal" and "undocumented" can have political implications as well as grammatical-conceptual difficulties.
13. "The Hispanic Population: Census 2000 Brief". May, 2001. Washington, DC: U.S. Census Bureau. http://www.census.gov/prod/2001pubs/c2kbr01-3.pdf

References

1. Kochhar, Rakesh. 2008. *"Latino Labor Report, 2008: Construction Reverses Job Growth for Latinos."* Washington, DC: Pew Hispanic Center. http://pewhispanic.org/files/reports/88.pdf (last accessed 2 Oct 2010).

2. Tienda, Marta. 2007. "Hispanics at the Age Crossroads: Opportunities and Risks." *Focus*, 25: 27–32.

3. Fraga, Luis R., and David L. Leal. 2004. "Playing the 'Latino Card': Race, Ethnicity, and National Party Politics." *Du Bois Review: Social Science Research on Race*, 1: 297–317.

4. Catanzarite, Lisa, and Lindsey Trimble. 2007. "Latinos in the United States Labor Market." In *Latinas/os in the United States: Changing the Face of América*, eds. Havidán Rodríguez, Rogelio Sáenz and Cecilia Menjívar, 149–164. New York: Springer.

5. Myers, Dowell. 2007. *"Immigrants and Boomers: Forging a New Social Contract for the Future of America."* New York: Russell Sage.

6. Tienda, Marta, and Faith Mitchell 2006. *"Multiple Origins: Uncertain Destinies: Hispanics and the American Future."* Washington, DC: National Academies Press.

7. Bean, Frank D., Stephen J. Trejo, Randy Capps, and Michael Tyler. 2001 February. *"The Latino Middle Class: Myth, Reality, and Potential."* Los Angeles, CA: Tomás Rivera Policy Institute.

8. Duncan, Brian, V. Joseph Hotz, and Stephen J. Trejo. 2006. "Hispanics in the U.S. Labor Market." In *Hispanics and the Future of America*, eds. Marta Tienda and Faith Mitchell, 228–290. Washington, DC: National Academies Press.

9. Card, David, and Ethan G. Lewis. 2007. "The Diffusion of Mexican Immigrants During the 1990s: Explanations and Impacts." In *Mexican Immigration to the United States*, ed. George J. Borjas, 193–227. Chicago: University of Chicago Press.

10. Moskos, Charles. 1977. "From Institution to Occupation: Trends in Military Organization." *Armed Forces and Society*, 4(1): 41–50.

11. Moskos, Charles. 1978. "The Emergent Military: Calling, Profession, or Occupation?" In *The Changing World of the American Military*, ed. Franklin Margiotta, 199–206. Boulder, CO: Westview Press.

12. Moskos, Charles. 1986. "Institutional/Occupational Trends in Armed Forces: An Update." *Armed Forces and Society*, 12(3): 377–382.

13. Fischer, Mary J., and Marta Tienda. 2006. "Redrawing Spatial Color Lines: Hispanic Metropolitan Dispersal, Segregation, and Economic Opportunity." In *Hispanics and the Future of America*, eds. Marta Tienda and Faith Mitchell, 100–137. Washington, DC: National Academies Press.

14. Borjas, George J. 2003. "The Labor Demand Curve is Downward Sloping: Reexamining the Impact of Immigration on the Labor Market." *Quarterly Journal of Economics*, 118(4): 1335–1374.

15. Card, David. 2009. "Immigration and Inequality." *American Economic Review: Papers & Proceedings*, 99(2): 1–21.

16. Fry, Richard. 2008. *"Latino Settlement in the New Century."* Washington, DC: Pew Hispanic Center. http://pewhispanic.org/files/reports/96.pdf (last accessed 3 Nov 2010).

17. Passel, Jeffrey S., and D'Vera Cohn. 2008. *"Trends in Unauthorized Immigration: Undocumented Inflow Now Trails Legal Inflow."* Washington, DC: Pew Hispanic Center. http://pewhispanic.org/files/reports/94.pdf (last accessed 3 Nov 2010).

Part I
K-12 Education

Chapter 2
The Hispanic Diaspora and the Public Schools: Educating Hispanics

Richard Fry

Abstract Reflecting the geographic concentration of the Hispanic population in the Southwest, as recently as 1990 the bulk of Hispanic children were educated in public schools in 48 metropolitan areas. Schools in the Los Angeles and New York metropolitan areas alone educated more than one quarter of Hispanic students in the early 1990s. The Hispanic diaspora, however, has resulted in very large Hispanic public school enrollment growth in 30 "new settlement" metropolitan areas (such as Atlanta and Charlotte). The percentage of the nation's Latino public school students that are educated in the schools of the new settlement areas has nearly doubled since 1993. The quality of public schools varies across states and metropolitan areas. On average, the public schools educating Hispanics in the 30 new settlement areas have different characteristics than the schools in the 48 traditional Hispanic metro areas. Examination of the rudimentary characteristics of the public schools educating Latinos in the new settlement areas suggests that the diaspora has not necessarily diminished the educational context of Hispanic youth. The new settlement public schools are more suburban. They tend to be smaller, are less likely to be high poverty schools (as measured by Title I status), and have smaller pupil-to-teacher ratios. At the school level, Hispanic students in the new settlement schools have more exposure to white students than their peers educated in schools in the traditional Hispanic metros. The impact of the Hispanic enrollment boom in the 30 new settlement metros was concentrated in about one-out-of-eight public schools. Compared to other public schools in the new settlement metros, the high Hispanic growth schools experienced abrupt changes since 1993. The highly impacted schools went from being majority white schools to majority minority schools by 2004. Unlike other schools, they grew substantially in size in spite of white student enrollment declines. These changes are noteworthy because although only about one-in-eight schools was affected, these schools educate 40% of Latinos in the new settlement areas.

R. Fry (✉)
Pew Hispanic Center, Washington, DC, USA
e-mail: rfry@pewhispanic.org

D.L. Leal, S.J. Trejo (eds.), *Latinos and the Economy*, Immigrants and Minorities, Politics and Policy, DOI 10.1007/978-1-4419-6682-7_2,
© Springer Science+Business Media, LLC 2011

Introduction

In addition to its high growth rate, an important feature of recent Hispanic population dynamics has been its dispersion to new communities. The migration trends include not only movement to new settlement communities (e.g., Atlanta and Salt Lake City) as opposed to long-standing Hispanic communities (e.g., Los Angeles and Miami), but also movement to the suburbs within metropolitan areas. To date, researchers have performed very little formal analysis of the implications of these new residence patterns on the quality of public education for Latino children. This chapter quantifies the extent of dispersion and suburbanization of Hispanic public school students since the early 1990s. It then examines the basic characteristics of the new public schools educating Latinos and compares these to the characteristics of public schools that have traditionally educated Latinos. Given the long-standing concerns about the quality of the education that Latino children were receiving in over-burdened central city schools in the nation's largest cities, this analysis shows that the Hispanic diaspora could potentially improve the schooling context of Latino children.

The diaspora of Hispanics away from the southwest and other traditional immigrant gateway cities has drawn intense interest and been well-documented by scholars (e.g., 1, 2). Most of this literature has examined the migration of the entire Hispanic population; it has not focused on the growth of Hispanic children or students in the new settlement areas. The dispersion has not been neutral in terms of the characteristics of the new Hispanic residents. Research suggests that many of the Latino migrants into the new settlement areas are immigrants. "Thus, the increasing distribution of Hispanics, as a group, is driven mostly by the new geographical trends in settlement among Mexican and Central American immigrants" (3, p. 93.) Foreign-born Hispanics have different characteristics than native-born Hispanics. For example, foreign-born Hispanic adults are disproportionately male; in addition, the median age for foreign-born Hispanics is about 35, but it is about 17 for native-born Hispanics.[1]

In regard to immigration from Mexico, Durand, Massey, and Capoferro (1, p. 15) report that "tabulations suggest that this shift away from traditional destinations was not led by a random cross-section of Mexican immigrants, but by a particular subset of migrants composed predominantly of working-age men working disproportionately in agriculture." The recent Mexican arrivals in the new destination states were less likely to be married than those in traditional states.

These considerations suggest that overall Hispanic population growth in the new areas need not have resulted in corresponding school enrollment growth. This chapter analyzes public school enrollments to assess the dispersion of Hispanic children; it examines how many schools in new settlement communities have experienced large Hispanic growth and discusses the consequences of that growth.

Case studies of the education of Latino children in new settlement areas have uncovered great challenges and indicate that schools have had difficulties incorporating their new students and developing the resources and curriculum to educate these new populations. "While scholars' findings point to a somewhat positive overall environment for Latinos in the South (with significant exceptions), Latino public education in emerging immigrant communities has been quite troubled" (4, p. 12). Systematic analysis of the educational outcomes of Hispanic children in new destination areas versus traditional Latino areas has not been performed. Nor have evaluations of the instructional resources and student expenditures been undertaken.

This chapter carefully examines an important—albeit limited—set of public school characteristics to further our knowledge of the nature of the schools educating Hispanics. Are the public schools educating Hispanics in new settlement areas different from those educating Hispanics elsewhere? Many parents and educators believe that schools matter. Empirical research suggests that school conditions affect adolescent academic performance (5, 6). Part of an assessment of Hispanic education in the wake of the diaspora requires an investigation of the schools as well as student outcomes, family background, and public expenditures. This chapter provides a description of the basic characteristics of public schools educating Hispanic children and how they vary spatially.

Examining the educational attainment of foreign-born adult Latinos that came to the US during childhood (and thus are a product of US schools), Stamps and Bohon (7) report that Latino immigrants in new settlement areas are more educated than their counterparts in established Latino metros. One possible explanation is that new settlement areas offer greater economic rewards to highly educated Latinos and that, therefore, the more highly educated migrated to the new settlement areas. Alternatively, the more highly educated adult Latinos might have grown up and been educated in the new settlement areas, so perhaps the new Latino communities are conducive to Latino education relative to traditional Hispanic metros. The evidence presented in this chapter is consistent with this latter explanation. The public schools that Hispanics attend in new settlement areas, on average, have more favorable characteristics than the public schools that Hispanics attend in traditional Hispanic metros.

A less-heralded but also noteworthy shift in the residence patterns of Hispanics is their growing suburbanization. Suro and Singer (8, p. 7) summarize their findings in regard to the entire Hispanic population: "The Latinos, in short, are becoming suburbanites." If Hispanic children are also becoming suburbanites, one might surmise that this would have fortuitous consequences for their education. On average, central city schools are believed to be more crowded, less adequately funded, have higher concentrations of poverty (9, 10), and are associated with less favorable student outcomes, for example, higher student dropout rates (11) and lower average scores in reading and mathematics assessments (12). Migration to the suburbs (or the areas the National Center for Education Statistics refers to as "the urban fringe of the metro area") means that Latino children are potentially attending better schools. Again, little formal analysis has documented Hispanic children's suburbanization and the implications for their education.

Following a discussion of the data source on public schools, the analysis documents the extent to which Hispanic students dispersed and suburbanized since the 1993–1994 school year. It then concentrates on the differences in the quality of public schools educating Hispanics and whites. A necessary condition for differences is that students not attend the same public schools. A simple, standard measure suffices to show that suburban Hispanic and white students largely do not go to the same schools. Then differences in the typical characteristics of public schools are examined spatially.

Data

This analysis is based on the Public Elementary/Secondary School Universe Surveys in the Common Core of Data (CCD) collected by the US Department of Education (13). These annual surveys are a census of public elementary and secondary schools. State education agencies submit the data. For school year 2004–2005, 93,295 schools reported enrolling students (14). In 2004–2005, Tennessee and Nevada did not report student enrollments by race/ethnicity. Idaho did not report such enrollments in school year 1993–1994. To facilitate comparisons over time, public schools in Tennessee, Nevada, and Idaho are omitted from the analysis. In school year 2004–2005, 90,389 public schools had students in 47 states and the District of Columbia.

Following recent analyses of residential dispersal of the entire Hispanic population, the analysis is limited to enrollment patterns and changes in urban metropolitan schools (2, 8). Hispanics are heavily urbanized, and urban metropolitan schools educated 86% of the nation's 9.1 million Hispanic public students in 2004–2005.[2]

Although rural schools outside of metropolitan areas are educating much greater numbers of Hispanic students, their relative importance in Hispanic public education is declining. In 1993–1994, nonmetropolitan rural schools educated 9% of Hispanic students. By 2004–2005, these schools educated 7% of Latino public school enrollment.[3]

Further simplification is possible by focusing on the 100 largest urban metropolitan areas in terms of Hispanic public school enrollments. The 100 largest Hispanic areas educated 82% of Hispanics in 2004–2005. Not much dispersion beyond the top 100 largest Hispanic urban metro areas has occurred as these areas educated 83% of Latinos in 1993–1994.[4] The remainder of this chapter concentrates on the schooling of Latino public school students in the nation's 100 largest Hispanic areas (7.4 million Hispanic students in 2004–2005).

The Dispersion and Suburbanization of Hispanic Schooling

Dispersion

Over the 11-year period examined, Hispanic youth have dispersed considerably from traditional urban metro areas in the Southwest. The largest 100 Hispanic urban metro areas can be subdivided into traditional Hispanic urban metros, new settlement metros, and other urban metros (Table 2.1 provides the full listing). Nearly half of the largest 100 Hispanic urban metros are traditional Hispanic metros and are in California, New York, Arizona, and Texas (sans Dallas-Fort Worth) or are traditional immigrant gateways including Chicago and Miami. As Table 2.2 shows, the 48 traditional Hispanic urban metro areas continue to educate the bulk of Hispanic students, but their share has markedly declined. In the 1993–1994 school year, public schools in traditional Hispanic areas educated 85% of Hispanic students. This share declined to 78% by 2004–2005.

Table 2.1 Hispanic public school enrollment in the top 100 Hispanic urban metropolitan areas

	Metro	Hispanic enrollment		2004–2005 Hispanic enrollment rank	Percent growth in Hispanic enrollment 1993–2004
		1993–1994	2004–2005		
	New settlement areas				
1	Dallas-Fort Worth-Arlington, TX	141,132	328,002	6	132
2	Washington-Arlington-Alexandria, DC-VA-MD-WV	43,678	107,425	15	146
3	Orlando, FL	25,357	72,076	21	184
4	Atlanta-Sandy Springs-Marietta, GA	9,994	66,961	25	570
5	Tampa-St. Petersburg-Clearwater, FL	22,094	56,731	29	157
6	Seattle-Tacoma-Bellevue, WA	14,931	41,483	36	178
7	Portland-Vancouver-Beaverton, OR-WA	11,419	36,375	37	219
8	Salt Lake City, UT	11,246	29,577	40	163
9	Minneapolis-St. Paul-Bloomington, MN-WI	7,409	26,376	44	256
10	Kansas City, MO-KS	7,367	22,817	49	210
11	Oklahoma City, OK	7,276	20,624	54	183
12	Charlotte-Gastonia-Concord, NC-SC	1,397	16,790	58	1,102
13	Naples-Marco Island, FL	4,695	14,811	62	215
14	Salem, OR	5,743	14,601	64	154
15	Cape Coral-Fort Myers, FL	3,563	13,363	68	275
16	Lakeland, FL	4,007	12,732	71	218
17	Omaha-Council Bluffs, NE-IA	3,303	12,279	74	272
18	Grand Rapids-Wyoming, MI	1,460	11,803	75	708
19	Wichita, KS	5,115	11,456	77	124
20	Indianapolis, IN	1,367	11,355	79	731
21	Sarasota-Bradenton-Venice, FL	3,565	10,959	80	207
22	Ogden-Clearfield, UT	4,456	10,859	82	144
23	Tulsa, OK	2,470	10,846	83	339
24	Fayetteville-Springdale-Rogers, AR-MO	777	10,466	86	1,247
25	Baltimore-Towson, MD	3,176	10,381	87	227

Table 2.1 (continued)

Metro	Hispanic enrollment 1993–1994	2004–2005	2004–2005 Hispanic enrollment rank	Percent growth in Hispanic enrollment 1993–2004
26 Virginia Beach-Norfolk-Newport News, VA-NC	3,981	8,709	92	119
27 Jacksonville, FL	3,086	8,672	93	181
28 Raleigh-Cary, NC	977	8,466	94	767
29 Rockford, IL	2,604	7,843	96	201
30 Provo-Orem, UT	2,063	7,772	98	277
Traditional Hispanic areas				
31 Los Angeles-Long Beach-Santa Ana, CA	932,383	1,290,083	1	38
32 New York-Northern New Jersey-Long Island, NY-NJ	537,809	705,441	2	31
33 Houston-Baytown-Sugar Land, TX	223,307	396,046	3	77
34 Riverside-San Bernardino-Ontario, CA	199,839	374,434	4	87
35 Chicago-Naperville-Joliet, IL-IN-WI	208,629	367,342	5	76
36 Miami-Fort Lauderdale-Miami Beach, FL	182,366	310,977	7	71
37 Phoenix-Mesa-Scottsdale, AZ	99,443	240,012	8	141
38 San Diego-Carlsbad-San Marcos, CA	129,003	199,224	9	54
39 San Antonio, TX	148,891	188,836	10	27
40 McAllen-Edinburg-Pharr, TX	110,259	160,214	11	45
41 San Francisco-Oakland-Fremont, CA	93,987	145,623	12	55
42 El Paso, TX	114,015	139,059	13	22
43 San Jose-Sunnyvale-Santa Clara, CA	74,414	94,007	16	26
44 Fresno, CA	60,166	87,847	17	46
45 Brownsville-Harlingen, TX	63,745	77,131	18	21
46 Austin-Round Rock, TX	41,870	75,145	19	79
47 Bakersfield, CA	43,412	73,378	20	69
48 Sacramento–Arden-Arcade–Roseville, CA	36,455	68,180	23	87
49 Albuquerque, NM	46,023	59,873	26	30
50 Oxnard-Thousand Oaks-Ventura, CA	39,029	59,031	27	51
51 Tucson, AZ	38,790	58,837	28	52
52 Laredo, TX	37,588	51,490	30	37
53 Visalia-Porterville, CA	25,724	51,370	31	100
54 Stockton, CA	25,629	49,799	32	94
55 Corpus Christi, TX	44,991	47,477	33	6
56 Salinas, CA	30,071	47,367	34	58

Table 2.1 (continued)

Metro	Hispanic enrollment 1993–1994	Hispanic enrollment 2004–2005	2004–2005 Hispanic enrollment rank	Percent growth in Hispanic enrollment 1993–2004
57 Modesto, CA	18,099	44,817	35	148
58 Santa Barbara-Santa Maria-Goleta, CA	23,587	35,549	38	51
59 El Centro, CA	23,212	28,878	42	24
60 Merced, CA	14,883	28,179	43	89
61 Yuma, AZ	13,099	25,724	45	96
62 Las Cruces, NM	16,105	21,913	52	36
63 Santa Rosa-Petaluma, CA	8,364	19,717	55	136
64 Vallejo-Fairfield, CA	9,437	17,530	57	86
65 Lubbock, TX	13,889	15,825	59	14
66 Santa Cruz-Watsonville, CA	11,460	15,639	60	36
67 Odessa, TX	13,009	15,548	61	20
68 Madera, CA	8,039	13,343	69	66
69 Hanford-Corcoran, CA	8,664	12,687	72	46
70 Amarillo, TX	7,579	12,614	73	66
71 Poughkeepsie-Newburgh-Middletown, NY	5,165	11,403	78	121
72 Killeen-Temple-Fort Hood, TX	7,055	10,929	81	55
73 Santa Fe, NM	8,379	10,263	88	22
74 Midland, TX	7,126	9,960	89	40
75 Waco, TX	5,823	9,480	90	63
76 Victoria, TX	7,267	8,924	91	23
77 San Luis Obispo-Paso Robles, CA	3,998	7,778	97	95
78 Napa, CA	3,878	7,613	100	96
Other Areas				
79 Denver-Aurora, CO	51,764	107,470	14	108
80 Boston-Cambridge-Quincy, MA-NH	45,911	69,651	22	52
81 Philadelphia-Camden-Wilmington, PA-NJ-DE-MD	41,423	67,185	24	62
82 Providence-New Bedford-Fall River, RI-MA	15,307	31,372	39	105
83 Hartford-West Hartford-East Hartford, CT	21,484	29,302	41	36
84 Milwaukee-Waukesha-West Allis, WI	13,413	24,276	46	81
85 New Haven-Milford, CT	13,177	24,161	47	83
86 Detroit-Warren-Livonia, MI	10,419	23,079	48	122
87 Springfield, MA	15,694	22,099	50	41
88 Yakima, WA	14,468	22,075	51	53
89 Bridgeport-Stamford-Norwalk, CT	14,401	21,500	53	49

Table 2.1 (continued)

	Metro	Hispanic enrollment		2004–2005 Hispanic enrollment rank	Percent growth in Hispanic enrollment 1993–2004
		1993–1994	2004–2005		
90	Allentown-Bethlehem-Easton, PA-NJ	8,640	17,789	56	106
91	Colorado Springs, CO	8,022	14,661	63	83
92	Worcester, MA	9,286	14,287	65	54
93	Kennewick-Richland-Pasco, WA	6,850	14,003	66	104
94	Cleveland-Elyria-Mentor, OH	9,408	13,436	67	43
95	Reading, PA	5,703	13,138	70	130
96	Greeley, CO	6,693	11,492	76	72
97	Pueblo, CO	9,481	10,693	84	13
98	Rochester, NY	7,907	10,551	85	33
99	Lancaster, PA	4,832	7,979	95	65
100	Boulder, CO	3,688	7,627	99	107

Source: US Department of Education, Common Core of Data (CCD), Public Elementary/Secondary School Universe Survey

Table 2.2 Hispanic urban metropolitan public school enrollment: top 100 Hispanic areas

Area type	1993–1994		2004–2005	
	Students	%	Students	%
Traditional Hispanic areas (48)	3,825,955	85	5,802,536	78
New settlement areas (30)	359,708	8	1,022,610	14
Other areas (22)	337,971	7	577,826	8
Total	4,523,634	100	7,402,972	100

Source: US Department of Education, Common Core of Data (CCD), Public Elementary/Secondary School Universe Survey

Declining Hispanic populations in urban metro areas in California, Texas, and New York account for the waning importance of traditional Hispanic areas. Metro areas in each of these states educated relatively fewer Hispanics. The movement out of LA-Long Beach-Santa Ana schools can entirely account for the decline in California. Schools in this one urban metro area educated 21% of the nation's Hispanics in the 1993–1994 school year. By 2004–2005, LA-Long Beach-Santa Ana educated 17% of Hispanic students.[5]

Not only did public schools in the 30 new settlement urban metro areas at least double their Hispanic enrollments (indeed, Fayetteville, AR public schools enrolled 13 times more Latinos in school year 2004–2005 than in school year 1993–1994), they also educated a rising proportion of the nation's Hispanics. Public schools in the new settlement areas educated 8% of Hispanic urban metropolitan enrollments in 1993–1994. By 2004–2005, these areas educated 14% of Hispanics. With the

exception of Dallas-Fort Worth,[6] these public schools are all outside California and
the southwest; one obvious question is how public schools attended by Hispanics in
the new settlement areas compare to public schools in the traditional Hispanic urban
metros.

Suburbanization

A second recent significant Hispanic population development has been the dispersion of Hispanics within, rather than across, metropolitan areas. During the 1990s,
all racial/ethnic groups began to move to suburban areas in greater numbers than
ever before (15). Though blacks have shown the greatest increase in suburban
residence, almost half of Hispanic persons are suburbanites.

Hispanic public school enrollments have also shifted from the central city to the
urban fringe of the metro area (more commonly known as suburbia). In 1993–1994,
40% of Hispanic enrollment was educated in "urban fringe" schools (Table 2.3).[7]
By 2004–2005, this percentage had risen to 45%. The dispersal of students within
an urban metropolitan area from 1993 to 2004 occurred in traditional Hispanic metros nearly as much as in the new settlement areas. In the 30 new settlement areas,
however, Hispanic students were more likely than their peers in other metro areas
throughout the country to be educated in schools in the urban fringe.

Table 2.3 Suburbanization of Hispanic public school enrollment: Top 100 Hispanic areas

	1993–1994			2004–2005		
Area type	Students	Students in urban fringe schools	% in urban fringe schools	Students	Students in urban fringe schools	% in urban fringe schools
Traditional Hispanic areas (48)	3,825,955	1,516,822	40	5,802,536	2,594,997	45
New settlement areas (30)	359,708	170,461	47	1,022,610	544,838	53
Other areas (22)	337,971	101,035	30	577,826	204,929	35
Total	4,523,634	1,788,318	40	7,402,972	3,344,764	45

Source: US Department of Education, Common Core of Data (CCD), Public Elementary/
Secondary School Universe Survey

The pace of suburbanization of Hispanic children should not be overemphasized.
Almost half (46%) of the large Hispanic enrollment growth between 1993 and 2004
occurred in central city schools (Table 2.4). In comparison, white enrollment in
central city schools declined over the period. Black and Asian enrollment in central
city schools did increase from 1993 to 2004, but much more of the black (83%) and
Asian enrollment growth (66%) occurred in urban fringe schools in comparison to
Latinos (54%). Latino students were suburbanizing, but less so than other students.

Table 2.4 Suburbanization of public school enrollment: top 100 Hispanic areas

	1993–1994			2004–2005			% of growth that occurred in urban fringe
Race	Students	Students in urban fringe schools	% in urban fringe schools	Students	Students in urban fringe schools	% in urban fringe schools	
Hispanic	4,523,634	1,788,318	40	7,402,972	3,344,764	45	54
NH white	11,514,647	8,001,661	69	11,256,601	8,281,134	74	100
NH black	3,838,242	1,301,905	34	4,595,082	1,927,356	42	83
NH Asian	1,177,733	525,059	45	1,637,139	828,812	51	66
All students	21,179,866	11,680,842	55	25,065,053	14,477,530	58	72

Source: US Department of Education, Common Core of Data (CCD), Public Elementary/Secondary School Universe Survey

Suburban Schooling

It is well known that Hispanics do not attend the same public schools as whites. Logan (16) reports that 78% of Hispanics went to majority minority public schools in 2000; only 11% of whites attended these same public schools. In part, Hispanics do not attend the same schools as whites because more whites reside in the urban fringe of the metropolitan area, rather than the central city. Although central city schools are more heavily minority, even Hispanics and whites that reside in the urban fringe do not attend the same schools.

Suburbanization is not the great equalizer in that suburban white and Hispanic students attend different schools. In the suburbs of the top 100 Hispanic urban areas, 75% of Hispanic students went to majority minority schools in 2004. In these same suburbs, 13% of white students went to these schools (Table 2.5). Again, spatial differences between Hispanics and whites contribute to this difference. Whites are more likely to reside and be educated in metros other than the 48 traditional Hispanic areas. As Table 2.5 reports, areas outside the 48 traditional Hispanic areas tend to have fewer students in majority minority schools.

Geographic differences are not the whole explanation, however, because within the same metropolitan area type, suburban whites and suburban Hispanics do not go

Table 2.5 Urban fringe students in majority minority schools, 2004–2005

Area type	Race	Urban fringe of top 100 Hispanic urban metropolitan areas	In majority minority schools	% majority minority schools
Top 100 Hispanic	Hispanic	3,344,764	2,517,295	75
urban metropolitan	NH white	8,281,134	1,106,454	13
areas	NH black	1,927,356	1,349,784	70
	NH Asian	828,812	359,284	43
	All students	14,477,530	5,363,584	37
Traditional Hispanic	Hispanic	2,594,997	2,142,923	83
areas (48)	NH white	3,222,458	719,864	22
	NH black	857,475	694,859	81
	NH Asian	498,212	278,604	56
	All students	7,208,516	3,855,786	53
New settlement areas	Hispanic	544,838	291,584	54
(30)	NH white	2,773,788	301,724	11
	NH black	799,310	524,619	66
	NH Asian	224,581	70,385	31
	All students	4,389,555	1,196,778	27
Other areas (22)	Hispanic	204,929	82,788	40
	NH white	2,284,888	84,866	4
	NH black	270,571	130,306	48
	NH Asian	106,019	10,295	10
	All students	2,879,459	311,020	11

Source: US Department of Education, Common Core of Data (CCD),
Public Elementary/Secondary School Universe Survey

to the same schools. In the 30 new settlement areas, for example, 54% of suburban Hispanics went to majority minority schools. In comparison, 11% of their white peers attended these schools.

It is not the case that in every metro area suburban whites were less likely to attend majority minority schools than suburban Hispanics.[8] But in 82 out of the 100 top Hispanic metros, suburban whites were less likely than suburban Hispanics to attend majority minority schools. Consider, for example, the New York/Northern New Jersey/Long Island metro area. Over 70% of suburban Hispanics in the NY metro area enrolled in majority minority schools. Less than 10% of their suburban white peers attended these schools.

The Impact of Dispersion on Hispanic Education Conditions

The CCD does not have extensive information on the characteristics of schools. The rudimentary characteristics available suggest that the dispersion of students out of traditional Hispanic metros has tended to improve the educational context of Hispanic public school students. Table 2.6 shows the characteristics of the schools attended by the typical Hispanic student. Schools attended by Hispanics in the traditional Hispanic metros tend to be larger, poorer, more segregated, and have fewer instructional resources than schools attended by Hispanics in the new settlement metros.

The typical Hispanic student's school in the traditional Hispanic metros has 1,240 students. In comparison, the average Hispanic student's school in the new destination metros has 986 students.[9] Although the relationship between school size and educational outcomes may not be linear, bigger schools are associated with higher student attrition rates and lower educational achievement (9, 17).

Hispanic students in traditional Hispanic metros are more likely to attend Title I schools. Title I funds are targeted on public schools with larger concentrations of low-income students. Nearly 75% of Hispanic students in traditional metros attend Title I eligible schools, in comparison to 58% of Hispanic students in the new settlement metros. Title I status has at least two direct implications. On the one hand, since Title I schools tend to be high-poverty schools, they tend to have lower achievement levels. On the other hand, Title I status implies additional Title I funding and the ability to offer supplemental services and school-wide programs.

A widely used measure of school segregation is the exposure index (18). The Hispanic-white exposure index is the percent of the student body that is white at the school of the average Hispanic student. As Table 2.6 reports, the Hispanic-white exposure score is 38 in new settlement areas and 18 in traditional Hispanic areas. The schools attended by Hispanics in new settlement areas are less segregated than the schools attended by Hispanics in traditional Hispanic areas.

In terms of instructional resources, Hispanic schools in new settlement areas seem to be better staffed than Hispanic schools in traditional Hispanic areas. The student-to-teacher ratio is about 17 at the school attended by the average Hispanic student in new settlement areas versus 20 in traditional Hispanic metros.

Table 2.6 Mean characteristics of schools attended by Hispanics: Top 100 Hispanic urban metropolitan areas, 2004–2005

Public schools attended by Hispanics	Characteristic										
	% Hispanic	% black	% white	% free/reduced lunch	Size	Student to teacher ratio	% Title I eligible	% school-wide Title I	% magnet	% charter	% urban fringe
Traditional Hispanic areas (48)	65	11	18	56	1,240	19.6	74	58	11	2	45
New settlement areas (30)	37	19	38	56	986	16.6	58	49	11	2	53
Other areas (22)	44	17	35	59	840	17	74	55	1	4	

Source: US Department of Education, Common Core of Data (CCD), Public Elementary/Secondary School Universe Survey

Note: These are the average characteristics of public schools, where the weight a school receives is the number of Hispanic students. Schools educating more Hispanics receive higher weight in computing the average.

Public School Changes in New Settlement Areas

The above comparison is simply based on the most recent characteristics of public schools in the 30 new settlement metros. It also is based on the average of the public schools. Some of the public schools in new settlement metros experienced very large changes since 1993–1994 that may have had an impact on the quality of education.

Although Hispanic enrollment in the new settlement metros nearly tripled from 1993–1994 to 2004–2005 (Table 2.2), public schools in the new settlement metros as a whole did not widely experience this increase. The increases in Hispanic enrollment heavily occurred at 1,400 public schools termed "high Hispanic growth" schools. By definition, these public schools gained at least 100 Hispanic students and at least doubled their Hispanic enrollment from 1993–1994 to 2004–2005. Of the 11,065 public schools in operation during 2004–2005 in the new settlement areas, about 13% experienced "high Hispanic growth."[10] This subset of public schools in the new settlement areas experienced the bulk of the Hispanic enrollment boom. As Table 2.7 shows, 44% of the increase in Hispanic enrollment in the new settlement areas occurred at these 1,400 public schools. The high Hispanic growth schools are consequential presently because they educate 40% of Hispanic students in the new settlement metros.

The rapid growth of Latinos at these public schools was accompanied by other changes as well (Table 2.8). While the size of the student population at most public schools remained stable, rapid Latino growth at the high Hispanic growth schools was accompanied by an increase in the size of the school. The typical high Hispanic growth school increased in size from 860 students in 1993–1994 to 986 students in 2004–2005. High Hispanic growth schools markedly increased in size in spite of the fact that white enrollments were declining. White enrollments were declining at most public schools from 1993–1994 to 2004–2005, but the declines were particularly marked at the high Hispanic growth schools. In 1993–1994, the typical high Hispanic growth school had 573 white students and was 64% white. By 2004–2005, these schools had 417 white students and whites had declined to 38% of the student body. Family affluence at the high Hispanic growth schools also markedly declined. In 1993–1994, 31% of the students at these schools qualified for free lunches under the National School Lunch Act. By 2004–2005, 48% of the students qualified for free lunches.

Thus, although dispersion generally has led to improvement in the measured characteristics of public schools educating Hispanics relative to the public schools in the traditional Hispanic metros, a subset of public schools in the new settlement metros have clearly undergone radical, and perhaps traumatic, changes in the past decade. These public schools are fewer than one-in-seven public schools in the new settlement metros, but they educated 40% of new settlement Hispanics in 2004–2005. How well these schools are coping with the influx of Latinos and meeting their educational needs deserves more investigation.

Table 2.7 Public school enrollment in the 30 new settlement urban metropolitan areas

Race	1993–1994			2004–2005			
	Students	Students in high Hispanic growth schools	% in high Hispanic growth schools	Students	Students in high Hispanic growth schools	% in high Hispanic growth schools	% of growth that occurred in high Hispanic growth schools
Hispanic	359,708	111,168	31	1,022,610	405,452	40	44
NH white	3,929,374	802,537	20	3,814,417	583,357	15	16
NH black	1,235,232	226,101	18	1,650,821	293,644	18	15
NH Asian	219,796	55,156	25	358,749	75,460	21	15
All students	5,795,732	1,204,526	21	6,920,414	1,369,349	20	15

Source: US Department of Education, Common Core of Data (CCD), Public Elementary/Secondary School Universe Survey

Note: In the 2004–2005 school year there were 11,065 public schools in the 30 new settlement areas. "High Hispanic Growth School" refers to the 1,400 public schools that gained at least 100 Hispanic students and at least doubled their Hispanic enrollment from 1993–1994 to 2004–2005.

Table 2.8 Change in the mean characteristics of schools in 30 new settlement urban metropolitan areas

Characteristic								
Public school type	Year	Hispanic enrollment	Black enrollment	White enrollment	% white	% free lunch	Size	Student to teacher ratio
Not a high Hispanic growth school	1993–1994	35	137	439	68	27	639	18.2
	2004–2005	62	153	363	56	35	621	16.4
High Hispanic growth school	1993–1994	79	162	573	64	31	860	18.4
	2004–2005	290	210	417	38	48	986	16.5

Source: US Department of Education, Common Core of Data (CCD), Public Elementary/Secondary School Universe Survey

Note: Unlike Table 5, the average characteristics are the simple average for the schools. The average is not weighted by enrollment. A small school receives the same weight as a large school.

The Impact of Suburbanization on Hispanic Education Conditions

Though the magnitude of suburbanization of Hispanic students from 1993–1994 to 2004–2005 seems modest, suburbanization does seem to have improved the characteristics of the schools attended by Hispanic students. Table 2.9 reports the typical 2004–2005 characteristics of schools attended by Hispanic students in central city areas versus the urban fringe of the central city. Suburban schools are smaller, their student bodies have a smaller percentage qualifying for free/reduced price lunches, and they are more integrated: the typical Hispanic school in the suburbs is a school with 30% white student enrollment versus central city schools with 16% white student enrollment. The pupil-to-teacher ratio varies little across central city and suburban schools attended by Hispanics. Suburban schools attended by Hispanics are much less likely to be Title I eligible than their central city counterparts.

Suburban Hispanic students not only attend different schools than their suburban white counterparts, the average characteristics of Hispanic schools in the suburbs are inferior to the schools attended by suburban whites. Table 2.9 documents that the average urban fringe school attended by whites has fewer students, has fewer students eligible for the reduced/free lunch program, has fewer students per teacher, and is much less likely to be Title I eligible in comparison to the average characteristics of urban fringe schools attended by Hispanics. Although suburbanization does improve the educational context of Hispanic youth, on average, suburban Hispanics are not educated in schools with similar characteristics to suburban white schools.

Conclusions

Until 1990, schools in California, Texas, and New York largely dominated the public schooling of Hispanic youth. Public schools in these three states educated nearly seven-in-ten Hispanic public students. As a result of the changing settlement patterns of the Hispanic diaspora, these states no longer have a near monopoly on the education of Latino youth. These three large states tend to have large, urban public schools, and partly because Hispanics were concentrated in these states, Hispanics have been educated in public schools with distinct, generally unfavorable characteristics (10). While the diaspora presented public schools in new settlement areas with the challenge of educating Hispanic youth that they had little experience educating, it also resulted in Hispanics being educated in new school contexts that may be more favorable.

While the rise of Hispanic students in the South and other new settlement areas has drawn scholarly attention (e.g.,19), there has been little formal empirical analysis of the effect on public schools and the implications for Hispanic education. Perhaps not surprisingly, the dispersion of Hispanic enrollments in new areas of the country has not been evenly distributed across schools. Hispanic population growth has been concentrated in certain communities, and most public schools in the 30 new settlement areas did not experience a much different change than the national

Table 2.9 2004–2005 Mean characteristics of schools: Central city versus urban fringe areas

Characteristic	% Hispanic	% black	% white	% free/reduced lunch	Size	Student to teacher ratio	% Title I eligible	% school-wide Title 1	% magnet	% charter
Central city public schools attended by Hispanics	64	13	16	59	1,182	18.8	80	67	13	3
Urban fringe public schools attended by Hispanics	54	11	30	54	1,163	19.1	61	42	5	1
Urban fringe public schools attended by whites	12	8	75	22	1,025	17.7	31	9	3	1
Traditional Hispanic areas										
Central city public schools attended by Hispanics	68	11	14	57	1,258	19.4	81	67	15	3
Urban fringe public schools attended by Hispanics	61	10	24	56	1,217	19.8	65	45	5	1
Urban fringe public schools attended by whites	19	7	67	22	1,125	18.2	36	11	2	2
New settlement areas										
Central city public schools attended by Hispanics	46	21	28	67	921	16.6	71	64	13	2

Table 2.9 (continued)

Characteristic	% Hispanic	% black	% white	% free/reduced lunch	Size	Student to teacher ratio	% Title I eligible	% school-wide Title 1	% magnet	% charter
Urban fringe public schools attended by Hispanics	29	18	46	47	1,043	16.6	47	36	10	1
Urban fringe public schools attended by whites	9	10	75	26	1,051	18.1	26	11	4	1
Other areas										
Central city public schools attended by Hispanics	51	22	23	69	862	17.0	82	69	1	5
Urban fringe public schools attended by Hispanics	30	9	56	40	802	17.0	60	27	1	2
Urban fringe public schools attended by whites	5	6	85	15	854	16.4	33	4	3	1

Source: US Department of Education, Common Core of Data (CCD), Public Elementary/Secondary School Universe Survey
Note: These are enrollment weighted averages. Calculations for Hispanics put more weight on schools with more Hispanic students. Calculations for whites put more weight on schools with greater white enrollment.

trends in public education over the past 15 years (i.e., they slightly shrank in size, they became less white in both absolute and percentage terms, and their students grew slightly poorer as measured by eligibility for free school lunches). In the new settlement areas, fewer than one-in-seven public schools absorbed much of the Hispanic enrollment boom.

In terms of the kinds of public schools Latinos are attending in new settlement communities, on average, Latino students in new settlement areas are educated in schools with no worse measured characteristics than Latino students in traditional Hispanic metros. The typical Hispanic student educated in a new settlement metro is, in fact, more likely to attend a suburban school, a smaller school, and a more affluent school than his/her counterpart in a traditional Hispanic metro. That is not to say that Hispanics in new settlement areas are attending the same kinds of schools as white students. Hispanics in new settlement areas are much more likely to be educated at majority minority schools than white students in new settlement areas.

Comparing the educational conditions of Hispanic students in new settlement areas to those in traditional Hispanic areas indicates that the diaspora may not have had the dire consequences for Hispanic education that is oft asserted. The "proof of the pudding" is, however, not the characteristics of the schools but the educational outcomes of Hispanic public school students. Little formal analysis investigates the educational attainment (e.g., high school completion and college attendance) and educational achievement (e.g., English acquisition, standardized test scores, and curriculum) of Hispanic students educated in new versus traditional Hispanic schools. An examination of high school completion rates reveals that Hispanic youth in new settlement areas are less likely to finish high school than their Hispanic counterparts in traditional Hispanic metropolitan areas (20). However, white and African American youth also do not finish high school at the same rate if they are educated in the new settlement areas versus the traditional Hispanic areas. This suggests that the educational disparities that Latinos may encounter in their new metropolitan areas are not distinctly Latino but rather reflect long-standing educational disparities between different areas of the country. High school completion is far from the only metric of educational success, however, and more research is needed to understand how Hispanic youth are faring in new communities of settlement.

Acknowledgement The views expressed in this chapter are those of the author and do not necessarily reflect those of the Pew Hispanic Center or The Pew Charitable Trusts. The author appreciates the comments by Lindsay Lowell, Cordelia Reimers, Richard Santos, and the editors on an earlier draft.

Notes

1. Two-thirds of the Hispanics in 36 new settlement counties in the South were foreign born. Nationally, four-in-ten Latinos were born outside the United States. These immigrant men were less likely to be married than their counterparts elsewhere in the United States (21).
2. Though the terms urban and metropolitan are often used interchangeably, metropolitan areas, in fact, can include both rural and urban territory. Although the meaning of the term "suburbanization" is arbitrary, linguistic meaning would seem to dictate that rural areas not be

included in the analysis. Thus, the focus is limited to schools in urban metropolitan areas, not just metropolitan areas.

3. This is consistent with trends in the settlement of the foreign-born population. Gurak and Kritz (22) note that the percentage of the foreign-born population residing in non-metropolitan areas has been declining.

4. Fischer and Tienda (2) note the metropolitanization of Hispanics since 1980, when 77% of Hispanics resided in the 100 largest metro areas. By 2000, 79% of Hispanics lived in these areas.

5. The relative decline of LA-Long Beach-Santa Ana may reflect the location decisions of recently arrived Mexican immigrants. Card and Lewis (23, p. 225) report that the "most important trend in the destination choices of new Mexican immigrants [is] the move away from Los Angeles."

6. The Dallas-Fort Worth metro is considered a "new settlement area" due to the inordinate growth of its Hispanic population since 1980 and the relatively recent settlement of Hispanics in that area. In regard to Dallas, Suro and Singer (8, p. 6) observe that it has not "played a longstanding role as a major gateway for Latino immigrants."

7. The term "urban fringe" reflects the school locale classification used by the National Center for Education Statistics. The locale reflects the location of the school's buildings, not necessarily the residence of its students. "Urban fringe" refers to urban places or territories in metropolitan core based statistical areas that are not in the principal city of the CBSA (13).

8. In some suburban areas (e.g., Fayetteville, Arkansas or Provo, Utah), there are no majority minority schools. In some suburban areas of Texas (e.g., McAllen or El Paso) all suburban schools are majority minority schools.

9. Comparisons of the characteristics of public schools in the two areas are not biased by differences in the school level of Hispanic students. Hispanic students in new settlement areas are not much more likely than their counterparts in the traditional areas to be enrolled in primary schools as opposed to middle schools and high schools. About 56% of Hispanic students in new settlement areas and 54% in traditional Hispanic areas were enrolled in primary schools in 2004–2005.

10. Not all 11,065 public schools can be categorized as a "high Hispanic growth school" or not. Some of the 11,065 schools in 2004–2005 did not exist in 1993–1994; they opened more recently. For a school to be deemed "high Hispanic growth," it must have operated in both 1993–1994 and 2004–2005.

References

1. Durand, Jorge, Douglas S. Massey, and Chiara Capoferro. 2005. "The New Geography of Mexican Immigration." In *New Destinations: Mexican Immigration in the United States*, ed. Victor Zuniga and Ruben Hernandez-Leon, 1–20. New York: Russell Sage Foundation.

2. Fischer, Mary J., and Marta Tienda. 2006. "Redrawing Spatial Color Lines: Hispanic Metropolitan Dispersal, Segregation, and Economic Opportunity." In *Hispanics and the Future of America*, ed. Marta Tienda and Faith Mitchell, 100–137. Washington DC: National Academies Press.

3. Durand, Jorge, Edward Telles, and Jennifer Flashman. 2006. "The Demographic Foundations of the Latino Population." In *Hispanics and the Future of America*, ed. Marta Tienda and Faith Mitchell, 66–99. Washington DC: National Academies Press.

4. Wainer, Andrew. 2004. *"The New Latino South and the Challenge to Public Education: Strategies for Educators and Policymakers in Emerging Immigrant Communities."* Los Angeles, CA: Tomás Rivera Policy Institute.

5. Hanushek, Eric A., and Steven G. Rivkin. 2006. "School Quality and the Black – White Achievement Gap." NBER Working Paper No. 12651. Cambridge, MA: National Bureau of Economic Research.

6. Pong, Suet-ling, and Lingxin Hao. 2007. "Neighborhood and School Factors in the School Performance of Immigrants' Children." *International Migration Review*, 41(1): 206–241.
7. Stamps, Katherine, and Stephanie A. Bohon. 2006. "Educational Attainment in New and Established Latino Metropolitan Destinations." *Social Science Quarterly*, 87(5): 1225–1240.
8. Suro, Roberto, and Audrey Singer. 2002. *"Latino Growth in Metropolitan America: Changing Patterns, New Locations."* Washington, DC: Brookings Institution Center on Urban and Metropolitan Policy.
9. Wirt, John, Susan Choy, Stephen Provasnik, Patrick Rooney, Anindita Sen, and Richard Tobin. 2003. *"The Condition of Education 2003."* NCES 2003067. Washington, DC: National Center for Education Statistics.
10. Schneider, Barbara, Sylvia Martinez, and Ann Owens. 2006. "Barriers to Educational Opportunities for Hispanics in the United States." In *Hispanics and the Future of America*, ed. Marta Tienda and Faith Mitchell, 179–227. Washington, DC: National Academies Press.
11. Rumberger, Russell W. 1995. "Dropping out of Middle School: A Multilevel Analysis of Students and Schools." *American Educational Research Journal*, 32(3): 583–625.
12. Wirt, John, Patrick Rooney, William Hussar, Susan Choy, Stephen Provasnik, Gillian Hampden-Thompson. 2005. *"The Condition of Education 2005."* NCES 2005094. Washington, DC: National Center for Education Statistics.
13. Shen, Quansheng. 2006. *"Documentation to the NCES Common Core of Data Public Elementary/Secondary School Universe Survey: School Year 2004–2005."* NCES 2006339. Washington, DC: National Center for Education Statistics.
14. Sable, Jennifer, and Jason Hill. 2006. *"Overview of Public Elementary and Secondary Students, Staff, Schools, School Districts, Revenues, and Expenditures: School Year 2004–2005 and Fiscal Year 2004."* NCES 2007309. Washington, DC: National Center for Education Statistics.
15. Frey, William H. 2001. *"Melting Pot Suburbs: A Census 2000 Study of Suburban Diversity."* Washington, DC: Brookings Institution Center on Urban and Metropolitan Policy.
16. Logan, John 2004. *"Resegregation in American Public Schools? Not in the 1990s."* Albany, NY: Lewis Mumford Center for Comparative Urban and Regional Research, University at Albany.
17. Rumberger, Russell W., and Scott L. Thomas. 2000. "The Distribution of Dropout and Turnover Rates Among Urban and Suburban High Schools," *Sociology of Education*, 73(1): 39–67.
18. Logan, John. 2002. *"Choosing Segregation: Racial Imbalance in American Public Schools, 1990–2000."* Albany, NY: Lewis Mumford Center for Comparative Urban and Regional Research, University at Albany.
19. Hernandez-Leon, Ruben, and Victor Zuniga. 2005. "Applachia Meets Aztlan: Mexican Immigration and Intergroup Relations in Dalton, Georgia." In *New Destinations: Mexican Immigration in the United States*, ed. Victor Zuniga and Ruben Hernandez-Leon, 244–274. New York: Russell Sage Foundation.
20. Fry, Richard. 2008. "The Enrollment and Attainment of Hispanic Youth in the New Settlement Areas." Paper presented at the 2008 Population Association of America meetings, New Orleans, LA.
21. Kocchar, Rakesh, Roberto Suro, and Sonya Tafoya. 2005. "The New Latino South: The Context and Consequences of Rapid Population Growth." Paper presented at Immigration to New Settlement Areas, the Pew Research Center, Washington, DC.
22. Gurak, Douglas T., and Mary M. Kritz. 2005. "Immigrant Settlement Patterns in the United States in the 1990s: Can Existing Theories Explain the Changes?" Paper presented at the 2005 Population Association of America meetings, Philadelphia, PA.
23. Card, David, and Ethan G. Lewis. 2007. "The Diffusion of Mexican Immigrants During the 1990s: Explanations and Impacts." In *Mexican Immigration to the United States*, ed. George J. Borjas, 193–227. Chicago: University of Chicago Press.

Chapter 3
System of Elections, Latino Representation, and School Policy in Central California Schools

Belinda I. Reyes and Max Neiman

Abstract If representation of a group on a governing board enhances the policy responsiveness of that body to such groups, then under-representation might deprive particular groups of needed programs and benefits. This chapter, therefore, examines the demographics of school boards in Central California, the potential barriers to representation, and differences between Latino and white board members in their perceptions of the issues, needs, and priorities in their districts. We analyze data from the California Department of Education, National Center for Education Statistics, and the National Association of Latino Elected Officials (NALEO), as well as a survey of all superintendents, board members, and a sample of principals in school districts in Central California. We include all unified, elementary, and high school districts that were open in the 2003–2004 academic year (325 districts), concentrating on the years 1995–2004. We find a positive relationship between Latino representation and the proportion of Latino students. However, it is not until Latinos are the overwhelming majority of the district, well over 60% of the students, that we see increased numbers of Latinos on school boards. In addition, the system by which school board members are elected to office is strongly associated with Latino representation, even when we account for the size of the Latino population and party affiliation. Furthermore, the system of electing board members appears to influence local policy. The findings of this study point towards potential changes in policy with changes in Latino representation on school boards.

Introduction

On July 15, 2004, a lawsuit on behalf of Latino voters was filed in Kings County Superior Court. The central claim in the case was that the Hanford Joint Union High School District's at-large system of electing trustees[1] to its board violated the

B.I. Reyes (✉)
San Francisco State University, San Francisco, CA, USA
e-mail: reyesb@sfsu.edu

D.L. Leal, S.J. Trejo (eds.), *Latinos and the Economy*, Immigrants and Minorities, Politics and Policy, DOI 10.1007/978-1-4419-6682-7_3, © Springer Science+Business Media, LLC 2011

California Voting Rights Act of 2001.[2] The school district, which was 39% Latino as of the 2000 Census, did not have a Latino representative among the five-member Board of Trustees for the previous 20 years.

The Hanford school district lawsuit is consistent with a general concern of many scholars and policy makers regarding the impact of institutions on the civic engagement of previously marginalized groups (1, 2). Systems of representation among cities and a host of special purpose districts have come under persistent political and legal scrutiny because there are reasons to believe that certain election systems dilute the voting strength of racial and ethnic groups, leading to the under-representation of socially disadvantaged groups. In fact, such electoral systems were specifically implemented for the purpose of excluding immigrants, among others, from local governance during the Progressive Era (3). For instance, Leal, Martinez-Ebers, and Meier (4, p. 5) noted that at-large elections were "one prong in a larger effort to isolate school boards and city councils from the influence of political parties, immigrants, those of lower socioeconomic status, and the vagaries of the democratic process generally."

If the presence of minority group members on a governing board enhances policy responsiveness to that group, then under-representation might deprive particular groups of needed programs and benefits, which could present particular challenges for the educational mission of schools. School administrators, although largely sympathetic to the needs of all children, may not be able to completely represent the needs of the communities they are tasked to serve if they themselves do not represent the diversity of their communities. Hence, the concern about diversity in governing boards is not simply about "descriptive representation"; diversity may make a difference in terms of policy.

The matter is particularly pressing in places such as our study sites in Central California, where the Latino population has exploded in recent decades. While there are certainly substantial increases in Latino representation on government bodies, Latino political incorporation lags behind relatively when compared to the size of the Latino population (5, 6). Furthermore, a serious challenge for school boards in Central California is the low educational achievement of Latino students. In a recent study, Danenberg, Jepsen, and Cerdan (7, p. vii) examined student outcomes in the California Central Valley and found that "although the Central Valley has one of the fastest growing populations in California, the region is faring worse than the rest of the state on several dimensions, including student socioeconomic outcomes (SES), test scores, college preparation, and college attendance."

The purpose of this chapter is to examine Latino representation in school boards in Central California, the factors that may be contributing to under-representation, and the potential implication of under-representation on policy outcomes. In particular, we examine whether the system of electing school board members affects the number of Latinos on school boards in Central California and whether Latino representation is related to the adoption of Latino-relevant policies.

Review of the Literature

There is a long-standing research literature that examines the relationship between systems of representation and local public policy (8). The range of policy topics is wide and includes such matters as adopting fluoridation, spending and tax levels, responding to the needs of the poor, and the rate at which localities adopt policy innovations. Aspects of local representation systems include whether party labels are on the ballot, what kind of executive system exists (e.g., council-manager, commissioner, or mayor), and whether local elections are organized around ward or at-large systems. This chapter converges with this more general basic research by asking the question "do institutions matter?"

On the one hand, we are interested in learning whether at-large elections systems affect Latino representation. Most of the initial research on at-large elections dealt with city councils and the under-representation of African Americans. Although there are a few exceptions, the evidence strongly suggested that at-large elections diminished the representation of African Americans and thereby reduced the benefits of public policies that would otherwise have been more responsive to them. With the exception of Fraga and Elis (9), similar studies of Latino cities and school boards also indicated that shifts from at-large to ward systems, single-member districts produced very strong representational benefits for Latino communities (10). Two recent studies of national and Texas school boards support these findings (4, 11).

Not only does the system of electing representatives affect the backgrounds of such legislators as city councilmen and school board members, but it apparently also shapes the substance of local policy. In a seminal article, Karnig and Welch (12) found that the way in which chief executives were elected affected how responsive local spending policies were to African Americans. Stewart et al. (13) found that shifting away from at-large school board elections was noticeably related to increasing the numbers of African American teachers and administrators. An analysis of a national sample of school districts by Leal, Martinez-Ebers, and Meier (4) provided similar findings. Even more suggestive for this project is the finding in a Texas study showing that increases in minority teachers and administrators are associated with improved student performance (11).

Of course, in addition to the actual policy consequences of differing election systems on Latino representation and their subsequent influence on board policy, the issues are also related to varying perceptions of legitimacy, concerns regarding civic engagement, and increasing litigation concerning compliance with the California Voting Rights Act of 2001. Indeed, increasingly rancorous disputes over extending voting rights to non-citizens is apparently instigated, in part, because of the perceptions among Latino civil rights activists that Latino populations are not being adequately represented on local governing bodies such as school boards and city councils. In short, the perception among significant segments of the Latino community about a lack of legitimacy among local governing boards might be contributing to other conflicts, with the possible result of increasing the level of acrimony that may be spilling over into larger disputes about immigration policy.[3]

Data and Methods

The research in this chapter focused on the school districts in the San Joaquin Valley (Kern, Tulare, Kings, Fresno, Madera, Merced, Stanislaus, and San Joaquin counties) and Central Coast Region (Monterey, San Benito, San Luis Obispo, Santa Barbara, Santa Cruz, and Ventura counties). We refer to these counties as Central California. We included all unified, elementary, and high school districts that were open during the 2003–2004 academic year. School districts that closed or merged with other districts before 2003–2004 were excluded from the analysis. In all, we concentrated our analysis on 325 districts and gathered data for the years between 1995 and 2004.

Generally speaking, Central California districts are poor—on average, 53% of the children in these districts are on free lunch programs and 10% of the population received TANF (formerly AFDC) in 2003–2004 (see Table 3.1). Also, parents have limited educational levels—over a quarter of parents have not graduated from high school—and student achievement is lower than at other regions of the state (7). Although board members in these districts face significant challenges in general, Latino board members face additional disadvantages. Districts with Latinos on the

Table 3.1 Characteristics of districts in Central California and by whether or not there is a Latino on the school board

	All districts Central California	Latino board member	
		No	Yes
Average number of schools	6.4	5.1	8.8
Average number of students in the district	3,523.39	2,662.63	5,252.88
Number of students in the average school	434.52	390.55	522.88
Average number of Latinos in the district	1,787.27	1,064.40	3,239.71
Number of Latinos in the average school	230.03	159.72	371.29
Average number of EL in the district	922.57	518.33	1,700.24
Number of EL in the average school	122.84	78.25	208.62
Percent of districts with Democrat in the assembly	54.46	48.11	66.37
Percent of parents without a high school education_0304	25.17	18.49	37.38
Percent of population in AFDC_0304	10.11	9.32	11.60
Average % students in free lunch_0304	53.32	45.78	67.46
Percent of teachers that are Latino	11	7	19
Average teacher experience	12.93	13.15	12.52
Percent of teachers with BA or Less	14.8	13.8	16.7
Percent of teachers with emergency or waived credentials	4.1	3.0	4.3
Percent of teachers with bilingual training	7.3	5.0	11.45

school board are poorer, they have a higher proportion of Latinos and English Learners (EL), and they have teachers with slightly less education and experience than districts without Latino board members.

In this chapter, we examine the socioeconomic conditions of the districts, representational issues, and policy using the following wide range of data sources: 1) we merged multiple files (CBEDS, The Language Census, and the Academic Performance Index) from the California Department of Education to generate measures of student outcomes, school and teacher characteristics; 2) Census Demographic Data at School District Level from the National Center for Education Statistics to gather data on population demographics and socioeconomics; 3) data from the National Association of Latino Elected Officials (NALEO) on Latino elected officials in California to gain insights into Latino representation; and 4) data from a survey instrument to include key process and decision-making variables that are not available in published form.[4]

The survey instrument was developed and administered via mail and website for all superintendents, board members, and a randomly representative sample of principals.[5] The survey gathered information on board member characteristics, including age, gender, education, and party affiliation. It asked participants about the level of electoral competition, their expenditures in the last school board election, and their reasons for running for office. It queried participants on what they perceive as the major problems confronting their district, the needs of Latino students, the priorities of the districts, and their views on federal/state mandates. We were also interested in their views on the election system in their districts and the need for Latino representation.

Table 3.2 shows some of the characteristics of the survey respondents. On average, board members, superintendents, and principals are in their early fifties, and most are males, white, and college graduates. Principals and superintendents have significantly more education than school board members—22% of school board members have less than a college education—and most school board members are not conversant in a language other than English. Most school board members in Central California are Republicans, while most superintendents and principals are Democrats.

We employed standard correlation statistics and two sets of multivariate regression models to explore the representation of Latinos in school boards as well as the potential implications of under-representation. The first set of models explores the factors that affect Latino representation in school boards (Table 3.6).[6] The model captures the probability that a district would have Latino representation in the board using logistic regressions, while controlling for factors that could affect representation, such as the proportion of Latino students in the district, poverty in the districts, party affiliation of public officials, and the system of electing board members in the district.

The second set of models captures the potential impact of Latino representation on school policies (see Table 3.7).[7] We estimated a set of OLS equations to examine the proportion of Latino and bilingual teachers, student teacher ratios, and teacher education, while controlling for economic conditions in the district, party affiliation

Table 3.2 Selected comparative characteristics of school boards and superintendents

Selected characteristics	School board members $N = 344$	Superintendents $N = 104$	Principals N=119
Survey recipients	1540	299	602
Response rates	22.3%	34.8%	19.8%
Mean age	54 years old	54 years old	51 years old
Gender	57 % male	75% male	53% male
	43% female	25% female	47% female
Race/ethnicity	1% African American	1% African American	2% African American
	2% Native American	1% Native American	0% Native American
	84% White	85% White	82% White
	2% Asian/Pacific	2% Asian/Pacific	3% Asian/Pacific
	12% Mexican/Latino	11% Mexican/Latino	13% Mexican/Latino
Years lived in district	29 years	16 years	24 years
Years served current position	8 years	6 years	8 years
Partisan identification	10% Strong Democrat	7% Strong Democrat	13% Strong Democrat
	27% Democrat	27% Democrat	41% Democrat
	13% Independent	25% Independent	14% Independent
	39% Republican	33% Republican	28% Republican
	12% Strong Republican	7% Strong Republican	7% Strong Republican
Education	22% Less than College	2% College Grad	5% College Grad
	41% College Grad	59% Masters	82% Masters
	27% Masters	39% Doctoral	13% Doctoral
	10% Doctoral		
Conversant in other language	31% other language	30% other language	33% other language

of public officials, enrollment growth, proportion of EL and Latino students, and the representation of Latinos in the board. Finally, we employed simple descriptive statistics to explore the differences in attitudes, perceptions, and policies between Latino and white school administrators and board members that emerge from our survey. These last results are available in Table 3.8.

Latino Representation in Central California Schools

The Latino population is growing throughout California, but in no place is this growth more dramatic than in California schools. There were 2.1 million Latino children in school in California in the 1995–1996 school year. Nine years later, 3.0 million Latino children attended California schools—a nearly 43% increase in a decade, although the state's overall population only grew by approximately 14%. In the San Joaquin Valley and Central California Coast, the Latino student population increased from under 400,000 to over 580,000 students. They constituted 49% of the students in Central California and were the majority of the students in half of the districts in the 2003–2004 academic year.

Even though the Latino population is growing dramatically, its growth in the political leadership in Central California's schools has been sluggish. Latino representation increased from 136 Latino board members in the mid 1990s to 219 in 2002–2004 (see Table 3.3), but Latinos still only comprise 15% of the 1,602 school board members in the region. In about two third of districts, no Latino school board member was elected in the entire period between 1995 and 2004.

Table 3.3 Number of Latino board members over time, by election system and size of the Latino student population in the district[8]

	1996–1997	1999–2001	2002–2004
Average number of Latino board members	136	146	219
Districts with Latino board member			
No	251	259	212
Yes	74	66	113

There are more Latinos in school districts with Latino board members. In 2004, 62% of the students in districts with Latino representation were Latinos, while Latinos were 40% of the students in districts with no Latino board member. We also find Latino board members in districts with a higher concentration of Latinos. As Table 3.4 illustrates, the average Latino student in a district with a Latino board member was in a school that was 21% white, while the average Latino in a district without a Latino board member was in a school that was 51% white. Even in districts with no Latino school board members, the proportion of Latino students was large.

Table 3.4 The relationship between Latino representation in school boards and the proportion of Latinos and whites in Central California districts[9]

	Latino Board Member 2004		
Data	No	Yes	All Districts
Percent Latino in average school	39%	70%	49%
Percent Latino in school district	40%	62%	51%
Exposure index	51%	21%	40%
Latinos 60% or more of students in the district (37% of districts)		68%	
Latinos 40–60% of students in the district (20% of the districts)		17%	
Latinos under 40% of students in the district (43% of the districts)		14%	

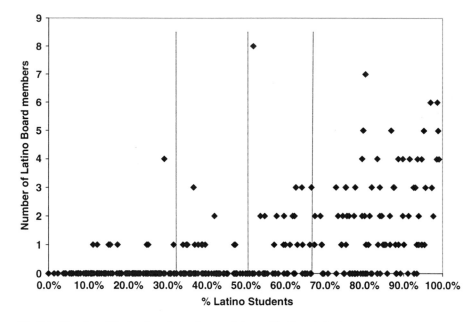

Fig. 3.1 Number of Latino board members and share of Latino students

In order for a district to elect a Latino board member, Latinos need to comprise a large proportion of the district's population. Latino representation is minimal in districts with less than 60% Latino students. Latinos were represented in only 17% of the districts with a Latino student population between 40 and 60% of students. Even when the district has 60% Latino students, Latinos were not represented on about one third of the school boards. Figure 3.1 shows how Latino representation increases with the proportion of Latino students in the districts, but it is not until Latinos are a supermajority of the district, over 60% of the students, that we see more Latino representation.

Factors apart from size of the Latino population in the districts could also affect Latino representation in school boards. Table 3.5 examines the system by which school board members are elected in the region. Few districts (about 5% in Central California) use ward (also known as "trustee") elections. Therefore, most Latino school board members are elected to school boards through at-large elections. However, the proportion of Latino board members increases in jurisdictions that use ward elections. While 32% of at-large district elections have a Latino on the board, 81% of districts with ward elections have at least one Latino on the board. This is also the case for districts with a majority of Latino students. While 65% of the districts with at-large elections and a student population over 60% Latino had a Latino in the board, 85% of districts with ward elections and over 60% Latino students elected Latinos to the board. However, ward elections may have more of an impact on representation in districts where Latinos are not the majority; we test this possibility in the next set of equations.

Table 3.5 The relationship between Latino representation in school boards and the system by which board members are elected at the district

	%
Districts with trustee elections	4.92
At-large elections with Latino board members	32.36
Trustee elections with Latino board members	81.25
Districts with Latino student 60% or more of students	
- With Latino board members	67.77
- Trustee with Latino board member	84.62
- At-large with Latino board member	65.74
Districts with Latino student 40–60% of students	
- With Latino board members	17.19
- Trustee with Latino board member	100.00
- At-large with Latino board member	14.52

Modeling Latino School Board Representation

In this section, we examine the factors that structure Latino representation in school boards. As shown in Table 3.6, the proportion of Latino board members increases with the proportion of Latinos in the districts. Party affiliation has an insignificant impact on Latino representation in Central California school districts, but the system by which school board members are elected has a significant impact on Latino representation.

Figure 3.2 uses the results in Table 3.6 to simulate the relationship between the size of the Latino population and the election system on Latino representation holding constant for other factors. The first two bars show the simulated probability of a Latino board member with at-large elections. The next two bars show the same probability with ward elections. In districts where Latinos are not a majority of the students that use an at-large system of elections (second bar), there is a 9% chance that a Latino would be elected to the school board. Changing the election system to ward elections increases the probability that a Latino would be elected to 27%, even if Latinos are not the majority in the district (first bar). If Latinos are both the majority and there is a ward system of elections (third bar), there is a 66% chance that a Latino would be elected to the board.

However, these results should be considered cautiously since it is difficult to separate the effect of the system of election from those associated with the rate of Latino residents and party affiliation. It is likely that a high proportion of Latinos is correlated with a shift from Republicans to Democrats (14), and one might expect increasing pressures and demands to shift from at-large to trustee elections, especially if Latinos are residentially segregated. There has long been a notion that institutional arrangements such as at-large and nonpartisan elections tend to have a "Republican" bias (15, 16). The implication is that Democratic communities are more likely to change from at-large to ward level elections. Since Latinos tend to vote Democratic, and Democrats are more likely to advocate ward elections, some of the impact of the election system could be due to party affiliation. We

Table 3.6 Regression Results. Logistic equations of the probability of having Latino board members and of having more than one Latino board member

	At least one Latino in the board			More than one Latino in the board		
	Model 1	Model 2	Model 3	Model 4	Model 5	Model 6
Trustee	7.18** (0.66)	3.96* (0.705)	4.72** (0.71)	4.29** (0.62)	4.6* (.72)	4.24** (0.74)
Democrat assembly	1.86** (.25)	1.29 (.279)	1.27 (.28)	1.5 (0.36)	1.52 (.42)	1.16 (.42)
No Latino majority		0.188*** (.366)	0.189*** (0.37)	0.057*** (0.68)	0.097*** (0.73)	0.096*** (0.72)
% Free lunch		1.01 (0.0066)	1.01 (0.007)	1.01 (0.009)	1.01 (.01)	1.01 (.01)
Trustee*Lesst60%Latino			0.001 (789)			2.74 (2.72)
Latino board member 1996–1997					11.7*** (0.39)	11.62*** (0.39)
Likelihood ratio	21.78***	84.5***	85.3***	95.4***	141.5***	141.7***
Wald	17.4***	65.9***	65.2***	43.97***	70.6***	69.9***
Number of observations	325	325	325	325	325	325

Note: *** Significant at a 1% level. ** Significant at a 5% level. * Significant at a 10% level.
The table shows odds ratios instead of regression coefficients. An odds ratio smaller than one means that as the independent variable increases, or the dichotomous variable has a value of one, the odds of having a Latino in the board decrease. A value greater than one indicates that as the variable increases, or a dichotomous variable has a value of 1, the odds of having a Latino in the board increase. Standard errors are in parentheses.

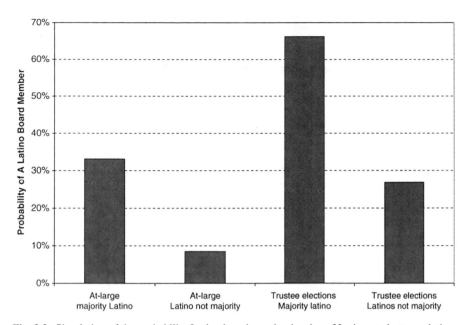

Fig. 3.2 Simulation of the probability Latino board member by size of Latino student population and the election system: 2002–2004

therefore ran models separately for Republican and Democratic districts, but we still find that the system of elections has a large and significant correlation with Latino representation.

Undoubtedly, having a Latino board member is better than having no Latino board member, but they may not be able to have sufficient influence in policy if they are marginalized on the board. About two-thirds of the districts in Central California had no Latino representation (see Fig. 3.3). Of those with Latinos on the school boards, 44% had only one Latino trustee on the board. The majority of the districts with more than one Latino school board representative were places that had very large Latino majorities among the residents and district students.

In addition to the size of the Latino population, what would lead to greater Latino representation in school boards? Although model 4 in Table 3.6 shows that the size of the Latino population is critical, so is having another Latino in the board, as is having trustee elections. Figure 3.4 shows a simulation of the probability of having more than one Latino in the school board using the results from Table 3.6. In a given year, it is unlikely that a district would have more than one Latino in the board if there were no Latino board member in prior years, but the system of elections appears to correlate with the number of Latino board members. There is a 6% chance of having more than one Latino board member if the district has at-large elections and there is no prior Latino representation, even when Latino students are the majority of the district. However, if there are district elections, the probability of having more than one Latino in the board increases to 24%. Once a Latino

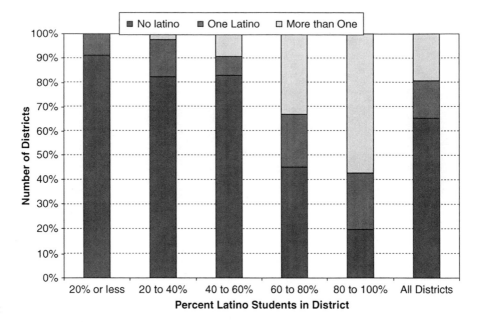

Fig. 3.3 Latino representation by the proportion of Latino students in the district: 2002–2004

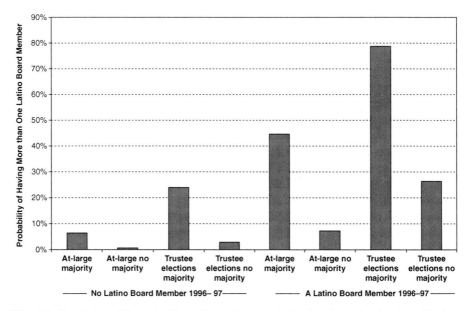

Fig. 3.4 Simulation of the probability of more than one Latino board member by size of Latino student population and the election system: 2002–2004

is elected to the school board, the chances of electing a second Latino increases significantly—there is a 45% chance of electing a second Latino to the board if Latino students are the majority and the community uses at-large elections. On the other hand, if Latino students are the majority and there are ward elections, the probability of having multiple Latino board members increases to 80%. Therefore, for Latinos, getting the first Latino in office is critical to increasing the probability of a second Latino board member. In school districts with no Latinos in office, only ward elections have a large and significant correlation with having multiple Latino board members.

These findings strongly suggest the importance of the system by which board members are elected and its effect on Latino representation in Central California. Without ward elections, Latinos are unlikely to win office, even in cases where they are the majority of the student population. Changing the system of elections in Central California could have a significant impact on Latino representation in school boards.

The Impact of Latino Representation on Policy

As pointed out earlier, representation is important not only because it may have an impact on descriptive representation, but it may also shape the substance of local policy. In this study we find that Latino representation is correlated with the proportion of Latino teachers and bilingual teachers (see Table 3.7 for the results). In Fig. 3.5, we illustrate a simulation of the correlation between Latino board members and the proportion of Latino and bilingual teachers, holding constant for other factors. Districts with at least one Latino board member have more Latino and bilingual teachers than districts with no Latino representation, after controlling for the size of the Latino student population and the growth in the district. Latinos are less than 1% of the teachers in districts with no Latino representation but close to 7% of the teachers in districts with new Latino representation, as measured by having a Latino board member in 2002–2004. In districts that had Latino representation for a longer period of time (since 1999–2000), one of every 10 teachers was a Latino. Similar patterns are also clear for bilingual education. In districts without a Latino board member, 6% of the teachers can teach bilingual education. In districts with Latino representation, at least 10% of the teachers can teach bilingual education.

Districts with Latino representation have more students than districts without Latino representation. On average there are over 5,000 students in districts with Latino board members as compared to 2,600 students in districts without Latino representation. In Fig. 3.6, we see that districts with Latino board members also have greater student-teacher ratios. However, over time, Latino representation correlates with reduced class size. While class sizes have a positive correlation with Latino representation in 2002–2004, it does not with Latino representation in 1999–2000. Furthermore, we find a correlation between Latino representation in 2002–2004 and the proportion of teachers with a BA or less. But just as with class size, in school districts with longer periods of Latino representation, this is less of a problem. There is

Table 3.7 Parameter estimates for OLS equation of bilingual teacher training, Latino teacher, class size, and teacher education: 2003–2004 academic year and 2000–2001 academic year

	% Bilingual teachers 0304	% Bilingual teachers 0304	% Bilingual teachers 0001	% Latino teachers 0304	Mean class-size 0304	Mean class-size 0304	% Teachers BA or less 0304	% Teachers BA or less 0304
Intercept	0.01557** (0.01588)	0.02027 (0.0158)	1.83782** (0.92007)	–0.034** (0.01462)	18.7*** (0.693)	18.9*** (0.6955)	0.12*** (0.01853)	0.12*** (0.01876)
Latino board 0204	0.03588 (0.01629)			0.061*** (0.01449)	1.29541** (0.50407)		0.03075* (0.01842)	
Latino board 9900		0.05594*** (0.01793)				0.16097 (0.5975)		0.01805 (0.02184)
Latino board 9697			1.82455* (0.99452)					
Democrat	0.01352 (0.01372)	0.01169 (0.0136)	–0.185 (0.82974)	0.047*** (0.01254)	–0.35 (0.42)	–0.31829 (0.4294)	–0.00921 (0.01595)	–0.0075 (0.01604)
% students free lunch_0304	0.00016 (0.0003)	0.0001 (0.0003)	–0.0373** (0.01825)	0.0018*** (0.0002)	–0.00324 (0.0096)	–0.00149 (0.0097)	0.000549 (0.0003)	0.00065** (0.0003)
% LEP students district_0304	0.11121** (0.0483)	0.1129** (0.04602)	22.659*** (2.76011)					
# Latino students district	0.000001 (0.000002)	0.0000 (0.0000)	0.0003** (0.0001)	0.000003* (0.00000)			–0.000003 (0.00000)	–0.000003 (0.00000)
Latino students mean school					–0.00126 (0.002)	0.0007 (0.0023)		
# of students mean school					0.0064*** (0.00139)	0.006*** (0.0014)		
Enrollment growth_9504	0.01243 (0.02603)	0.01031 (0.02578)	1.86903 (2.24074)	0.02805 (0.02101)			–0.00273 (0.02648)	–0.00279 (0.02658)
R square	0.1276	0.1451	0.3334	0.3412	0.2326	0.2168	0.0316	0.025
Observation	293	293	277	308	323	323	310	310

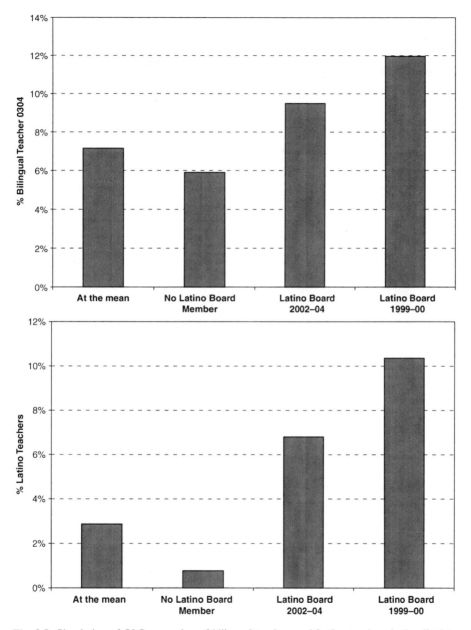

Fig. 3.5 Simulation of OLS regression of bilingual teachers and Latino teachers in the district, 2003–2004 academic year

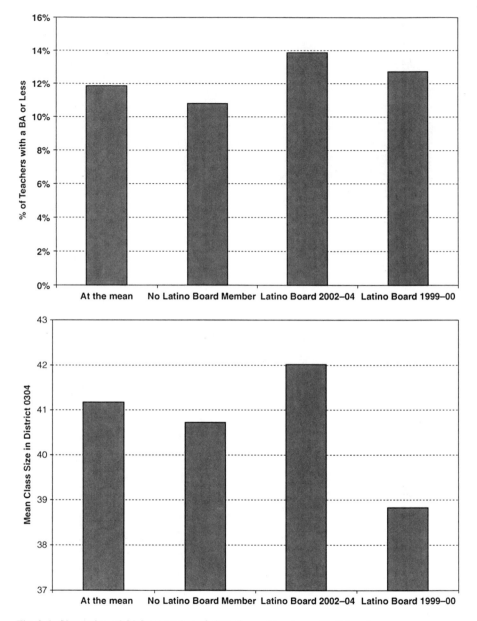

Fig. 3.6 Simulation of OLS regression of class size and teachers with BA or less

no statistically significant correlation between Latino representation in 1999–2000 and teacher education.

These findings point towards potential changes in policy with Latino representation in school board after controlling for the size of the student population, growth in the district, and the economic conditions of the district. Latino representation may increase the number of bilingual teachers and the number of Latino teachers, but they may also increase student teacher ratios and reduce the education of teachers in the district. There may be a decline in student teacher ratios as Latinos remain on the board for longer periods of time.

Views about Challenges and Priorities in the District

In addition to these policy changes, Latino representation may change the environment in schools. Latino school board members may bring different perspectives to the boards and change the priorities of the districts. In the following pages, we compare the views of Latino and white school board trustees, superintendents, and principals. Ideally, we would account for the characteristics of the district—election systems in the district as well as the social and economic conditions of the district and its schools—when looking at the opinions of district's administrators, since the realities of the district could dictate the views and priorities of school officials. This section only shows the general patterns without controlling for other factors. In future research, we would explore the opinions of school administrators while controlling for the conditions in the district. Therefore, these results only suggest differences in views and priorities.

There were 567 respondents in the survey: 470 of them were white and only 62 Latino (37 school board trustees and 25 superintendents and principals). Although consistent with the patterns of representation in Central California, the sample size is too small to make major generalizations about Latino school officials. However, they are nevertheless suggestive of potential differences between Latino and white school officials. In order to increase the level of confidence in the findings, we would like to interview a larger sample of school officials in the future.

We presented respondents with a list of issues or problems (see Table 3.8). They were asked to determine which issues were serious in their district. Figures 3.7 and 3.8 show the percent of respondents that felt the problem or issue was serious, very serious, or extremely serious in their district. As pointed out earlier, while districts in Central California are at a disadvantage compared to other districts in the rest of the state (7), districts with Latino representation appear to have greater challenges. This may reflect the differences in what Latinos and white school board members view as the more serious problems in their schools.

The only issue the majority of white school board members mentioned as a serious problem in their district was federal and state mandates, but only about one-third mentioned having problems meeting those standards. Although many white board members mentioned funding as a problem, most did not—46% of white board members mentioned insufficient funds as a serious issue in their schools. The story is very different for Latino board members: 64% of them mentioned the lack of sufficient funds and having a cohort of students with language limitations in their districts (they also have a higher proportion of English learners than the typical district without Latino representation in Central California). Only 39% of the Latino respondents

Table 3.8 Combined percentage for serious, very serious, extremely serious responses for trustees, principals and superintendents

	Trustees		Superintendents		Principals	
	%	N	%	N	%	N
Mandates from federal/state government	54	333	61	103	67	117
Students' language limits	40	329	51	101	65	117
Problems meeting federal/state standards	30	339	47	103	53	118
Lack of parental involvement	33	334	30	102	43	115
Learning disabilities among students	28	340	30	102	42	117
Insufficient funds	45	337	43	103	37	116
Teacher salaries	20	336	27	102	30	118
Lack of representation for some groups on boards	9	339	8	103	23	118
School over-crowding	18	338	10	103	20	116
Teacher training	10	334	8	103	17	115
Quality of school board trustees	6	338	5	103	17	118
Instructional use of computers	10	336	15	103	15	118
Community conflicts	9	338	14	101	15	114
Student discipline	13	337	6	102	14	115
Quality of superintendent	6	339	1	96	10	113
Substandard buildings	8	336	1	103	7	116
Poor classroom materials	3	334	1	103	6	115

rated state and federal mandates as a serious problem in their district. More important for them was the lack of access to computers and that of parental involvement in schools. They were also concerned with student discipline and the quality of their facilities.

White and Latino board members disagreed on the importance of representation and the level of group conflict in their communities. Although Central California has a significantly diverse population throughout Central California, Latinos are more represented in the more diverse districts, where there is potentially more conflict and more need for descriptive representation. About 20% of Latino board members mentioned community conflict and representation as critical issues in their districts, but only 7% of white board members saw these as serious issues in their districts. The picture that emerges from our interviews is that Latino respondents clearly viewed their schools as under stress in a number of unsurprising ways with regard to student preparation and school resources, while the major issue for white board members, even in districts with high proportions of Latinos and English learners, is federal and state standards.

Turning to the Latino and white superintendents and principals, they tend to agree with each other more than Latino and white board members. They are also in more direct contact and more accountable for the problems in their schools than school

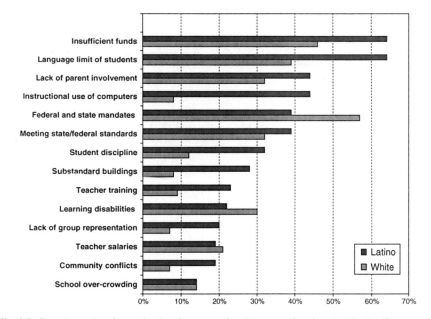

Fig. 3.7 Board members' perceived seriousness of problems confronting the district (Percent who responded the issue was serious, very serious, or extremely serious). Note: Results generated from survey

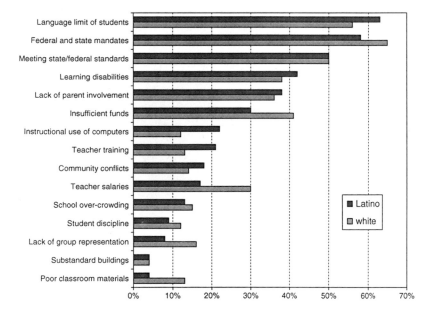

Fig. 3.8 Superintendents and principals perceived seriousness of problems confronting the district (Percent who responded the issue was serious, very serious, or extremely serious). Note: Results generated from the survey

board members. The majority of them see the language limitations of their students and meeting mandates and standards as serious problems confronting their districts. A similar proportion also spoke about insufficient funds, lack of parental involvement, and being able to educate students with learning disabilities. Superintendents rated the two resource items more seriously (insufficient funds and teacher salaries), while the principles tended to focus on the quality of the pedagogical environment— the quality or preparation of the students and the physical environment of teaching. Latinos and white superintendents and principals also shared similar views on the importance of group conflict and issues of representation in their districts. In fact, more white superintendents and principals mentioned representation as a serious problem in their district than Latinos—16% of the white respondents versus 8% of Latino superintendents and principals. With so few Latino superintendents or principals, we view these results as highly tentative and suggestive, rather than conclusive.

Figure 3.8 focuses on processes associated with elections and representation. Perhaps responding to the slow turnover in school board memberships in Central California, Latino trustees indicate more than whites that there is very little turnover in board membership; indeed 61% of the Latino trustees indicate that there is very little turnover on their boards, compared to 42% of white respondents. Furthermore, Latino school board members are more likely than their white counterparts to believe that an at-large election system decreases the district's ability to represent constituents, although less than a majority of the Latino respondents feel that way (47% versus 30% of the white respondents). Significantly, a higher proportion of Latino board members (25% versus 10%) believes that changing the election system is either important or fairly important in their districts. This is perhaps because Latinos see themselves as better representing the needs of Latino students in their district. Seventy-two percent of Latino trustees believe that they are influential or very influential in representing Latino students in their districts, as compared to 53% of white board members. There is also a relationship between being a Latino school board trustee and believing that Latino residents want to increase both the number of Latino trustees and the number of Latino teachers.

Looking at superintendents and principals, there is again significant agreement between whites and Latinos. The main area of disagreement among white and Latino school administrators is the issue of changing the election system. School administrators tend to agree on most other issues, but when talking about representation, Latino administrators are more than three times as likely as whites to claim that changing the school board election system is important for their district. Furthermore, an overwhelming majority (78%) of Latino administrators believe that Latino residents in their districts desire to increase the number of Latino teachers in their districts. However, this is also an important issue for white administrators. Almost 60% of white principals and superintendents believe that Latino residents desire to increase the number of Latino teachers.

Finally, given the importance of federal and state standards, we asked respondents about the effectiveness of the No Child Left Behind Act in responding to the needs of under-served students in their district. More than 60% of white and

Latino trustees, principals, and superintendents agreed that the Act *has not* made the schools in their districts more responsive to the needs of under-achieving students. In fact, Latino school officials are slightly more likely to say the Act has made their districts more responsive, but the difference is not statistically significant.

Notwithstanding the tentative nature of the data, the results suggest that whether or not a school board trustee is Latino or white is associated with a host of important issues regarding representation, policy, and election systems. Of special interest for this research, Latinos see conflict and representation as critical issues for their districts to address. They also bring a different set of priorities to the district and concentrate more on resources needs and the quality of the pedagogical environment in their schools. This, however, may correspond to the needs of their districts as having a greater host of challenges than the average district represented by white board members. Additional data would allow us to model these interactions and be able to explore if Latinos bring a different set of perspectives to districts, while holding constant other possibly important characteristics of the districts.

Conclusion and Policy Implications

We find that there are distinctive socioeconomic patterns in districts that have Latino school board trustees as compared to those that do not. Our data suggest that Latino trustees and Latino school district administrators, such as superintendents and principals, may think of priorities, problems, and processes differently than their white counterparts. As others have shown (4), Latino representation is linked to the electoral structure of school boards, with at-large systems potentially hindering Latino representation. We found that there is a significant correlation between bilingual teachers in a district and Latino school board membership. Additionally, having more Latino administrators appears to produce higher numbers of Latino teachers. Insofar as a greater presence of Latino administrators and teachers ultimately produces policies or provides environments that are conducive to improved performance among otherwise under-performing students, the system of electing school board members might be a critical, albeit indirect, factor shaping Latino student performance.

We believe that two major considerations need further work. First, it is necessary to greatly increase the reach of the study by including a number of additional regions from the state, particularly some of the urban regions in both the northern and southern regions, as well as some of the other rural, less developed areas of the state. Moreover, we would like to concentrate on districts with low-SES schools and/or Latino-predominant school districts, to more effectively control for the social environment in the districts.

Despite the data limitations, the study strongly supports the claim that election systems matter. The data also underscore the point that Latinos differ from whites in their perceptions of problems and priorities. Insofar as these differences in perceptions are also linked to differences in student performance, the clear

Table 3.9 Trustee, superintendents/principals compared by whether respondent is White or Latino

	Trustees		Superintendents and principals	
	White	Latino	White	Latino
Competition				
How often trustees turn over (% Very little)	42%	61%	52%	46%
How competitive trustee elections (% Very little)	37%	28%	38%	21%
Perception of efficacy				
Effect of election system on representing constituents (% decreases ability)	30%	47%	43%	42%
How influential is a board member in representing Latino students (% influential/very influential)	53%	72%	68%	73%
Election system as issue				
Issue of changing election system (% fairly important or important)	10%	25%	12%	40%
Do Latino residents desire to increase number of Latino trustees (% Yes)	18%	55%	33%	33%
Do Latino residents desire to increase number of Latino teachers (% Yes)	34%	68%	58%	78%
Impact of accountability				
NLCB made schools more responsive (% agree/strongly agree)	26%	33%	40%	41%

implication is that policies designed to improve the descriptive representation of Latinos might be an important part of the overall effort to enhance Latino student performance.

Acknowledgement The authors would like to thank Joaquin Avila for his contribution to this report. As a consultant on this project, his help was invaluable in disentangling the legal implications of this research. We are grateful to the California Policy Research Center (CRPC) for their funding and to Andres Jimenez, the Director of CPRC, for his support and mentoring. We benefited greatly from the work of Jason Martinez, Renatta DeFever, and Diego Valencia, who provided research support on this project. Our survey would have been impossible without the help of Jorge Aguilar and his staff at the Center for Educational Partnership, Melissa Mayorga, Rei Suryana, and Xuanning Fu, who ran the survey for us. Finally, we are indebted to the Public Policy Institute of California for generously providing us with space and resources to complete this research.

Notes

1. The form of local elections varies from school district to school district. Some cities elect their local representatives by district, some have at-large elections, and some have both. In an at-large system of voting, all candidates for school board are elected by all of the city's voters. In district elections, however, council members are selected from a geographical section of the city, or ward. Some cities combine these two methods and elect some council members at large

and some from districts. One of the arguments against at-large elections is that it diminishes the representation of particular groups, especially if the group is concentrated in a specific ward. For more information on election systems throughout the United States, visit the National League of Cities website at http://www.nlc.org/about_cities/cities_101/168.aspx.

2. Recent California law has made it easier to sue to challenge at-large elections. The California Voting Rights Act of 2001 expands the voting rights granted under the federal Voting Rights Act by, among other things, granting standing to groups who are too geographically dispersed to elect their candidate of choice from a single member district. The Act prohibits at-large voting if evidence shows that such voting "impairs the ability" of a minority group "to elect candidates of its choice or its ability to influence the outcome of an election."

3. There have been increasing calls among some groups to permit non-citizens to vote in school board and municipal elections, and the issue has fueled increasingly intense reactions among groups that have expressed opposition to Latino immigrants. In this sense, the issue of representation of Latinos has the potential of spilling into other policy areas.

4. Most of the data on student and teacher characteristics was obtained from Christopher Jepsen, who graciously shared his data on Central California with us.

5. Using multiple mailings, web surveys, and preparatory contact with respondents, we achieved a response rate of 23%. A survey list of these respondents was generated from the districts' administrators and principals as well as county boards of education. To retrieve this information, the project used a mailed survey sent to a list of key administrators and principals. We also contacted all the districts in the region of analysis to gather information about the type of election system available in the district.

6. Table 3.6 shows logit regressions for Latino representation. The first three columns present the probability of having Latinos in the board. The last three columns examine the probability of getting more than one Latino in the board.

7. Table 3.7 presents a set of OLS equations for class size, percent of bilingual and Latino teachers, and for the educational level of the teachers in the district. We explore the impact of a long Latino presence on the board examining the impact of Latino representation at multiple years on the outcomes in the 2003–2004 academic year.

8. We looked at 325 districts in the Central Valley and the Central Coast and 1,602 board members.

9. We measure concentration using the exposure index. The exposure index captures the exposure the average Latino student has to white students by calculating the percent of white students in the school attended by the average Latino student.

References

1. Abney, F. Glenn, and John D. Hutcheson, Jr. 1981. "Race, Representation, and Trust: Changes in Attitudes after the Election of a Black Mayor." *Public Opinion Quarterly*, 45(1): 91–101.
2. Browning, Rufus P., Rogers Dale Marshall, and David H. Tabb. 1986. *Protest Is Not Enough*. Berkeley, CA: University of California Press.
3. Tyack, David. B. 1974. *The One Best system: A History of American Urban Education*. Cambridge, MA: Harvard University Press.
4. Leal, David, Valerie Martinez-Ebers, and Kenneth J. Meier. 2004. "The Politics of Latino Education: The Biases of at-Large Elections." *Journal of Politics*, 66(4): 1224–1244.
5. Hero, Rodney. 1992. *Latinos and the Political System: A Two-Tiered Pluralism*. Philadelphia, PA: Temple University Press.
6. Meier, Kenneth, and Joseph Stewart, Jr. 1991. *The Politics of Hispanic Education: Un paso pa'lante y dos pa'tras*. Albany, NY: State University of New York Press.
7. Danenberg, Anne, Christopher Jepsen, and Pedro Cerdán. 2002. "*Student and School Indicators for Youth in California's Central Valley*." San Francisco, CA: Public Policy Institute of California.

8. Bowler, Shaun, Todd Donovan, and David Brockington. 2003. *Electoral Reform Minority Representation: Local Experiments and Alternative Elections*. Columbus, OH: Ohio State University Press.
9. Fraga, Luis R., and Roy Elis. 2009. "Interests and Representation: Ethnic Advocacy on California School Boards." *Teachers College Record*, 111(3): 659–682.
10. Polinard, Jerry L., Robert D. Wrinkle, Tomas Longoria, and Norman Binder. 1994. *Electoral Structure and Urban Policy: the Impact on Mexican American Communities*. Armonk, New York: M.E. Sharpe.
11. Meier, Kenneth J. and Eric Gonzalez-Juenke. 2003. "Electoral Structure and the Quality of Representation: The Policy Consequences of School Board Elections." Paper presented at conference on School Board Politics, Program on Education Policy and Governance, Taubman Center for State and Local government Center for American Political Studies, John F. Kennedy School of Government, Harvard University, October 15–17.
12. Karnig, Albert K. 1980. *Black Representation and Urban Policy*. Chicago: University of Chicago Press.
13. Stewart, Joseph, Jr., Robert E. England, and Kenneth J. Meier. 1989. "Black Representation in Urban School Districts: From School Board to Office to Classroom." *Western Political Quarterly*, 42(2): 287–305.
14. Gimpel, James G., and Karen Kaufman. 2001. *"Impossible Dream or Distant Reality? Republican Efforts to Attract Latino Voters."* Backgrounder, August. Washington, DC: Center for Immigration Studies.
15. Hagensick, A. Clarke. 1964. "Influences of Partisanship and Incumbency on a Nonpartisan Election System." *Western Political Quarterly*, 17 (1): 117–124.
16. Williams, Oliver P., and Charles R. Adrian. 1959. "The Insulation of Local Politics under the Nonpartisan Ballot." *American Political Science Review*, 53(4): 1052–1063.

Part II
Higher Education

Chapter 4
Does Reducing College Costs Improve Educational Outcomes for Undocumented Immigrants? Evidence from State Laws Permitting Undocumented Immigrants to Pay In-State Tuition at State Colleges and Universities

Aimee Chin and Chinhui Juhn

Abstract Ten states, beginning with Texas and California in 2001, have passed laws permitting undocumented students to pay the in-state tuition rate—rather than the more expensive out-of-state tuition rate—at public universities and colleges. We exploit state-time variation in the passage of the laws to evaluate the effects of these laws on the educational outcomes of Hispanic childhood immigrants who are not US citizens. Specifically, through the use of individual-level data from the 2001–2005 American Community Surveys supplemented by the 2000 US Census, we estimate the effect of the laws on the probability of attending college for 18- to 24-year-olds who have a high school degree and the probability of dropping out of high school for 16- to 17-year-olds. We find some evidence suggestive of a positive effect of the laws on the college attendance of older Mexican men, although estimated effects of the laws, in general, are not significantly different from zero. We discuss various reasons for the estimated zero effects. Two important considerations are that little time has elapsed since the state laws were passed and that unchanged federal policy on financial aid and legalization for undocumented students may dampen the state laws' benefits. Thus, the longer-run effects of the laws may well differ from the short-run effects presented in this chapter.

Introduction

State colleges and universities typically charge a much lower tuition to students who have established residency in the state than to students who reside elsewhere. Debate has ensued over how to treat undocumented immigrants who arrived in the United States as children. They may have grown up in the state, but because they are in

A. Chin (✉)
University of Houston, Houston, TX, USA; National Bureau of Economic Research (NBER), Cambridge, MA, USA
e-mail: achin@uh.edu

D.L. Leal, S.J. Trejo (eds.), *Latinos and the Economy*, Immigrants and Minorities, Politics and Policy, DOI 10.1007/978-1-4419-6682-7_4,
© Springer Science+Business Media, LLC 2011

the United States without legal authorization, it is not clear whether they have met the residency requirements for in-state tuition. State governments define residency requirements, and thereby have the ability to determine whether an undocumented student who has been living in that state qualifies for in-state tuition. Ten states, beginning with Texas and California in 2001, have passed laws permitting undocumented students to enroll in public universities and colleges as state residents. In this chapter, we evaluate the impact of such laws on the educational outcomes of undocumented immigrants.

An evaluation of these laws is of interest for a number of reasons. First, additional states are considering passing similar laws. Evidence for whether these laws help intended beneficiaries would assist states in deciding whether to adopt them. Second, the lower educational attainment of Hispanic immigrants and their children relative to non-Hispanics has been a major domestic policy concern. Undocumented immigrants are predominantly from Mexico and Central America and make up a disproportionate share of less-educated Hispanics.[1] It would be useful to understand the extent to which the high price of college education is responsible for the poor educational outcomes of undocumented immigrants. Access to affordable college education may induce high school graduates to go on to college, and perhaps even induce children who would have dropped out of high school (because there was no hope of attending college) not to drop out. Might reducing the price of college education increase educational attainment for undocumented immigrants?

We exploit state-time variation in the passage of the laws permitting undocumented immigrants to pay in-state tuition to evaluate the effects of these laws. Specifically, we are not comparing outcomes in a particular state before and after the law is passed to determine the effect of the law, nor are we comparing outcomes in states that have the law to states that do not have the law. Instead, we are using a difference-in-differences-type identification strategy in which the change in outcome over time for states that passed the law earlier are compared to the change over time for states that passed the law later or that have not passed it; that is, the identifying assumption is that without the law, changes in outcome would have been the same between earlier passers and later/never passers.[2] We explore the validity of this assumption by examining US-born Hispanics—they are legal US residents but arguably experience similar conditions in terms of obstacles to higher education in the state.

We apply our identification strategy to individual-level data from the 2001–2005 American Community Surveys supplemented by the 2000 US Census. To preview the results, although we find some evidence suggestive of a positive effect of the laws on the college attendance of Mexican men, estimated effects of the laws, in general, are not significantly different from zero. We discuss various reasons for the estimated zero effects. Two important considerations are that little time has elapsed since the state laws were passed and that unchanged federal policy on financial aid and legalization for undocumented students may dampen the state laws' benefits. Thus, the longer-run effects of the laws may well differ from the short-run effects presented in this chapter.

This chapter is organized as follows. In the next section, we provide a brief background on these laws permitting undocumented students to pay in-state tuition and discuss related literature. Following that, we propose a theoretical and empirical framework. We then discuss the data and present our results. We discuss the findings in the last section.

Background

Legislative Background

The rise in the number of undocumented immigrants has been an impetus for state laws permitting them to pay in-state tuition at public colleges or universities. In 2004, there were an estimated 10.3 million undocumented immigrants in the United States, which constitute 29% of the foreign-born population in the country (1). Undocumented immigration has grown dramatically in recent decades, such that undocumented immigrants represent a larger share of recent immigrants than immigrants who have lived in the United States a long time. For example, in 1995, nearly half (an estimated 45%) of recent immigrants were undocumented, in contrast to 28% in 1980 and 5% in 1970 Smith (2).[1] Many of the undocumented immigrants were born in Mexico and other countries in Latin America. In 2004, 57% of undocumented immigrants were born in Mexico and 24% were born in the rest of Latin America (1).

Among these undocumented immigrants are foreign-born children who followed their parents to the United States; in 2004, 14% of all undocumented immigrants were undocumented children (1). US law requires education through grade 12 to be provided irrespective of legal status, thus providing full access to public schools up through grade 12 to these undocumented children.[3] Proponents of the laws permitting undocumented students to pay in-state tuition argue that undocumented children who grew up in the state should continue to have the same access to the state's educational institutions as their legally resident classmates even after high school. An important premise is that the undocumented children should not be penalized for their parents illegally entering and/or staying in the United States; if their undocumented children have performed well in school, they should be rewarded with the same opportunity to attend college as their legally resident classmates.

California and Texas are the two states with the most undocumented immigrants—California has 24% of the nation's unauthorized immigrants and Texas has 14%—and were the first two states to adopt these laws permitting undocumented immigrants to pay in-state tuition. Between 2002 and 2006, eight more states passed these laws (see Table 4.1), some with a substantial number of undocumented immigrants (e.g., New York with 7% of the total unauthorized population and Illinois with 4%) and others with relatively few (e.g., Nebraska with under 0.5%). Typically, out-of-state tuition is over twice the amount of in-state tuition. In the 10 states that

---

[1] Table 4 which uses data from Passel.

Table 4.1 State laws allowing undocumented students to pay in-state tuition

State	Name of law	Date law was passed	First semester law was effective
Texas	H.B. 1403	May 2001	Fall 2001
California	A.B. 540	April 2001	Spring 2002
Utah	H.B. 331	March 2002	Fall 2002
New York	S.B. 7784	August 2002	Fall 2002
Washington	H.B. 1079	May 2003	Fall 2003
Oklahoma	S.B. 596	May 2003	Fall 2003
Illinois	H.B. 60	May 2003	Fall 2003
Kansas	H.B. 2145	May 2004	Fall 2004
New Mexico	S.B. 582	April 2005	Fall 2005
Nebraska	L.B. 239	April 2006	Fall 2006

Source: Education Commission of the States (2006).

passed the law, the differential between in-state and out-of-state tuition amounted to a saving of $3,326 per year per student in 2003 (3).

Since the intended beneficiaries are undocumented immigrants who were brought over to the United States by their parents and who grew up in the state, only a limited subset of undocumented immigrants qualify for the in-state tuition. In general, to qualify, the prospective student must have: 1) attended a high school in the state for a certain number of years (typically, 2–4 years); 2) graduated from high school or completed a GED in the state; and 3) signed an affidavit stating that they intend to legalize their status as soon as they become eligible.

As of August 2006, 28 states had considered legislation allowing undocumented immigrants to pay in-state tuition (4).[4] The federal government itself has been considering legislation that makes it easier for states to adopt such legislation, and to make it more worthwhile for undocumented students to take advantage of such legislation. The Dream Act, introduced in Congress in 2001, would provide a route to legal permanent residency status for undocumented students[5] and remove penalties on states that allow undocumented students to pay in-state tuition.[6] Understanding the effects of laws allowing undocumented immigrant students to pay in-state tuition would help states and Congress in their decision-making process.

Related Literature

We are not aware of published studies that use rigorous methods to study the effect of the laws permitting undocumented immigrants to pay in-state tuition on their educational outcomes, probably because most laws have only recently passed.[7] Indeed, the 2006–2007 school year is only the sixth school year in which the law has been in effect for the earliest implementer (Texas), and fewer than four school years have elapsed for six of the 10 states. There may not yet be measurable outcomes in terms of completing a college degree, years of educational attainment, and labor market outcomes. Moreover, it may take time for undocumented immigrants to find out about the laws or for them to adjust their behavior in K-12 to put themselves in a position for college. Therefore, the effects may not be immediate.

Although there are currently no academic studies evaluating these laws, a story by Lewis (5) in the *Boston Globe* attempts to examine the enrollment effects. In Texas, enrollment of undocumented students increased from 1,500 in Fall 2001[8] to 8,000 in Fall 2006. In California's University of California system—the state's most selective tier of higher education institutions—357 undocumented students were enrolled in the 2004–2005 school year, which is the third school year with the law. Data were also provided for the University of New Mexico system, University of Utah system, University of Washington system, and all public institutions in Kansas, which revealed few undocumented students. The story's conclusion is revealed in the title: "In-state tuition is not a draw for many immigrants."

Our study is also interested in the effect of the laws on college enrollment, but we will examine enrollment in all higher education institutions rather than restricting the focus to state flagship systems (as undocumented immigrants for various reasons may be unlikely to attend a flagship institution) and also control for secular changes over time in the enrollment that have nothing to do with the laws. Moreover, we will consider the possibility that the law might have dynamic effects, such as raising high school graduation rates first, because now there is the prospect of attending college in the future.

There are also studies estimating the fiscal impact of these laws (6, 7). These studies examine the impact of the law on tuition revenue, with downward pressure coming from charging undocumented students the in-state tuition rate instead of the out-of-state tuition rate and an upward pressure coming from the entry of students who would otherwise not have attended a public college. In this study, we ignore the cost side and focus on the first-order question of whether the law raises educational attainment for undocumented students. If the law does not provide benefits to the intended beneficiaries, it should be eliminated because its cost — whatever the exact level is — is non-zero.[9]

Besides being (among) the first to estimate the effect of these laws on the educational outcomes of undocumented immigrants, this study adds to the more general literature on the effect of college costs on educational outcomes. Although this is a large literature, few studies have rigorously addressed the problem of endogeneity of college cost in estimating the effect of college cost on educational outcomes.[10] Moreover, none of the studies that do address the problem of endogeneity have focused on the behavior of the children of immigrants. Among children under age 18 in the United States, 13.5 million (or 18.7%) are either immigrants themselves or have at least one parent who is an immigrant based on 2002 data (8). The upsurge in immigration in recent decades means that children of immigrants will be a growing share of the US population into the foreseeable future. It is therefore an urgent policy problem that the children of immigrants lag behind the children of natives in economic and educational achievement. These concerns are especially acute for immigrants from Latin America. Hispanic immigrants and their descendents do not converge to native levels of education as quickly as non-Hispanic immigrants and their descendents (see, for example 9–11). The impact of college costs on the children of immigrants may not necessarily be the same as the impact on other subpopulations, and this chapter goes part of the way toward filling the gap by examining the impact on undocumented immigrants.

The few studies that do treat the endogeneity of college costs convincingly include the following. Kane (12), using within-state changes in tuition at public institutions, finds that a $1,000 decrease in tuition at public institutions raises college attendance by 3.7%. Dynarski (13), using a natural experiment involving the elimination of the Social Security student benefit program, finds that a $1,000 increase in grant aid increases the probability of attending college by 3.6% points and the years of completed schooling by 0.16 years. Dynarski (14), using a natural experiment involving the introduction of a large-scale merit aid program in Georgia, finds that a $1,000 increase in aid raises the college attendance rate by 3.7–4.2%. Dynarski (15) finds that the large-scale merit aid programs in Arkansas and Georgia increased not only college attendance but also college completion. The effect is larger for women than men, and especially large for Hispanic and non-white women; Dynarski attributes this to the fact that girls outperform boys in high school, with the female advantage even starker among Hispanics and non-whites.

Although the four studies just described use distinct identification strategies, they reach a similar conclusion: college attendance and years of college education completed are highly sensitive to costs. However, studies of the Pell Grant program suggest smaller and close to zero effects on college attendance (16–18). Arguably, the typical undocumented student may resemble a Pell Grant beneficiary—most of the $13 billion in Pell Grants given annually are to students from families with income under $40,000; perhaps we should not expect the laws to have any impact on educational outcomes. On the other hand, Dynarski (15) did find that Hispanic and non-white women experienced the largest gains in college attendance and degree completion among all race/ethnicity-gender groups as a result of the Arkansas and Georgia merit aid programs—these programs targeted low- and middle-income families during the time the affected cohorts considered in her paper would have been applying to college; perhaps it is not unreasonable to expect laws permitting undocumented students to pay in-state tuition to improve educational outcomes.

Theoretical and Empirical Framework

Theoretical Considerations

The laws allowing undocumented immigrants to pay in-state tuition effectively lower the price of attending college. Instead of paying the out-of-state price, undocumented immigrants meeting the criteria pay the in-state price, which, as we noted above, is an average annual savings of $3,326. In the framework of an individual deciding whether to invest in a college education (perhaps together with his or her parents), since the cost of college education has decreased, we can expect demand for education to rise. This is because the reduction in price causes some people who did not "value" college education at the out-of-state tuition rate to now buy a college education. Moreover, given that the cost of attending 4-year institutions far exceeds the cost of attending 2-year institutions, the reduction in price might also cause people who would have stopped with a 2-year degree to pursue a 4-year degree.[11] These people would have valued college education at least as much as the out-of-state 2-year college price but less than the out-of-state 4-year college price. The average in-state price at 4-year colleges is lower than the average out-of-state price at 2-year colleges, so these associate's degree holders will now enroll at the 4-year institution for additional schooling, such as for a bachelor's degree.

It should be pointed out that a college education may still be prohibitively expensive for most undocumented immigrants even after the passage of the laws. Most undocumented children are from low-income families. Federal financial aid, which consists of grants (Pell Grants and Supplemental Educational Opportunity Grants), loans (Stafford and Perkins loans), and work-study programs, is the main source of help for students from low-income families, but it is only available to US citizens, US nationals, and "eligible non-citizens." The latter category does not include undocumented immigrants, and it is comprised primarily of permanent residents. The reduction in price of a college education may be insufficient to draw some undocumented children away from the corner solution (for the poorest, the corner is no college education; for the less poor, the corner might be completing an associate's degree only).

The reason for the corner solution does not have to involve low valuation placed on a college education, but could just be the result of credit constraints. Relaxing credit constraints could lead not only to more years of college education, but also to a different composition of years of college education. In particular, it may cause undocumented immigrants to consume more education at 4-year institutions. The reasons stem from the fact that attending 4-year institutions is much more expensive than attending 2-year institutions. In 2003, in the states that passed the law, the average out-of-state price of a year of college was $9,767 for 4-year public institutions and $4,365 for 2-year public institutions. The laws enable undocumented students to pay the in-state price of $3,620 for 4-year public institutions and $2,099 for 2-year public institutions on average. Thus, as mentioned earlier in this subsection, some students who previously would have only attended 2-year institutions will now continue their education at a 4-year institution (thus, fraction of years spent at a 4-year institution rises from nil to at least 50% if a BA is completed).

Additionally, some students may substitute completely away from 2-year colleges toward 4-year colleges (fraction of years spent at a 4-year institution rises from nil to 100%). These students value the higher quality of education at 4-year colleges, such as higher quality faculty, greater course diversity, and additional student services, but due to credit constraints are only able to pay as much as the out-of-state tuition rate at 2-year colleges. The average in-state price at 4-year colleges is lower than the average out-of-state price at 2-year colleges, so now students can afford the higher-quality good. Thus, it is possible that even if we do not observe an increase in years of college education completed, there may be a change in composition of these college years toward higher quality; this compositional change would still be beneficial for the student and society.

There might be substitution not only away from 2-year institutions toward 4-year institutions, but also away from private colleges toward public colleges. Attending a private 4-year institution is more expensive than attending a public 4-year institution, but after the law, the relative price is even higher. In 2003, the average tuition and fees at a private 4-year institution is 1.37 times higher than at a public 4-year institution at out-of-state prices but 3.38 times higher at in-state prices. There might exist some people who would choose a private college before the law who now choose a public college; though they value education at the private institution, they do not value it enough to pay more than triple the price.

The laws could have dynamic effects as well. If one plans on attending college, then one might take a more rigorous set of classes and apply more effort in high school and perhaps even in earlier grade levels. On the other hand, if one does not anticipate attending college, one might apply less effort at school and possibly even not bother completing high school. This suggests that the laws may not necessarily raise college enrollment immediately among undocumented students, because the first cohorts to be of college-going age while the law is in effect may have inadequate preparation for college and, therefore, not be in a position to take advantage of the law. For example, it might be too late for a high school junior to adjust her behavior so that she can have the coursework and grades to get into a competitive 4-year college. By contrast, later cohorts would have time to make adjustments to place themselves in the position of applying for college in the senior year of high school. In summary, given the fact that ability to get into college and perform well in college depends on past schooling investments, it could be that the law has no impact on cohorts who were juniors in high school or older at the time the law passed. Also, it could be that the law, by increasing student expectations of attending college, raises high school completion rates for younger cohorts.

Besides reducing the cost of attending a public post-secondary institution, the laws may have other effects that, in turn, affect schooling decisions. One such possibility is that the laws change perceptions about the future return to education. The Immigration Reform and Control Act (IRCA) of 1986 made it illegal for employers to knowingly hire an undocumented worker, and penalties include fines and prison time. The laws allowing undocumented students to pay in-state tuition make post-secondary education cheaper, but do not change the legal status of undocumented students. Only the federal government can make legislation dealing with immigration in this respect, and currently Congress is considering the Dream Act, which provides a mechanism through which undocumented students (as well as those who serve in the armed forces) can become US permanent residents. With legal status, undocumented immigrants would be able to apply to a much wider set of jobs and would not be restricted to the fringe economy that is less visible to IRCA enforcers.

This means that if undocumented immigrants want a college degree only for an increase in future earnings, the laws allowing undocumented students to pay in-state tuition may have negligible effects on college enrollment and completion.

This is because even with a college degree, undocumented students would still be unable to get good jobs at US firms. For example, a *Wall Street Journal* article by Jordan (19) reports on the experience of the first graduating class to benefit from the Texas law, summarizing: "They are educated, but unable to get work because of their immigration status." On the other hand, it is possible that legislation allowing undocumented students to pay in-state tuition makes undocumented immigrants in that state more optimistic about the passage of the Dream Act.[12] These more optimistic undocumented immigrants will have higher expectations of their return to education—since they believe they will gain legal status and therefore get better jobs—relative to undocumented immigrants in other states. There is good empirical evidence that legalization raises a worker's wages, and much of the wage gain comes from increases in returns to human capital (20).[13] Since undocumented immigrants in states with the laws have higher expectations for legalization, their educational outcomes should improve relative to undocumented immigrants in other states. This legalization-based story might increase enrollment even in educational institutions whose prices for undocumented students are not affected by the laws, such as private colleges.

To summarize this subsection on theoretical considerations, the laws allowing undocumented immigrants to pay in-state tuition should increase (or eventually increase) college enrollment. Additionally, they may change the composition of post-secondary education (2-year/4-year, public/private). The primary stories for these effects are the reduction in the price of college and the increase in expectations about the return to education for undocumented immigrants in states with these laws.

Empirical Framework

We wish to estimate the effect of the laws permitting undocumented immigrants to pay in-state tuition on the educational outcomes of undocumented immigrants. Our main identification strategy relies on the state-time variation in adopting the law. The law has been in effect since the Fall of 2001 semester in Texas, and the latest date of implementation is the Fall of 2006 in Nebraska, the 10th (and most recent) state to pass such a law. On the other hand, there are numerous states that have never had the law, although some are considering it. We can use states that passed the law later or never as controls for secular changes over time in outcomes for states that passed it earlier. To fix ideas, consider estimating the following regression model using repeated cross sections on young adults who are likely to be undocumented immigrants:

$$y_{ist} = \alpha + \beta \, INSTATE_{st} + \delta_s + \gamma_t + x_{ist}'\rho + \varepsilon_{ist}. \qquad (4.1)$$

For individual i born in state s observed at time t, y_{ist} is the outcome (e.g., college attendance), $INSTATE_{st}$ is a binary variable indicating whether state s has a law permitting undocumented immigrants to pay in-state tuition at time t, δ_s is state fixed effects, γ_t is time fixed effects, and x_{ist} is a vector of exogenous explanatory variables (e.g., age and sex of individual, time-varying state attributes).

This is a difference-in-differences-type identification strategy. In order to interpret the OLS estimate of β in Eq. (4.1) as the effect of the laws, we must assume that without the laws, the outcomes would have changed over time by the same amount in the states that passed the laws earlier and the other states (this is known as the parallel trend assumption). It is not possible to directly test this identifying assumption; however, there are ways in which we might try to assess its validity. In this study, we will use legal residents to assess the validity of the parallel trend assumption. The simple intuition is that the law does not impact legal residents—both before and after the law is passed, legal residents can pay in-state tuition when attending an in-state public college or university. However, legal residents are impacted by other changes over time (e.g., economic conditions, tuition, attitudes toward education) that the affected group (undocumented immigrants) also experiences. Thus, we can estimate Eq. (4.1) using a sample of legal residents and test if the estimate of β is zero. This estimate of β using legal residents is essentially an estimate of the differential trend, i.e., it is the difference in outcome that would exist between states that passed the laws earlier and other states *even if there were no such laws at all.* If this estimated differential trend is zero, then we have increased confidence that the parallel trend assumption holds. If it is not zero, we can still recover an estimate of the effect of the laws on undocumented immigrants by subtracting this differential trend away from the estimated β using a sample of undocumented immigrants. More formally, estimate using a pooled sample of undocumented immigrants and legal residents:

$$y_{istj} = \alpha_j + \kappa \; INSTATE_{st} \times I(j = 1) + \lambda \; INSTATE_{st} + \delta_{sj} + \gamma_{tj} + x_{ist,j}'\rho_j + \varepsilon_{istj} \quad (4.2)$$

for individual i born in state s observed at time t where $j = 1$ for an undocumented immigrant (i.e., the affected group, whose opportunities are changed by the laws) and $j = 0$ for legal residents (i.e., the comparison group, whose opportunities are unchanged). $I(\cdot)$ is the indicator function. Since all the parameters are allowed to vary by j, λ of Eq. (4.2) is equal to the estimated β from Eq. (4.1) when using the comparison group individuals and κ of Eq. (4.2) is the difference between the estimated β from Eq. (4.1) when using the affected group individuals and λ. In other words, the estimated effect of the laws on undocumented immigrants is given by κ, which is the estimated β using a sample of undocumented immigrants adjusted for the differential trend provided by the legal residents.

For κ to be a convincing estimate of the effect of the laws permitting undocumented immigrants to pay in-state tuition, we must find a comparison group that adequately captures the differential trends in educational outcomes between states that passed the laws earlier and the other states. The comparison group we use is US-born Hispanics. Since they are native-born American citizens, the laws do not change anything for them. At the same time, given the history of US immigration and the relative recentness of immigration inflows from Latin

America, a majority of US-born children who are Hispanic are of the second generation (i.e., have at least one foreign-born parent). Thus, we can think about US-born Hispanics as a group filled predominantly with children of immigrants. We might believe that US-born children of immigrants and undocumented children living in a particular state experience many similar things, such as changes over time in the state's educational policies, economic conditions, population changes, and attitudes toward foreign-looking or foreign-sounding people. At the extreme, imagine a nuclear family containing undocumented parents, some undocumented children, and some US-born children—then we might believe that all siblings experience similar things except that the undocumented siblings would benefit from the new laws.[14] So it seems that US-born Hispanics could provide a credible estimate of differential trends in educational outcomes.

Data

To implement our identification strategy, we require a dataset that is large enough to provide an adequate number of observations on a narrow subpopulation: foreign-born young adults who are likely to be undocumented. First, we focus on young adults because they are the primary candidates for attending college—although more and more people are taking college courses later in their lives, for the most part, college students come straight from high school or within a few years of leaving high school. For this chapter, we will focus on individuals aged 18–24 with a high school degree when examining measures of college attendance. When we examine dropping out of high school as an outcome, we will examine people aged 16–17.

Second, although ideally we would like the affected group to be restricted to undocumented immigrants, the reality is that there are no nationally representative individual-level data sets that indicate whether someone is an undocumented immigrant; obviously, legal status is sensitive information and difficult to elicit. In this study, we will define the affected group, which is known to contain many more undocumented immigrants than any of the comparison groups, as follows: The affected group contains Hispanic individuals who are foreign-born and not US citizens who arrived in the US after 1981 by age 14 (excluding Puerto Ricans).[15] Our inability to separate the legal from undocumented immigrants does not invalidate our identification strategy, but it does reduce its power. Since there are legal residents mixed in with undocumented immigrants in this affected group, any detectable effect of the law on undocumented immigrants will be averaged over everyone in the affected group, which makes it harder to detect a statistically significant effect.

To implement our identification strategy, we use individual-level data from the American Community Survey (ACS). The ACS is modeled after the Census of Population and Housing long questionnaire; it is an annual survey begun in 2000 to provide reliable intercensal data. We use the 2001–2005 ACS, and merge in the 2000 1% Census public use microdata sample (PUMS) files to get more "before" data.[16] The 2005 ACS is the largest ACS sample to date—it is a 1-in-100 national random sample of the population—and older ACS samples are only one-half to one-third of that size.

We define the state law variable, $INSTATE_{st}$, as follows. Table 4.1 shows the first semester the law would have taken effect in each state passing the law. When a law takes effect in the fall semester of a particular year, we code $INSTATE_{st} = 1$ beginning the following year. For example, although the law took effect in Fall 2001 for Texas, $INSTATE_{st} = 0$ up through the 2001 survey year and $INSTATE_{st} = 1$ beginning in 2002. California, the only state for which the policy did not begin in the fall (it began in Spring 2002), has $INSTATE_{st} = 1$ beginning 2002.

Because these laws were passed so recently and the latest ACS we use is from 2005, there will be few post-law years of data.[17] In fact, the most recent passer, Nebraska, will not have any years of post-law data since Fall 2006 is the first semester the law came into effect. This will reduce the power, since there are few state-time cells where the law is effective. In the future, with more years of post-law data, we will be able to measure a wider range of outcomes (e.g., ultimate educational attainment, labor market outcomes) and be able to use more flexible functional forms that allow treatment effects to vary by state and years of exposure. For this chapter, we will focus on attendance-related outcomes and a single average treatment effect.

Table 4.2 shows descriptive statistics for the ACS/Census sample for the educational outcomes which we will analyze below. In the affected group (i.e., Hispanic non-US-citizen immigrants), 32% of 18–24 year-olds with a high school degree are currently attending college or university, and 11% of 16–17 year-olds have dropped out of high school. Educational outcomes are worse for men than women, and for Mexicans than Hispanics overall (Mexicans make up about 60% of the affected group). Additionally, the affected group is doing worse than the US-born comparison group (i.e., US-born Hispanics: Columns 7–12), which is, in turn, doing worse than US-born non-Hispanic whites.[18] Finally, the affected group has a lower propensity to attend private colleges/universities than either the US-born comparison group or the US-born non-Hispanic whites.

Of course the identification strategies described by Eqs. (4.1) and (4.2) do not involve just taking differences between groups to obtain effects of the law, and instead rely on differences in the evolution of educational outcomes over time following the passage of the law between states with the law and states without the law. Thus, it is useful to graph educational attainment measures by year for states with the law and states without the law. These graphs of the raw data are useful for discerning pre-existing trends in the measures and see trend breaks, if any, starting from the passage of the laws.[19] Panel A of Fig. 4.1 shows the graph of college attendance among 18–24 year-olds with a high school degree for the affected group. The survey years 2000 and 2001 are both "before" years for every state. Then in 2002, the law comes into effect in Texas and California.

Table 4.2 Descriptive statistics

| | Hispanic | | | Mexican | | | | | | | | | US-born non-Hispanic Whites |
| | Non-US-citizen immigrants | | | Non-US-citizen immigrants | | | US-born Hispanics | | | US-born Mexicans | | | |
	Total (1)	Men (2)	Women (3)	Total (4)	Men (5)	Women (6)	Total (7)	Men (8)	Women (9)	Total (10)	Men (11)	Women (12)	(13)
A. Individuals aged 18–24 with high school degree													
Attending college/university	0.3205 (0.4667)	0.2866 (0.4522)	0.3547 (0.4785)	0.2822 (0.4501)	0.2484 (0.4322)	0.3172 (0.4655)	0.3975 (0.4894)	0.3635 (0.4810)	0.4290 (0.4949)	0.3777 (0.4848)	0.3430 (0.4747)	0.4096 (0.4918)	0.4233 (0.4941)
Attending public college	0.2837 (0.4508)	0.2479 (0.4319)	0.3197 (0.4664)	0.2603 (0.4389)	0.2213 (0.4152)	0.3006 (0.4586)	0.3392 (0.4734)	0.3089 (0.4620)	0.3672 (0.4820)	0.3320 (0.4710)	0.2996 (0.4581)	0.3619 (0.4806)	0.3339 (0.4716)
Attending private college	0.0368 (0.1884)	0.0387 (0.1929)	0.0350 (0.1837)	0.0219 (0.1464)	0.0271 (0.1624)	0.0166 (0.1276)	0.0584 (0.2344)	0.0546 (0.2272)	0.0618 (0.2408)	0.0456 (0.2087)	0.0434 (0.2038)	0.0477 (0.2131)	0.0895 (0.2854)
B. Individuals aged 18–21 with high school degree													
Attending college/university	0.3691 (0.4826)	0.3286 (0.4698)	0.4096 (0.4919)	0.3264 (0.4690)	0.2900 (0.4539)	0.3633 (0.4811)	0.4638 (0.4987)	0.4226 (0.4940)	0.5011 (0.5000)	0.4379 (0.4961)	0.4015 (0.4902)	0.4710 (0.4992)	0.5301 (0.4991)
Attending public college	0.3276 (0.4694)	0.2857 (0.4518)	0.3696 (0.4828)	0.3032 (0.4597)	0.2620 (0.4399)	0.3448 (0.4754)	0.3967 (0.4892)	0.3606 (0.4802)	0.4294 (0.4950)	0.3855 (0.4867)	0.3513 (0.4774)	0.4165 (0.4930)	0.4211 (0.4937)
Attending private college	0.0414 (0.1993)	0.0429 (0.2027)	0.0400 (0.1959)	0.0233 (0.1508)	0.0280 (0.1649)	0.0185 (0.1348)	0.0671 (0.2502)	0.0620 (0.2412)	0.0717 (0.2579)	0.0524 (0.2229)	0.0502 (0.2183)	0.0545 (0.2270)	0.1090 (0.3116)
C. Individuals aged 22–24 with high school degree													
Attending college/university	0.2398 (0.4271)	0.2176 (0.4128)	0.2625 (0.4402)	0.2072 (0.4054)	0.1797 (0.3842)	0.2366 (0.4252)	0.3133 (0.4638)	0.2901 (0.4538)	0.3353 (0.4721)	0.3027 (0.4594)	0.2716 (0.4448)	0.3319 (0.4709)	0.3069 (0.4612)
Attending public college	0.2107 (0.4079)	0.1859 (0.3891)	0.2359 (0.4247)	0.1875 (0.3905)	0.1540 (0.3612)	0.2235 (0.4168)	0.2660 (0.4419)	0.2447 (0.4299)	0.2863 (0.4520)	0.2655 (0.4416)	0.2364 (0.4249)	0.2929 (0.4551)	0.2387 (0.4263)

Table 4.2 (continued)

| | Hispanic | | | Mexican | | | US-born Hispanics | | | US-born Mexicans | | | US-born non-Hispanic Whites |
| | Non-US-citizen immigrants | | | Non-US-citizen immigrants | | | | | | | | | |
	Total (1)	Men (2)	Women (3)	Total (4)	Men (5)	Women (6)	Total (7)	Men (8)	Women (9)	Total (10)	Men (11)	Women (12)	(13)
Attending private college	0.0292 (0.1684)	0.0317 (0.1754)	0.0266 (0.1610)	0.0196 (0.1388)	0.0257 (0.1583)	0.0131 (0.1139)	0.0473 (0.2122)	0.0454 (0.2082)	0.0490 (0.2159)	0.0372 (0.1892)	0.0351 (0.1842)	0.0391 (0.1937)	0.0682 (0.2521)
D. Individuals aged 16–17													
Dropped out of High school	0.1125 (0.3160)	0.1273 (0.3334)	0.0962 (0.2949)	0.1330 (0.3396)	0.1507 (0.3578)	0.1132 (0.3170)	0.0495 (0.2169)	0.0451 (0.2075)	0.0541 (0.2262)	0.0533 (0.2247)	0.0478 (0.2134)	0.0592 (0.2360)	0.0530 (0.2241)

Notes: The sample consists of individuals from the 2000 Census 1% PUMS files and the 2001–2005 American Community Survey with additional restrictions as follows. In Columns 1–6, people are foreign-born and not US citizens, having arrived in the US after 1981 and by age 14, and Hispanic (excluding Puerto Ricans). In Columns 7–12, people are US-born and Hispanic (excluding Puerto Ricans). In Column 13, people are US-born, white and non-Hispanic. Observations with allocated age, birthplace, year of immigration, and school attendance were dropped. Currently attending college variables are constructed based on the IPUMS variables school attendance (*school*), grade attending (*gradeatt*) and school type (*schtype*), with observations with allocated values for *school* and *schtype* dropped. Dropped out of high school variable is constructed based on the IPUMS variables educational attainment (*educ99*) and school attendance (*school*), with observations with allocated values for *educ99* and *school* dropped. A person is coded as a high school dropout if he/she has completed fewer than 12 years of schooling and is not currently attending school.

It would be incorrect to attribute all differences between 2001 and 2002 in Texas and California to the laws permitting undocumented students to pay in-state tuition, however, since there appear to be secular changes over time (as indicated by the college attendance in states without the law yet in 2002—the later-law states and never-law states on the graph—experiencing changes between 2001 and 2002). In Eq. (4.1), we use states that passed the laws later or never passed the law to control for secular time changes. This may not be wholly satisfactory since Panel A of Fig. 4.1 suggests that prior to any state implementing the law, the trend in college attendance does not appear similar between the earlier-law states and other states. It is, therefore, useful to take a comparison group of people whose opportunities are not impacted by the laws to correct for the differential trend, which is what Eq. (4.2) does. Our comparison group for obtaining the differential trend will be US-born Hispanics; Panel B of Fig. 4.1 graphs college attendance among 18–24 year-olds with a high school degree for this group.

On a separate note, we can obtain consistent estimates of the parameters in Eqs. (4.1) and (4.2) via ordinary least squares (OLS) only if all the right-hand side variables are exogenous. Thus, it is important to consider whether $INSTATE_{st}$ can plausibly be viewed as exogenous. Our reading of the circumstances surrounding the passage of these laws is that the laws were passed out of fairness considerations—it was believed that children who grew up in the state and performed well in K-12 deserved to have the same opportunity to attend college as their legally resident classmates, and should not be punished for the fact that their parents entered and stayed in the United States illegally. These laws were not a response to perceptions that educational outcomes for undocumented students were getting worse or better. Thus, it seems reasonable to consider the dummy for having the law as exogenous to educational outcomes. However, it could be a concern that states that passed these laws are also passing other laws to help undocumented immigrants or improving their attitudes about undocumented immigrants over time. More specifically, although state fixed effects allow states to differ in how they treat undocumented immigrants, there remains room for bias caused by time-varying state attributes (e.g., other policies, changes in unmeasured state attributes over time). Using US-born Hispanics as a comparison group helps mitigate bias associated with state-specific changes in policies and attitudes toward immigrants since many of them are children of immigrants.[20]

Results

Effect on College Attendance

First, we examine the effect of the laws on the probability of attending college among people who are currently aged 18–24 and possess a high school degree. Using ACS/Census data, we are able to distinguish between college attendance in public and private institutions.[21] In Table 4.3, we present the results of estimating Eq. (4.1) using individuals in the affected group.

Panel A. Hispanic Non-U.S.-Citizen Immigrants (Affected Group)

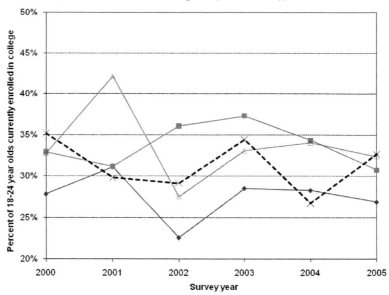

Panel B. U.S.-Born Hispanics (Comparison Group)

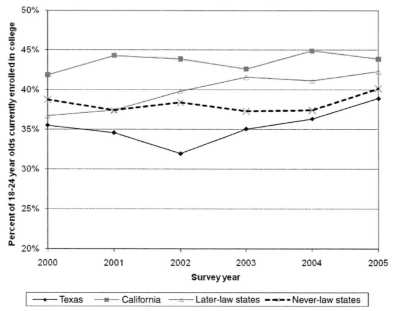

Fig. 4.1 College Attendance Among 18–24 Year Olds, 2000–2005. **A.** Hispanic Non-US-Citizen Immigrants (Affected Group). **B.** US-born Hispanics (Comparison Group). Notes: The sample consists of individuals from the 2000 Census 1% PUMS files and the 2001–2005 American Community Survey who are currently age 18–24 and Hispanic (excluding Puerto Ricans) with additional restrictions as follows. In Panel **A**, people are foreign-born, and not US citizens, and

The general result is that there are no statistically significant effects at conventional levels of significance (e.g., 5% or better). In Panel A, when a sample pooling men and women is used, we detect no effect for either Hispanics overall or Mexicans only, although it can be said that the point estimates for 22–24 year-olds tend to be positive and of greater magnitude than for the 18–21 year-olds. In Panel B, restricting focus to men, we notice larger positive point estimates for 22–24 year-olds compared to the pooled sample, which lead to more positive point estimates for men overall that are sometimes significant at the 10% level of significance. The positive effects come largely from the increased probability of attending public colleges— the point estimates for attending private colleges is close to zero. These findings are consistent with the laws having an impact since the laws would operate through attendance at state institutions (the laws do not change prices for anyone at private institutions).

In Panel C, restricting the focus to women, most of the point estimates are actually negative. The only significant effects for women are for the private college attendance of Mexican women aged 22–24—and they are positive! The results for Mexican women are puzzling, since we would not have expected negative effects of the laws on public college attendance but positive effects on private college attendance. To summarize the findings of Table 4.3, there is a suggestion of a benefit of the laws on older Mexican men, although differential trends appear to be an important issue that must be considered before drawing conclusions.

To explore the problem of differential trends, we estimate Eq. (4.1) for the US-born comparison group. Since the laws do not change anything for the US-born comparison group, the estimated β can be thought of as an estimate of the differential trend prevailing between states with the law and states without the law. The results are displayed in Table 4.4, and are generally statistically insignificant, which is evidence in support of the parallel trend assumption. Interestingly, in Panel B, the point estimates for public Mexicans' college attendance would have fallen in states with the law relative to states without the law; this means the corrected estimates will reveal an even larger benefit of the laws on Mexican men than is suggested in Table 4.3 (which shows uncorrected estimates).

In Table 4.5, we present estimates of the effect of the laws on the affected group that are adjusted for differential trends. Specifically, we subtract Table 4.4 estimates (which are estimates of the differential trends using the US-born comparison group) from the Table 4.3 estimates.[22] For example, in Table 4.3, Panel B, the coefficient is 0.0603 for Hispanic men aged 18–24 in the affected group.

Fig. 4.1 have arrived in the US after 1981 and by age 14. In Panel **B**, people are US-born. Means are weighted by IPUMS weights. The laws would have become effective in the 2002 survey year for Texas and California. The laws would have become effective after 2002 for the "Later-law states": UT, NY, WA, OK, IL, KS, NM, and NE. The states that do not have the law as of August 2006 are in the "Never-law states" category

Table 4.3 Effect of state laws on college attendance of non-US-citizen immigrants

	Hispanic immigrants			Mexican immigrants		
	Attending College (1)	Attending Public College (2)	Attending Private College (3)	Attending College (4)	Attending Public College (5)	Attending Private College (6)
A. Men and women						
Age 18–24	0.0199 (0.0329)	0.0047 (0.0334)	0.0152 (0.0110)	0.0120 (0.0448)	−0.0042 (0.0439)	0.0162 (0.0097)
Age 18–21	0.0122 (0.0299)	−0.0090 (0.0357)	0.0212 (0.0134)	−0.0067 (0.0512)	−0.0143 (0.0520)	0.0076 (0.0126)
Age 22–24	0.0374 (0.0557)	0.0360 (0.0430)	0.0015 (0.0163)	0.0354 (0.0655)	0.0022 (0.0551)	0.0332* (0.0183)
B. Men only						
Age 18–24	0.0603* (0.0344)	0.0387 (0.0356)	0.0216 (0.0134)	0.0648* (0.0347)	0.0469 (0.0294)	0.0179 (0.0140)
Age 18–21	0.0324 (0.0528)	0.0064 (0.0516)	0.0259 (0.0195)	−0.0187 (0.0455)	−0.0234 (0.0451)	0.0047 (0.0219)
Age 22–24	0.0623 (0.0783)	0.0560 (0.0661)	0.0063 (0.0216)	0.1177 (0.0746)	0.1094* (0.0635)	0.0083 (0.0254)

4 Does Reducing College Costs Improve Educational Outcomes?

Table 4.3 (continued)

	Hispanic immigrants			Mexican immigrants		
	Attending College (1)	Attending Public College (2)	Attending Private College (3)	Attending College (4)	Attending Public College (5)	Attending Private College (6)
C. Women only						
Age 18–24	−0.0208	−0.0305	0.0096	−0.0306	−0.0568	0.0262**
	(0.0452)	(0.0449)	(0.0178)	(0.0896)	(0.0864)	(0.0122)
Age 18–21	−0.0305	−0.0463	0.0158	−0.0284	−0.0496	0.0211
	(0.0507)	(0.0506)	(0.0217)	(0.1076)	(0.1038)	(0.0184)
Age 22–24	0.0201	0.0236	−0.0035	−0.0316	−0.0783	0.0467***
	(0.0502)	(0.0490)	(0.0139)	(0.0838)	(0.0787)	(0.0120)

Notes: The sample consists of individuals from the 2000 Census 1% PUMS files and the 2001–2005 American Community Survey who are currently aged 18–24, foreign-born and not U.S. citizens, having arrived in the US after 1981 and by age 14, Hispanic, and have a high school degree. Each cell is from a separate regression that is weighted by IPUMS weights and contains dummies for the survey year, state of residence, age, age at arrival, race, and sex; Columns 1–3 additionally control for Hispanic origin dummies (Mexican, Cuban, and Other). Robust standard errors from clustering by state of residence are shown in parentheses. Asterisks denote significance levels (*=0.10, **=0.05, ***=0.01). For analysis of Hispanic immigrants in Columns 1–3, there are 7,152 observations (3,652 women and 3,500 men). For analysis of Mexican immigrants in Columns 4–6, there are 4,643 observations (2,340 women and 2,303 men).

Table 4.4 Effect of state laws on college attendance of US-born comparison group

	US-born Hispanics			US-born Mexicans		
	Attending College (1)	Attending Public College (2)	Attending Private College (3)	Attending College (4)	Attending Public College (5)	Attending Private College (6)
A. Men and women						
Age 18–24	−0.0166	−0.0184	0.0018	−0.0061	−0.0107	0.0046
	(0.0149)	(0.0170)	(0.0075)	(0.0197)	(0.0217)	(0.0072)
Age 18–21	−0.0094	−0.0125	0.0031	−0.0016	−0.0118	0.0102
	(0.0147)	(0.0182)	(0.0092)	(0.0213)	(0.0261)	(0.0101)
Age 22–24	−0.0261	−0.0248	−0.0013	−0.0143	−0.0104	−0.0038
	(0.0199)	(0.0190)	(0.0093)	(0.0246)	(0.0214)	(0.0097)
B. Men only						
Age 18–24	−0.0206	−0.0280	0.0074	−0.0298	−0.0433*	0.0135
	(0.0168)	(0.0214)	(0.0104)	(0.0199)	(0.0240)	(0.0110)
Age 18–21	−0.0263	−0.0275	0.0013	−0.0342	−0.0494	0.0152
	(0.0239)	(0.0253)	(0.0140)	(0.0321)	(0.0332)	(0.0163)
Age 22–24	−0.0206	−0.0323	0.0117	−0.0337*	−0.0433**	0.0096
	(0.0191)	(0.0236)	(0.0150)	(0.0182)	(0.0205)	(0.0109)

Table 4.4 (continued)

	US-born Hispanics			US-born Mexicans		
	Attending College (1)	Attending Public College (2)	Attending Private College (3)	Attending College (4)	Attending Public College (5)	Attending Private College (6)
C. Women only						
Age 18–24	-0.0138	-0.0088	-0.0050	0.0120	0.0164	-0.0043
	(0.0234)	(0.0208)	(0.0085)	(0.0322)	(0.0288)	(0.0103)
Age 18–21	0.0062	0.0019	0.0044	0.0278	0.0218	0.0060
	(0.0269)	(0.0242)	(0.0125)	(0.0377)	(0.0363)	(0.0110)
Age 22–24	-0.0370	-0.0204	-0.0166*	-0.0080	0.0111	-0.0191
	(0.0292)	(0.0246)	(0.0089)	(0.0353)	(0.0292)	(0.0155)

Notes: The sample consists of individuals from the 2000 Census 1% PUMS files and the 2001–2005 American Community Survey who are currently aged 18–24, US-born, Hispanic (excluding Puerto Ricans), and have a high school degree. Each cell is from a separate regression that is weighted by IPUMS weights and contains dummies for the survey year, state of residence, age, age at arrival, race, and sex; Columns 1–3 additionally control for Hispanic origin dummies (Mexican, Cuban, and Other). Robust standard errors from clustering by state of residence are shown in parentheses. Asterisks denote significance levels (* = 0.10, *** = 0.05, *** = 0.01). For analysis of Hispanic immigrants in Columns 1–3, there are 41,418 observations (22,107 women and 19,311 men). For analysis of Mexican immigrants in Columns 4–6, there are 29,648 observations (15,726 women and 13,922 men).

Table 4.5 Effect of state laws on college attendance of non-US-citizen immigrants, adjusted for differential trend using the US-born comparison group

	Hispanic immigrants			Mexican immigrants		
	Attending College (1)	Attending Public College (2)	Attending Private College (3)	Attending College (4)	Attending Public College (5)	Attending Private College (6)
A. Men and women						
Age 18–24	0.0365	0.0231	0.0134	0.0181	0.0065	0.0116
	(0.0371)	(0.0335)	(0.0111)	(0.0524)	(0.0503)	(0.0127)
Age 18–21	0.0216	0.0035	0.0181	−0.0051	−0.0025	−0.0026
	(0.0358)	(0.0403)	(0.0142)	(0.0592)	(0.0633)	(0.0169)
Age 22–24	0.0636	0.0608	0.0028	0.0497	0.0126	0.0371*
	(0.0612)	(0.0468)	(0.0207)	(0.0686)	(0.0546)	(0.0219)
B. Men only						
Age 18–24	0.0809**	0.0667**	0.0142	0.0946**	0.0902***	0.0043
	(0.0316)	(0.0308)	(0.0171)	(0.0379)	(0.0338)	(0.0196)
Age 18–21	0.0586	0.0340	0.0247	0.0155	0.0260	−0.0105
	(0.0541)	(0.0554)	(0.0275)	(0.0654)	(0.0654)	(0.0313)
Age 22–24	0.0830	0.0883	−0.0053	0.1514**	0.1527***	−0.0013
	(0.0830)	(0.0693)	(0.0303)	(0.0725)	(0.0545)	(0.0327)

Table 4.5 (continued)

	Hispanic immigrants			Mexican immigrants		
	Attending College (1)	Attending Public College (2)	Attending Private College (3)	Attending College (4)	Attending Public College (5)	Attending Private College (6)
C. Women only						
Age 18–24	−0.0071	−0.0217	0.0146	−0.0426	−0.0731	0.0305
	(0.0590)	(0.0533)	(0.0185)	(0.1091)	(0.1005)	(0.0191)
Age 18–21	−0.0367	−0.0482	0.0114	−0.0562	−0.0714	0.0152
	(0.0678)	(0.0624)	(0.0212)	(0.1294)	(0.1224)	(0.0231)
Age 22–24	0.0571	0.0440	0.0131	−0.0236	−0.0894	0.0658***
	(0.0582)	(0.0536)	(0.0161)	(0.0940)	(0.0835)	(0.0204)

Notes: This table reports the difference between the effect on non-US-citizen immigrants reported in Table 4.4 and the effect on the US-born comparison group reported in Table 4.1 for a given outcome, age, and Hispanic/Mexican group. Asterisks denote significance levels (*0.10, **0.05, ***0.01). In practice, these adjusted effects were obtained from regressions pooling the affected (immigrant) and comparison (US-born) groups and allowing all coefficients to differ between the two groups; the reported coefficient is the coefficient for the interaction between being in the affected group and the "INSTATE" variable.

In Table 4.4, Panel B, the coefficient is −0.0206 for Hispanic men aged 18–24 in the comparison group. In Table 4.5, Panel B, the coefficient is 0.0809 [=0.0603−(−0.0206)] for Hispanic men aged 18–24. The estimated effect of the laws on males in the affected group, adjusted for differential effects using US-born Hispanic males, is 8.09%. That is, the laws raised college attendance 8.09% among Hispanic men aged 18–24 who are foreign-born and not US citizens.

Because the Table 4.4 results were typically around zero, and for males of opposite sign, all the effects found in Table 4.3 are carried through to Table 4.5. In particular, the overall small and near-zero effects found for the pooled sample of men and women mask positive effects for men and negative effects for women. The positive effect for men derives from the significantly higher likelihood that older (aged 22–24) Mexican men are attending public colleges. Puzzlingly, older Mexican women, though no more likely to attend public colleges (if one takes the point estimates literally, they are actually less likely), are more likely to attend private colleges.

To summarize the results of Tables 4.3, 4.4 and 4.5, we find some evidence suggestive of a positive effect of the laws on the college attendance of Mexican men, but, in general, estimated effects of the laws are not significantly different from zero. In an earlier section, we provide some reasons for the insignificant results. Here, we discuss the effect on Mexican men in more detail.

The point estimate of the effect on the college attendance of Mexican men is large—in Table 4.5, the effect of the laws on the probability that Mexican men aged 22–24 who are foreign-born and not US citizens are currently attending college is 15%, which is more than half of the mean college attendance rate for Mexican men—although quite imprecise (the 95% confidence interval is 0.6% to 29.7%).[23] In contrast, the point estimates of the effect on Mexican women and younger Mexican men are not only insignificant but also much less than 15%. Why should the effect be larger for men than women and larger for older men (aged 22–24) than younger men (aged 18–21)?

At first blush, it is surprising that men alone benefit since females tend to do better than males in K-12, which puts females in a better position to apply successfully to college and succeed in college. Dynarski (15) found that Hispanic and non-white women experienced the largest gains in college attendance and degree completion among all race/ethnicity-sex groups as a result of the Arkansas and Georgia merit aid programs. Why would we find the opposite here? First, it is important to point out that these laws allowing undocumented students to pay in-state tuition do not provide *merit-based* benefits. The law does not only benefit undocumented immigrants with good grades who are eligible to pay in-state tuition rates; all undocumented immigrants who attended high school and received a high school degree in that state can benefit.

Second, although it is true that women, including Mexican women in the affected group, are more likely to obtain a high school degree, the fact is that our analysis is *conditional* on having a high school degree. Only people with high school degrees are eligible to benefit from the law, hence we have focused on them in our analysis of high school attendance. It is possible that males who graduate from high school have different underlying ability than females who graduate from high school, since the former drop out of high school at much higher rates. If we assumed that men and women each had the same ability distribution and that people of lower ability are more likely to drop out, then the higher high school dropout rate for males would suggest that the smaller pool of male high school graduates have higher average ability. It is plausible that the law impacts people of higher ability more, which leads to a larger estimated benefit of the laws for men than women. If we had not conditioned on having a high school degree, then results by sex would likely be different than what we found here.[24]

It may also be surprising that older Mexican males benefit more than younger Mexican males (also, the point estimates for the effect of the laws on public college attendance are higher for older Hispanic females than for younger Hispanic females, although none of these point estimates are significant). Why should the effect of the laws differ by age? Seftor and Turner (18, p. 349) estimate that availability of federal financial aid increases the college enrollment of older students: "The behavioral effects for the traditional college-aged students associated with changes in the availability of Pell funding are modest, but the responsiveness among older students is marked." The main reason offered for the differential effects by age is that older students may face greater credit constraints than younger students. Older students may be less able to get funding from parents, as they are less likely to be living with the parents—and from banks, as they are attending community colleges instead of traditional 4-year colleges. In the case of undocumented immigrants, while greater credit constraints may well be present for older youths, we believe there is another important reason for the greater effects on older youths.[25] Undocumented immigrants may wish to take advantage of the law, but they have a competing desire to conceal the undocumented status of their family. Given the United States' unstable attitudes toward immigrants, undocumented immigrants face a constant threat of deportation and may be reluctant to have an official government record (e.g., student record at a public college) that indicates undocumented status and contains family information. Compared to the 18–21 year-olds, 22–24 year-olds are more likely to be living on their own. People who live on their own cannot easily be linked to their family. Hence, older Mexicans are more likely than younger Mexicans to take advantage of laws permitting undocumented immigrants to pay in-state tuition.

Effect on Dropping Out of High School

It could be that the law, by increasing student expectations of attending college, raises high school completion for younger cohorts. In this subsection, we examine the effect of the laws on the dropping out of high school among people who are currently aged 16–17. We define dropping out of high school as not having a high school degree and not currently attending school. Note that many people who will eventually drop out have not yet done so by age 17, thus by focusing on 16–17 year-olds we are capturing early dropout behavior.

Table **4.6** Effect of state laws on dropping out of high school for 16–17 year olds

	Hispanics	Mexicans
	(1)	(2)
A. Men and women		
Unadjusted effect	−0.0162	−0.0008
	(0.0244)	(0.0305)
Adjusted effect	−0.0145	−0.0022
	(0.0237)	(0.0310)
B. Men only		
Unadjusted effect	−0.0253	0.0068
	(0.0221)	(0.0319)
Adjusted effect	−0.0267	0.0008
	(0.0239)	(0.0406)
C. Women only		
Unadjusted effect	−0.0220	−0.0255
	(0.0481)	(0.0606)
Adjusted effect	−0.0157	−0.0186
	(0.0461)	(0.0612)

Notes: The sample consists of individuals from the 2000 Census 1% PUMS files and the 2001–2005 American Community Survey who are currently aged 16–17 with additional restrictions as follows. The affected group is Hispanic, foreign-born and not US citizens, who arrived in the US after 1981 by age 14 (Column 2 is restricted to Mexicans). The comparison group is born in the US and Hispanic (excluding Puerto Ricans; only Mexicans are used for comparison in Column 2). The "unadjusted effect" is the coefficient for "INSTATE" from Eq. (4.1) estimated using data on the affected group. The "adjusted effect" is the coefficient for interaction between being in the affected group and "INSTATE" from Eq. (4.2) using data on the affected group and comparison group. Robust standard errors from clustering by state of residence are shown in parentheses. Asterisks denote significance levels (*=0.10, **=0.05, ***=0.01).

Table 4.6 shows the estimated effects of the tuition laws on dropping out of high school. The general conclusion from this table is that neither the unadjusted estimates (obtained by estimating Eq. (4.1) using the affected group) nor the adjusted estimates (which were obtained by estimating Eq. (4.2) using the affected group combined with the US-born Hispanic comparison group) suggest any significant effects of the laws on dropout behavior. However, it is true that the point estimates are generally negative, consistent with a decline in dropping out as a consequence of the laws. If indeed high school dropout rates are declining in response to the laws, we might expect an increase in college attendance in the future as these 16–17 year-olds come of age and wish to attend college.

Conclusion

The staggered adoption of state laws permitting undocumented students to pay in-state tuition provides a natural experiment for evaluating the effects of such laws. We found some evidence suggestive of a positive effect of the laws on the public college attendance of older Mexican men. For younger, female, and non-Mexican members of the affected group, however, the effects of the laws on college attendance were typically not significantly different from zero. Additionally, there were no significant effects of the laws on high school dropout behavior among 16–17 year olds. Thus, our main finding is that estimated effects tend not to be significant. At this point, we do not wish to put too much emphasis on the significant effects for older Mexican men. On the one hand, they are sensitive to the specific comparison group used to correct for differential trends in college attendance. On the other hand, given the sheer number of regressions we have estimated, it is to be expected that a small handful of these regressions will show significant effects. In future work, we will further scrutinize the positive effect on the college attendance of older Mexican men.

The most obvious interpretation of this finding—of no significant effects—is that the laws truly do not affect the educational outcomes of undocumented students. This could be for a number of reasons. First, although the laws made attending college cheaper, the in-state tuition rates may still be prohibitively expensive for undocumented students. Undocumented students do not qualify for federal financial aid, the chief source of financial aid for college students. Second, the laws do not change the legal status of undocumented immigrants, and due to IRCA employer sanctions, undocumented immigrants will continue to be unable to access good jobs even with a college degree. These first two reasons suggest that without corresponding changes in the federal government's treatment of undocumented students (e.g., setting qualifications for federal financial aid or creating a legalization process) it may be unreasonable to expect significant increases in educational attainment due to these laws.

A third reason that there might truly be no effect is that too little time has elapsed since the laws were passed. The most recent data we were able to obtain are from 2005, but the earliest any state implemented the law was Fall 2001—at the time of this writing, a maximum of 5 years and a median of 3 years have elapsed since the adoption of the laws. Because of the newness of the law, perhaps undocumented immigrants may not even be aware of its existence. Or, perhaps they are aware, but have not accumulated the credentials (e.g., a high school degree, rigorous high school classes) to place themselves in a position to take advantage of the law. This third reason suggests that the short-run effect of the law may well differ from the longer-run effect. As information spreads about these laws, the estimated effect might change.[26] Also, younger cohorts would have had time to accumulate the right credentials to attend college, and the estimated effect on them could well differ from the effect on people who made schooling choices not expecting to attend college but then are unexpectedly given the opportunity to do so.

Another interpretation of the finding is that the laws *do* affect the educational outcomes of undocumented students, but our statistical tests lack the power to detect these effects. There were so few observations exposed to the law—given the recent passage of these laws, only a few state-time cells are "treated" to the law—that we have sufficient power only to detect relatively large effects on educational outcomes. The inability to distinguish undocumented immigrants from other non-citizen immigrants exacerbates the problem, since it means that among the observations coded as exposed to the law, only a subset would actually have experienced a change in opportunities (e.g., legal immigrants lumped into the treated group would not have experienced any change in opportunities). Thus, we cannot rule out that modest short-run effects existed, but statistically we cannot distinguish that from a zero effect. We have, however, ruled out large short-run effects.[27]

In the future, it will be useful to assess the longer-run effects of the laws permitting undocumented students to pay in-state tuition. There is good reason to believe that the longer-run effects differ from the short-run effects. Using the same empirical methodology used in this chapter, we would be able to look at outcomes related to college persistence (e.g., completion of an associate's or bachelor's degree) after more time has elapsed.[28] Additionally, with more data, we would be able to test whether effects vary by state; it is conceivable that states differ in how effectively they have advertised the law, which may have implications for the estimated effect on undocumented immigrants.

Acknowledgement We thank Peter Mieszkowski, Stephen Trejo, and the participants in the IUPLR Conference in April 2007 for helpful comments and discussion. We also thank Aly Capetillo, Serguei Chervachidze, and Parul Mathur for research assistance. Financial support from Rice University's Baker Institute for Public Policy is gratefully acknowledged. The authors bear sole responsibility for the content of this chapter.

Notes

1. Smith (2), Table 2 reports that while average years of schooling was 12.99 for all US-born in 1996, it was 12.64 for legal immigrants, and 10.79 for illegal immigrants. For Hispanics, years of schooling were 11.52 for the US-born, 10.12 for legal immigrants, and 6.90 for illegal immigrants.
2. In other words, we will always have state-fixed effects and time-fixed effects in the estimated regressions. Details are provided in the Related Literature section.
3. As required by the *Plyler v. Doe* Supreme Court decision in 1982 and subsequent laws.
4. Alaska and Virginia have considered legislation explicitly preventing undocumented students from paying in-state tuition and are not counted among the 28.
5. In particular, the law pertains to undocumented immigrants who have been in the United States for at least 5 years, having arrived at age 15 or younger, and graduates from high school would be granted 6 years of legal residence. At the end of the 6 years, if the undocumented immigrant has completed a 2-year degree, completed at least 2 years of a 4-year degree or served at least 2 years in the US military, he/she will be granted permanent residence.
6. The 1996 Illegal Immigration Reform and Immigrant Responsibility Act does not permit states to provide benefits in post-secondary education to undocumented immigrants that are not available to US citizens. The Dream Act would remove any federal constraints on a state's ability to define "resident" for the purpose of receiving in-state tuition.
7. Since the working paper version of this chapter was issued in January 2007 by Rice University's Baker Institute for Public Policy, we have become aware of Kaushal (21) and Flores (22), which evaluate these laws using Current Population Survey data.
8. Fall 2001 is the first semester in which the law was in effect in any state; the law was passed on June 16, 2001, which is too late to affect the application process and decision about

which institution to attend for high school graduates wanting to attend a competitive public institution.

9. Technically, tuition revenue could increase overall with the law since the law could cause the enrollment of undocumented students to increase in a way that more than offsets the reduced revenue on a per-undocumented-student basis. However, it seems inaccurate to characterize the costs associated with the law as negative since there are marginal costs associated with increased enrollment, like a decrease in school inputs (e.g., faculty, facilities) on a per-student basis and spending on more school inputs.

10. Some reasons for endogeneity are as follows. For example, financial aid awarded based on need may provide downward bias on aid's benefits because the estimated effect of aid will conflate the true effect of the aid and the effects of coming from a low-income family. Conversely, financial aid awarded based on merit may bias upwards the effect of aid on educational outcomes because the estimated effect also encapsulates the effect of the student attributes that earned him or her a merit-based award in the first place. Furthermore, comparing educational outcomes in states with lower and higher costs of attending public colleges and universities might be biased due to other differences between states that affect public tuition, such as in quality of education or returns to education.

11. In 2003, public 4-year institutions in the United States had average in-state tuition of $4,507 and out-of-state tuition of $11,125 (3). In contrast, public 2-year institutions had average in-state tuition of $2,217 and out-of-state tuition of $5,076 (3).

12. Alternatively, undocumented immigrants in states with the law may be more aware of the Dream Act itself (because information about it is found in the same place that information about the laws is provided), whereas those in other states do not know about the Dream Act. In this case, the former has higher expectations that legal status will be granted in the future than the latter.

13. This study uses individual-level panel data to deal with the problem faced by other studies of the effect of legal status on wages that individual characteristics differ between legal and illegal immigrants. The variation in legal status is driven by IRCA, which provided amnesty to undocumented immigrants arriving in the US before January 1, 1982. The authors deal with secular changes in wages over time by using a comparison group not experiencing any change in legal status.

14. In our empirical analysis, we will not be able to use within family variation in legal status to identify the effect of the laws. This is because there are no large data sets connecting adult siblings in the United States; for example, in the Census, we know family connections among individuals only if they reside in the same household. In this chapter, we rely on a cross section of young adults, and use the US-born Hispanics as a comparison group for the foreign-born children of immigrants, but the intuition of the within-family approach applies.

15. A few clarifications: First, IRCA enabled immigrants who arrived in the United States by January 1, 1982, to become legal residents. It makes sense to ignore immigrants arriving in 1981 and earlier when seeking a group of people with high likelihood of being undocumented. Second, age at arrival in the United States is calculated as [current age−(survey year−year of immigration to the United States)]. Since the laws require attending high school in the state for a certain number of years, it makes sense not to include immigrants who arrived at a later age—they simply would not meet the state qualifications for in-state tuition. Third, people born in Puerto Rico are US citizens, so Puerto Ricans are not affected by the laws.

16. We downloaded the data from the IPUMS website in October 2006 (23).

17. The 2006 ACS has become available since the working paper version of this chapter was issued in January 2007, and adding these data to the analysis does not meaningfully change the results we report here.

18. We will not use US-born non-Hispanic whites in our regression analysis below. We present their descriptive statistics here only to provide a reference point.

19. Unfortunately, given that the ACS in 2001–2004 are only one-third to one-half of a percent of the US population, and that some states have little immigration, some state-year cells will

have few observations for the affected group, leading to a noisy series. It is preferable to pool data to gain efficiency, as we do in the regression analysis below.

20. Moreover, we considered several alternative comparison groups: (1) Asian immigrants; (2) non-Hispanic and non-Asian immigrants; and (3) Hispanic immigrants who are naturalized US citizens. These groups, as immigrants themselves, might better control for state-specific changes in policies and attitudes toward immigrants. Since the results using these alternative comparison groups are qualitatively similar to those using the US-born Hispanic comparison group, we do not report them.

21. Unfortunately, the ACS/Census data do not distinguish between 4-year and 2-year institutions. Future analysis using data from the Current Population Survey can examine whether the laws impacted attendance at 4-year and 2-year institutions differently.

22. In practice, we obtain the effects shown in Table 4.5 by estimating Eq. (4.2) by OLS. Estimating in regression form makes it easier to get the standard errors associated with the effects.

23. So far, we have estimated the effect of the law on the affected group. Of course the affected group contains both undocumented immigrants and legal immigrants. To get the effect of the law on the undocumented immigrants, we would have to divide the estimated effect on the affected group by the fraction of the affected group that is undocumented. We do not know the exact fraction, but based on the fact that 52% of the stock of Mexican immigrants is undocumented and that new immigrant inflows from Mexico are increasingly illegal over time, then we would guess that fraction is in excess of 50%. This means that to obtain an upper bound on the effect of treatment on the undocumented immigrants, we can multiply the reported estimated effects on the affected group by two (the reciprocal of .5 is 2).

24. Future analysis will model the differential selectivity of men and women into the sample.

25. It is possible to imagine older students being less, not more, credit constrained. Older youths would have worked and saved money for longer, which enables them to attend college if they wished (so when the passage of the laws presents the opportunity to attend college, older people can respond quickly whereas younger people must wait and save). Older students being less credit constrained may be the more likely situation for undocumented immigrants since they come from very poor families that cannot spare enough money for college even if the parents were supportive of college.

26. Education policymakers should undertake actions to spread the word about these laws to undocumented students, guidance counselors in junior high and high schools serving undocumented students, and leaders in communities with undocumented students. This would remove the possibility that the estimated results relate to a failure to provide information about the law to the intended beneficiaries, and it would improve our confidence that the estimated results truly relate to the impact of the law itself.

27. Given the standard errors, an effect in excess of 6% to 10% (depending on the subsample) would be detectable as a significant effect. For older Mexican men, we did detect a large short-run effect on college attendance—the point estimate was 15% according to Table 4.5. For all other groups and outcomes, we can rule out effects larger than 6% to 10%.

28. Dynarski (15) reports: "In the 2000 Census, just 57 percent of those age 22–34 with any college experience had completed an associate's or bachelor's degree. Thirteen percent had not completed even a year" (p. 1). The Hoxby (24) edited volume emphasizes the distinction between college attendance and college persistence. This chapter has focused on college attendance, and given the low proportion of Hispanic immigrants who have attempted college, access to college may be a major problem for this subpopulation, and it is of policy interest to raise college attendance.

References

1. Passel, Jeffrey S. 2005. "Unauthorized Migrants: Numbers and Characteristics." Washington, DC: Pew Hispanic Center. http://pewhispanic.org/files/reports/46.pdf (accessed September 2006).
2. Smith, James P. 2006. "Immigrants and the Labor Market." *Journal of Labor Economics*, 24(2): 203–233.
3. U.S. Department of Education, National Center for Education Statistics. 2003. Integrated Postsecondary Education Data System, "IPEDS State Tables 2003." http://nces.ed.gov/das/library/tables_listings/state2003_price.asp (accessed September 2006).
4. Krueger, Carl. 2006. "In-state Tuition for Undocumented Immigrants." Education Commission of the States State Notes: Tuition and Fees, August. http://www.ecs.org/clearinghouse/61/00/6100.htm (accessed October 2006).
5. Lewis, Raphael. 2005. "In-State Tuition Not a Draw for Many Immigrants." *Boston Globe*, November 9.
6. Institute of Public and International Affairs, University of Utah. 2006. "Mexico and Utah: The Complex Relationship." http://www.ipia.utah.edu/programs/utah_mexico/full_text.pdf (accessed September 2006).
7. Martin, Jack. 2005. "Breaking the Piggy Bank: How Illegal Immigration is Sending Schools into the Red." Federation for American Immigration Reform Report. http://www.fairus.org/site/PageServer?pagename=research_researchf6ad (accessed December 2005).
8. Capps, Randy, Michael Fix,and Jane Reardon-Anderson. 2003. "Children of Immigrants Show Slight Reductions in Poverty, Hardship." In *Snapshots of American Families III, No13*. Washington, DC: Urban Institute.
9. Card, David, John DiNardo, and Eugena Estes. 2000. "The More Things Change: Immigrants and the Children of Immigrants in the 1940s, the 1970s, and the 1990s." In *Issues in the Economics of Immigration*, ed. George J. Borjas, 227–270. Chicago: University of Chicago Press.
10. Grogger, Jeffrey, and Stephen J. Trejo. 2002. "*Falling Behind or Moving Up? The Intergenerational Progress of Mexican Americans.*" San Francisco, CA: Public Policy Institute of California.
11. Smith, James P. 2003. "Assimilation Across the Latino Generations." *American Economic Review Papers and Proceedings*, 93(2): 315–325.
12. Kane, Thomas J. 1994. "College Entry by Blacks since 1970: The Role of College Costs, Family Background and the Returns to Education." *Journal of Political Economy*, 102(5): 878–911.
13. Dynarski, Susan M. 2003. "Does Aid Matter? Measuring the Effect of Student Aid on College Attendance and Completion." *American Economic Review*, 93(1): 279–288.
14. Dynarski, Susan M. 2000. "Hope for Whom? Financial Aid for the Middle Class and Its Impact on College Attendance." *National Tax Journal*, 53(3): 629–661.
15. Dynarski, Susan M. 2008. "Building the Stock of College-Educated Labor." Journal of Human Resources, 43(3): 576–610
16. Hansen, W. Lee. 1983. "The Impact of Student Financial Aid on Access." In *The Crisis in Higher Education*, ed. Joseph Froomkin, 84–96. New York: Academy of Political Science.
17. Kane, Thomas J.1995. "Rising Public College Tuition and College Entry: How Well Do Public Subsidies Promote Access to College." NBER Working Paper 5164.
18. Seftor, Neil, and Sarah Turner. 2003. "Back to School: Federal Student Aid Policy and Adult College Enrollment." *Journal of Human Resources*, 37(2): 591–617.
19. Jordan, Miriam. 2005. "Illegal Immigrants' New Lament: Have Degree, No Job." *The Wall Street Journal*, April 26: Section B, 1 and 7.
20. Kossoudji, Sherrie A., and Deborah A. Cobb-Clark. 2002. "Coming out of the Shadows: Learning about Legal Status and Wages from the Legalized Population." *Journal of Labor Economics*, 20(3): 598–628.

21. Kaushal, Neeraj. 2008. "In-State Tuition for the Undocumented: Education Effects on Mexican Young Adults."*Journal of Policy Analysis and Management*, 27(4): 771–792.
22. Flores, Stella M. 2010. "State Dream Acts: The Effect of In-State Resident Tuition Policies on Undocumented Latino Students." The Review of Higher Education, 33(2): 239–283.
23. Ruggles, Steven, Matthew Sobek, Trent Alexander, Catherine A. Fitch, Ronald Goeken, Patricia Kelly Hall, Miriam King, and Chad Ronnander. 2004. "Integrated Public Use Microdata Series: Version 3.0." Minneapolis, MN: Minnesota Population Center. http://www.ipums.org (accessed October 2006).
24. Hoxby, Caroline M., ed. 2004. *College Choices: The Economics of Where to Go, When to Go, and How to Pay for It*. Chicago: University of Chicago Press.
25. Education Commission of the States. 2006. "Recent State Policies/Activities, Tuition and Fees – In-state Tuition for Undocumented Immigrants." Education Commission of the States State Policy Database. http://www.ecs.org/ecs/ecscat.nsf/WebTopicView?OpenView&count=-300&RestrictToCategory=Tuition/Fees–In–State+Tuition+for+Undocumented+Immigrants (accessed October 2006).

Chapter 5
Is There a Link Between Hispanics and First-Generation College Students? The Importance of Exposure to a College-Going Tradition

Arturo Gonzalez[1]

Abstract It is well documented that Hispanics have some of the lowest earnings and highest poverty rates of any group in the US. Increasing their college graduation rate is perhaps the most obvious way to foster and accelerate the pace of their economic mobility. At the same time, this is a very challenging public policy goal, partly because such a small percentage of Hispanics presently have a 4-year college degree. Currently, 13% of all Hispanics 25 years and older have graduated from college, compared to 33% of non-Hispanic whites. Not only is scale an issue, but policies must also overcome the paradox that college graduates generally come from college-educated households. According to this view, "first-generation" college students—the first in their family to go to college—are different from their socioeconomic and college-going peers in a multitude of ways and will, therefore, have differential educational outcomes. The descriptive analysis in this chapter reveals that first-generation college students of all ethnic backgrounds have lower 4-year completion rates and are also more likely to enroll in community colleges than in 4-year colleges. Such findings are not surprising considering that a multitude of family background factors, such as the emphasis given to learning, have a strong, but difficult to measure, impact on educational outcomes. The analysis shows that Hispanic college students stand out as being primarily first-generation college students—65% of all Hispanics—even when compared to blacks (50%). The chapter concludes with a brief discussion of the programs designed to overcome the challenges facing first-generation college students, and hence the issues that simultaneously affect Hispanic college students.

Introduction

The economic disparity between individuals with and without a bachelor's degree is well documented. Table 5.1 shows the positive association between earnings in 2008

A. Gonzalez (✉)
Office of the Comptroller of the Currency, Washington, DC 20219, USA
e-mail: arturo.gonzalez@occ.treas.gov

D.L. Leal, S.J. Trejo (eds.), *Latinos and the Economy*, Immigrants and Minorities, Politics and Policy, DOI 10.1007/978-1-4419-6682-7_5,
© Springer Science+Business Media, LLC 2011

95

Table 5.1 2008 Average income by educational attainment for persons 25 years old and over

Education	All races	White alone	Hispanic any race	Black alone	Asian alone
Less than 9th grade	$21,491	$21,895	$21,337	$17,605	$20,700
Grades 9th through 11th	$24,686	$25,630	$23,671	$20,940	$23,171
High school graduate	$33,618	$34,513	$29,318	$29,139	$30,747
Some college, no degree	$38,676	$39,726	$34,814	$32,376	$37,832
Associate's degree	$41,226	$42,108	$38,885	$35,552	$40,461
Bachelor's or higher degree	$69,155	$70,571	$57,944	$54,259	$70,240
Bachelor's degree	$60,954	$62,383	$50,023	$48,031	$59,799
Master's degree	$71,236	$72,454	$75,096	$58,481	$72,019
Professional degree	$125,622	$128,492	$81,969	$107,026	$117,090
Doctoral degree	$99,995	$100,317	$96,070	$92,998	$101,487
Total	$46,547	$47,734	$32,880	$35,695	$54,431

Source: US Census Bureau, Current Population Survey, 2009 Annual Social and Economic Supplement.

and education for workers 25 years and older. The gap between all workers with a bachelor's degree and high school graduates is over $27,000. While not causal, this table illustrates the positive return—over 40% since the 1990s—to a college education that has persisted since the 1980s, due in part to the relative decline in the supply of college educated young workers (1–3). This gap is likely to grow as the demand for college-educated workers increases at a faster rate than their supply (1, 4, 5).

Table 5.1 also highlights the low mean income for adult Hispanic workers. While the average income for all workers in 2008 is about $46,550, the average income for Hispanics is just under $33,000—a gap of about $13,670. Yet Hispanics with higher levels of education earn more; the average income for Hispanics with at least a bachelor's degree is nearly $58,000. Putting aside important factors such as immigration and experience, it is clear that having 4-year college degree leads to higher earnings.

Policymakers aiming to end the cycle of poverty for low-income Hispanic families must confront the challenge of increasing the 4-year college enrollment *and* graduation rates of Hispanics (6, 7). While most policymakers would agree with this policy goal, it may be difficult to achieve in practice because college graduates tend to come from the ranks of the middle- and upper-classes, which is made up mostly of college graduates. Without specific attention paid to this issue, children of parents that never went to college are in danger of following in their parents' footsteps. Being the first in a family to attend and graduate from a 4-year college—the "first generation"—requires overcoming multiple challenges, including academic, financial, peer, familial, and cultural challenges (8). Students whose parents have a college degree would be expected to experience these challenges to a lesser extent.

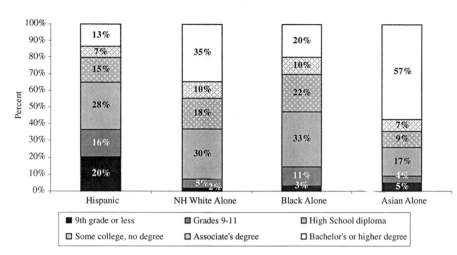

Fig. 5.1   Educational attainment of family householder, 2008, CPS

Figure 5.1 presents the extent of the "first generation" challenge facing Hispanic college students by looking at the highest education level completed by the family householder,[2] which better reflects the education background faced by children at home than using an overall population measure. In 2008, 13% of Hispanic family householders had a bachelor's degree. Hispanics would have to nearly double their current 4-year college graduation rate in order to overtake blacks (20%) and nearly *triple* their graduation rate in order to overtake non-Hispanic whites (35%). The gap between Hispanic and non-Hispanic family householders is lowest for associates degree and some college; the gap with non-Hispanic whites is about 25% for some college, and 50% for community college. These are very stark statistics facing policymakers and Hispanic students.

Figure 5.1 also illustrates a characteristic unique to Hispanic students—over 35% of Hispanic householders do not have a high school diploma (comprised mostly of householders with less than a 9th grade education), compared to less than 2–5% for other groups. This difference is explained by immigration status, as countries in Latin America provide limited educational opportunities (9). However, even after several generations in the US, a significant percentage of Hispanics have not reached parity with their non-Hispanic counterparts (10).

The cumulative effects of being raised in non-college educated households put Hispanic college students at risk of diverging from students that are raised in college-educated households. One such outcome is the disproportionate number of Hispanics that attend community colleges. This non-traditional postsecondary path taken by Hispanic students may reflect a combination of factors linked to not having college-educated parents, such as lower academic preparation, lower educational aspirations, and lack of information regarding the availability and quality of postsecondary institutions. Low income is also recognized as an important factor distinguishing students at community colleges from those at 4-year colleges (6–8). Taking this path is potentially problematic as 2-year colleges are characterized with lower levels of achievement (8, 11, 12). What are the implications of this different path for the levels of education obtained by first-generation college students?

The rest of this chapter considers the descriptive evidence for whether or not the choice of postsecondary institution (4-year, 2-year, and less-than-2-year colleges) differs by college generation. Additionally, I examine whether starting at a 2-year college and then transferring to a 4-year college is a better strategy than initially enrolling in a 4-year college. Although not causal, the evidence suggests that first-generation college students that enroll in 4-year colleges do better than those that enroll in 2-year colleges. This possibility is particularly relevant for Hispanic college students, many of whom are first-generation college students, who enroll in community colleges (8, 13).

The Data and Sample

The data used in this chapter come from the 1996 cohort of first-time college enrollees in the Beginning Postsecondary Student survey (BPS:96/01). These students were interviewed multiple times, first in 1996, and then, for the last time, in 2001. The final sample consists of 8,087 eligible respondents who participated in all rounds of the survey and had valid information on generation and degree status. Consistent with other studies, first-generation college students are defined as having a parent without any postsecondary experience, second-generation college students are defined as having at least one parent that attended college but did not attain a bachelor's degree, and third-generation students are defined as having at least one parent who graduated from college with a bachelor's degree or higher (14–16).

Table 5.2 provides the characteristics of the sample by college generation. The first generation comprises the largest share of all college students, 42%, which is double the percent of second-generation students, and five percentage points more than students who have at least one parent with a bachelor's degree (37%). Whites account for 71% of all postsecondary students in the sample, with blacks (12%) and Hispanics (11%) representing the next two largest groups. Asians (5%) and others (1%) make up the remainder of the BPS:96/01 sample. Women make up 55% of the sample, consistent with the trend of increasing numbers of women in postsecondary institutions. Average parental income in 1995 was $54,593 and the average high school student grade was about a B.

The characteristics of the students in the BPS:96/01 survey differ by college generation. Compared to their overall postsecondary share of 11%, Hispanics make up a disproportionate higher share of first-generation college students, 17%, and lower shares of second- and third-generation college students, 8% and 6%, respectively. This distribution of Hispanic first-generation college contrasts with the distribution for whites and Asians, who are more likely to comprise a greater share of third-generation college students, 79% vs. 71% and 6% vs. 5%, respectively. Like Hispanics, blacks disproportionately make up a higher proportion of first-generation college students, 14% first-generation vs. 12% overall. Together, Hispanics and

Table 5.2   Selected mean characteristics of BPS:96/01 sample, by college generation

	Total	First generation	Second generation	Third generation
Generation	1.00	0.42	0.21	0.37
	(0.00)	(0.49)	(0.37)	(0.48)
White	0.71	0.63	0.74	0.79
	(0.45)	(0.48)	(0.44)	(0.41)
Black	0.12	0.14	0.15	0.08
	(0.33)	(0.35)	(0.35)	(0.27)
Hispanic	0.11	0.17	0.08	0.06
	(0.32)	(0.38)	(0.28)	(0.24)
Asian	0.05	0.04	0.03	0.06
	(0.21)	(0.20)	(0.17)	(0.24)
Other race/ethnicity	0.01	0.01	0.01	0.01
	(0.10)	(0.11)	(0.08)	(0.10)
Age, 1995	21.72	24.82	20.14	19.14
	(7.61)	(10.08)	(4.73)	(3.17)
Female	0.55	0.60	0.58	0.47
	(0.50)	(0.49)	(0.49)	(0.50)
Married, 1995	0.12	0.20	0.09	0.04
	(0.32)	(0.40)	(0.29)	(0.20)
Foreign born	0.10	0.13	0.05	0.10
	(0.30)	(0.33)	(0.22)	(0.30)
English spoken as a child?	0.90	0.84	0.95	0.93
	(0.30)	(0.37)	(0.22)	(0.25)
Parents' income, 1995	$54,593	$38,110	$45,889	$71,077
	($58,584)	($61,929)	($31,669)	($62,111)
High school GPA[1]	5.7	5.5	5.5	5.9
	(1.2)	(1.2)	(1.2)	(1.1)
Maximum sample size[2]	8,087	2,918	1,525	3,644

Notes: Includes individuals with non-missing information on generation, degree/enrollment status, and eligible students that participated in all three waves of the BPS:96/01. Standard deviation in parenthesis. Estimates are weighted.
[1] High school GPA is measured on a seven-point scale: 1 = D- to D, 2 = D to C-, 3 = C- to C, 4 = C to B-, 5 = B- to B, 6 = B to A-, 7 = A- to A.
[2] The number of non-missing observation is 7,803 for foreign born, 7,826 for English, 7,031 for parents' income, and 5,684 for high school GPA. All other variables have 8,087 observations with non-missing values.

blacks make up about one-third of all first-generation college students, whites nearly two-thirds, and Asians and others the remaining 5%.

First-generation college students differ from other students in other important ways: they come from poorer families and have slightly lower grades than other students. Parental income for first-generation college students is $33,000 less than for third-generation students and the GPA of first-generation students is nearly one-half points lower than thrid-generation students on a seven-point scale. Married (20%), foreign-born (13%), and non-native English speaking students (16%) are also over-represented among the first generation. As first-generation college students are

Table 5.3 Postsecondary educational outcomes in 2000–2001, by college generation, BPS:96/01

	Total	First generation	Second generation	Third generation
Bachelor's	29.5%	15.7%	22.8%**	49.0%**
Associate's	10.4%	11.2%	10.3%	9.6%
Certificate	11.8%	18.2%	10.9%**	5.1%**
None, Enrolled	14.5%	12.2%	17.2%**	15.4%*
None, Not Enrolled	33.8%	42.7%	38.8%	20.9%**

Notes: Sample size is 8,087. See Table 5.2 for sample restrictions. **,* denotes that the difference in proportion between first-generation college students and higher generation is statistically significant at the 1% and 5% levels, respectively. Estimates are weighted.

4 years older than other students, this is one likely explanation for the difference in marital status between the generations. Many of these characteristics (income, foreign-born, English ability) also distinguish Hispanics from non-Hispanics and suggest a link between college-generation and Hispanic status. Exploring the role of college-generation status on college completion thus serves to better understand the process of educational achievement for Hispanics.

Descriptive Findings

A. Outcomes in Postsecondary Education by Generational Status

Table 5.3 reports the educational outcomes of students at the end of the 2000–2001 academic year, 6 years after first enrolling in a postsecondary institution in 1995–1996. For any given academic year from 1995–1996 through 2000–2001, students are categorized as either having attained a bachelor's degree, associate's degree, a certificate, no degree but still enrolled, or no degree and not enrolled in any postsecondary institution. After 6 years of enrolling, first-generation college students have lower levels of degree completion and are less likely to still be enrolled than are other students. By the 2000–2001 academic year, 42.7% of first-generation college students have not completed any kind of degree or certificate and are not enrolled in a postsecondary institution. This percentage is twice as much as for third-generation college students, 20.9%. First-generation college students are also less likely be persisting toward a degree by three–five percentage points, than students whose parents have more college experience.

Slightly less than 16% of first-generation college students completed a bachelor's degree by 2000–2001, compared to 22.8% and 49.0% of second- and third-generation college students. Only at the community college level do first-generation college students seem to do as well as higher college-generation students, with about 10% of all students completing an associate's degree by 2000–2001. First-generation college students are significantly more likely to attain a certificate, by as much as a factor of three compared to third-generation college students. Thus, with the important exception of community college programs, first-generation college students seem to fare less well in academic institutions than other students.

The longitudinal information in the data permits an analysis of postsecondary education attainment for each generation of college students. Figures 5.2a–5.2c show the cumulative (highest) postsecondary educational outcome for each college generation in each academic year of the survey. The figures provide insight into changes in attainment of postsecondary education for each generation as well as differences in attainment across generations.

The first figure (Fig. 5.2a) shows that growth in attainment for first-generation college students is generally limited to the first 2 years after enrollment. For instance, the percentage of students with a certificate increases from about 5% in 1995–1996 to over 15% in 1997–1998, and remains relatively flat thereafter. The same pattern is observed for an associate's degree: the frequency of first-generation college students with an associate's degree rises steeply from the initial year to the second year, from 3% to 9%, and then increases only slightly in subsequent years. The pattern of increasing attainment also holds for bachelor's degrees. Seven percent of first-generation college students attained this degree in 1998–1999 (the traditional time-to-degree), 13% in 1999–2000, and 16% in 2000–2001. As the percentage of first-generation students that complete a bachelor's degree continually increases 4–6 years after enrollment, this suggests that first-generation college students may take longer than the 4-year timetable to complete a bachelor's degree and may not conform to the traditional timetable of many colleges and universities.

Throughout most of the 6-year period of the survey, the percentage of first-generation college students that are neither enrolled nor have completed a degree is falling. By the end of their first year, nearly 20% stopped attending a postsecondary institution without completing any kind of program—reflecting the enrollment decisions of those that take time off from school or dropped out during their first year of college. This percentage increases to 40% in 1997–1998 and remains relatively constant thereafter. On the other hand, the percentage of enrolled students without a degree declines throughout the 6-year period. Combined with the observation of continually increasing completion rates, especially for bachelor degrees, this suggests that the 6-year period of the study most likely does not capture the full extent of educational achievement by first-generation college students. Furthermore, with rates of attainment for associate's and certificate programs increasing only slightly, any future growth in degree completion is likely to be observed more for bachelor degrees.

Second-generation college students exhibit similar patterns as the first generation, except that by 2000–2001, the former group is more likely to have completed a bachelor's degree, still be enrolled in college (without having attained a degree), and be less likely to have obtained a certificate. In addition, the second generation also has a greater year-to-year increase in the percentage with a bachelor's degree: the percentage increases from 10% in 1998–1999 to 19% in 1999–2000, and to 23% in 2000–2001. Since attainment percentages for associate's degrees and certificates is unchanged from the fifth to sixth year, it is possible that the majority of those still

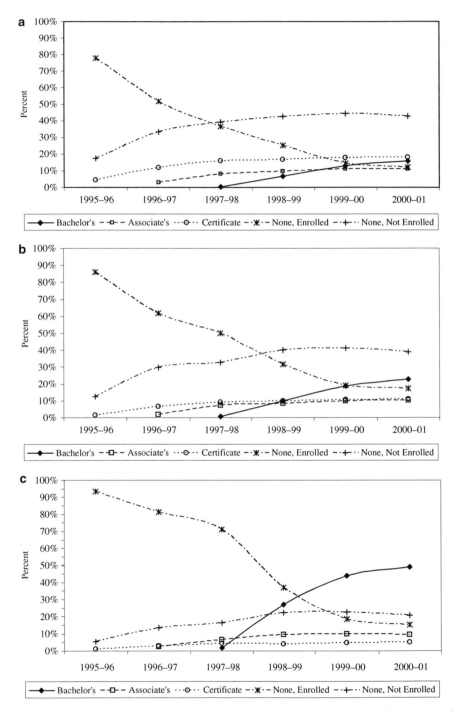

Fig. 5.2 a. Cumulative outcome of first-generation college students. **b**. Cumulative outcome of second-generation college students. **c**. Cumulative outcome of third-generation college students

enrolled in college without a degree (17%) will complete a bachelor's degree if they eventually finish their degree program.

Third-generation college students have the highest percentage of students that complete a bachelor's degree in any year during the 6 years of the BPS:96/01. In 1998–1999, 27% of these students have a 4-year degree, and it increases to 44% and 49% in subsequent years. These percentages are twice and three times as large as for second- and first-generation college students in the same academic year. Similarly, about one-in-five students stop going to college without having attained any type of degree or certificate, a proportion that is half as much as lower-generation students. Finally, in contrast with first-generation college students, only 5% and 10% of third-generation college students complete a certificate program or an associate's degree, respectively by 2000–2001.

These figures reinforce the basic findings of Table 5.3 that students raised in households with no college-educated parents are not just at greater risk of not completing a bachelor's degree, but they are also less likely to complete any degree program. In addition, when they do, they are more likely to stop with a certificate's degree (18%). Furthermore, while the evidence is limited, it is possible that first- and second-generation students take more than 6 years to complete a bachelor's degree.

B. What Kind of Institutions Do First-Generation College Students Attend?

College-generation status is also highly correlated with the type of postsecondary institution in which students initially enroll in. According to Fig. 5.3, slightly more

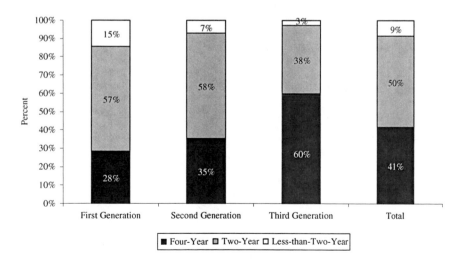

Fig. 5.3 First postsecondary institution attended in 1995–1996, by college generation

than one-quarter of first-generation college students initially enroll in a 4-year college, in contrast to 35% and 60% for second- and third-generation college students, respectively. Instead, the majority (57%) of first-generation students initially enroll in 2-year colleges. Although this percentage is nearly identical for second-generation students (58%), first-generation college students are twice as likely as second-generation college students to enroll in less-than-2-year colleges: 15% vs. 7%.[3] On the other hand, third-generation college students are significantly less likely to enroll in either of these two institutions—38% enrolled in 2-year colleges and 3% in less-than-2-year colleges. The educational paths taken by students should be a fundamental consideration in analyses of educational outcomes by each generation of college students, especially if the initial choice may reduce the likelihood of completing a bachelor's degree.

Students that start at 2-year colleges attain a bachelor's degree only if they transfer, an outcome that is not always realized even among those that intended to transfer when they first enrolled in a 2-year college (8, 12, 13, 17). Fig. 5.4 considers the transfer outcomes for each college generation in the BPS:96/01 sample by type of institution first attended. The percentage of students that start in 4-year institutions and transfer is very similar across all college generations, with about 25% of all students transferring at least once during the 6-year period.

In contrast to 4-year colleges, transfer status varies more by generation at 2-year institutions. Among those starting at 2-year institutions, first-generation college students are less likely to transfer than other students by about 15–35 percentage points. Similarly, first-generation college students that start at less-than-2-year institutions are more likely to never transfer, 87% compared to less than 80% for other students starting in the same institutions. Among transfer students starting at 2-year colleges,

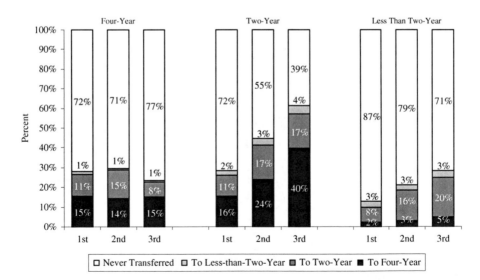

Fig. 5.4 Transfer status in 2000–2001, by college generation and first institution attended

about 55% of first- and second-generation students transfer to a 4-year college and nearly 40% transfer to another 2-year college. The remainder, about 7%, transfers to less-than-2-year institutions. On the other hand, among third-generation students at community colleges that transfer, 65% transfer to a 4-year college.

Above all, Fig. 5.4 shows that for students in 2- or less-than-2-year institutions, no more than 40%, at best, of students transfered to a 4-year college during the study period. Furthermore, among transfers, first-generation college students at community colleges are less likely than third-generation college students to transfer to a 4-year college (roughly 55% vs. 65%). Additionally, while the proportion of students that transfer to a 4-year college from a less-than-2-year institution is the same for all generations (about 15%), the remainder of first-generation college students are twice as likely to transfer to another less-than-2 year institution than second- or third-generation students (25% vs. 12%). Lastly, among those who start at 4-year colleges, first- and second-generation college students are more likely than their third-generation peers to "transfer down." Compared to 45% and 52% of first- and second-generation college transfer students that transfer down, 65% of third-generation transfer students make a lateral transfer, i.e., transfer to another 4-year college.

Hispanic and College Generation Status

Education experts and policy makers recognize that increasing the postsecondary education of Hispanics and blacks is a worthy policy goal. Are the findings about the differential postsecondary outcomes for first-generation college students applicable to Hispanics? Specifically, what is the link between Hispanic educational attainment and generational status? The ethnic and racial composition of each generation given in Table 5.2 is more representative of non-Hispanic whites since they make up over 70% of the total BPS:96/01 sample. For this reason, Fig. 5.5 considers the college-generation composition for each ethnic and non-Hispanic racial group (American Indian and "other" represent about 1% of the sample and are not included for simplicity).

This exercise reveals interesting differences not captured in Table 5.2. Fig. 5.5 shows that the majority of Hispanics (64%) and non-Hispanic blacks (50%) are first-generation college students. In contrast, one third of non-Hispanic white and Asian students fall in this category. Only one-in-five Hispanic students have at least one parent with a bachelor's degree, five percentage points less than blacks, and at least 20% points less than whites and Asians. Nearly half (48%) of Asian students in postsecondary institutions have at least one parent with a bachelor's degree, reflecting in part the self-selection of immigrants (18). Black students are similar to white students in terms of having a parent with some college experience (second generation)—26% and 22%, respectively.

In sum, although whites account for the bulk of first-generation students in postsecondary education due to their population size, their share of the total white college-student population is only about 35%. On the other hand, Hispanics are

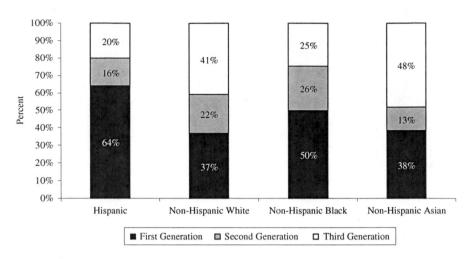

Fig. 5.5 Distribution of college generation by ethnicity/race

more likely to be first-generation college students, 64%, than other college generation. Hispanics also comprise the largest minority group among first-generation college students and the smallest minority group among third-generation students, 17% and 6%, respectively (see Table 5.2). First-generation college status is thus a defining characteristic of Hispanic college students.

The variety in the ethnic composition of each generation has potentially important implications for interpreting the outcomes of minority students. Fig. 5.6 explores the highest educational attainment in 2000–2001 by various ethnic groups.

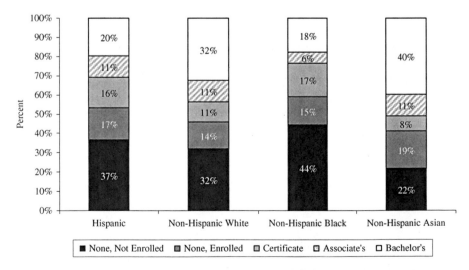

Fig. 5.6 Education attainment by ethnic/racial group, 2000–2001

Relatively few blacks and Hispanics have completed a bachelor's degree by this academic year, 18% and 20%, respectively, while the completion rate is about twice as
high for whites (32%) and Asians (40%). In addition, blacks and Hispanics have the
highest fraction without any kind of degree in 2000–2001: 44% for blacks and 37%
for Hispanic. Blacks and Hispanics also have the highest percentage of students that
earn a certificate (about 16%), but blacks (6%) are less likely than all three other
groups (11%) to have an associate's degree.

Conclusions and Policy Implications

This chapter argues that family educational background of college students is
associated with the choice of postsecondary institution and with postsecondary
achievement. Specifically, first-generation college students—students whose parents do not have any college experience—are different than other postsecondary
students. Understanding the postsecondary experiences of first-generation college
students provides insights into the achievements of Hispanics in postsecondary institutions because about two third of them are first-generation college students. The
findings in this chapter support the argument that first-generation college students
at less-than-4-year institutions may have lower educational achievements than other
students. The transfer status of first-generation college students also suggests that
first-generation college students are on an educational path that seems to divert them
from a bachelor's degree.

There are two inter-related factors affecting whether or not first-generation
students attain a bachelor's degree. The first is whether first-generation students
have the same completion rates as second- and third-generation college students,
conditional on being on the same educational path. On average it seems that first-
generation college students have lower college completion rates 6 years after first
enrolling in college. This finding in the BPS:96/01 data is consistent with studies that find a significant negative effect of first-generation college status on the
probability of completing a bachelor's degree (see below).

The second question pertains to the educational path taken by first-generation
college students. Specifically, the first generation is disproportionately more likely
to start off in a less-than-4-year institution than third-generation college students. It
is important to understand what factors lead to this outcome—is it due to lower academic goals, lack of counseling or information about the 4-year colleges as viable
options, and less preparation? Is this a condition that should concern policy makers?
If so, what are the possible remedies that would put first-generation college students
in a better position to complete a bachelor's degree? How early in life should such
policies be implemented? What programs are cost-effective from a policy evaluation
perspective?

Both questions are related, but the first question has received more attention.
Studies find that first-generation college students are less likely to complete a bachelor's degree than their peers (14–16). For instance, after controlling for student,

parent, and institutional characteristics, first-generation college students are eight percentage points less likely to complete a bachelor's degree (16). Furthermore, this estimate decreases only slightly to six percentage points when only students that start in 4-year colleges are considered (16). It is possible that other factors, such as academic goals, the burden of loans, adjustment to a new academic lifestyle, and pressure to support their family might account for the remaining achievement gap.

Yet one shortcoming of such studies is that they do not control for self-selection into the academic/college-preparatory track, as opposed to the less rigorous non-academic track. The lower academic preparation of first-generation college students documented by the US Department of Education (15)—which also affects the likelihood of completing a degree—might be the result of the lower quality schooling available or a lack of understanding regarding career options after graduating from a 4-year college. Variables that account for how first-generation college students make investment decisions in education need to be incorporated into future studies of achievement.

Most programs that aim to increase the achievement of first-generation college students specifically, or low-income or minority students more generally, tend to deal with one or several of the issues facing these students. Instead, programs that integrate financial support, academic, and social counseling, and other related factors are likely to be more successful than programs with a limited focus (19). More importantly, if students are making decisions early in their life that affect the options available to them in the future, then it may be worthwhile to begin programs or interventions many years before students start high school. An example of one such program is the First Graduate program in San Francisco, which provides a wide range of programs, starting in the 7th grade and continuing for 10 years, with the aim of helping them to become the first in their family to graduate from college.[4] In addition to the services provided to the students, First Graduate also engages parents in the process so that students can receive a level of emotional support that first-generation college students may otherwise not receive.

The fact that a large percentage of Hispanics in postsecondary institutions also happen to be first-generation college students suggests that discussions and policy implications for first-generation college students will disproportionately impact Hispanic students. Affirmative action programs were the primary means by which the higher education system addressed the lower attainment of minority students. Recently, such programs have come under attack throughout the country, especially in states with large minority populations such as California, Michigan, and Texas. Recent disputes over affirmative action plans in higher education have challenged the ability of states to target ethnic and racial groups in admissions and retention programs. California and Texas, for instance, eliminated postsecondary affirmative action programs. While the US Supreme Court ruled that such programs are not necessarily unconstitutional, not every state—or every university within a state—currently uses them. However, focusing on college-generation status may make it possible for policymakers to address the low college-graduation rates of minorities without having to target them on the basis of race or ethnicity. For this reason, further research is needed to answer the question of the extent to which first-generation status accounts for the observed college graduation gaps between Hispanics and non-Hispanic whites.

Another interesting issue raised by these descriptive findings is the role played by 2-year colleges in the educational outcomes of college students. Community colleges are an attractive instrument for policy makers desiring to increase access to postsecondary education. Compared to 4-year institutions, 2-year colleges have lower admissions standards, lower tuition, and cost less to operate. California, for instance, eases access to the 2-year college system by locating more than 100 campuses throughout the state and charging relatively low fees. Thus, the availability of such institutions may draw students into the postsecondary system that may otherwise never enroll, perhaps increasing the number of 2- and 4-year graduates in the process. However, the low levels of degree completion at community colleges may reflect the fact that access is misaligned with funding and fee policies, restrictions on spending of funding and hiring, and the role of institutions in guiding students in their programs (20).

It is also possible that some students diverted to 2-year colleges may be better served by 4-year institutions. These students may linger in 2-year colleges and never transfer or, if they do transfer, they may receive a lower quality education in their first 2 years, leaving them less prepared for their junior or senior years. These two possibilities reduce the likelihood that students in 2-year colleges attain a bachelor's degree, undermining the cost savings of steering students toward 2-year colleges.

Yet, as noted previously, the same factors that drive the choice of institution may be correlated with educational outcomes. In other words, picking a first-generation college student in a 2-year college at random and putting her at a 4-year college may not remedy the observed difference between the three generations of students. It is important to explain the choice of first institution attended in order to understand why first-generation college students are less likely to attain 4-year degrees.

Notes

1. Disclaimer: The opinions expressed in this chapter are those of the author, and do not necessarily reflect the views of the Office of the Comptroller of the Currency or the Department of the Treasury.
2. A family householder is the owner or renter of the housing unit who is also in a family (in the case of a couple, the householder can be either partner).
3. Less-than-2-year institutions are generally referred to as "technical," "vocational," or "career" schools, and offer courses that train students in a specific career or skill and that result in a terminal degree or certificate.
4. Full disclosure: As of September 2010, the author is on the Board of Directors of First Graduate.

References

1. Card, David, and Thomas Lemieux. 2001. "Can Falling Supply Explain the Rising Return to College for Younger Men? A Cohort-Based Analysis." *Quarterly Journal of Economics*, 116(2): 705–746.

2. Katz, Lawrence F., and David Autor. 1999. "Changes in the Wage Structure and Earnings Inequality." In *Handbook of Labor Economics*, Volume 3A, ed. Orley C. Ashenfelter and David Card, 1463–1555. Amsterdam: North-Holland.

3. Katz, Lawrence F., and Kevin M. Murphy. 1992. "Changes in Relative Wages, 1963–1987: Supply and Demand Factors." *The Quarterly Journal of Economics*, 107(1): 35–78.

4. Ashenfelter, Orley, Colm Harmon, and Hessel Oosterbeek. 1999. "A Review of Estimates of the Schooling/Earnings Relationship, with Tests for Publication Bias." *Labour Economics*, 6(4): 453–470.

5. Johnson, Hans P., and Deborah Reed. 2007. "Can California Import Enough College Graduates to Meet Workforce Needs?" *California Counts*, 8(4): 1–24.

6. Haveman, Robert, and Timothy Smeeding. 2006. "The Role of Higher Education in Social Mobility." *Opportunity in America*, 16(2): 125–150.

7. Kane, Thomas J. 2001. *"College-Going and Inequality: A Literature Review."* New York: Russell Sage Foundation.

8. Bailey, Thomas, Mariana Alfonso, Juan Carlos, Calcagno, Davis Jenkins, Gregory Kienzl, and Tim Leinbach. 2004. *"Improving Student Attainment in Community Colleges: Institutional Characteristics and Policies."* New York: Community College Research Center, Teachers College, Columbia University.

9. Ribando Seelke, Clare. 2007. "Overview of Education Issues and Programs in Latin America." CRS Report for Congress. Congressional Research Service, Library of Congress.

10. Smith, James P. 2003. "Assimilation across the Latino Generations." *American Economic Review*, 93(2): 315–319.

11. Sandy, Jonathan, Arturo Gonzalez, and Michael J. Hilmer. 2006. "Alternative Paths to College Completion: The Effect of Attending a Two Year School on the Probability of Completing a Four Year Degree." *Economics of Education Review*, 25(5): 463–471.

12. Wellman, Jane V. 2002. "State Policy and Community College–Baccalaureate Transfer." National Center Report #02-6. The National Center for Public Policy and Higher Education and The Institute for Higher Education Policy.

13. Gonzalez, Arturo, and Michael J. Hilmer. 2006. "The Role of 2-Year Colleges in the Improving Situation of Hispanic Postsecondary Education." *Economics of Education Review*, 25(3):249–257.

14. Nunez, Anne-Marie, and Stephanie Cuccaro-Alamin. 1998. "First-Generation Students: Undergraduates Whose Parents Never Enrolled in Postsecondary Education." Statistical Analysis Report, NCES 98-082. U.S. Department of Education, Office of Education Research and Improvement.

15. Warburton, Edward C., Rosio Bugarin, and Anne-Marie Nunez. 2001. "Bridging the Gap: Academic Preparation and Postsecondary Success of First-Generation Students." Statistical Analysis Report, NCES 2001-153. U.S. Department of Education, Office of Education Research and Improvement.

16. Chen, Xianglei. 2005. "First-Generation Students in Postsecondary Education: A Look at Their College Transcripts." Statistical Analysis Report, NCES 2005-171. U.S. Department of Education, Institute of Education Sciences.

17. Leigh, Duane E., and Andrew M. Gill. 2002. "Do Community Colleges Really Divert Students from Receiving a Bachelor's Degree?" *Economics of Education Review*, 21(1): 23–30.

18. Borjas, George J. 1994. "The Economics of Immigration." *Journal of Economic Literature*, 34(4): 1667–1717.

19. Tym, Carmen, Robin McMillion, Sandra Barone, and Jeff Webster. 2004. "First-Generation College Students: A Literature Review." Texas Guaranteed Student Loan Corporation. http://www.tgslc.org/pdf/first_generation.pdf (accessed on March 19, 2010).

20. Shulock, Nancy, and Colleen Moore. 2007. *"Rules of the Game: How State Policy Creates Barriers to Degree Completion and Impedes Student Success in the California Community Colleges."* Sacramento, CA: Institute for Higher Education Leadership & Policy, California State University, Sacramento.

Part III
Legalization and Naturalization

Chapter 6
The Effects of Legalization on Migrant Remittances

Catalina Amuedo-Dorantes and Francesca Mazzolari

Abstract Remittances to Latin America have been increasing at rather dramatic rates in recent years. As some countries have grown accustomed to remittances, policy-makers have become increasingly worried about the stability of these transfers. US immigration policy, via its impact on immigration inflows and the immigrant stock, can significantly affect future remittances. This study investigates how a generalized amnesty, a provision in the 1986 Immigration Reform and Control Act (IRCA), affected remitting patterns of immigrants from Latin America. Using the Legalized Population Survey—a nationally representative sample of undocumented immigrants who benefited from IRCA's main amnesty program—we find that legalization had a statistically and economically significant negative impact on remittances sent home, particularly among Mexicans. Indeed, back-of-the-envelope calculations show that a current amnesty would significantly lower remittances sent to Mexico, and this would, in turn, result in sizeable foregone investment and education funds.

Introduction

Until the recent economic slowdown, remittances had been increasing in size at a very rapid rate. As noted by the Inter-American Development Bank (IADB), remittances to Latin America and the Caribbean (LAC) region stood at $45 billion in 2004 (1), increased to $53.6 billion in 2005, and then to $62.3 billion in 2006—a 38% increase in only 2 years. Within the LAC region, Mexico received the most (about half) of the total remittance flows, which make up around 3% of its GDP. In smaller immigrant-sending countries, remittances make up even strikingly higher shares of national income—as high as 18% in El Salvador and 23% in Honduras. These magnitudes are impressive, exceeding combined inflows of foreign direct investment

C. Amuedo-Dorantes (✉)
San Diego State University, San Diego, CA, USA; IZA – Institute for the Study of Labor,
Bonn, Germany
e-mail: catalina.amuedo.dorantes@gmail.com

D.L. Leal, S.J. Trejo (eds.), *Latinos and the Economy*, Immigrants and Minorities, Politics and Policy, DOI 10.1007/978-1-4419-6682-7_6,

113

and official development assistance. Furthermore, remittance flows have proven to be quite stable at a macroeconomic level, even during economic downturns (2). As a result, remittance inflows have been regarded as an important source of external funding for fueling economic development (3).

However, as some developing economies have grown accustomed to remittances, policy-makers have become increasingly worried about the potentially transitory versus permanent nature of international money transfers. This concern has been aggravated by recent news regarding the drop in migrant remittances for some economies, as is the case with Mexico (4).[1] A variety of factors are likely to affect the temporary versus long-lasting character of remittance inflows, such as changes in the cost of remitting funds, changes in the composition and magnitude of migration flows, and changes in the characteristics of the existing immigrant stock. As a result, US immigration policy, via its impact on both the immigration inflows and the immigrant stock, can have a significant impact on the volume of remittances.

In this chapter, we examine the impact of generalized amnesty—a provision in the 1986 Immigration Reform and Control Act (IRCA)—on immigrants' remitting patterns. Amnesty can improve the well-being of newly legalized immigrants via higher wages (5–7), in which case immigrants may have more disposable income to remit to their families and communities back home. Alternatively, the acquisition of legal permanent resident (LPR) status may facilitate family reunification and, as such, curtail migrants' remitting incentives (8, 9). In addition to its impact on immigrants' remitting patterns via changes in family income and composition, the acquisition of LPR status might further affect remittances by changing an immigrant's perceived degree of uncertainty regarding his migration experience. To the extent that legalization reduces deportation risk and possibly income uncertainty by opening up new job opportunities to the now-legal migrant, the propensity to remit might decrease among recently legalized immigrants that primarily remitted for self-insurance purposes.

This study addresses a policy question that is increasingly important in the light of recent discussions in the US Congress on a comprehensive immigration bill that would allow a path to legalization for most of the undocumented population residing in the United States—a population recently estimated at around 12 million (10). Despite an extensive debate on the pros and cons of such a generalized amnesty for the United States, much less attention has been devoted to the potential effects of such a policy on immigrant-sending regions. Since no evidence of the impact of past amnesty programs on immigrants' remitting patterns post-legalization is available, this study sheds some light on the consequences that a generalized amnesty may have on the persistence of these money flows to developing regions in the world and, in particular, to Latin American countries.

To assess the impact of legalization on remittance behavior, we use data from the Legalized Population Survey—a nationally representative sample of undocumented immigrants who benefited from IRCA's main amnesty program—to examine changes in Latin American immigrants' remitting patterns between 1987 (before they became legal) and 1991 (after they became legal). Since IRCA legislation was passed in 1986 after being debated for years, even if individuals in our sample had not yet legalized by 1987, they may have planned to do so, and may have already cut back on remittances, instead re-focusing their investments on the future they expected to have as legalized immigrants in the United States. If so, post-legalization changes in remittances estimated in the Legalized Population Survey would understate the decline in remittances actually associated with legalization.

To preview our findings, we estimate that legalization did have a statistically and economically significant negative effect on remittances sent home by Mexicans and by other Latin Americans, both at the extensive (probability to remit) and intensive (amount remitted) margin in the former group, and only at the intensive margin in the latter. Based on the estimated effects of legalization for Mexicans, and current figures on the undocumented population from Mexico residing in the United States and on the amounts they remit home, back-of-the-envelope calculations show that a current amnesty would cause drops in remittances to Mexico that would, in turn, result in foregone investment and education funds of sizable magnitude when compared to some of the main programs promoted by the Mexican government to foster investment and education.

Theoretical Framework

The primary objective of this study is to examine the consequences of legalization occurring via a generalized amnesty program for the remitting patterns of newly legalized immigrants. In this regard, it is helpful to first overview some of the motives for remitting as discussed in the literature.

Migrants remit money home for a myriad of motives. Altruism is one of the key motives for remitting money home (11, 12). If migrants primarily remit altruistically, remittances should vary with migrants' remitting capacity and the needs of friends and family back home. A second reason for remitting money back home often discussed in the literature is to make a specific purchase (e.g., a plot of land or a house) or investment (e.g., setting up a small business). This is particularly common among short-term or temporary migrants who migrate for the specific purpose of accumulating financial assets for consumption smoothing or future retirement (13, 14). Finally, a third motive for remitting contemplated in the literature is insurance.[2] Because migration is fraught with uncertainties, it is prudent for migrants to cover for these risks by remitting funds home. In this way, migrants maintain a "good standing" with family members in the home country, securing a place within the family in the face of an unsuccessful migration experience (15, 16).

Depending on the motive behind migrants' remitting behavior, we may expect legalization to affect remittances differently. If migrants remit for primarily altruistic or saving/investment purposes, legalization may result in larger remittance flows to the extent that the acquisition of LPR status is associated with higher earnings. Additionally, legalization may facilitate family reunification and reduce remittances sent for altruistic purposes. Consequently, controlling for family income and composition should account for changes in remittance flows sent for altruistic and saving/investment purposes. However, remittances sent for self-insurance purposes depend on the migrant's perceived uncertainty regarding the migratory experience.

To the extent that legalization reduces deportation risk and possibly income uncertainty by opening up new job opportunities, there might be a residual effect of LPR status on migrants' remitting patterns even after controlling for ongoing changes in family composition and income. If that is the case, we should find a negative "residual" effect of legalization on migrants' remitting patterns.

The 1986 Immigration Reform and Control Act

Enacted in 1986, IRCA granted legalization to many unauthorized workers already present in the United States. Specifically, about 1.6 million individuals who could demonstrate continuous presence in the United States since 1982 legalized through the general amnesty program.[3]

Under the rules included in section 245A of the Immigration and Nationality Act (INA), undocumented migrants that intended to legalize through this general amnesty had to apply for adjustment of status during the 12-month period beginning on a date (not later than 180 days after November 6, 1986) designated by the Attorney General. They also had to prove continuous unlawful residence since January 1, 1982, as well as continuous physical presence since the enactment of the law. As proof of their continued residence in the United States, migrants were allowed to use a variety of documents, such as a driver license, gas, electric or telephone bills, or bank statements.[4] Lastly, migrants had to demonstrate "good moral character," primarily established on the basis of not having been convicted of any felony or three or more misdemeanors in the United States.

Filing fees were approximately $185 (17), but poor families were eligible for fee waivers.[5] Eighteen months after obtaining temporary residence status, migrants could apply for permanent residence status (i.e., for a "green card"). At that point, migrants had to prove "basic citizenship skills," such as a minimal understanding of English, US history, and government. Migrants could prove such knowledge by passing a test or with proof of having satisfactorily pursued a course of study (e.g., a certificate of completion of English and/or US history/government course from a community college).

It is estimated that most undocumented migrants applied for legalization (18, 19). After application, an immigrant's process of legalization lasted an average of 2 years—about 99% of legalizations took place between 1989 and 1992. These applications had a high rate of success—about 9 out of 10 applicants obtained legalization (20).

Data

To assess the impact of legalization on remittance patterns, this study analyzes data from the Legalized Population Survey (LPS)—a nationally representative sample (the only one available) of the population that was legalized through IRCA's general amnesty program.[6]

The LPS is a two-wave, nationwide longitudinal survey. The universe for the first wave (LPS1) was the population of adult legalization applicants. Interviews took place between February and June of 1989 and collected information from 6,193 individuals who had applied for temporary residence status—the first step towards legalization—by January 31, 1989. In this first wave of the survey, respondents were asked about the dollar amount remitted to family and friends in other countries during 1987. In the follow-up survey wave (LPS2), conducted between April and September of 1992, about 4,012 LPS1 respondents who were granted legal permanent residence by January 1992 were re-interviewed and asked about the dollar amount remitted to family and friends in other countries during 1991. The universe for the follow-up survey excluded 1,193 individuals who were either randomly selected for exclusion because of resource limitations (691 individuals) or found to be ineligible because they were not legalized by January 1992 (502 individuals, most of which were still waiting for a decision). Of the remaining 5,000 individuals sampled for the LPS2, 890 were non-respondents and 98 individuals were later found ineligible.

LPS1 includes information on the respondent's country of origin, the year of first and last entry in the United States, and the number of times the respondent entered the United States and stayed for longer than 3 days. We approximate the length of residence in the United States as the number of years elapsed since the immigrant first entered the United States and stayed longer than 3 days.

Both waves include information on family composition at the time of the interview. In particular, for married respondents, we have information on whether the spouse lived in the US (either in the same household or elsewhere) or abroad. We also know the number of children (as well as of parents and siblings) living in the same household in the United States, but we do not have enough information to infer the composition of the family residing abroad at the time of each wave.

Table A1 in the appendix provides a description of the LPS variables used in the analysis, while Table 6.1 shows the summary statistics for the LPS1 and the LPS2 samples. About 63% of the LPS1 sample remitted approximately $2,200 home in 1987. Both the percentage of individuals who remit and the average dollar amount remitted decreased by 1991: the former drops to 54% and the latter to approximately $1,600. Between 56% and 58% of the respondents in the LPS1 and LPS2 samples are men. Respondents are 32 years old, on average, when interviewed in 1989. About 72% of them do not have a high-school degree. Approximately 56% of the sample resides in California and the vast majority had been in the US for about 10 years by 1987. Most immigrants in our sample have family incomes anywhere between $12,000 and $25,000 in both sample years, although a larger fraction of households had income over $30,000 by 1991.[7] There is, however, a decline in the employment rate of respondents, from 80% to 77%.

Finally, we observe changes in family composition—a larger proportion of migrants declare having their spouse as well as more children in the United States by 1991. Because the drop in the fraction of respondents with spouses abroad is significantly smaller than the increase in the percentage of respondents with spouses in

Table 6.1 Descriptive Statistics

Sample: immigrants from	All countries 1987	1991	Mexico 1987	1991	Other Latin American countries 1987	1991	Other countries 1987	1991
Fraction remitting	0.63	0.54	0.64	0.52	0.69	0.63	0.37	0.39
Amount remitted (if >0)	2,194.5	1,656.5	2,300.3	1,619.4	1,843.4	1,566.5	2,355.1	2,411.6
Male	0.58	0.56	0.59	0.57	0.53	0.51	0.64	0.62
Age	32.25	36.26	31.17	35.21	33.68	37.78	36.94	40.68
Less than 12 years of education	0.72	0.72	0.83	0.83	0.60	0.60	0.17	0.16
California	0.56	0.58	0.62	0.65	0.44	0.48	0.34	0.35
Years in US	9.91	13.86	10.41	14.39	8.44	12.42	9.67	13.30
Undocumented at last entry	0.76	0.76	0.86	0.85	0.71	0.74	0.14	0.13
Family income								
Less than $15,000	0.36	0.28	0.37	0.29	0.40	0.29	0.27	0.15
$15,000–$29,999	0.36	0.37	0.36	0.39	0.35	0.36	0.33	0.28
$30,000 or more	0.17	0.26	0.15	0.23	0.15	0.26	0.33	0.50
Employed	0.80	0.77	0.78	0.75	0.84	0.80	0.82	0.85
Spouse in the US	0.45	0.60	0.47	0.63	0.39	0.52	0.39	0.57
Spouse abroad	0.06	0.04	0.06	0.03	0.04	0.04	0.06	0.05
Children in the US	1.47	2.11	1.66	2.27	1.15	1.79	0.76	1.43
Parents in the US	0.24	0.17	0.26	0.17	0.19	0.16	0.15	0.17
Siblings in the US	0.74	0.47	0.88	0.54	0.53	0.33	0.24	0.23
Observations	5,894	3,874	2,799	1,879	2,183	1,436	918	565

Source: Legalized Population Survey.

the United States, new marriages may have played a role in the observed changes in family composition. A bit more puzzling is the fact that the number of parents or siblings living in the United States declines. Given that family composition pertains to individuals residing in the same household, parents and siblings may be moving out of the household as they settle in the United States. Alternatively, some elderly parents may have passed away by the second wave.

Table 6.1 also distinguishes between Mexicans, other Latin Americans, and migrants from other countries. The analysis in the next sections is restricted to the first two groups because they are numerically more relevant. It is worth noting the particularly large decline in the percentage of Mexican migrants who remit, as well as in the amount remitted by Mexicans, although both are larger than among other Latin Americans. Other notable differences between the two groups include the lower educational attainment, the longer US migration experience, and the higher percentage of undocumented migrants among Mexicans. In light of these differences, we carry the analysis separately for Mexicans and other Latin Americans.

Research Strategy

We examine whether IRCA affected remittance patterns of undocumented immigrants by estimating the 1987–1991 change in the propensity to remit among LPS respondents. Using pooled data from the two LPS waves, we estimate the following regression model:

$$R_{it} = \beta_0 + \beta_1 \, yearsUS_{it} + \beta_2 \, X_{it} + \gamma_{1991} + \varepsilon_{it} \qquad t = 1987, 1991 \qquad (6.1)$$

where

R_{it} is either an indicator for whether individual i remitted any amount of money in year t, or the amount remitted, if positive;

γ_{1991} is a dummy that takes the value one if the observation comes from the second wave, and zero otherwise;

$YearsUS_{it}$ measures the number of years since the respondent first entered in the United States (we include linear, quadratic, and cubic terms in the estimated equation);

X_{it} is a vector of individual and family characteristics that are either time-invariant (gender, state of residence[8]) or vary over time (age, education, family income, employment status).[9]

If IRCA were the only factor affecting remittances between 1987 and 1991, then the estimated γ_{1991} from Eq. (6.1) would arguably represent the causal effect of legalization on remittance behavior. IRCA was close to being a universal program, so that selection effects, if any, are a second-order concern. First, the take-up rate of IRCA's general amnesty program is estimated to have been very large, between two thirds (19) and 100% (18). Second, there is no clear reason to expect the incomplete take-up rate (if any) to be systematically related to unobservable personal characteristics that also affect remittance behavior. The administrative filing costs should not have disproportionally deterred low-income people from applying for amnesty because poor families were eligible for fee waivers. The other key requirement for obtaining general amnesty was the ability to prove continuous residence in the United States since 1982. However, given that a large variety of documents were accepted to that end, this requirement should not have significantly affected the composition of the pool of eligible applicants.

Assuming a negligible selectivity bias, the main identification issue in Eq. (6.1) arises from the fact that the estimated γ_{1991} captures not only the effect of legalization, but also the effect of any other time-varying factor contemporaneous with IRCA. The 1991–1992 economic downturn is one such event that might have affected the lives of immigrant families over the relevant period of analysis. Equation (6.1), however, includes controls for those time-varying characteristics—family income and the respondent's employment status—through which most of the business cycle effect on a migrants' remitting capacity is likely to take place. Hence, we argue that γ_{1991} should be purged from the first-order effects of the business cycle, and reasonably capture the effects of legalization.

How could legalization affect remittances once we control for employment and income variables? Following our discussion on remitting motives, we expect two main components in the effects of legalization: (1) Legalization may facilitate family reunification (or family formation in the United States) and reduce remittances sent home to relatives for altruistic purposes; (2) To the extent that legal status reduces deportation risk, and, more generally, an immigrant's perceived uncertainty about her migration experience, then legalization might reduce remittances sent for insurance purposes. Both channels predict that the estimated γ_{1991} should be non-positive. Alternatively, if we expand Eq. (6.1) to include time-varying family characteristics, the sign and magnitude of the estimated time dummy might directly serve as a test for the existence and strength of insurance motives for remittances.

Last, it is worth discussing a final identification issue. One might be worried that a before-after estimate of the effects of legalization on remittances in a sample of legalized immigrants does not adequately control for changes that, even in the absence of legalization or of any other time-varying shock, would have happened over time as a result of an immigrant's "assimilation." For example, as long as greater assimilation is expected to weaken altruistic and insurance motives for remitting, the fact that 4 years have elapsed (between 1987 and 1991) should be associated with a certain degree of remittance decay. Equation (6.1), however, controls for this effect through the inclusion of the term $YearsUS_{it}$. The estimated γ_{1991}, thus, represents the average change in remittances over time, once the effects of assimilation have been partialled-out by the inclusion of $YearsUS_{it}$.[10] We have also estimated various models in which we allow the effects of additional years of residence in the United States to be different before and after legalization. This amounts to including interactions between $YearsUS_{it}$ (and its quadratic and cubic transformation) and γ_{1991}. However, the coefficients of these interactions are not statistically different from zero and, therefore, have been omitted from our final specifications.

Results

Changes in the Likelihood of Remitting Money Back Home

Table 6.2 displays the results from estimating Eq. (6.1), with and without controls for time-varying characteristics such as employment, family income, and family composition. The dependent variable is an indicator for whether an immigrant remitted any amount of money home.[11] Given the differences between the two groups, the estimation is run separately for Mexicans (columns 1 and 2) and Latin Americans (columns 3 and 4).

Table 6.2 Before-after estimates of the likelihood of remitting money to Mexico

Country of origin	Mexico		Other Latin American countries	
Model specification:	Column 1	Column 2	Column 3	Column 4
Year 1991	−0.062***	−0.067***	0.009	0.021
	(0.015)	(0.016)	(0.020)	(0.021)
Male	0.171***	0.063***	0.074***	0.012
	(0.017)	(0.019)	(0.018)	(0.019)
Age	0.051***	0.026*	0.062***	0.044**
	(0.012)	(0.014)	(0.016)	(0.018)
Age squared	−0.095***	−0.039	−0.109***	−0.069
	(0.028)	(0.031)	(0.036)	(0.042)
Age cubic	0.001**	0.000	0.001*	0.000
	(0.000)	(0.000)	(0.000)	(0.000)
Undocumented at last entry	0.120***	0.089***	0.144***	0.091***
	(0.025)	(0.025)	(0.022)	(0.026)
Years in US	−0.050***	−0.037***	−0.053***	−0.044**
	(0.009)	(0.009)	(0.020)	(0.021)
Years in US quadratic	0.002***	0.001***	0.002	0.001
	(0.000)	(0.000)	(0.001)	(0.001)
Years in US cubic	−0.000***	−0.000*	−0.000	−0.000
	(0.000)	(0.000)	(0.000)	(0.000)
Education				
At most 5th grade		0.181***		0.167***
		(0.038)		(0.034)
6th–11th grade		0.126***		0.137***
		(0.036)		(0.028)
12th grade/HS diploma		0.070*		0.091***
		(0.040)		(0.030)
California		−0.007		0.019
		(0.017)		(0.019)
Family Income				
$3,000–$5,999		0.020		0.076
		(0.055)		(0.069)
$6,000–$8,999		0.084*		0.199***
		(0.049)		(0.064)
$9,000–$11,999		0.126**		0.153**

Table 6.2 (continued)

Country of origin	Mexico		Other Latin American countries	
Model specification:	Column 1	Column 2	Column 3	Column 4
		(0.049)		(0.063)
$12,000–$14,999		0.196***		0.162***
		(0.048)		(0.062)
$15,000–$19,999		0.247***		0.198***
		(0.048)		(0.062)
$20,000–$24,999		0.313***		0.217***
		(0.048)		(0.062)
$25,000–$29,999		0.291***		0.206***
		(0.051)		(0.064)
$30,000 or more		0.324***		0.268***
		(0.048)		(0.062)
Employed		0.126***		0.118***
		(0.021)		(0.025)
Spouse in the US		−0.042**		0.046**
		(0.019)		(0.021)
Spouse abroad		0.165***		0.201***
		(0.028)		(0.033)
Children in the US		−0.048***		−0.041***
		(0.006)		(0.008)
Parents in the US		−0.122***		−0.085***
		(0.018)		(0.023)
Siblings in the US		−0.008		0.030***
		(0.007)		(0.010)
Constant	−0.001	0.060	−0.103	−0.205
	(0.151)	(0.177)	(0.213)	(0.247)
Observations	4,626	4,008	3,604	3,051
R-squared	0.08	0.17	0.08	0.13

Notes: Dependent variable: Dummy equal to one if the family remitted a positive amount of money to family or friend abroad. Pooled OLS estimates. Standard errors (in parentheses) account for correlation across observations for the same individual.
*significant at 10%; ** significant at 5%; *** significant at 1%.
Sample: LPS unbalanced panel.

Among Mexicans, we find that, post legalization, the probability of remitting fell by six percentage points (Table 6.2, column 1). Importantly, adding controls for individual educational attainment and employment status, as well as for family income and family composition, leaves the estimated impact of legalization virtually unchanged (column 2). On the contrary, among other Latin Americans, we do not find evidence of a significant reduction in the likelihood of sending money home post legalization.

Despite this difference, the remaining regressors are found to have similar effects on the likelihood of remitting for the two migrant groups. For instance, in both groups, male, less educated, and more recent migrants display a greater likelihood of remitting money home relative to their female, more educated, or less recent migrant counterparts. Additionally, migrants' remitting likelihood is positively correlated with respondents' economic capability to remit, as proxied by their employment status and family income. Finally, as we expected, family composition—signaling family responsibilities back home and in the host country, is an important determinant of migrants' remitting patterns. For example, having parents or more children in the United States lowers the likelihood of remitting money home, whereas having a spouse back home increases it. In the case of Latinos who are not from Mexico, we also find that having a spouse or siblings in the United States increases the likelihood of remitting money home. This effect, which arises in 1991,[12] may signal a greater remitting capacity (e.g., if the spouse contributes economically to the household), or social pressure to fulfill family responsibilities (e.g., coming from other family members in the United States who are contributing to the household back home).

As noted above, the business cycle between 1987 and 1991 may have affected migrants' remitting patterns. To the extent that most of the impact of economic fluctuations in the United States on migrants' remitting patterns is captured by changes in their employment status and family income, then the before-after estimate of the impact of legalization proposed in Eq. (6.1) should not be confounded by the effects of the US business cycle. However, if, for example, the economic downturn in the early 1990s affected low-skill workers to a greater extent than high-skill workers, then changes in migrants' remitting patterns observed post legalization would potentially be driven by the lower likelihood of remitting among the low-skill population.

A similar concern would arise from the existence of differential effects of the business cycle on other subgroups of migrants, such as those living in some states, or those with shorter working experience in the United States. Finally, business cycles in the origin communities (i.e., an economic boom), which Eq. (6.1) does not control for, may as well result in a reduction of migrants' remitting patterns. To partially assess the robustness of the estimates presented in Table 6.2 to the aforementioned effects, we re-estimate Eq. (6.1) for different sub-samples: 1) for California versus other regions, 2) for individuals with and without a high-school diploma, and 3) for migrants from Mexico originating from poorer versus richer states.[13] Additionally, to explore differences across other socio-demographic groups, we also distinguish by gender, age (up to 30 years old or older), legal status (undocumented versus visa-overstayers), and year of first entry in the United States (before or after 1976).[14]

Overall, the results indicate that, after legalization, the probability of remitting money home dropped uniformly for practically all sub-samples of LPS Mexican migrants anywhere between 6% and 13% points. Interestingly, the only exceptions are women and young migrants, who appear to be more consistent remitters. It is possible that women and young migrants' remitting patterns are less tied to new family responsibilities emerging in the United States after legalization when compared to those of men and older migrants.

What are the key findings for the various sub-samples of Latin Americans other than Mexicans? Even if Latin Americans do not seem to experience a reduced likelihood of remitting money back home when we work with the full sample, we find evidence of (1) a statistically significant reduction in the likelihood of remitting money back home among more recent immigrants (entered after 1976) and (2) an increase in the likelihood of remitting among younger and more educated immigrants. These exceptions could be linked to a variety of factors, ranging from economic cycles in migrants' countries of origin to improvements in money transferring mechanisms (e.g., lower remitting costs).

Changes in the Dollar Amount Remitted Back Home

Did the amounts sent home by migrants who continued to remit drop following legalization? Table 6.3 displays the results from estimating Eq. (6.1) when the dependent variable is the logarithm of the dollar amount remitted home by LPS migrants. As in Table 6.2, we distinguish between Mexicans and other Latin Americans.

Table 6.3 Before-after estimates of the (log) dollar amount remitted to Mexico

Country of origin	Mexico		Other Latin American countries	
Model specification:	Column 1	Column 2	Column 3	Column 4
Year 1991	−0.250***	−0.310***	−0.035	−0.124**
	(0.049)	(0.050)	(0.057)	(0.059)
Male	0.621***	0.319***	0.341***	0.174***
	(0.051)	(0.056)	(0.049)	(0.052)
Age	0.024	0.025	0.070	0.129**
	(0.046)	(0.052)	(0.059)	(0.060)
Age squared	−0.069	−0.045	−0.120	−0.278*
	(0.113)	(0.131)	(0.145)	(0.147)
Age cubic	0.001	0.000	0.000	0.002
	(0.001)	(0.001)	(0.001)	(0.001)
Undocumented at last entry	−0.050	0.091	0.184***	0.282***
	(0.087)	(0.078)	(0.065)	(0.074)
Years in US	−0.141***	−0.098***	−0.146***	−0.135**
	(0.037)	(0.036)	(0.050)	(0.054)
Years in US quadratic	0.006***	0.004**	0.007**	0.007**
	(0.002)	(0.002)	(0.003)	(0.004)
Years in US cubic	−0.000***	−0.000**	−0.000	−0.000
	(0.000)	(0.000)	(0.000)	(0.000)
Education				
At most 5th grade		−0.150		0.004
		(0.118)		(0.094)
6th–11th grade		−0.032		0.121
		(0.113)		(0.077)
12th grade/HS diploma		−0.089		−0.088
		(0.125)		(0.085)
California		−0.021		−0.031
		(0.047)		(0.051)

Table 6.3 (continued)

Country of origin	Mexico		Other Latin American countries	
Model specification:	Column 1	Column 2	Column 3	Column 4
Family Income				
$3,000–$5,999		0.494***		0.415*
		(0.184)		(0.228)
$6,000–$8,999		0.624***		0.391*
		(0.162)		(0.221)
$9,000–$11,999		0.819***		0.455**
		(0.164)		(0.218)
$12,000–$14,999		0.959***		0.661***
		(0.157)		(0.214)
$15,000–$19,999		0.924***		0.845***
		(0.159)		(0.213)
$20,000–$24,999		1.094***		0.970***
		(0.161)		(0.214)
$25,000–$29,999		1.382***		1.035***
		(0.167)		(0.218)
$30,000 or more		1.508***		1.208***
		(0.163)		(0.212)
Employed		0.164**		0.159**
		(0.070)		(0.071)
Spouse in the US		−0.272***		−0.091
		(0.057)		(0.056)
Spouse abroad		0.668***		0.456***
		(0.097)		(0.114)
Children in the US		−0.141***		−0.124***
		(0.017)		(0.021)
Parents in the US		−0.306***		−0.169***
		(0.057)		(0.061)
Siblings in the US		0.002		0.061**
		(0.024)		(0.031)
Constant	7.335***	6.318***	6.280***	4.722***
	(0.554)	(0.644)	(0.735)	(0.794)
Observations	2,739	2,418	2,418	2,089
R-squared	0.10	0.26	0.05	0.15

Notes: Dependent variable: Logarithm of amount remitted to family and friends abroad. Pooled OLS estimates. Standard errors (in parentheses) account for correlation across observations for the same individual.
*significant at 10%; ** significant at 5%; *** significant at 1%.
Sample: LPS unbalanced panel.

In a specification that only controls for characteristics that are time-invariant or vary deterministically over time (column 1), the estimated drop in the dollar amount remitted among Mexicans post-legalization is about 25%. Adding controls for education, income, employment, and family composition (column 2) actually raises the estimated drop to 31%. But, perhaps, what is more interesting to note is the significantly smaller reduction in the dollar amount remitted home among other Latinos (columns 3 and 4). For them, remittances only dropped by approximately 12%, and only once we include controls for education, employment, family income, and family composition.

We find other notable differences between Mexicans and other Latin Americans. For instance, while the amount remitted by Mexicans does not seem to be correlated with age, older non-Mexican Latinos appear to remit larger amounts than their younger counterparts. Likewise, non-Mexican Latinos who entered the United States without documents remit up to 28% more than those who entered with documents but overstayed their visas. Finally, as opposed to Mexicans, other Latin American migrants do not remit less when they are married and their spouses live in the United States.

Yet various factors seem to have a similar impact on the dollars remitted by Mexicans and other Latin American migrants. For instance, as in Amuedo-Dorantes and Pozo (15), we find that every additional year of residence reduces the dollar amount migrants remit home by approximately 10–14%, although at a decreasing rate. Migrants who are employed and have greater family incomes are not only more likely to remit (as shown in Table 6.2), but they also remit larger dollar amounts. Finally, family composition as well determines the dollar amount sent home. For instance, having a spouse back home raises remittances anywhere between 46% and 67%. Likewise, the presence of children or parents in the United States significantly lowers the dollar amount remitted by migrants by as much as 14% for each additional child and by up to 30% for each additional parent living in the same household.

As in the case of the likelihood of remitting money home, a concern is that the legalization effect (as captured by the estimated dummy for 1991) might be confounded by the effects of economic cycles (in the US or Mexico) that are not fully controlled in the model. Therefore, we first test the robustness of our estimates in sub-samples defined by US state of residence, education, and Mexican state of origin, given that these are all factors that might help predict differences in business cycle effects. Likewise, we study post-legalization changes in the dollar amount remitted by different socio-demographic groups (e.g., by gender, age, legal status, and year of first entry into the United States). Overall, all groups of Mexican migrants display a significant drop in the dollar amount remitted home, which declines anywhere between $288 and $859 after legalization. However, in the case of Latin Americans, the reduction in the dollar amount remitted home is statistically different from zero only among older, undocumented, high school graduates, or male migrants, as well as for those residing in California. In sum, the impact of business cycles is likely to be limited among Mexicans, for whom we find generalized reductions in the likelihood of remitting and/or in the dollar amount remitted home regardless of their demographic characteristics, geographic location in the US, or state of origin in Mexico. However, there seems to exist more variability in the remitting practices of other non-Mexican Latin Americans depending on a variety of demographic characteristics.

Concluding Remarks

While the literature has paid close attention to issues such as the reasons for a migrant's propensity to remit money home or the uses of these money flows in the receiving countries, we are unaware of any work examining the impact of specific US policies on a migrant's remitting patterns. Our study addresses this void in the literature with an analysis of how legalization through a generalized amnesty (such as the one included in IRCA) may impact the remitting patterns of immigrants from Latin American countries. This analysis is of particular interest in light of recent bipartisan discussions in the US Congress on a comprehensive immigration bill that would offer legal status to most of the nation's 11.5–12 million undocumented immigrants estimated to be living in the United States (10, 21). About 57% of the undocumented population is estimated to originate in Mexico and another 24% from Central and South America.[15] While comprehensive reform did not pass during the Bush administration, it remains on the agenda of the Obama White House.

Our analysis suggests that legalization may have a significant negative effect on newly legalized migrants' remitting patterns not accounted for by migrants' personal characteristics, length of residence in the United States, family income, employment, and family composition. In particular, this result suggests that one of the motives behind migrants' remitting patterns may be self-insurance. Specifically, the acquisition of legal status may reduce the migrant's perceived uncertainty about her/his migration experience and, therefore, may also reduce remittances sent by migrants to maintain a "good standing" with family members in the home country in the event of an unsuccessful migration experience.

The reduction in remittances following migrants' legalization is particularly large among Mexican migrants. For them, on average, legalization appears to have reduced the probability of remitting money home by six percentage points and reduced the dollar amount remitted by approximately 30%. These estimated effects remain quite stable when we re-estimate our models for different sub-samples of migrants. We argue that the stability of the results across groups defined by characteristics such as state of residence in the United States and state of origin in Mexico can be interpreted as evidence that the estimated post-legalization drops in migrants' remitting patterns are not driven by business cycle effects.

The effects of legalization on the remitting patterns of other Latin Americans are estimated to be smaller and more heterogeneous across socio-demographic groups. Non-Mexican Latin Americans, as a group, do not experience any drop in the likelihood to remit post-legalization. Even if the average dollar amount they remit home per year drops by 12%, the large variability across socio-demographic groups in the remitting patterns post-legalization makes it difficult to rule out the existence of factors other than legalization (e.g., business cycles in the origin countries) possibly driving the observed changes in the years following the implementation of the generalized amnesty.

In light of the drop in remittances among Mexicans as a consequence of the legalization program included in the 1986 Immigration Reform and Control Act, we can speculate on the impact of a hypothetical current universal legalization program on the remittance flows sent by Mexican migrants to family and friends back home. In particular, back-of-the envelope calculations based on (1) the impact of legalization estimated in this study, (2) the number of undocumented Mexican migrants estimated to be residing in the United States as of the early 2000s,[16] and (3) the fraction of undocumented Mexicans remitting money home and the dollar amount sent,[17] show that a generalized amnesty might cause an overall remittance loss to Mexico of approximately \$3.2 billion per year.[18] Around one-fourth of this loss is attributable to fewer migrants remitting money home, while the remaining loss is due to the smaller amounts remitted.

How much of these potential losses would result in lower investments in Mexico? Researchers have found that remittances are primarily used to pay for daily expenses, such as food and rent, with the rest being used to improve housing conditions, education, and health, along with other purposes. For instance, Durand et al. (22) found that about 76% of Mexican remittance receivers use the funds for consumption purposes, 14% spend them on housing, and about 10% use remittances for productive purposes—a figure that coincides with the one reported by Amuedo-Dorantes and Pozo (15) and Amuedo-Dorantes (forthcoming) for Mexico. Likewise, Suro (23) reports that, for Mexico, about 9% of remittances are either invested or saved, with up to 7% being used for educational purposes. Therefore, using these lower-bound estimates, about \$289 million in investment funds and \$225 million in education could be lost per year.

How significant are these sums for Mexico? To serve as a reference, we compare the estimated figures to government funds dedicated to investment and education purposes in Mexico. In an International Food Policy Research Institute' report, Skoufias (24) discusses one of the investment programs promoted by the Mexican government, FONAES (National Social Enterprise Fund), which promotes employment and income opportunities by financing productive projects. In 2000, this program had a budget of \$80 million, a much smaller sum compared to the \$289 million in investment funds that would be lost with the reduction in remittance inflows.

The loss in educational funds due to the drop in remittances is not as large, but still quite significant, when compared to the budgets of other Mexican institutions or programs created with the purpose of fostering education. For instance, CONAFE (Consejo Nacional de Fomento Educativo), which is part of the Secretary of Public Education and distributes school supplies to children as well as teachers in isolated areas, had an estimated budget of \$400 million in 2000 (24). The program PROGRESA (Programa Nacional de Educación, Salud y Alimentación), which provides cash transfers to mothers as long as their children attend school and go to regular health check-ups, had a budget of \$800 million in 2000 (25) when the program (created in 1997) reached about 10% of Mexican families. The estimated loss in funds promoting education that would stem from remittance drops caused by an amnesty program is quite large, representing about half and one-fourth of CONAFE's and PROGRESA's budgets, respectively.

In sum, while legalization is likely to improve the welfare of the migrant and her/his family, the findings in this study suggest that amnesty programs can also significantly reduce the aggregate flow of remittances received by the migrant-sending country. This finding highlights the importance for developing nations to gain a better understanding of the impact that immigration policies in immigrant-receiving countries can have on the incoming stream of remittance flows.

Notes

1. Remittances to Mexico did not significantly increase during the first half of 2007 over the $11.4 billion sent in the first half of 2006; by contrast, remittances increased by 23% in the same time period between 2005 and 2006.
2. Self-insurance is a well-recognized motive for remitting money back home which relates to the migrant's desire to insure himself against an unsuccessful migration experience. This type of insurance is different from the migration motive behind the so-called *New Economics of Labor Migration* (NELM) literature, according to which migration is a family strategy to diversify income and fight income risk.
3. In addition, around 1.1 million individuals who demonstrated 60 days of seasonal agricultural work between May 1985 and May 1986 legalized through the Special Agriculture Worker (SAW) Program included in IRCA. Due to data limitations, this study focuses on the effects of the general amnesty provision that applied to long-term ("pre-1982") undocumented immigrants.
4. From discussions with practice lawyers, we gathered that almost any kind of document was accepted for the purpose of proving residence.
5. Fee waivers could be requested using Form EOIR-26A.
6. The SAW population was not surveyed.
7. Because information on family income is available by brackets and the income brackets are the same in the two waves, this income variable cannot be deflated.
8. We treat state of residence as time-invariant because only a negligible number of respondents are observed to move. Effort to relocate LPS respondents in Wave 2 focused in their state of residence in 1989, so that out-of-state migrants are likely to be underrepresented.
9. Equation (6.1) is estimated with pooled Ordinary Least Squares (OLS). Given that multiple observations for the same individuals are likely to induce serial correlation in the error term ε_{it} , standard errors are estimated allowing for clustering at the individual level.
10. If we used an individual fixed model to estimate Eq. (6.1), instead of pooled OLS, we would not be able to clean the 1987–1991 drop from the effects of increasing length of residence in the United States. In fact, years of residence in the United States are perfectly collinear with interview year and year of entry in the United States—and the latter cannot be identified in a fixed effect model, since it is time-invariant.
11. Since the dependent variable is in this case a dummy variable, we calculate the fraction of predictions that fall outside the unit interval and find that this fraction is never higher than 6% across different specifications (in most of the cases it is below 2%). This suggests a fair goodness-of-fit for a linear probability model.
12. Differences over time in the marginal effect of socio-demographic characteristics on a migrant's likelihood to remit are explored by running separate analyses on samples drawn either from the LPS1 or the LPS2 (results not reported).

13. Information on the state of residence in the country of origin is only available for migrants originating from Mexico.
14. These results are not displayed for the sake of brevity, but are available from the authors upon request.
15. About 9% come from Asia, approximately 6% from Europe, and the remaining 4% from various other locations (21).
16. Passel (26) estimates that about 4.7 million undocumented immigrants from Mexico and about 2 million from other countries in Latin America were living in the United States in 2000.
17. On data from the Mexican Migration Project (MMP), we find that approximately 75% of undocumented Mexican migrants remitted in 2000 and, on average, they sent about $200 per month.
18. The total loss is calculated as the sum of (1) the remittances lost because fewer migrants remit money home, given the amount remitted; and (2) the remittances lost because of the smaller amount remitted, given the fraction of the population remitting money home. Using information on the estimated undocumented Mexican population from Passel (26) along with information regarding the remitting patterns of Mexican migrants from the MMP, we calculate the total loss as follow: $[(4.7 \text{ million}) * (-0.06) * \$2,400] + [(4.7 \text{ million} * 0.75) * [\$2,400/\text{yr} * (-0.30)]] = \$3.2 \text{ billion/yr}$.

Appendix

Table A1 Variable description (Legalized Population Survey)

Fraction remitting	=1 if respondent (and her family) sent money to family and friends in other countries; 0 otherwise.
Dollar remitted	Amount of money sent to family and friends excluding zeros and in 1991 dollars (adjusting for inflation using consumer price index).
Year 1991	=1 for year 1991 (post legalization period); 0 otherwise.
Male	=1 if respondent is male; 0 otherwise.
Age	Age of the respondent (16+). Linear, quadratic, and cubic terms included.
Education	Four dummy variables indicating highest grade completed: at most 5th grade, between 6th and 11th, 12th or HS diploma, at least some college.
State of residence	=1 if respondent lives in California; 0 otherwise.
Undocumented at last entry	=1 if respondent entered the US without documents; 0 if overstayed his visa.
Years in the US	Number of years since the respondent first entered the United States and stayed longer than 3 days. Linear, quadratic, and cubic terms included.
Family income	Nine dummy variables indicating total family income from all sources and from all family members living in the United States in the same household as the respondent: less than $3,000; $3,000–$5,999; $6,000–$8,999; $9,000–$11,999; $12,000–$14,999; $15,000–$19,999; $20,000–$24,999; $25,000–$29,999; $30,000 or more.
Employed	=1 if the respondent worked during the year; 0 otherwise.
Spouse in the US	=1 if the respondent is married and the spouse lives in the US; 0 otherwise.

Table A1   (continued)

Spouse abroad	=1 if the respondent is married and the spouse lives abroad; 0 otherwise.
Children in the US	Number of children living in the United States.
Parents in the US	Number of parents living in the same household in the United States.
Siblings in the US	Number of siblings living in the same household in the United States.

References

1. Terry, Donald F. 2005. "Remittances as a Development Tool." In *Beyond Small Change*, ed. Donald F. Terry and Steve R. Wilson, 3–19. Washington, DC: Inter-American Development Bank.

2. Ratha, Dilip. 2004. "Understanding the Importance of Remittances." Migration Information Source. Washington, DC: Migration Policy Institute. http://www.migration information.org/Feature/display.cfm?ID=256 (accessed on October 5, 2010).

3. Taylor, Edward J. 1999. "The New Economics of Labour Migration and the Role of Remittances in the Migration Process." *International Migration*, 37(1): 63–88.

4. Preston, Julia. 2007."Fewer Mexican Immigrants Are Sending Money Back Home, Bank Says." *The New York Times*, August 9.

5. Kossoudji, Sherrie A., and Deborah Cobb-Clark. 2002. "Coming Out of the Shadows: Learning about Legal Status and Wages from the Legalized Population." *Journal of Labor Economics*, 20(3): 598–628.

6. Kossoudji, Sherrie A., and Deborah Cobb-Clark. 2004. "IRCA's Impact on the Occupational Concentration and Mobility of Newly-Legalized Mexican Men." In *How Labor Migrants Fare*, ed. Klaus F. Zimmermann and Amelie Constant, 333–350. Heidelberg and New York: Springer.

7. Kaushal, Neeraj. 2006. "Amnesty Programs and the Labor Market Outcomes of Undocumented Workers." *Journal of Human Resources*, 61(3): 631–647.

8. Grieco, Elizabeth. 2003. *The Remittance Behavior of Immigrant Households: Micronesians in Hawaii and Guam*. New York: LFB Scholarly Publishing LLC.

9. Grieco, Elizabeth. 2004. "Will Migrant Remittances Continue Through Time? A New Answer to an Old Question." *International Journal on Multicultural Societies (IJMS)*, 6(2): 243–252.

10. Passel, Jeffrey S. 2006. *"Estimates of the Size and Characteristics of the Undocumented Population."* March Report. Washington, DC: Pew Hispanic Center.

11. Becker, Gary S. 1974. "A Theory of Social Interactions." *Journal of Political Economy*, 82(6): 1063–1093.

12. Stark, Oded. 1991. *The Migration of Labor*. Oxford: Basil Blackwell.

13. Ahlburg, Dennis A., and Richard P. C. Brown. 1998. "Migrants' Intentions to Return Home and Capital Transfers: A Study of Tongans and Samoans in Australia." *The Journal of Development Studies*, 35(2):125–151.

14. Glytsos, Nicholas P. 1997. "Remitting Behaviour of 'Temporary' and 'Permanent' Migrants: the Case of Greeks in Germany and Australia." *Labour*, 11(3): 409–435.

15. Amuedo-Dorantes, Catalina, and Susan Pozo. 2006. "Remittances and Insurance: Evidence from Mexican Migrants." *Journal of Population Economics*, 19(2): 227–254.

16. Lucas, Robert E.B., and Oded Stark.1985. "Motivations to Remit: Evidence from Botswana." *Journal of Political Economy*, 93(5): 901–918.

17. Cooper, Betsy, and Kevin O'Neil.2005. *"Lessons from the Immigration Reform and Control Act of 1986."* Migration Policy Institute Policy Brief No. 3. Washington, DC: Migration Policy Institute.

18. Hoefer, Michael D. 1991. "Background of U.S. Immigration Policy Reform." In *U.S. Immigration Policy Reform in the 1980s: A Preliminary Assessment*, ed. Francisco L. Rivera-Batiz, Selig L. Sechzer, and Ira N. Gang, 17–44. New York: Praeger.
19. Warren, Robert. 2000. *Annual Estimates of the Unauthorized Population Residing in the United States and Components of Changes: 1987 to 1997*. Washington, DC: U.S. Immigration and Naturalization Service.
20. Rytina, Nancy. 2002. "IRCA Legalization Effects: Lawful Permanent Residence and Naturalization through 2001." Working Paper, Office of Policy and Planning, Statistics Division, U.S. Immigration and Naturalization Service.
21. Pew Hispanic Center Factsheet. 2006. http://pewhispanic.org/files/factsheets/17.pdf (accessed on October 6, 2010).
22. Durand, Jorge, William Kandel, Emilio A. Parrado, and Douglas S. Massey. 1996. "International Migration and Development in Mexican Communities." *Demography*, 33(2): 249–264.
23. Suro, Roberto. 2003. *Remittance Senders and Receivers: Tracking the Transnational Channels*. Washington, DC: Pew Hispanic Center.
24. Skoufias, Emmanuel. 2001. *"PROGRESA and its Impacts on the Human Capital and Welfare of Households in Rural Mexico: A Synthesis of the Results of an Evaluation by IFPRI."* Washington, DC: International Food Policy Research Institute.
25. Easterly, William. 2006. "Multilateral Development Banks: Promoting Effectiveness and Fighting Corruption." Hearing before the Committee on Foreign Relations, United States Senate, One Hundred Ninth Congress, Second Session, Tuesday, March 28.
26. Passel, Jeffrey S. 2002. *"New Estimates of the Undocumented Population in the United States."* Migration Information Source.Washington, DC: Migration Policy Institute.

Chapter 7
Naturalization and Its Determinants Among Immigrants from Latin America: The Role of Dual Citizenship Rights

Francesca Mazzolari

Abstract This chapter presents an empirical analysis of US citizenship acquisition among immigrants from Latin America in the 1990s. While immigrants from Latin America have had historically lower propensity to naturalize than immigrants from other parts of the world, they are observed to experience the largest hikes in naturalization in the 1990s. Welfare and illegal immigration reforms—that made access to public benefits and other selected rights increasingly dependent on citizenship—are among the explanations that have often been offered for the surge in naturalizations in the 1990s. Other explanations include changes in immigration laws in the late 1980s, which allowed large numbers of immigrants to apply for citizenship in the mid-1990s, and anti-immigrant reform attempts (such as in California). The common denominator of the available explanations is that they are about domestic administrative and political changes, and neglect to consider those sending-country policies that might have affected immigrants' propensity to naturalize in the 1990s. Notably, between 1991 and 1996, some important Latin American sending countries (Colombia, the Dominican Republic, Ecuador, Costa Rica, and Brazil) changed their laws and granted their expatriates the right to naturalize in the receiving country without losing their nationality of origin. Immigrants from these countries are expected to be more likely to naturalize because of the decrease in a major cost of naturalization, specifically the need to forfeit rights in their country of origin. The analysis presented in this chapter suggests that these laws are associated with an increase of 10 percentage points in the probability of naturalization of immigrants coming from Colombia, the Dominican Republic, Ecuador, Costa Rica, and Brazil. These effects are sizable, explaining one sixth of the overall rise in the naturalization rate of non-Mexican Latin Americans in the 1990s.

F. Mazzolari (✉)
Centro Studi Confindustria, Rome, Italy
e-mail: francesca.mazzolari@gmail.com

D.L. Leal, S.J. Trejo (eds.), *Latinos and the Economy*, Immigrants and Minorities, Politics and Policy, DOI 10.1007/978-1-4419-6682-7_7,

Introduction

Naturalization is the process by which US citizenship is conferred upon a foreign national after she fulfills the admission, age, and residency requirements established by Congress in the Immigration and Nationality Act. Naturalization is the gateway for immigrants to full membership and political participation in US society. After naturalization, foreign-born individuals enjoy the same benefits, rights, and responsibilities that the Constitution gives to native-born US citizens, such as the right to vote.

This chapter presents results of an analysis of citizenship acquisition among immigrants from Latin America in the 1990s. It is a well-known fact that immigrants from Latin America have the lowest propensity to naturalize. In 1995, only 19% of Mexican immigrants eligible to naturalize had done so, compared to 66% of immigrants from Europe and Canada, and 56% of immigrants from Asia (1). Rates of naturalization among immigrants from other Latin American countries (40% on average) were higher than for Mexicans, but still lower than among immigrants from the rest of the world.

Another well-known phenomenon is the large surge in naturalizations since the mid-1990s. This time, the largest hikes in naturalizations occurred among immigrants from Latin America: by 2001, the share of eligible Mexicans who had naturalized rose from 19% to 34% and the corresponding share among Latin Americans rose from 40% to 58%, while the share of Europeans and Canadians held constant and the share of Asians rose from 56% to 67%. These two stylized facts—the traditionally low rates of American citizenship acquisition among Latinos and the recent high spikes in naturalizations—make the analysis of citizenship acquisition among immigrants from Latin America in the 1990s of particular interest.

Immigrants who meet the requirements for naturalization decide whether or not to apply for citizenship. Their decision depends on the perceived benefits and costs of naturalization and the weights attached to them. The importance of citizenship has risen since the mid-1990s, when both welfare and illegal immigration reforms made access to public benefits and other selected rights increasingly dependent on citizenship. These legislative changes are the most commonly cited explanation for the surge in naturalization in the 1990s, but the empirical literature on this issue is limited and offers mixed findings. In support of the existence of behavioral responses to welfare reform, Borjas (2) finds that the national origin groups most likely to receive public assistance in the pre-PRWORA period experienced the largest increase in naturalization after 1996. However, against the notion that immigrants naturalize to retain (or acquire) welfare eligibility, Fix et al. (1) estimate that in 2001 recently naturalized immigrants use public benefits (except for Supplemental Security Income) at slightly lower rates than do the pool of immigrants currently eligible for naturalization.

Besides the alleged incentive to become a citizen in order to retain access to social benefits, there are also a number of other influences that might have affected an immigrant's propensity to naturalize in the 1990s. In particular, between 1991 and 1996, some important sending countries in Latin America (Colombia, the Dominican Republic, Ecuador, Costa Rica, and Brazil) changed their laws and granted their expatriates the right to naturalize in the receiving country without losing their nationality of origin. Immigrants from these countries may be more likely to naturalize because of the decrease in a major cost of naturalization—specifically the need to forfeit rights in their country of origin. The main goal of the empirical analysis discussed in this chapter is to assess whether recognition of dual citizenship rights in the 1990s affected the propensity to naturalize among immigrants from Latin America. The proposed identification strategy consists in comparing the 1990–2000 change in naturalization rates of immigrants coming from countries that have recently legalized dual citizenship to the change over time in naturalization rates of immigrants from Latin American countries that did not change the law.

The estimation results provide strong support for the hypothesis that changes in dual citizenship laws caused naturalization rates to rise. This finding shows the importance of going beyond unilateral explanations for the surge in naturalization in the 1990s. In the aftermath of welfare reform, the public debate has centered on whether many immigrants would choose to become citizens not because they want to fully participate in the US political system but because naturalization is the price to pay to receive welfare benefits. Evidence presented in this chapter shows that immigrants from Latin America may have naturalized at high rates in the 1990s because recently granted dual citizenship rights provided a means for them to reconcile memberships in both their countries of origin and the United States.

This chapter also directly relates and contributes to the long-standing debate over the pros and cons of dual nationality. From the point of view of receiving states, dual nationality has been criticized as a sort of political bigamy—a way of devaluing the meaning of citizenship and impeding assimilation in the destination country. This chapter begins to answer this question by presenting a way to empirically identify the effects of dual citizenship on naturalization. When the same research design is used to identify the effects of dual citizenship on economic outcomes (3), the analysis shows that immigrants coming from countries that have recently allowed dual citizenship are not only more likely to naturalize, but they also experience relative employment and earnings gains, and lower their reliance on welfare. These findings support the view that dual nationality might indeed foster assimilation in the receiving country.

The next section presents institutional details on the process of naturalization in the United States and discusses the role of dual citizenship rights in understanding and modeling an immigrant's decision to naturalize. The following section explains the proposed identification strategy for the effects of dual citizenship rights on an immigrant's propensity to naturalize. Then I describe the recognition of dual citizenship in the 1990s by the five Latin American countries that are the focus of this chapter. The empirical analysis follows, including a description of: (1) the data drawn from the 1990 and 2000 censuses and the sample restrictions; (2) the empirical model; (3) other influences besides changes in dual citizenship laws that could explain naturalization trends in the United States in the 1990s, and (4) how the empirical model controls for them. The chapter next provides estimation results for the relationship between naturalization and dual citizenship and concludes with a discussion about policy implications.

Modeling an Immigrant's Decision to Naturalize in the United States

Under US immigration law, immigrants granted legal permanent residence (holding a "green card") are eligible to naturalize once they are at least 18 years old[1] and have continuously resided in the United States for 5 years (or 3 years if the immigrant is the spouse of a US citizen). In a utility maximizing framework, immigrants who fulfill the requirements to naturalize decide to apply for citizenship if the benefits exceed the costs. Citizenship grants immigrants certain political and social rights to which permanent residents are not entitled, such as the ability to vote and, therefore, to influence political decisions and policy outcomes. Citizenship also makes it easier to sponsor relatives. The importance of citizenship has risen since the mid-1990s. The welfare legislation passed in 1996 (Personal Responsibility and Work Opportunity Reconciliation Act) restricted foreign-born eligibility for a wide range of public programs, with all restrictions on welfare use by foreign-born persons lifted once an immigrant becomes a naturalized citizen. A consequence of illegal immigration reform (the 1996 Illegal Immigration and Immigrant Responsibility Act) is that only foreign-born people who have naturalized are granted the right to "residential security," that is, the right to remain in the country and not be deported for minor crimes or misdemeanors.

Citizenship also entails costs. First, there are costs related to the naturalization process. To naturalize, applicants must: (1) pay a fee ($320 in 2006, plus $50 for fingerprinting); (2) demonstrate the ability to read, write, speak, and understand English; and (3) pass an examination on US government and history. Second, depending on the dual citizenship laws in the country of origin, those who naturalize in the United States might be obliged to forfeit rights in their home country. Both practical and psychological costs could arise from being denied dual nationality. Immigrants might be hesitant to give up the instrumental benefits of a second passport, such as the right to travel freely back and forth to the country of origin without special visas, the right to work in the country of origin, or have full access to public services and social benefits. They might also be reluctant to give up the right to vote and influence the political outcomes in their home country. Psychologically, they may wish to continue to identify themselves as citizens of their country of birth and be able to pass their national identity to their children.

Identifying the Effects of Dual Citizenship
Rights on an Immigrant's Propensity to Naturalize

Even if the Immigration and Nationality Act does not explicitly accept dual nationality on the part of naturalizing immigrants, neither does it take a position against it. Foreign-born migrants who naturalize in the United States are formally required to state under oath that they are renouncing their old citizenship,[2] but the requirement of renunciation is something of an empty verbal gesture (4). Enforcement of the declaration of renunciation is nonexistent; for example, the US Department of State does not require official notification that naturalized US citizens have formally renounced their nationality of origin.[3]

Given that dual citizenship rights are recognized in practice in the US, immigrants coming from countries that allow these rights to their expatriates are expected, everything else being equal, to be more likely to acquire American citizenship than immigrants coming from countries that deny these rights. Previous studies have proposed two main empirical approaches to test for this prediction, using either cross-sectional or time-series variation in dual citizenship recognition by sending countries. Apparently against the hypothesis that dual citizenship encourages naturalization, the cross-sectional correlation between dual citizenship recognition by sending countries and the likelihood of naturalization in the United States of different national origin groups has been found to be non-positive (5, 6). By contrast, Jones-Correa (7) finds that, for nine Latin American immigrant groups from countries that started to grant dual nationality between 1965 and 1997, the naturalization rate increased in the period after the sending countries recognized dual nationality.

However, not only do the two empirical approaches used in the literature deliver opposite results, but neither credibly identifies the causal effect of dual citizenship rights on naturalization. On the one hand, cross-sectional analyses are likely to be confounded by the existence of country-of-origin specific characteristics that are correlated with dual citizenship laws but that also directly affect immigrants' preferences for naturalization. On the other hand, before-after strategies might be confounded by the existence of trends over time in the rate of change of naturalization of immigrants in the United States (e.g., due to changes in US policies).

In order to identify whether dual citizenship rights have a causal effect on American citizenship acquisition, this chapter compares the change over time in naturalization rates of immigrants coming from countries that have recently legalized dual citizenship (the "treatment" group) to the change over time in naturalization rates of immigrants from Latin American countries that have not changed the law (the "control" group). As compared to cross-sectional or before-after analysis, this identification strategy, commonly referred to as *difference-in-differences* analysis, has the advantage to control, in a parsimonious way, for (1) differences in the propensity to naturalize across origin groups that are constant over time, and (2) changes over time in the propensity to naturalize that are constant across origin groups.

For the proposed identification strategy to hold, we need to rule out that other incentives to naturalize during the 1990s (such as welfare reform and citizenship outreach programs) had *differential* effects by country of origin. As a way to address this identification issue, the empirical analysis is run on individual-level data from the 1990 and 2000 US censuses and models the effects of these other incentives as a function of place of residence and socio-demographic characteristics (not available by year and country of origin in administrative data). In these model specifications, changes in dual nationality policies are arguably the only source of systematic differences over time in the incentive to naturalize by country of origin. For example, if citizenship were indeed sought after welfare reform to protect access to social benefits, then this effect should mainly depend on place of residence (because different states implemented very different welfare reform programs) and on personal characteristics (such as education, gender, and age) that predict eligibility for means-tested categorically-restricted benefits such as the ones offered by the US welfare system.

Changes in Dual Citizenship Laws in the 1990s

Ideally, identification of the effects of the recognition of dual nationality rights on the propensity to naturalize would stem from an experiment that randomly assigns changes in the laws to some countries, and not to others. To mimic this approach, I exploit a so-called "natural" experiment (8), defined on the base of *observed* changes in the laws. Five countries in Latin America granted dual nationality in the 1990s: Colombia made this change in 1991, the Dominican Republic in 1994, Costa Rica and Ecuador in 1995, and Brazil in 1996. As documented in Jones-Correa (7), there are differences in the process of recognition of dual nationality in these countries. Colombia, Ecuador, and the Dominican Republic decided to recognize dual nationality primarily as a response to pressures from their overseas compatriots (in particular, those residing in New York City), while Brazil and Costa Rica allowed it with little concerted pressure from the immigrant community abroad. In particular, Costa Rica seems to have passed its dual nationality amendments in response to dismay among the public that the first Costa Rican astronaut was going into space as an American citizen, not as a Costa Rican.

Concerns about the internal validity of the proposed natural experiment research design would arise if legal changes took place as a response to rising naturalizations (a so-called problem of "policy endogeneity"), rather than the legal changes causing rising naturalizations. Sending countries might be willing to grant dual citizenship to foster ties with their expatriates, hoping these ties pay off in terms of current remittances or future investments. If so, rising naturalizations might indeed predate the policy changes, and this would invalidate the research design. As a way to address this concern, I explored trends in naturalization rates in the treatment and control groups (immigrants from Colombia, the Dominican Republic, Costa Rica, Ecuador, and Brazil, and immigrants from other Latin American countries, respectively) before the passage of the laws, that is, between 1980 and 1990. I find no evidence of increases in the number of naturalizations that predate the passage of the laws (3).

In 1996, Mexico also granted its citizens dual nationality rights, but only of a temporary and limited nature. A non-loss of nationality provision (passed in December 1996) took effect in March 1998 and allowed Mexicans who had become US citizens to apply for dual citizenship until March 20, 2003. After that date, Parliament subsequently extended the dual nationality rights. In the summer of 1996, Mexico also recognized the right of citizens residing abroad to vote,[4] but there were such delays in the implementation of the reform that Mexican citizens in the United States could not exercise their right to vote in the 2000 Mexican presidential elections. The temporary and limited nature of the dual citizenship rights granted to Mexicans suggests that immigrants from Mexico might not belong either to the treatment or the control group. For this reason (and a further reason explained in the next section), immigrants of Mexican origin are excluded from the main analysis.

Two other countries in the world granted dual citizenship rights in the 1990s: Italy and Hungary. However, I restrict the analysis to immigrants from Latin American countries, a choice that increases comparability between treatment and control group.

Empirical Analysis

Data

The empirical analysis uses microdata from the 1990 and 2000 US censuses (9) and is restricted to working-age, foreign-born individuals from Latin American countries who were at least 18 when they arrived in the United States and who have been living in the United States for at least 5 years (3 years if married to a US citizen).[5]

The age and residency restrictions might not be sufficient to identify immigrants eligible to naturalize. There are ineligible foreign-born individuals in the census, such as non-immigrants and undocumented immigrants. The likelihood of including non-immigrants in the sample is reduced by the length-of-residence sample restriction[6] and, further, by limiting the analysis to Latin American immigrants.[7] The inclusion of illegal immigrants in the sample is problematic to the extent that rates of illegal immigration vary over time by country of origin. The five Latin American countries allowing dual citizenship in the 1990s experienced particularly large increases in the estimated unauthorized resident population from 1990 to 2000 (10), and this should work against finding effects of dual citizenship laws on naturalization in samples drawn from census data. In the empirical investigation, the problem of changing rates of unauthorized immigration is addressed by dividing individual data on naturalization status by the probability of legal status by country of origin and census year. This procedure allows for estimates of naturalization rates among the eligible legal population.

Probabilities of legal status, conditional on country of origin, census year, and at least 5 years of residence in the United States, are obtained from comparisons of the immigrant population represented in the census, adjusted for the estimated undercount (11, 12), with estimates of the inflows of the unauthorized population developed by the INS (10, 13). The latter estimates exclude from the undocumented population some immigrant groups that received legal status through special amnesties at some point after entering the United States. For this reason, the derived probabilities of legal status might not be reliable in two cases: first, when involving immigrants from countries granted special temporary amnesties or Temporary Protected Status in the 1980s and 1990s (Guatemala, El Salvador, Honduras, and Nicaragua); second, when involving immigrants who were legalized under the 1986 Immigration Reform and Control Act (IRCA) provisions. (These latter immigrants, still illegal in 1985, were mostly legalized by 1990, but at that time were still ineligible to naturalize). Of the 2.7 million unauthorized aliens who applied for legal permanent status under IRCA, 75% were from Mexico and another 9% were from El Salvador and Guatemala. Excluding immigrants from these countries from the analysis should alleviate the problems posed by special temporary amnesty programs and by IRCA when deriving probabilities of legal status.

The socio-demographic characteristics included in the empirical analysis are state of residence, education, age, and gender. Also, nine cohorts of entry in the United States[8] and 23 specific countries of origin are defined.[9]

Table 7.1 presents descriptive data on the characteristics of immigrants from different countries in 1990. Excluding Mexico and the Central American countries

Table 7.1 Selected descriptive statistics for foreign-born by country of origin, 1990

	CR, DR, BZ, CO, and EC	MX, ES, GU, HO, and NI	Other Latin American countries
Naturalized citizen	0.33	0.24	0.45
Probability legal status	0.82	0.41	0.89
Living in the United States >10 Years	0.65	0.65	0.67
Female	0.56	0.47	0.52
Age	43.6	41.1	46.9
Education			
<12 Years	0.37	0.72	0.29
> = 12 years	0.63	0.28	0.71
State of residence			
CA	0.10	0.56	0.10
FL, IL, NJ, NY, TX	0.76	0.32	0.76
Other states	0.14	0.12	0.14
Number of observations	58, 620	328, 024	121, 222

Sample: 1990 and 2000 IPUMS, born in Latin American countries, less than 65 years old, arrived in the US at least 18 years old and stayed for at least 5 years. The sample sizes pertain to the combined total for 1990 and 2000. Legend: CR: Costa Rica, DR: Dominican Republic, BZ: Brazil, CO: Colombia, EC: Ecuador, MX: Mexico, ES: El Salvador, GU: Guatemala, HO: Honduras, NI: Nicaragua whose expatriates to the United States were granted special amnesties in the 1990s notably increases the comparability between average characteristics of immigrants from the five "treated" countries and immigrants from the Latin American countries that serve as controls. Still, immigrants in the treatment group have lower naturalization rates (the difference somewhat shrinks once we correct for probability of legal status). They are also more likely to be female, younger, and less educated. The two groups have instead almost the same proportion of immigrants that arrived in the United States more than 20 years ago and a similar geographic distribution across the states.

Empirical Model

The difference-in-difference strategy described in the previous sections can be cast in the following regression framework, that is, a model of the decision to naturalize for individual i born in country c residing in state s and observed in year $t = 1990$ or 2000:

$$N_{icst} = \alpha + \gamma_c + \gamma_t + \delta\,(\Delta DC_c \gamma_t) + \gamma_s + X_{it}\Gamma_1 + X_{it}\gamma_t\Gamma_2$$
$$+\gamma_t\gamma_s + X_{it}\gamma_t\gamma_s\Gamma_3 + \varepsilon_{icst}, \tag{7.1}$$

where N_{icst} is a dummy variable indicating whether the individual is a naturalized citizen, γ_c is a country-of-origin fixed effect, γ_t is a dummy for year 2000, ΔDC_c is a dummy for those countries that allowed dual citizenship during the 1990s, γ_s is a state-of-residence fixed effect, and X_{it} is a vector of individual socio-demographic characteristics (listed in the previous section).[10]

In Eq. (7.1), δ (the coefficient of the interaction term $\Delta DC_c \gamma_t$) captures the mean differential 1990–2000 change in naturalization rates between immigrants from countries that changed their laws and immigrants from other Latin American countries. Country-of-origin fixed effects (the γ_c's) control for systematic differences in the propensity to naturalize among immigrants from different countries that are constant over time, while the time dummy γ_t controls for changes in the propensity to naturalize over time that are common to different origin groups. The difference-in-differences (DD) parameter δ, then, identifies the effect of dual citizenship laws under the assumption that shocks other than changes in the laws had no *differential* effects on immigrants coming from different countries. The next section reviews other shocks in the 1990s and discusses why allowing the effects of socio-demographic characteristics and state of residence to vary over time (through the inclusion in Eq. (7.1) of interactions between socio-demographics and the time dummy γ_t) should strongly increase the case for this assumption to hold.

Other Influences on the Propensity to Naturalize in the 1990s

Besides changes in dual citizenship laws, a number of other factors explain rising naturalization in the 1990s. The Green Card Replacement Program, begun in 1992 by the Immigration and Naturalization Service (INS), required that long-term permanent residents replace their resident cards with new, more counterfeit-resistant cards. Many immigrants chose to naturalize rather than apply for new cards (14). There is no clear reason for the Green Card Replacement Program to differentially affect people coming from different countries, once cohort of entry in the United States is controlled for, and the cohort's effects on naturalization are allowed to be different between 1990 and 2000.

In August 1995, the INS started the Citizenship USA program, which was aimed at reducing the significant backlog of naturalization applications accumulated in INS offices. The number of petitions for naturalization increased from 206,668 in 1991 to 959,963 in 1995, but INS resources to adjudicate naturalization applications evidently did not keep pace with the increase in filing given that, by summer 1995, the pending caseload was nearly 800,000 and waiting times in the largest offices exceeded 2 years. The goal of Citizenship USA was to reduce the processing time per petition to no more than 6 months. The key cities identified for the effort were those with the largest number of pending cases: Chicago, Los Angeles, Miami, New York, and San Francisco. A different geographical concentration of resources would explain higher naturalization rates as the result of this program among immigrant populations concentrated where the backlogs were higher. When controlling for place of residence and its interaction with the year 2000, however, there should not be any reason for this campaign to differentially affect the propensity to naturalize by country of origin.

Political events taking place in the 1990s may have led to increased naturalization among eligible immigrants. Proposition 187 was passed in California in 1994 in an attempt to curtail social services to unauthorized immigrants, and in 1995–96 the nation was debating the virtues of restricting benefits to legal immigrants. The media and some scholars argue that Proposition 187 and the perceived anti-immigrant sentiment encouraged many immigrants to naturalize to protect their rights and cast their vote against anti-immigrant legislation. If the anti-immigrant rhetoric of the early 1990s affected an immigrant's propensity to naturalize depending on the intensity of anti-immigrant campaigns in the state of residence, then the inclusion of place of residence (and its interaction with year 2000) will control for its effect in Eq. (7.1).[11]

Finally, the passage of 1996 welfare reform, restricting federal public benefits for non-citizens, may have increased the incentive to naturalize as a way of retaining access to social programs. If citizenship were indeed sought after welfare reform to protect access to social benefits, then this effect should mainly depend on state of residence (because different states implemented specific welfare reform programs; see (15)) and on personal characteristics (such as education, gender, and age) that predict eligibility for means-tested categorically-restricted benefits such as the ones offered by the US welfare system.[12]

In sum, most of the factors listed in this section should not differentially affect naturalization rates by country of origin once observable socio-demographic characteristics are controlled for and their effects are allowed to vary over time. The estimated coefficient δ in Eq. (7.1), then, arguably captures the effect of newly granted dual citizenship rights on naturalization.

Estimation Results

Effects of Changes in Dual Citizenship Rights on the Probability of Naturalization

Tables 7.2–7.4 report difference-in-differences estimates of the effects of recognizing dual citizenship on the decision to naturalize, that is the estimated δ in Eq. (7.1). The first two columns of Table 7.2 include people born in Mexico in the treatment and control group, respectively. In both cases the DD estimate is positive, but only in the second case is it precisely estimated. As discussed above it is problematic to assign people from Mexico to either the treatment or the control group, so I exclude them from the rest of the analysis. As shown in column 3, when excluding the Mexican-born population, the naturalization rate of immigrants from Colombia, Ecuador, Costa Rica, the Dominican Republic, and Brazil is estimated to rise by 4.5 percentage points between 1990 and 2000 relative to the naturalization rate of immigrants from other Latin American countries.

Table 7.2 Difference-in-difference estimates of dual citizenship on naturalization status

Sample	Mexico in the treatment group	Mexico in the control group	Excluding Mexico	Excluding Mexico 20 yrs or more in the US	Excluding Mexico less than 20 yrs in the US
Mean of dependent variable	*0.33*	*0.33*	*0.42*	*0.71*	*0.32*
	(1)	(2)	(3)	(4)	(5)
ΔDual*year 2000	0.012	0.044**	0.045**	0.060***	0.020
	[0.012]	[0.018]	[0.017]	[0.022]	[0.017]
Observations	507,847	507,847	243,685	67,236	176,449
R-squared	0.20	0.20	0.25	0.11	0.15

Notes: Dependent variable: naturalization status. Standard errors (clustered by country of origin and census year) are in brackets. * denotes statistical significance at the 90% level of confidence, ** 95%, *** 99%. Sample: 1990 and 2000 IPUMS, born in Latin American countries, less than 65 years old, arrived in the US at least 18 years old and stayed for at least 5 years. $\Delta Dual = 1$ for immigrants born in Costa Rica, Dominican Republic, Brazil, Colombia, Ecuador (and Mexico in column 1 only). All specifications include controls for state of residence, education, age, gender, cohort of entry in the US, country-of-birth, census year, and interaction terms between year 2000 by: state of residence, education, age, gender, cohort of entry; year 2000 by state by education; year 2000 by state by gender).

Table 7.3 Difference-in-difference Estimates of Dual Citizenship on adjusted naturalization status

Sample	Excluding Mexico		Excluding Mexico, El Salvador, Guatemala, Honduras, and Nicaragua		
	All	Less than 20 yrs in US	All	Less than 20 yrs in US	All
Mean of dependent variable	0.54 (1)	0.42 (2)	0.54 (3)	0.41 (4)	0.54 (5)
ΔDual * year 2000	0.188*** [0.048]	0.159*** [0.047]	0.104*** [0.027]	0.068** [0.025]	0.104*** [0.020]
Observations	243,685	176,449	179,839	122,731	179,839
R-squared	0.17	0.10	0.21	0.13	0.21

Notes: Dependent variable: naturalization status divided by probability of legal status (by country of origin and year). Standard errors (clustered by country of origin and census year) are in brackets. * denotes statistical significance at the 90% level of confidence, ** 95%, *** 99%. Sample: 1990 and 2000 IPUMS, born in Latin American countries, less than 65 years old, arrived in the US at least 18 years old and stayed for at least 5 years. $\Delta Dual = 1$ for immigrants born in Costa Rica, Dominican Republic, Brazil, Colombia, and Ecuador. All specifications include controls for state of residence, education, age, gender, cohort of entry in the US, country-of-birth, census year, and interaction terms (year 2000 by: state of residence, education, age, gender, cohort of entry; year 2000 by state by education; year 2000 by state by gender). The specification in column 5 also includes interactions between year 2000 and naturalization and welfare use rates in 1990, and estimated outmigration rates by country.

Even if most illegal immigrants are from Mexico (10), dropping the Mexican-born population from the analysis might not be enough to address the potential bias arising from the presence of unauthorized immigrants in census samples. This concern is supported by large differences between estimates obtained for long-term immigrants versus more recent immigrants, given the different likelihood of illegal status in the two groups.[13] As shown in column 4 of Table 7.2, between 1990 and 2000 there is a rise in the naturalization rate of long-term immigrants in the treatment group, relative to the comparison group, of six percentage points, or 8% of the baseline naturalization rate. Among immigrants who have resided in the United States for at most 20 years (column 5), the estimated effect of dual citizenship on naturalization is smaller and imprecisely estimated. However, in this sample the high growth rates of illegal immigration from countries in the treatment group (10) might contribute a downward bias on the estimated effects of dual citizenship.

Tables 7.3 and 7.4 report results from regressions run on samples where individual naturalization status is divided by the probability of legal status by country of origin and census year. As shown in column 1 of Table 7.3, the DD estimate of the 1990–2000 change in the adjusted probability of naturalization is larger, both in absolute and proportional terms, than the one estimated on raw data. The same result holds when restricting the analysis to immigrants who have been in the United States for less than 20 years (column 2). As explained above in the description of the data, the probability of legal status might be imprecisely estimated for those countries

Table 7.4 Difference in differences estimates of dual citizenship on adjusted naturalization status, by length of residence in the United States, gender, and education

Sample	Excluding Mexico, El Salvador, Guatemala, Honduras, and Nicaragua				
	8–15 years in the US	Males	Females	Less than high school degree	High school degree or more
Mean of dependent variable	*0.40* (1)	*0.51* (2)	*0.58* (3)	*0.43* (4)	*0.61* (5)
ΔDual * year 2000	0.061** [0.026]	0.100*** [0.031]	0.105*** [0.026]	0.043 [0.032]	0.129*** [0.024]
Observations	60,007	83,547	96,292	48,531	131,308
R-squared	0.08	0.20	0.22	0.19	0.20

Notes: Dependent variable: naturalization status divided by probability of legal status (by country of origin and year). Standard errors (clustered by country of origin and census year) are in brackets. * denotes statistical significance at the 90% level of confidence, ** 95%, *** 99%. Sample: 1990 and 2000 IPUMS, born in Latin American countries, less than 65 years old, arrived in the US at least 18 years old and stayed for at least 5 years. $\Delta Dual = 1$ for immigrants born in Costa Rica, Dominican Republic, Brazil, Colombia and Ecuador. All specifications include controls for state of residence, education, age, gender (not columns 2 and 3), cohort of entry in the US, country-of-birth, census year, and interaction terms: year 2000 by: state of residence, education, age, gender (not columns 2 and 3), cohort of entry; year 2000 by state by education (not columns 4 and 5); year 2000 by state by gender (not columns 2 and 3).

that were granted special temporary amnesties in the 1980s and 1990s. To address this concern, the remaining specifications drop from the analysis immigrants from Guatemala, El Salvador, Honduras, and Nicaragua. As shown in column 3, between 1990 and 2000, there is a rise in the naturalization rate of immigrants from the five countries that granted dual citizenship (relative to the restricted set of other Latin American countries) of 10 percentage points, or 18% of the baseline naturalization rate. When restricting the analysis to immigrants who have been in the United States for less than 20 years (column 4), we estimate a rise in the naturalization rate of immigrants in the treatment group of seven percentage points, or 17% of the baseline naturalization rate.

Specification Checks

To address the concern that changes in the laws are correlated with other country-of-origin factors that affect the likelihood of naturalization over the 1990s, I test the robustness of the results to the inclusion of controls for some initial conditions at the country level that might differentially affect absolute changes in naturalization rates over the 1990s. Column 5 in Table 7.3 shows how stable the estimates are to the inclusion of interactions between year 2000 and naturalization and welfare participation rates in 1990, and a measure of outmigration rates.[14] To address the concern that other factors affecting the naturalization decision in the 1990s may have had a different impact on people granted (or not granted) dual citizenship rights, I restrict the comparison group either to countries that did allow dual citizenship in 1990 or to countries that did not, and find stable estimation results (not reported). The results are also robust to excluding those countries that granted dual citizenship in the 1970s and 1980s, and for which lagged effects of changes in dual citizenship laws might affect the results for the 1990s.[15]

Column 1 in Table 7.4 presents estimates obtained from a sample of immigrants who have resided in the country for at least 8 years but for less than 15. On one hand, I increase the minimum number of years of residence because the 5-year residency requirement included in the law applies to legal permanent residents, but every year only around half of the those newly granted legal permanent resident status are new entrants. The others adjust their status while already residing in the United States. On the other hand, limiting the length of residence to at most 15 years guarantees that respondents from the 2000 census could not have already been citizens in 1990; it also addresses the concern that the results in Table 7.3 are mechanically driven by different naturalization rates across treatment and control countries in 1990. Estimates are remarkably similar to the ones obtained in a sample of immigrants who stayed between 5 and 20 years (column 4 of Table 7.3): dual citizenship recognition is associated with a 6.1 percentage point increase (15% of the baseline) in the naturalization rate among immigrants from treatment countries.

I also estimate Eq. (7.1) on subsamples defined by gender and level of education. Splitting the sample by observable characteristics is problematic because it takes away some of the variation we rely on to control for the effects of welfare reform and other factors contemporaneous with changes in dual citizenship laws. However, to the extent that welfare reform primarily affected low-income families headed by single mothers,[16] estimation results obtained on samples of males or more-educated immigrants are less likely to be confounded by the effects of the reform. As shown in Table 7.4 (columns 2 through 5), the results are unchanged when splitting the sample by gender, although they differ by education. Dual citizenship rights raised the propensity to naturalize in the target group with at least a high school degree, but had a small and statistically insignificant effect on those without a high school degree. This finding suggests that the implied benefits of dual citizenship are higher for more educated immigrants, as we would expect if education were correlated with higher career and income benefits from transnational activities. This result is consistent with findings in Bloemraad (16):—using a unique feature of the Canadian censuses (that ask respondents to report multiple citizenships), she finds that those with higher human capital are more likely to identify themselves as dual citizens. She notices that higher education might correlate with a greater sense of personal political efficacy. If so, people with more education might perceive a higher implied cost in naturalization when dual citizenship rights are denied.

Conclusions

The analysis presented in this chapter shows that the new dual citizenship laws enacted by five Latin American countries in the 1990s positively affected the US naturalization rate among immigrants from those countries. The effects are sizable in magnitude, implying an increase of 10 percentage points in the probability of naturalization over the 1990s among immigrants coming from Colombia, the Dominican Republic, Ecuador, Costa Rica, and Brazil. This result shows that the surge in naturalization in the 1990s—often interpreted in the public debate as a response to welfare legislation restricting access to benefits for non-citizens—is a phenomenon that might have multiple explanations, not exclusively related to changes in US policy. In particular, changes in dual citizenship laws by sending countries are estimated to explain one sixth of the total 18-percentage-point rise in the naturalization rate of non-Mexican Latin Americans in the second half of the 1990s.[17]

This chapter also relates and contributes to the long-standing debate over the *pros* and *cons* of dual nationality. It has been argued that dual nationality might simply add to the sense of *"ni aquí ni allá"* and as such impede immigrants' progress in either the home or the destination country. However, integration into the United States carries a lower cost once dual nationality rights are recognized, and this might promote stronger attachment to the destination country. In favor of this notion, the empirical evidence presented in this chapter shows that dual citizenship rights do promote a higher propensity to naturalize in the receiving country.

International law and practice have generally regarded dual citizenship with disfavor because of more practical concerns on divided allegiance. Dual citizenship raises concerns for nations regarding diplomatic protection, military service, and voting rights. Beyond these more technical issues, there are deeper questions of divided loyalty, the most serious of which arises in times of war. Nowadays, however, political loyalty is a more relevant concern. The fear is that an immigrant who is a dual citizen could participate in the political system of the receiving state with the interest of the country of origin in mind, or could exploit dual citizenship status for personal gain, for example, for collecting government benefits. Against this notion, in other work I find that immigrants coming from countries that have recently allowed dual citizenship lower their reliance on welfare and experience improved labor outcomes (3). These findings support the view that dual nationality might indeed foster both political and economic assimilation in the receiving country, rather than impeding it or raising issues of divided loyalty. This result is important in light of the growing number of countries that have altered their laws to permit their citizens to retain nationality despite naturalization elsewhere.[18] It suggests that receiving countries such as the United States should not fear such changes but support them as a way of granting foreign-born residents a means to reconcile memberships in both their countries of origin and of current residence.

Notes

1. Children residing in the United States can naturalize with their parents.
2. The oath of allegiance taken by all who become US citizens begins: "I hereby declare, on oath, that I absolutely and entirely renounce and abjure all allegiance and fidelity to any foreign prince, potentate, state, or sovereignty of whom or which I have heretofore been a subject or citizen ..."
3. Despite the absence of enforcement, anecdotal evidence suggests that the renunciation oath deters some eligible immigrants from naturalizing. Some might not understand that the oath is not enforced, partly because the US government does not publicize the absence of enforcement. Even equipped with the knowledge of its lack of practical effect, others may refuse to take the oath on principle (17).
4. In this chapter I treat "dual nationality" and "dual citizenship" as synonymous. However, in the Mexican legal system they are not. In Mexico, nationality does not, by itself, include a right to vote; this pertains to Mexican election law.
5. Adulthood upon arrival in the United States is imposed to rule out cases of immigrants deriving citizenship from their parents' naturalization, in order to focus on the voluntary decision to naturalize. Another reason to exclude childhood immigrants is that younger arrivers likely differ from older arrivers with respect to language acquisition and other experiences affecting labor outcomes (18). The restriction on length of stay in the United States is imposed in light of the residency requirements for naturalization included in the US law.
6. Non-immigrant aliens (admitted as students, temporary workers, or foreign diplomats) usually cannot stay in the United States longer than 5 or 6 years with the same type of visa. The problem persists, though, for foreign-born individuals who entered the United States as non-immigrants and then adjusted their status to legal permanent residents while residing in the United States. As shown in the section discussing dual citizenship laws, estimation results are robust to increasing the length of residence restriction.
7. Temporary admissions are much less likely among immigrants from Latin America than from the rest of the world. For example, in fiscal year 1996, people from Latin American countries represented 42% of all legal permanent residents admitted to the United States but only 18% of the almost two million non-immigrants admitted, other than temporary visitors for pleasure or for business (14).
8. Before 1965, 1965–1969, 1970–1974, 1975–1979, 1980–1981, 1982–1984, 1985–1990, 1991–1994, 1995–1997.
9. Mexico, Belize, Costa Rica, El Salvador, Guatemala, Honduras, Nicaragua, Panama, Cuba, the Dominican Republic, Haiti, Jamaica, Trinidad and Tobago, British West Indies, Argentina, Bolivia, Brazil, Chile, Colombia, Ecuador, British Guyana, Peru, and Venezuela.
10. Equation (7.1) is estimated with Ordinary Least Squares (OLS). Standard errors are corrected for heteroskedasticity (naturally arising in a linear probability model) and adjusted for correlation across observations for immigrants from the same country and interviewed in the same census year.
11. However, this factor could nevertheless lead to differential effects by country of origin if the reaction to anti-immigrant sentiments, mainly targeting illegal immigrants, were bigger among immigrant populations with high rates of unauthorized residents.
12. The inclusion of cohort of entry by year effects further addresses the possibility that immigrant participation in the welfare system increases with time spent in the United States (19). If so, in the aftermath of welfare reform, the incentive to naturalize to retain access to social benefits might vary by length of residence.
13. Long-term immigrants are more likely to be legal because they have had time and opportunities to adjust their status. In particular, immigrants in census 2000 who entered illegally before 1982 should have been legalized under IRCA and been eligible to naturalize by the middle of the 1990s. Because of IRCA, it is helpful to split the sample between immigrants

who have been living in the United States for more or less than 20 years as a way of evaluating the differences due to the presence of illegal immigrants.

14. Naturalization and welfare participation rates are calculated using 1990 census data. I use estimates of the outmigration rate of 1970–1974 arrivals by 1980, calculated in Borjas and Bratsberg (20).

15. The excluded countries (and the years in which they granted dual citizenship) are: Belize (1981), Panama (1972), Peru (1980), and the British West Indies (since independence, from 1966 to 1983, except for the Bahamas which still denies dual citizenship). El Salvador granted dual citizenship in 1983, but it is already excluded from the sample.

16. The program for which eligibility rules changed more dramatically (Aid to Families with Dependent Children) is primarily offered to single-parent families.

17. The estimate is obtained by decomposing the rise in the naturalization rate among all Latin Americans other than from Mexico (from 40% to 58%) in a weighted average of the change in the naturalization rate of immigrants from the treatment group (Colombia, the Dominican Republic, Ecuador, Costa Rica, and Brazil), and from other countries. Since immigrants from the treatment group represented 28% of the total non-Mexican population from Latin America in 1990, and dual citizenship laws are found to have increased their rate of naturalization by 10 percentage points, then the total contribution of these laws can be estimated as $(0.28*0.10)/0.18 = 16\%$.

18. For instance, Sweden made this change in 2001, Australia in 2002, and the Philippines in 2003.

References

1. Fix, Michael E., Jeffrey S. Passel, and Kenneth Sucher. 2003. *"Trends in Naturalization."* Immigration Studies Program Brief No. 3. Washington, DC: The Urban Institute.
2. Borjas, George J. 2002. "Welfare Reform and Immigrant Participation in Welfare Programs." *International Migration Review*, 36(4): 1093–1123.
3. Mazzolari, Francesca. 2009. "Dual Citizenship Rights: Do They Make More and Richer Citizens?" *Demography*, 46(1): 169–191.
4. Aleinikoff, T. Alexander, and Douglas Klusmeyer. 2002. *Citizenship Policies for an Age of Migration.* Washington, DC: Carnegie Endowment for International Peace.
5. de la Garza, Rodolfo O. 1996. "Dual Citizenship, Domestic Policies, and Naturalization Rates of Latino Immigrants in the U.S." The Tomas Rivera Center Policy Brief, June.
6. Yang, Philip Q. 1994. "Explaining Immigrant Naturalization." *International Migration Review*, 28(3): 449–477.
7. Jones-Correa, Michael.2001. "Under Two Flags: Dual Nationality in Latin America and Its Consequences for Naturalization in the United States." *International Migration Review*, 35(4): 997–1029.
8. Meyer, Bruce D. 1995. "Natural and Quasi-Experiments in Economics." *Journal of Business and Economic Statistics*, 13(2): 151–161.
9. Ruggles, Steven, Matthew Sobek, Trent Alexander, Catherine A.Fitch, Ronald Goeken, Patricia Kelly Hall, Miriam King, and Chad Ronnander. 2004. *"Integrated Public Use Microdata Series: Version 3.0."* Minneapolis, MN: Minnesota Population Center.
10. U.S. Immigration and Naturalization Service.2003. "Estimates of the Unauthorized Immigrant Population Residing in the United States: 1990 to 2000." http://www.uscis.gov/graphics/shared/aboutus/statistics/Ill_Report_1211.pdf.
11. Costanzo, Joe, Cynthia Davis, Caribert Irazi, Daniel Goodkind, and Roberto Ramirez. 2001. "Evaluating Components of International Migration: The Residual Foreign Born." Working Paper Series No. 61, Population Division, U.S. Bureau of the Census.

12. Robinson, J. Gregory. 2001. *"ESCAP II: Demographic Analysis Results."* Executive Steering Committee for A.C.E. Policy II, Report No. 1. Washington, DC: U.S. Census Bureau.
13. Warren, Robert. 1995. *"Estimates of the Undocumented Immigrant Population Residing in the United States by Country of Origin and State of Residence: October 1992."* Unpublished, U.S. Immigration and Naturalization Service.
14. U.S. Immigration and Naturalization Service. 1997. *1996 Statistical Yearbook*, Washington, DC: U.S. Government Printing Office.
15. Zimmermann, Wendy, and Karen C. Tumlin. 1999. *"Patchwork Policies: State Assistance for Immigrants under Welfare Reform."* Assessing the New Federalism Occasional Paper 24. Washington, DC: The Urban Institute.
16. Bloemraad, Irene. 2004. "Who Claims Dual Citizenship? The Limits of Postnationalism, the Possibilities of Transnationalism, and the Persistence of Traditional Citizenship." *International Migration Review*, 38(2): 389–426.
17. Spiro, Peter J. 1998. "Embracing Dual Nationality." Carnegie Endowment for International Peace Occasional Paper No. 1.
18. Bleakley, Hoyt, and Aimee Chin. 2004. "Language Skills and Earnings: Evidence from Childhood Immigrants." *Review of Economics and Statistics*, 86(2): 481–496.
19. Borjas, George J., and Steve Trejo. 1991. "Immigrant Participation in the Welfare System." *Industrial and Labor Relations Review,* 44(2): 195–211.
20. Borjas, George J., and Bernt Bratsberg. 1996. "Who Leaves? The Outmigration of the Foreign-Born." *Review of Economics and Statistics*, 87(1): 165–176.

Part IV
Earnings

Chapter 8
The LEP Earnings Penalty Among Hispanic Men in the US: 1980 to 2005

Marie T. Mora and Alberto Dávila

Abstract Workers in the US lacking English-language fluency earn less on average than their English-proficient counterparts, although this limited-English-proficient (LEP) earnings "penalty" has not remained stable over time. Using Integrated Public Use Microdata Series data from the 1980, 1990, and 2000 decennial US censuses as well as the 2005 American Community Survey, we show that this average penalty seemingly fell between 1980 and 2005 for Hispanic men in the US. We interpret this decline as evidence that an increase in the relative demand for LEP Hispanics could have offset the increase in their relative labor supply, particularly during the 1980s. However, when comparing workers who completed high school with those who did not, this penalty increased among high school graduates during this time. This policy-relevant finding is consistent with the increasing returns to skill observed in the US during the past couple of decades.

Introduction

In the US, workers who lack English-language proficiency earn less on average than English-fluent workers. A variety of explanations have been used to address this limited-English-proficient (LEP) "earnings penalty." Starting with McManus et al. (1), this penalty has often been explained by human capital theory: English fluency represents a form of human capital that enhances workers' opportunities for trade and production, and, therefore, earnings. Others have argued that majority language proficiency may efficiently match workers' skills to available jobs (e.g., 2). Another possibility offered by extant literature is that employers interpret English fluency as an indicator of a worker's legal status, leading to statistical discrimination against those who lack such fluency (e.g., 3). Still others have suggested that English proficiency might reflect underlying socioeconomic characteristics, such as the quality of education (e.g., 4).

M.T. Mora (✉)
University of Texas – Pan American, Edinburg, TX, USA
e-mail: mtmora@utpa.edu

D.L. Leal, S.J. Trejo (eds.), *Latinos and the Economy*, Immigrants and Minorities, Politics and Policy, DOI 10.1007/978-1-4419-6682-7_8,
© Springer Science+Business Media, LLC 2011

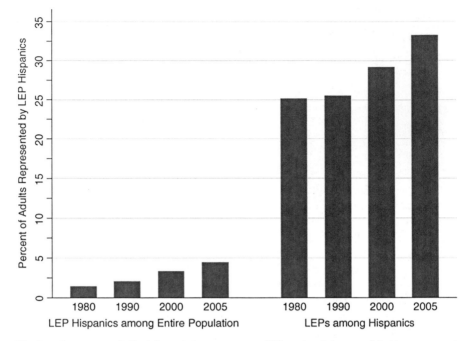

Fig. 8.1 Percentage of all adults and the percentage of Hispanic adults, ages 25–64, represented by LEP Hispanics in 1980, 1990, 2000, and 2005. Notes: This figure is based on the authors' estimates using data from the 1980, 1990, and 2000 US decennial censuses (1% sample) and the 2005 ACS, available in the IPUMS; the IPUMS-provided sampling weights are employed. The LEP are defined as those individuals who do not speak the English language well. This sample includes individuals between the ages of 25 and 64

   Independent of these explanations, recent studies have found that the relationship between English-language fluency and earnings has been evolving among Hispanic workers in the US (e.g., 5, 6). This is not surprising in light of the demographic shifts that have been occurring during the past few decades. For example, as observed in Fig. 8.1, the representation of LEP Hispanics among the adult population between the ages of 25 and 64 in the US more than tripled (from 1.4% to 4.4%) between 1980 and 2005. The increased representation of the LEP is not merely the outcome of the rapidly growing Hispanic population; even among Hispanic adults, the population share of the LEP rose from one-quarter to a third during this time.

   On the one hand, the growing proportion of the LEP Hispanic population indicates that their relative labor supply has risen over time, possibly magnifying the LEP-earnings penalty, particularly after 1990 when the population growth of LEP Hispanics accelerated. Socioeconomic and political events that occurred in the early 2000s (such as the terrorist attacks on September 11th) might have also added to this penalty by reducing the relative demand for these workers (e.g., 7), although this effect is difficult to quantify. On the other hand, Mora and Dávila (6) have suggested that socioeconomic and demographic changes beginning in the 1980s could have led to an increase in the relative demand for Spanish speakers, as discussed below.

Theoretically, these mostly concurrent increases in the relative demand and relative supply of LEP Hispanic workers exert opposing effects on their earnings. This chapter analyzes how the relative earnings of LEP Hispanic men in the US changed between 1980 and 2005 using nationally representative data. We also include policy implications stemming from our results.

Conceptual Issues

These introductory comments point to a simple relative supply and demand framework as a basis for understanding the potential changes in the earnings penalty and employment of LEP Hispanics in the US (6). Figure 8.2 provides this framework. The relative labor supply of the LEP is assumed to be positively affected by their relative wages; that is, the higher the earnings of the LEP vis-à-vis the English-fluent, the more willing are the LEP to work compared to the English-fluent. The relative labor demand for the LEP, in contrast, inversely relates to their relative earnings; an increase in the relative wages of the LEP presumably causes employers to hire fewer of them, other things being the same.

Recall that Fig. 8.1 illustrated the growth in the population representation of LEP Hispanics between 1980 and 2005, indicating that their relative supply has increased, especially since 1990. It follows that if relative labor demand conditions remained unchanged during this time, the average LEP-earnings penalty should have risen. As seen in Fig. 8.2, the increase in the relative labor supply of the

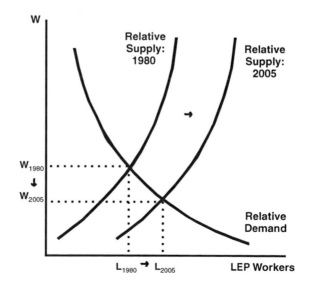

Fig. 8.2 The relative labor demand and supply model, with an increase in the relative supply of LEP workers between 1980 and 2005

LEP should have put downward pressure on their relative wages (W—defined as the ratio of wages earned by the LEP over the wages earned by the English fluent), from W_{1980} to W_{2005}, while their employment should have increased (from L_{1980} to L_{2005}).

Sociopolitical events in recent years, such as those following September 11th, could have magnified this potential widening of the earnings differential between LEP and English-fluent Hispanics. As discussed by Orrenius and Zavodny (7), employers might have been less likely to hire low-skilled Hispanic immigrants in fear of the legal ramifications stemming from new penalties associated with immigration law in the early 2000s. Because employers have used English-language proficiency to signal a worker's legal status (3, 8, 9), perhaps the LEP faced a disproportionate decline in job opportunities during this period.

Still, evidence suggests that the relative demand for Spanish-fluent workers has been increasing (5, 6), partly because the demand for labor is derived from product demand. Consider the visible growth in the demand for Hispanic-related products (including entertainment, clothing, and food), and the popularity of Spanish-language television networks has been growing nationwide. In fact, in cities such as Los Angeles and Miami, they now exceed English-language programming (e.g., 10). Such a product demand increase presumably stems from both the growing Hispanic population in the US and the rising popularity (or declining stigma) for "Hispanic" products. To the extent that the production of these goods and services is Spanish-language intensive, the relative demand for Hispanophones should have risen during this period. Given that nearly all LEP Hispanics speak Spanish, compared to three-quarters of English-fluent Hispanics,[1] the LEP conceivably experienced a relatively large part of this labor-demand increase.

Moreover, with the growth in the Hispanic population there is a stronger presence of Spanish-speaking managers: the share of individuals in managerial positions who spoke Spanish at home rose from 2.7% in 1980 to 6.5% in 2005.[2] This increase suggests growing employment opportunities for LEP Hispanic workers over time, as a larger share of managers would be able to effectively communicate with them.

Labor theory also suggests that the demand for labor relates to the ease of substitution between labor and other inputs. As discussed by Mora and Dávila (6), the ease of substitution between LEP and English-proficient Hispanic workers may have risen in recent years for at least two reasons. First, the growing numbers of Spanish speakers could have led to more efficient language and ethnic networks, possibly disproportionately benefiting the LEP, nearly all of whom speak Spanish. Second, while it has been argued that employers statistically discriminated against the LEP in the 1980s by interpreting English fluency as a signal of a worker's legal status (e.g., 3, 11), Immigration and Naturalization Service (8) records show that the *enforcement* of IRCA-related employer sanctions declined during the 1990s.[3] As noted by Mora and Dávila (6), the realization that the probability of facing such sanctions and losing specifically-trained workers through deportation was smaller than expected seemed to mitigate the perceived risks of hiring LEP Hispanics in recent years, hence increasing their substitutability with English-fluent workers.

It follows that a simultaneous increase in the relative labor demand and supply of LEP workers has a theoretically ambiguous net effect on the earnings of LEP

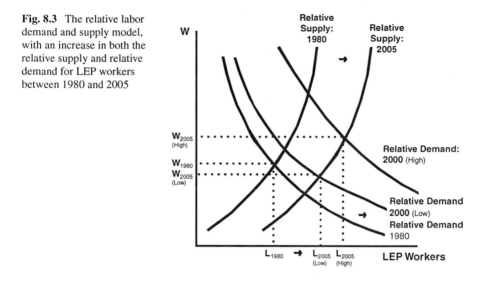

Fig. 8.3 The relative labor demand and supply model, with an increase in both the relative supply and relative demand for LEP workers between 1980 and 2005

Hispanics vis-à-vis their English-fluent peers. For example, consider Fig. 8.3 (similar to Fig. 8.2) that shows two hypothetical increases (a "High" increase and a "Low" increase) in the relative labor demand for the LEP. Regardless of the size of this increase, note that it counters the relative wage decline caused by the supply increase. In fact, under the case of a large increase in relative demand, the relative earnings of the LEP should *rise* [to W_{2005} (High)]. We turn to an empirical investigation of the LEP-earnings penalty with this conceptualization in mind.

Overview of LEP Earnings and Education Differentials

We use 1980, 1990, and 2000 decennial US census data, as well as 2005 American Community Survey (ACS) data, available in the 1% Integrated Public Use Microdata Series (IPUMS) provided by Ruggles et al. (12). These data contain statistical weights provided by the US Census Bureau to maintain the national representation of the samples. Our sample of interest includes US- and foreign-born Hispanic civilian men between the ages of 25 and 64 years who report wage and salary income. We focus on men here because gender significantly affects a variety of labor market outcomes among ethnic groups, including the LEP-earnings penalty (e.g., 6, 13, 14). We use the convention of identifying the LEP as those individuals who reported that they did not speak the English language "well."[4] To obtain a sample committed to labor market activities, individuals working less than 20 hours a week or under 32 weeks in the year prior to the census are excluded. Consistent with the literature, our base group of comparison contains civilians considered "assimilated"—US-born non-Hispanic whites who only speak English at home.

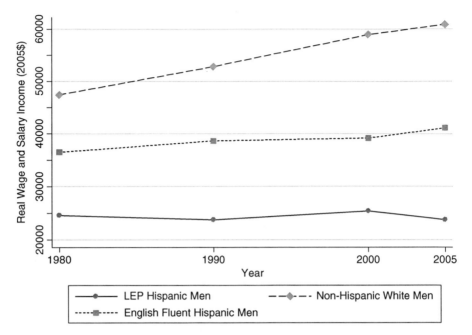

Fig. 8.4 Real wage and salary income (in 2005 Dollars) of Hispanic and non-Hispanic white men. Notes: These data are from the 1980, 1990, and 2000 decennial census (1% sample) and the 2005 ACS, available in the IPUMS; the IPUMS-provided sampling weights are employed. The salary figures are adjusted by the Consumer Price Index. This sample includes Hispanic and US-born monolingual English non-Hispanic white civilian men, 25–64 years old, who worked at least 20 hours per week for 32 weeks or more in the previous year, and who reported positive wage and salary income

Figure 8.4 provides the average wage and salary income for LEP Hispanic, English-fluent Hispanic, and non-Hispanic white men in 1980, 1990, 2000, and 2005. These numbers have been adjusted using the consumer price index (CPI) to denote values in 2005 dollars. While the earnings figures reported pertain to the year prior to the survey, for ease of discussion, we will refer to them here in terms of the survey year. As expected, LEP Hispanic men earned considerably less than English-proficient Hispanics and non-Hispanic whites in all 4 years. Of specific interest to this study, the real average earnings of LEP Hispanic men remained relatively flat during this time period (with a slight decline in the 1980s, a slight improvement in the 1990s, and a slight decline again in the early 2000s). English-fluent Hispanic men also had little real earnings growth between 1980 and 2005. Note, however, that the real average earnings of US-born non-Hispanic white men significantly increased between 1980 and 2005, such that the widening of the Hispanic/non-Hispanic-white earnings gap observed for the 1980s and 1990s did not lessen in the early 2000s.

These earnings differences at least partly reflect underlying differences in observable skills (such as education) as well as in the changes to skill returns that occurred

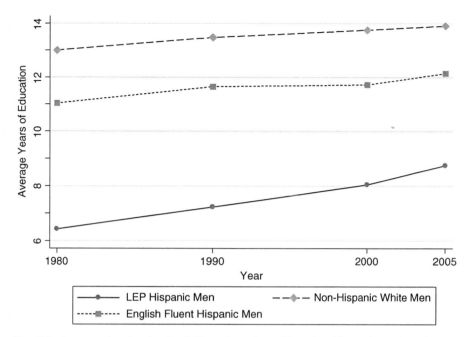

Fig. 8.5 Average education levels of Hispanic and non-Hispanic white male workers. Notes: These data are from the 1980, 1990, and 2000 decennial census (1% sample) and the 2005 ACS, available in the IPUMS; the IPUMS-provided sampling weights are employed. This sample includes Hispanic and US-born monolingual English non-Hispanic white civilian men, 25–64 years old, who worked at least 20 hours per week for 32 weeks or more in the previous year, and who reported positive wage and salary income. The LEP are defined as those individuals who did not speak the English language well

during this time. In particular, a salient feature in the US labor market during the past couple of decades has been the increasing returns to education (e.g., 15, 16). As Fig. 8.5 illustrates, LEP Hispanics have less education on average than English proficient workers,[5] although their schooling gap has been narrowing over time. In 1980, for example, LEP Hispanic men had 6.4 years of schooling, compared to 11 years for English-fluent Hispanics and 13 years for non-Hispanic white men. By 2005, these figures increased to 8.7, 12.1, and 13.9 years, respectively. Consistent with the widening earnings differentials between Hispanics and non-Hispanic whites observed in Fig. 8.4, however, Mora and Dávila (5, 6) have previously found that the relatively large increase in the average education levels of LEP Hispanic men was not enough to offset the increasing returns to education during the 1980s and 1990s.

Analyses of the Relative Earnings of the LEP

Given the impact that education has on labor market earnings, do the earnings differences in Fig. 8.4 mainly reflect the LEP/English-fluent schooling differentials, or can they be interpreted in terms of changes in the relative demand and supply of LEP workers? To address this question, we now analyze the changes in the LEP-earnings penalty for Hispanic men between 1980 and 2005 through the use of a wage decomposition technique (17).

Specifically, we first estimate a standard earnings function for each year to control for observable characteristics, including education, for English-fluent Hispanic and non-Hispanic white men:

$$\ln(W)_E = HC\, B_E + X\, A_E + u_E, \tag{8.1}$$

where $ln(W)_E$ represents the natural logarithm of hourly wages for the English fluent. Vector HC contains observed human capital characteristics, including education, experience (estimated by age − education − 5), and experience-squared, while Vector X includes sociodemographic characteristics, such as birthplace (foreign-versus US-born); immigrants' time in the US; Hispanic ethnicity (Mexican, Cuban, Puerto Rican, and "Other" Hispanic); geographic region (New England, North Central, South Central, Middle and South Atlantic, Mountain, and West—the base); residence outside of metropolitan areas; and a constant term. B_E and A_E depict vectors of coefficients to be estimated, and u_E represents the normally distributed error term. Note that B_E and A_E describe the structure of earnings structures for English proficient men in each year.

We then use the estimated coefficients from B_E and A_E to estimate how much LEP Hispanic men should have earned, given their characteristics, if they faced the same wage structure as English-fluent Hispanic and non-Hispanic white men. The difference between the actual average earnings of the LEP and these predicted earnings reflects the wage differential unexplained by differences in observable characteristics (such as education) between English-proficient men and English-deficient Hispanic men. Given that the quality and type of education might systematically vary between the LEP (almost all of whom are foreign-born) and English-fluent Hispanic and non-Hispanic white men, however, we will elaborate on whether distinguishing between immigrants' versus natives' education affects the estimated LEP earnings penalty later in this chapter.

The solid line in Fig. 8.6 (labeled "Entire Sample") presents the estimated average earnings penalties for LEP Hispanic men in the 4 years analyzed. Note that the magnitude of the LEP-earnings penalty fell for Hispanic men between 1980 and 2005; this decline is statistically significant at the 1% level. LEP Hispanic men earned around 11% less on average than their otherwise similar English-fluent Hispanic and non-Hispanic white counterparts in 1980; by 2005 this LEP-earnings penalty had dwindled to 2.3%.[6] The decline in this penalty is consistent with the large increase in the relative demand for LEP workers discussed above. That is, a large increase in the relative demand for LEP workers could have more than off-set the growth in their relative supply, particularly between 1980 and 1990, when the increase in their relative labor supply was modest. It should be noted that when comparing 2000 with 2005, the magnitude of the LEP penalty increased slightly (from 2.2% to 2.3%), although the change is not statistically significant

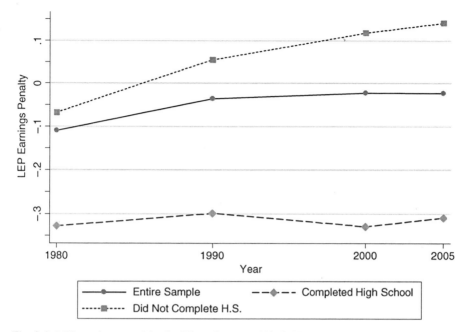

Fig. 8.6 LEP earnings penalties for Hispanic men: 1980–2005. Notes: These earnings penalties are estimated using a wage decomposition technique [see the discussion involving Eq. (8.1)]. The data are from the 1980, 1990, and 2000 decennial census (1% sample) and the 2005 ACS, available in the IPUMS; the IPUMS-provided sampling weights are employed. This sample includes Hispanic and US-born monolingual English non-Hispanic white civilian men, 25–64 years old, who worked at least 20 hours per week for 32 weeks or more in the previous year, and who reported positive wage and salary income. The LEP are defined as those individuals who did not speak the English language well. The lines for "Did Not Complete H.S." and "Completed High School" provide the average LEP penalties among men who did not finish high school, and then among those who had at least a high school diploma

at conventional levels. With regard to relative supply effects, this is not surprising, considering the relatively large growth in the LEP Hispanic population after 1990 (recall Fig. 8.1). Perhaps, also, some of the socioeconomic and political events in the early 2000s began to counter the rising relative labor demand for LEP Hispanic men that occurred in the previous decade.[7]

Hispanic Ethnicity and the LEP Penalty

Of course, the findings reported in Fig. 8.6 for the entire sample do not indicate that the LEP earnings penalty declined for all Hispanic workers in the US, but rather that a decline occurred on the average. Moreover, other work has shown that differences exist with respect to English-fluency returns across specific Hispanic populations (e.g., 6, 18). To address this issue, we further estimate the LEP-earnings penalties for Mexican American and Cuban men. These results (not shown to conserve space) indicate that Mexican American men experienced a declining LEP earnings penalty (from 11.4% in 1980 to 1.2% in 2005) that primarily mirrors the penalty shown in Fig. 8.6 for Hispanic men, in general. However, despite a decline in this penalty for Cuban men (from 15.7% to 7.3%) between 1980 and 1990, LEP Cuban men lost significant ground to their English-fluent counterparts with respect to wages after 1990; indeed, by 2005, their estimated LEP penalty was 17.1%—larger than it was in 1980. It follows that earnings trends observed for Hispanic men overall appear to be driven by Mexican Americans (the largest Hispanic ethnic group in the US, accounting for two third of the Hispanic population) and do not necessarily represent changes occurring among other Hispanic populations.

Education and the LEP Penalty

The observation that the LEP earnings penalty declined after 1980 appears to run counter to the increasing returns to skills observed in the 1980s and 1990s (4, 15, 16, 19). Nevertheless, McManus, Gould, and Welch (1), among others, have found that poor English-language fluency depresses the returns to other skills; this dampening effect on schooling returns became stronger for LEP Hispanic men during the 1980s (20).

As a result, Fig. 8.6 also provides the LEP earnings penalties distinguishing between workers with and without a high school diploma. Note that these results illustrate an erosion of limited English ability on the returns to education for Hispanic men between 1980 and 2005. The small dashed line (labeled "Did Not Complete H.S.") shows the average LEP-earnings penalty shrank in magnitude over the 25-year period (including between 2000 and 2005) for Hispanic men who did not finish high school. In fact, starting in 1990, among these less educated workers, LEP Hispanic men seemed to fare better on average than men who spoke English well or better, ceteris paribus. Nevertheless, the earnings penalty accrued by LEP workers with at least a high school education hovered around 30% and remained statistically unchanged over the entire time period. In short, the high school graduate/dropout earnings differential associated with poor English-language fluency widened among Hispanic men during the past 25 years.[8] This finding is consistent with the increasing returns to skill observed in the US in that English-language proficiency has become a more valued skill among educated Hispanic men.

Foreign Education and the LEP Penalty

The foregoing results indicate a declining LEP earnings penalty, particularly in the 1980s. However, one potential issue that arises when estimating earnings differentials between immigrants and natives using the methodology described thus far is that the returns to education and other skills might be overstated for the LEP. Previous studies have found that observed skill returns tend to be lower for immigrants than for US-born men (19, 21). LEP Hispanics are primarily immigrants, whereas English-fluent Hispanics include both the US- and foreign-born. As such, the estimated LEP earnings penalties displayed in Fig. 8.6 could be reflecting underlying differences in skill returns related to nativity in addition to the influence of limited English proficiency on earnings.

We address this issue by re-estimating Eq. (8.1) while interacting the human capital variables (education, experience, and experience-squared) with an immigrant binary variable. That is, Eq. (8.1) becomes:

$$\ln(W)_E = HC \, B_E + (HC \times Imm) \, \beta_E + X_E \, A_E + u_E \qquad (8.2)$$

In this version, the coefficient vector β_E allows for possible differences to be estimated with respect to the returns to human capital between Hispanic immigrants and US-born Hispanics and non-Hispanic whites. Figure 8.7 reports the LEP-earnings penalties using this modification.

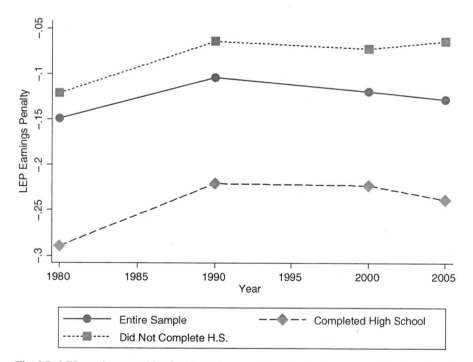

Fig. 8.7 LEP earnings penalties for Hispanic men while adjusting human capital returns for the foreign-born: 1980–2005. Notes: These earnings penalties are estimated using a wage decomposition technique that adjusts the returns to human capital according to birthplace (US- versus foreign-born) [see the discussion involving Eq. (8.2)]. The data are from the 1980, 1990, and 2000 decennial census (1% sample) and the 2005 ACS, available in the IPUMS; the IPUMS-provided sampling weights are employed. This sample includes Hispanic and US-born monolingual English non-Hispanic white civilian men, 25–64 years old, who worked at least 20 hours per week for 32 weeks or more in the previous year, and who reported positive wage and salary income. The LEP are defined as those individuals who did not speak the English language well. The lines for "Did Not Complete H.S." and "Completed High School" provide the average LEP penalties among men who did not finish high school, and then among those who had at least a high school diploma

Similar to Fig. 8.6, Fig. 8.7 shows that regardless of education, LEP Hispanic men fared better in a relative sense in 2005 than in 1980, even after controlling for potential differences in the returns to immigrants' versus natives' skills (see the solid line for the entire sample). However, Fig. 8.7 indicates that this relative gain primarily occurred in the 1980s, with little change between 1990 and 2005. Given that the post-1990 period was also associated with accelerated growth in the LEP Hispanic population (Fig. 8.1), potential relative labor demand effects appear to have been countered by these increases in the relative supply of LEP workers.

When considering differences between high school graduates and dropouts, as with Fig. 8.6, Fig. 8.7 shows that limited English skills were associated with a larger earnings penalty among the more educated workers. For example, in 2005, LEP Hispanic men without a high school diploma earned about 7% less than their English-proficient peers, while those with at least a high school education earned 24% less. Note also that after 1990, LEP Hispanic men without a high school diploma did not have an earnings premium as had been observed in Fig. 8.6, indicating that the LEP penalty could be understated when ignoring the issue of differences across birthplace.

Figure 8.7 further suggests that the high school graduate/dropout LEP-earnings differential remained fairly steady over time, except in the early 2000s. One possibility for this result is that the underlying skill distribution of LEP versus English-fluent immigrants has recently shifted in favor of the LEP. Recall that Fig. 8.4 indicated that the average education levels of LEP Hispanic men rose at a faster pace than for the English fluent between 1980 and 2005. Perhaps a similar trend occurred with respect to other unobservable characteristics (such as the quality of education, or motivation), enhancing the relative earnings of the LEP. These explanations can be explored more fully in future research.

Conclusion

Understanding the labor market implications of limited-English-proficiency has become increasingly important during the past few decades, given the large growth in the language minority population in the US. The primary findings reported in this chapter illustrate that the average LEP-earnings penalty among Hispanic men declined overall between 1980 and 2005, particularly between 1980 and 1990. Additional analyses suggest that this shrinking penalty occurred more so among Mexican immigrants and among workers with low education levels.

Following a relative labor demand and supply framework, we believe these changes reflect comparatively strong relative demand effects, especially during the 1980s, which outpaced the growth in the relative supply of LEP Hispanic workers. Our results beyond the 1980s, however, might be interpreted as showing relatively strong labor supply effects on the LEP earnings penalty.

These findings have several policy implications. Current policies favor stronger border enforcement aimed at reducing the flow of low-skill immigrants, who typically have poor English-language skills. To the extent that this enforcement is effective in the future, it might reduce the relative supply of LEP workers in the US and, thus, should put downward pressure on the foregoing LEP penalty, other things being the same. This would be an interesting labor-market outcome for several reasons. For one, other policies that have attempted to improve access to English-language programs might, therefore, not enhance labor market earnings unless such programs are coupled with other formal schooling or training opportunities.

For another, language-based policies that have aimed to improve English-language usage and fluency, including those related to bilingual education and official-English legislation, have parted from static assumptions about the importance of English in the labor market. Indeed, these policies have had relatively long implementation lags (such as the 34-year Title VII of the Elementary and Secondary Education Act—the Bilingual Education Act), and they are often not systematically administered.[9] Perhaps policies affecting the LEP should be designed with shorter implementation lags and/or more flexible and dynamic constructs to better reflect the fluidity of the returns to English proficiency in the US labor market.

Acknowledgement We would like to thank Stephen Trejo and the session participants at the SIGLO XXI—IUPLR Second Biennial Conference held in Austin, Texas on April 14, 2007 for their helpful comments. Much of the background discussion in this chapter is based on our unpublished manuscript titled "Changes in the Returns to English-Language Fluency for Hispanic Men between 1980 and 2000," The University of Texas–Pan American, 2004.

Notes

1. To illustrate, 73.9% of the 103,782 Hispanics (representing 12,836,275 Hispanics) between the ages of 25 and 64 who reported speaking English "well" or better in the 2005 American Community Survey spoke Spanish at home.
2. We estimated these figures by focusing on individuals aged 25–64 in the Integrated Public Use Microdata Series (IPUMS) who: (1) worked at least 20 hours per week for 32 or more weeks, (2) were not enrolled in school, and (3) reported a managerial occupation. Note that these figures probably understate the actual share of Spanish-fluent managers because the absence of the Spanish language in the household does not necessarily mean the person lacks Spanish-language fluency. Unfortunately, the IPUMS does not provide language-use information for the workplace. Recent evidence indicates that the growing demand for Spanish–English bilingual managers in the US has continued after 2005, as discussed in an October 2007 article in the *Financial Times* (22).
3. Mora and Dávila (6) note that, despite a doubling of the undocumented population in the US in the past decade, INS records show the number of employers fined for violating immigration law declined by 95% (from 1,063 to 53), and the number of warnings issued to employers declined by 80% (from 840 to 169) between fiscal years 1992 and 2001. Similarly, the number of completed work site investigations fell from 7,053 in 1992 to 1,595 in 2001—a 77% decline. Moreover, Orrenius and Zavodny (7) note that employer sanction caseloads continued to fall between 2001 and 2003, possibly because law enforcement efforts were directed to other activities, including interviewing thousands of Arab and Muslim men.

4. For individuals who speak a non-English language at home, these data provide self-reported categorical information on how well they speak English, with the possible responses of: "very well," "well," "not well," and "not at all." Combining the last two categories to define the LEP is fairly common in the literature; see Mora and Dávila (6) for a recent discussion of alternative measures.

5. Except for 1980, the data provide education levels in categories, not in a continuous format. We estimate the continuous education measure for 1990, 2000, and 2005 by taking the midpoint of the education categories or, where possible, the average number of years associated with certain schooling levels (e.g., 16 years for a college degree).

6. As a robustness test, we re-estimated the LEP-earnings penalties while also excluding workers who spoke the English language "well" from Eq. (8.1). Similar to Fig. 8.6, these results (not shown to conserve space) indicate that the relative earnings of LEP Hispanic men significantly improved between 1980 and 2005. The LEP earned 12.9% less in 1980 than their counterparts who either spoke English "very well" or only spoke English; this penalty had fallen to 4.3% in 2005. Moreover, the relative earnings of Hispanic men who spoke English "well" did not significantly change during this period; such men earned 3.9% less than their highly-English-fluent counterparts in 1980, and (a statistically similar) 4.5% less in 2005. It follows that while the relative earnings of LEP Hispanic men were higher in 2005 than in 1980, a similar improvement did not occur among Hispanic men who spoke the English language well. In fact, Hispanic men who spoke English well did not fare better with respect to labor market earnings than those with a lower grasp of the language in 2005, ceteris paribus.

7. It should be noted that when re-estimating the LEP-earnings penalties when further excluding workers who spoke the English language "well" from Eq. (8.1), this penalty significantly increased in magnitude from 2.1% in 2000 to 4.3% in 2005. This is an additional indication that the relative labor demand for LEP Hispanics might have been hindered after 2000.

8. When further separating high school graduates from college graduates (results not shown to conserve space), a similar pattern emerges: the college-graduate/high-school-graduate wage differential stemming from limited English skills significantly widened for Hispanic men between 1980 and 2005.

9. As Mora and Dávila (6) note, an example of this latter point is that despite the absence of a national language policy, over half of the states have some form of official-English legislation (the vast majority of which were passed since 1981); see US-English, Inc. (23) for more details. Yet, as noted by Crawford (24), state courts in two of them (Arizona and Alaska) recently deemed such legislation to be unconstitutional.

References

1. McManus, Walter, William Gould, and Finis Welch. 1983. "Earnings of Hispanic Men: The Role of English Language Proficiency." *Journal of Labor Economics*, 1(2): 101–130.
2. Grenier, Gilles. 1984. "The Effect of Language Characteristics on the Wages of Hispanic American Males." *Journal of Human Resources*, 19(1): 25–52.
3. Dávila, Alberto, Alok K. Bohara, and Rogelio Sáenz. 1993. "Accent Penalties and the Earnings of Mexican Americans." *Social Science Quarterly*, 74(4): 902–916.
4. Trejo, Stephen J. 1997. "Why Do Mexican Americans Earn Low Wages?" *Journal of Political Economy*, 105(6): 1235–1268.
5. Mora, Marie T., and Alberto Dávila. 2006a. "A Note on the Changes in the Relative Wages of LEP Hispanic Men between 1980 and 2000." *Industrial Relations*, 45(2): 169–172.
6. Mora, Marie T., and Alberto Dávila. 2006b. "Hispanic Ethnicity, Gender, and the Change in the LEP-Earnings Penalty in the US during the 1990s." *Social Science Quarterly* (Special Issue on Ethnicity and Social Change), 87(5): 1295–1318.

7. Orrenius, Pia M., and Madeline Zavodny. 2009. "The Effects of Tougher Enforcement on the Job Prospects of Recent Latin American Immigrants." *Journal of Policy Analysis and Management*, 28(2): 239–257.
8. Perotti, Rosanna. 1992. "IRCA's Antidiscrimination Provisions: What Went Wrong?" *International Migration Review*, 26(3): 732–753.
9. Phillips, Julie A., and Douglas S. Massey. 1999. "The New Labor Market: Immigrants and Wages after IRCA." *Demography*, 36(2): 233–246.
10. Authers, John. 2005. "Politicians Must Mind Their Language in Wooing Hispanic Vote." *Financial Times*, August 31, 4.
11. Immigration and Naturalization Service (INS). 1991–2001. *Statistical Yearbook of the Immigration and Naturalization Service.* (Currently part of the U.S. Citizenship and Immigration Services.) http://uscis.gov/graphics/shared/statistics/yearbook/index.htm (accessed February 17, 2006).
12. Ruggles, Steven, Matthew Sobek, Trent Alexander, Catherine A. Fitch, Ronald Goeken, Patricia Kelly Hall, Miriam King, and Chad Ronnander. 2007. *"Integrated Public Use Microdata Series: Version 3.0"* (machine readable database). Minneapolis, MN: Minnesota Population Center. http://www.ipums.org (accessed March 24, 2007).
13. Antecol, Heather, and Kelly Bedard. 2002. "The Relative Earnings of Young Mexican, Black, and Non-Hispanic Women." *Industrial and Labor Relations Review*, 56(1): 122–135.
14. Mora, Marie T., and Alberto Dávila. 1998. "Gender, Earnings, and the English-Skill Acquisition of Hispanic Americans in the United States." *Economic Inquiry*, 36(4): 631–644.
15. Juhn, Chinhui, Kevin M. Murphy, and Brooks Pierce. 1993. "Wage Inequality and the Rise in the Returns to Skill." *Journal of Political Economy*, 101(3): 410–442.
16. Welch, Finis. 2000. "Growth in Women's Relative Wages and in Inequality among Men: One Phenomenon or Two?" *American Economic Review Papers and Proceedings*, 90(2): 444–449.
17. Oaxaca, Ronald. 1973. "Male-Female Wage Differentials in Urban Labor Markets." *International Economic Review*, 14(3): 693–709.
18. Dávila Alberto, and Marie T. Mora. 2001. "Hispanic Ethnicity, English-Skill Investments, and Earnings." *Industrial Relations*, 40(1): 83–88.
19. Trejo, Stephen J. 2003. "Intergenerational Progress of Mexican-Origin Workers in the U.S. Labor Market." *Journal of Human Resources*, 38(3): 467–489.
20. Mora, Marie T. 1998. "Did the English Deficiency Earnings Penalty Change for Hispanic Men between 1979 and 1989?" *Social Science Quarterly*, 79(3): 581–594.
21. Chiswick, Barry R. 1978. "The Effect of Americanization on the Earnings of Foreign-Born Men."*Journal of Political Economy*, 86(5): 897–921.
22. McCullough, Debbi Gardiner. 2007. "Hispanic MBAs Find Themselves in High Demand." *Financial Times*, special section on Business Education, October 29, 13.
23. U.S.-English, Inc. 2007. www.us-english.org   (accessed April 12, 2007).
24. Crawford, James. 2003. "Issues in U.S. Language Policy: Language Legislation in the U.S.A." http://ourworld.compuserve.com/homepages/JWCRAWFORD/langleg.htm (accessed March 18, 2003).

Chapter 9
The Minimum Wage and Latino Workers

Pia M. Orrenius and Madeline Zavodny

Abstract Latinos comprise a large and growing share of the low-skilled labor force in the US and may be disproportionately affected by minimum wage laws as a result. We compare the effects of minimum wage laws on employment and earnings among Hispanic immigrants and natives with effects among non-Hispanic whites and blacks. We focus on adults who have not finished high school and on teenagers, groups likely to earn low wages. Conventional economic theory predicts that higher minimum wages lead to higher hourly earnings among people who are employed but lower employment rates. Data from the Current Population Survey during the period 1994–2007 indicate that there is a significant disemployment effect of higher minimum wages on Latino teenagers, although it is smaller for foreign- than native-born Latinos. Adult Latino immigrants' earnings are less affected by minimum wage laws than other low-education natives, and their employment rates appear to increase when the minimum wage rises. We investigate whether skill levels and undocumented status help explain these findings.

Introduction

Between 2007 and 2009, the federal minimum wage rose in three steps to $7.25 from $5.15. The increases were the first in a decade and were, in non-inflation adjusted terms, the largest rise in the minimum wage since its inception in 1938. It is important to understand how such a sizable increase might affect earnings and employment among low-skilled, low-wage workers. Because Latinos are the largest minority group in the US and tend to have relatively low levels of education and earnings, this chapter focuses on how minimum wage laws affected Latino workers' employment and earnings, compared with non-Latinos, during the period 1994–2007.

Previous research suggests that minimum wage laws may have sizable effects among Latino teenagers and young adults. Neumark and Wascher (1) indicate

P.M. Orrenius (✉)
Federal Reserve Bank of Dallas, Dallas, TX, USA
e-mail: pia.orrenius@dal.frb.org

D.L. Leal, S.J. Trejo (eds.), *Latinos and the Economy*, Immigrants and Minorities, Politics and Policy, DOI 10.1007/978-1-4419-6682-7_9,
© Springer Science+Business Media, LLC 2011

that higher minimum wages are associated with lower employment rates among Hispanics 16–24 years old, with the adverse employment effect increasing over time. Indeed, their results suggest that young Hispanics are more adversely affected than other racial and ethnic groups. Several studies also suggest that higher minimum wages are associated with more "idleness," or being neither enrolled in school nor working, among Hispanic and black teenagers (2, 3).

Minimum wage laws may particularly affect Latinos because of relatively low average education levels and high rates of limited English proficiency (LEP).[1] As of 2006, about 41% of Hispanics—and 52% of foreign-born Hispanics—ages 25 and older in the US did not have a high school diploma or equivalent. Less than 10% of non-Hispanic whites and 19% of blacks, in contrast, had not completed high school.[2] Data from the 2000 Census indicate that almost 82% of Hispanics aged 18–64 years old speak a language other than English at home, and almost 28% report that they speak English either "not well" or "not at all."[3]

This chapter assesses the incidence and impact of minimum wages on Latinos. We focus on Latino teenagers and low-education Latino adults because minimum wage laws will most likely affect these age/education groups. Although a few previous studies have examined the effect of minimum wages among Hispanics, most reported results that combined Hispanics with blacks. No previous research distinguished between Latino natives and immigrants, which we do here. Our examination of the effect of minimum wages on Latinos begins with an explanation of how minimum wages fit into a simple supply and demand model. We then discuss the data, which are from the Current Population Survey during 1994–2007, and our empirical methods.

The results indicate that the disemployment effect of higher minimum wages is smaller among foreign- than native-born Latino teenagers and is nonexistent for non-Hispanic white teens. Higher minimum wages do not adversely affect the employment rates of low-education adults. In fact, we find a *positive* employment effect for low-education foreign-and native-born Latino adults (and for whites). We investigate whether substitution across skill groups and undocumented status among immigrant Latinos underlie these results.

Theoretical Background

Conventional economic theory predicts that minimum wages raise hourly earnings and reduce employment. Figure 9.1 shows a simple version of this model. In the absence of a minimum wage, the labor market clears at the market wage, which is the wage at which the labor supply and labor demand curves intersect. In the figure, the number of workers employed at the market wage is labeled Qm. Imposing a "binding" minimum wage—one higher than the market-clearing wage—reduces the number of workers hired to the quantity labeled Qd but increases the number of individuals who are willing to work to the quantity Qs. The decline in the number of people employed is given by the quantity Qm—Qd. The quantity Qs—Qd represents the number of people unemployed.

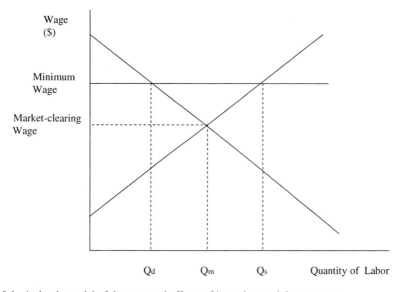

Fig. 9.1 A simple model of the expected effects of imposing a minimum wage

Further increases in the minimum wage would reduce the number of workers employed while raising the number of people who are unemployed. Economists usually focus on measuring the employment effect instead of unemployment since a higher minimum wage will cause people to enter the labor market, and not all of those workers will find jobs. The policy implications of this minimum wage-induced increase in unemployment are not clear. Moreover, unemployment statistics are misleading in that some people who cannot find a job stop searching and then are not counted as unemployed in official statistics.

The negative employment effect should be largest among workers who tend to earn low wages. Such workers usually are teenagers or young adults; many work at fast food restaurants. A number of studies have, therefore, focused on estimating the effect of minimum wage increases on employment among these groups and have typically found that a 10% increase in the minimum wage leads to a 1–3% decline in employment.[4] However, some research suggests that higher minimum wages are not necessarily associated with lower employment rates even though they raise workers' average hourly earnings (e.g., 4–8). Such results contradict the conventional model. One potential explanation for these results is that employers substitute more-skilled workers for less-skilled workers as the minimum wage increases, resulting in no net change in aggregate employment but changes across groups.[5] If Latinos are viewed as less skilled than non-Hispanic whites, employers might substitute non-Hispanic whites for Latinos. Another possibility is that employment rates based on surveys of individuals remain unchanged despite minimum wage increases because some individuals work "under the table" for wages below the legal minimum.[6]

From a theoretical standpoint, the impact of minimum wages is likely to be larger among Latinos than among non-Hispanic whites. As discussed above, Latinos, particularly those who are foreign-born, tend to have less education than non-Hispanic whites. If firms reduce employment of low-skilled workers when the minimum wage increases, Latinos should be affected more than other groups. Foreign-born Latinos should be particularly adversely affected since they are likely to have less US work experience than natives, as well as limited English skills. On the other hand, immigrants—especially undocumented immigrants—may be more likely than natives to work "off the books" and, therefore, not be adversely affected by changes in labor laws like the minimum wage. In a study of immigrants in the Chicago area in 2001, about 10% of undocumented immigrants (and 3% of legal immigrants) reported being paid less than the minimum wage (9). About 90% of the undocumented immigrants were from Latin America.

In addition, the measured employment effect of higher minimum wages might be closer to zero among immigrants if those who cannot find work when the minimum wage increases respond by moving. These unemployed workers might return to their home country or move within the US to an area that has a lower minimum wage (10). Immigrants who are not naturalized US citizens, and especially those illegally present in the US, have relatively little access to the public safety net (welfare benefits, unemployment insurance benefits, etc.). Because they have few alternatives, they are likely to move if they cannot find a job when the minimum wage rises.

Data

We use individual-level data to examine how minimum wage laws affect hourly earnings and employment during the period 1994–2007. The data are from the Current Population Survey, a large-scale survey conducted monthly among a representative random sample of households in the US. About 50,000 households per month participate in the survey and answer questions about household composition and demographic characteristics. Housing units are in the sample for 4 months, out for 8 months, and then back in the sample for 4 months. When a housing unit is in the fourth and eighth survey waves (the outgoing rotations), the survey asks about individuals' employment status and earnings. Our data consist of individuals who are in these outgoing rotation groups and who reported information about their demographic characteristics and labor market outcomes.

We constructed two samples from the outgoing rotation groups: teenagers and low-education adults. Teenagers are ages 16–19; low-education adults are ages 20–54 who do not have a high school diploma or equivalent. We focus on these groups since they tend to earn relatively low wages and hence are likely to be affected by minimum wage laws.

Our measure of the minimum wage is the higher of federal and state minimum wages (the "effective minimum wage") in each state. For simplicity and comparability to most previous studies, we do not examine federal and state "subminimum" wages (which allow employers to pay young or recently-hired workers a lower minimum wage); industry- or occupation-specific minimum wages (such as the tip credit

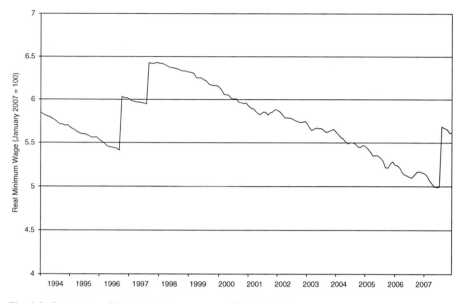

Fig. 9.2   Real value of federal minimum wage, 1994–2007

minimum wage for some restaurant workers); city-level minimum wages (which occurred in a few areas toward the end of our sample period); or "living wage" requirements.[7] The federal minimum wage increased twice early in our sample period, from $4.25 to $4.75 in October 1996, to $5.15 in September 1997, and to $5.85 in July 2007.[8] Fig. 9.2 shows the value of the real (inflation-adjusted) federal minimum wage during 1994–2007.

As inflation eroded the real value of the federal minimum wage, a number of states opted to pass higher minimum wages. The number of states with a minimum wage above the federal level at some point during the year ranges from a low of eight in 1998 to a high of 33 in 2007 (see Appendix Table 1). We use the effective minimum wage on the 12th of the month in the year in which individuals completed the survey (because the reference period for the labor force questions is the week including the 12th).

Table 9.1 reports descriptive statistics for three groups: (1) workers who earn exactly the minimum wage, (2) workers who are paid less than the minimum wage, and (3) workers who earn within 125% of the minimum wage. The table also reports (in the last column) descriptive statistics for all workers as a benchmark.[9] About one-third of all workers earning exactly the minimum wage are teenagers. Teens account for a slightly lower, but still considerable, fraction of workers earning less than the minimum wage and slightly above the minimum wage. About 27%, 16%, and 20% of workers earning exactly, less than, and slightly above the minimum wage, respectively, are Hispanic. Since Hispanics comprise only 14% of workers during our sample period, Hispanics are much more likely to be employed at low wages than other racial and ethnic groups. The majority of these low-wage Latino

Table 9.1 Characteristics of low-wage hourly workers

	Workers paid hourly earning			
	Exactly MW	Below MW	Within 125% of MW	All workers paid hourly
Average age	29.2	30.2	31.0	37.2
	(14.3)	(14.4)	(14.7)	(13.5)
Teen (ages 16–19)	0.33	0.26	0.27	0.08
	(0.47)	(0.44)	(0.44)	(0.27)
Young adult (ages 20–24)	0.21	0.24	0.22	0.14
	(0.41)	(0.43)	(0.41)	(0.35)
Latino	0.27	0.16	0.20	0.14
	(0.45)	(0.37)	(0.40)	(0.35)
Native-born Latino	0.09	0.06	0.08	0.06
	(0.29)	(0.25)	(0.27)	(0.25)
Foreign-born Latino	0.18	0.10	0.12	0.08
	(0.38)	(0.30)	(0.33)	(0.27)
White (non-Hispanic)	0.55	0.67	0.61	0.68
	(0.50)	(0.47)	(0.49)	(0.47)
Black (non-Hispanic)	0.12	0.11	0.14	0.13
	(0.33)	(0.31)	(0.35)	(0.33)
Female	0.59	0.64	0.59	0.50
	(0.49)	(0.48)	(0.49)	(0.50)
Less than high school graduate	0.46	0.34	0.37	0.17
	(0.50)	(0.48)	(0.48)	(0.38)
Sample size	29,441	47,795	165,491	1,440,822

Note: Shown are the means (standard deviations) based on individual-level data from the CPS-ORG during the period 1994–2007 for workers who report being paid hourly, weighted using the outgoing rotation weights. Workers who earn less than $1 per hour or more than $100 per hour are not included. Latinos are all individuals who identify themselves as Hispanic. Native-born Latinos are Hispanics born in the US, and foreign-born Latinos are Hispanics born outside of the US and outlying areas.

workers are foreign-born, although about one-third of low-wage Latino workers are US-born. Table 9.1 also indicates that women and individuals who have not completed high school are disproportionately employed in low-wage jobs.[10]

We examine four groups of teenagers and low-education adults: Latino immigrants, Latino natives, non-Hispanic whites, and non-Hispanic blacks. All individuals who identify themselves as being of Hispanic origin or descent are considered Hispanic (Latino) in this analysis. Latino immigrants are Hispanic individuals who were born in Latin America (Mexico, Central America, and South America), Cuba, or the Dominican Republic and were not US citizens at birth. Latino natives are Hispanic individuals who report being born in the US (not in an outlying area such as Puerto Rico) and who were US citizens at birth.[11] In this analysis, non-Hispanic whites and blacks are individuals who identified themselves as white or black but did not identify themselves as Hispanic. Hispanic individuals, therefore, can be of any race. Our samples do not include other non-Hispanic individuals, such as Asians, because sample sizes are relatively small for such groups. Non-Hispanic whites and blacks are not divided into immigrants and natives because very few (less than 2%) are immigrants.[12]

We analyze two labor market outcomes: average hourly earnings and employment. Individuals who are employed during the survey week report how much they earn per hour, week, or other time period. Our earnings analysis focuses on individuals who are paid hourly in order to reduce measurement error.[13] The earnings analysis also only includes individuals who earn at least $1 per hour and at most $100 per hour, again in order to reduce measurement error.[14] Earnings and the minimum wage are corrected for inflation with the monthly consumer price index for urban wage earners (CPI-W).

Table 9.2 reports descriptive statistics for our samples. Real average hourly earnings and employment are both considerably lower among teenagers than among adults who do not have a high school diploma. Reflecting the fact that most immigrants arrive as young adults and not as children, only 4% of the teenage sample is foreign-born Latino compared with 33% of the low-education adult sample. The proportions composed of native-born Latinos and non-Hispanic blacks are similar for the two samples at about 10% and 15%, respectively.

Table 9.2 Descriptive statistics for samples of teenagers and low-education adults

	Teenagers	Adults
Real hourly earnings	7.63	10.59
(Conditional on employment)	(2.89)	(4.99)
Employed	0.42	0.61
	(0.49)	(0.49)
Average age	17.5	36.1
	(1.1)	(10.0)
Foreign-born Latino	0.04	0.33
	(0.20)	(0.47)
Native-born Latino	0.11	0.09
	(0.32)	(0.29)
White (non-Hispanic)	0.69	0.44
	(0.46)	(0.50)
Black (non-Hispanic)	0.16	0.15
	(0.36)	(0.35)
Female	0.49	0.47
	(0.50)	(0.50)
Sample size, all	278,351	259,296
Sample size, hourly workers	110,199	116,601

Note: Shown are means (standard deviations) based on weighted individual-level data from the CPS-ORG during the period 1994–2007. Low-education adults do not have a high school diploma and are ages 20–54. The sample for average hourly earnings only includes workers who report being paid hourly and earn at least $1 per hour and no more than $100 per hour. Earnings are deflated using the CPI-W (January 2007 = 100). Latinos are individuals who identify themselves as Hispanic. Native-born Latinos are only Hispanics born in the US (not outlying areas), and foreign-born Latinos are Hispanics born in Latin America, Cuba, or the Dominican Republic.

As suggested by the age and education characteristics of low-wage workers, a large fraction of teenagers and low-education adults earn near the minimum wage. Figures 9.3 through 9.6 show the distribution of hourly earnings relative to the minimum wage among teenagers and low-education adults in our samples. Figures 9.3 and 9.5 show the fraction of workers in each race/ethnicity group earning various percentiles of the minimum wage (measured in 25% increments), and Figs. 9.4 and 9.6 show the cumulative density function (the cumulative fraction of workers earning various percentiles of the minimum wage) for each group.

The distributions indicate several interesting patterns. A large proportion of teens earn about 125% of the minimum wage, as indicated by the spike in the earnings distribution in Fig. 9.3. Very few teens earn more than 200% of the minimum wage, as shown in Fig. 9.4. Overall, given how close together the lines are on Figs. 9.3 and 9.4, the data suggest few differences in the distribution of hourly earnings by race/ethnicity/nativity among teens.

Among low-education adults, in contrast, more differences are apparent across these groups (Figs. 9.5 and 9.6). Latino immigrants and non-Hispanic blacks have the lowest earnings, followed by Latino natives. The earnings distribution is less centered on the minimum wage among low-education adults than among teenagers, suggesting that the minimum wage plays a larger role in the teens' labor market outcomes.

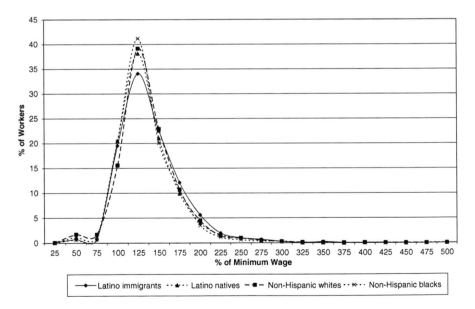

Fig. 9.3 Distribution of hourly earnings relative to minimum wage among teenagers

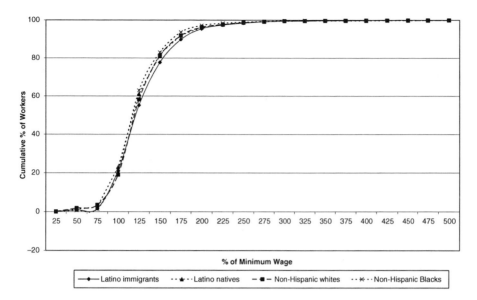

Fig. 9.4 Cumulative distribution of hourly earnings relative to minimum wage among teenagers

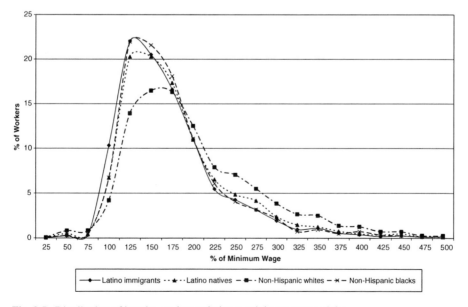

Fig. 9.5 Distribution of hourly earnings relative to minimum wage adults

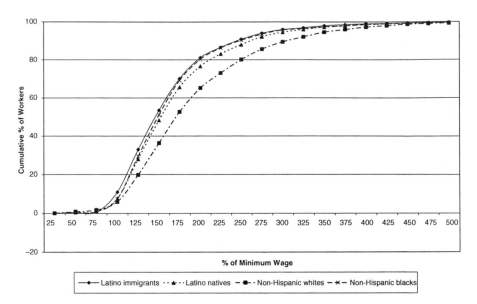

Fig. 9.6 Cumulative distribution of hourly earnings relative to minimum wage adults

Methods

We estimate two main regression models, one for hourly earnings and one for employment. The explanatory variable of interest in both models is the minimum wage. We expect to see a positive relationship between the minimum wage and hourly earnings, and a negative relationship between the minimum wage and employment. Our regression model for earnings, estimated using Ordinary Least Squares (OLS), is as follows:

$$\text{in Wage}_{ist} = \alpha + \beta_1 \ln \text{MW}_{st} + \beta_2 \text{Demographics}_i$$
$$+ \beta_3 \text{Business Cycle}_{st} + \beta_4 S_s + \beta_5 T_t + \varepsilon_{ist}, \tag{9.1}$$

where i indexes individuals, s indexes states, and t indexes time periods (survey month and year) in individual-level data. The dependent variable, $ln\ Wage_{ist}$, is the natural log of real hourly earnings for individual i, who lives in state s and is surveyed at time t. Again, only workers who are paid hourly are included in the earnings samples. Because the wage variables are measured in logs, the coefficient on the real minimum wage variable, β_1, gives the elasticity of average hourly earnings with respect to the minimum wage (the percentage change in wages if the minimum wage increases by 1%).

The regressions include several other variables besides the minimum wage. Variables measuring individuals' age and its square and an indicator variable for females are included to control for demographic characteristics that might be related to earnings. For example, females are more likely to work as wait staff, a job that often pays less than the minimum wage because of tips. We include several controls for state economic conditions (the business cycle): the natural log of real personal income per capita, the real contract value of residential building permits, the number of initial unemployment claims, and the state unemployment rate in that month and year.[15] The regressions include state fixed effects to control for any time-invariant factors that affect average wages within a state and time fixed effects to control for any time factors that are common across states, such as the national business cycle.

We pool the data for the various race/ethnicity/nativity groups and interact the minimum wage variable with an indicator variable for each group. We estimate separate regressions for teenagers and low-education adults since the coefficients may differ considerably across these groups. The standard errors are clustered on group, state, and time period to control for heteroscedasticity.

The regression model for employment is similar to the earnings model except that we use a probit model because the dependent variable, $Work_{ist}$, is a dichotomous variable that equals 1 if an individual is employed and 0 otherwise:

$$Work_{ist} = \Phi(\alpha + \beta_1 \ln MW_{st} + \beta_2 Demographics_i$$
$$+ \beta_3 Business\ Cycle_{st} + \beta_4 S_s + \beta_5 T_t + \varepsilon_{ist}), \tag{9.2}$$

where Φ is the standard cumulative normal distribution. For ease of interpretation, we report the derivatives of the estimated probit coefficients for the minimum wage variable (which is again interacted with indicator variables for the various race/ethnicity/nativity groups). These derivatives (changes in probability) are evaluated at the sample means for continuous variables. The reported results, therefore, can be interpreted like results from an OLS regression; they indicate the percentage point change in the probability of employment if the minimum wage increases by 1%. The employment regressions also include variables measuring age and its square, sex, business cycle controls, and state and survey month/year fixed effects. Observations are clustered on group, state, and survey month/year.

Results

The minimum wage has a major effect on earnings among teenagers and, to a lesser extent, among low-ducation adults. Table 9.3 shows the results from the earnings regressions, with teenagers in column 1 and adults in column 3. Among teenagers, average hourly earnings increase by about 1.9% when the minimum wage increases by 10% (column 1). The estimated elasticities are similar in magnitude for all four race/ethnicity/nativity groups of teenagers.[16] The results for low-education adults are smaller than those for teens and differ across groups. A 10% increase in the minimum wage raises average hourly earnings by about 0.4% among foreign-born Latino adults who do not have a high school diploma, 1% among native-born Latinos, 1.3% among non-Hispanic whites, and 0.6% among non-Hispanic blacks (column 3).

Applying the basic competitive model to the earnings results suggests that minimum wages will have a more adverse employment effect among teens than among

Table 9.3 Effect of the minimum wage on average hourly earnings and employment

	Teens		Low-education adults	
	Earnings	Employment	Earnings	Employment
Foreign-born Latino	0.195**	−0.065**	0.041†	0.101**
	(0.018)	(0.022)	(0.025)	(0.022)
Native-born Latino	0.191**	−0.085**	0.096**	0.044*
	(0.018)	(0.021)	(0.025)	(0.022)
White	0.195**	−0.012	0.126**	0.048*
(non-Hispanic)	(0.018)	(0.021)	(0.025)	(0.022)
Black	0.187**	−0.144**	0.064*	−0.029
(non-Hispanic)	(0.018)	(0.021)	(0.025)	(0.022)

$^{\dagger}p < 0.1$; $^{*}p < 0.05$; $^{**}p < 0.01$

Note: "Earnings" columns report estimated coefficients on the natural log of the real minimum wage from OLS regressions in which the dependent variable is the natural log of the real hourly earnings. "Employment" columns report derivatives of estimated coefficients on the natural log of the real minimum wage from probit regressions in which the dependent variable equals 1 if an individual is employed and 0 otherwise. All regressions include age, age^2, sex, business cycle controls, and state and survey month/year fixed effects. Less-educated adults are ages 20–54 and do not have a high school diploma; teens are ages 16–19. Robust, clustered standard errors are in parentheses. Observations are weighted using the outgoing rotation weights.

low-education adults and a more adverse effect among non-Hispanic white adults than among blacks or Latinos, particularly foreign-born Latinos. These predictions are only partially borne out in the employment results, which are also shown in Table 9.3. Column 2 reports the employment regression results for teenagers and column 4 for adults.

For both teens and low-education adults, the adverse employment effects of higher minimum wages appear to be greatest among non-Hispanic blacks. Among teenagers, the estimates indicate that a 10% increase in the minimum wage lowers the probability of employment by about 0.7 percentage points for foreign-born Latinos, 0.9 percentage points for native-born Latinos, and 1.4 percentage points for non-Hispanic blacks (column 2). There is no significant disemployment effect among non-Hispanic white teens. For low-education adults, higher minimum wages are not significantly adversely associated with employment among any of the groups examined here. The minimum wage is actually *positively* associated with employment among both foreign- and native-born Latinos and non-Hispanic whites. This positive impact is largest among foreign-born Latino adults, with a 10% increase in the minimum wage boosting the probability of employment by about one percentage point (column 4).

Taken together, the results suggest that higher minimum wages boost earnings among both teenagers and low-education adults and have adverse employment effects among most groups of teenagers. Our failure to find a negative employment effect among white teenagers and adults appears, at face value, to contradict the predictions of the simple supply and demand model presented above. The model predicts that if minimum wages are positively associated with earnings, then minimum wages should be negatively associated with employment. We next investigate two potential reasons for these rather anomalous results: substitution across skill groups and sub-minimum wages among undocumented immigrants.

Substitution across Skill Groups

Substitution across workers with different skill levels could help reconcile our results with the competitive model. Employers might replace the least-skilled workers with more skilled workers when the minimum wage increases. If higher minimum wages induce an increase in the quantity of labor supplied, as the simple model suggests would happen, then employers should be able to choose among workers and hire the more skilled ones. The results in Table 9.3 suggest that employers substitute adult workers—particularly foreign-born Latinos—for teenage workers when the minimum wage increases.

To further investigate this possibility, we examine the inter-relationship between minimum wages and age and education, which are proxies for skill.[17] If firms substitute more skilled workers for less skilled workers as the minimum wage increases, workers who are older and have more education should face less adverse employment effects than younger and less-educated workers. Wages among more-skilled workers also may be less tied to the minimum wage than among less-skilled workers, for whom the minimum wage may act as a binding floor. We estimated the following basic probit model to examine whether the employment effect of the minimum wage differs by age and education:

$$\text{Work}_{ist}$$
$$= \Phi \left(\begin{array}{l} \alpha + \beta_1 \ln \text{MW}_{st} + \beta_2 \ln \text{MW}_{st} * \text{Age}_i + \beta_3 \ln \text{MW}_{st} * \text{No high school}_i \\ + \beta_4 \text{Demographics}_i + \beta_5 \text{Business Cycle}_{st} + \beta_6 \text{S}_s + \beta_7 \text{T}_t + \varepsilon_{ist} \end{array} \right),$$
$$(9.3)$$

where the dependent variable is a dummy variable indicating whether an individual is employed. In the regressions for teenagers, the minimum wage variable is interacted with dummy variables for each of the four possible ages (16, 17, 18, and 19).[18] In the regression for low-education adults, the minimum wage is interacted with a linear age variable. The minimum wage variable is also interacted with a dummy variable that equals 1 if an individual has at most 8 years of education. These interactions allow us to examine how the effect of the minimum wage varies by age and education, our proxies for skill. All of these interactions are further interacted with dummy variables for the four race/ethnicity/nativity groups to allow us to examine how the effects differ across these groups.

The regressions also include demographic controls for age and sex, a dummy variable for having at most 8 years of education, controls for the business cycle, and state and month/year fixed effects. As in all regressions here, observations are weighted using the CPS outgoing rotation group weights and the standard errors are clustered on race/ethnic group, state, and survey date. We report derivatives of the

Table 9.4 Effects of the minimum wage on employment by age and education

	Foreign-born Latino (1)	Native-born Latino (2)	White (3)	Black (4)
Teens				
Minimum wage* age 16	−0.144*	−0.125**	−0.120**	−0.134**
	(0.067)	(0.045)	(0.031)	(0.049)
Minimum wage* age 17	−0.064	−0.061	−0.058*	−0.093*
	(0.066)	(0.044)	(0.029)	(0.047)
Minimum wage* age 18	0.058	0.037	0.001	−0.022
	(0.064)	(0.045)	(0.030)	(0.047)
Minimum wage* age 19	0.085	0.082†	0.020	0.005
	(0.064)	(0.046)	(0.032)	(0.048)
Minimum wage* no high school	−0.083	−0.255**	−0.282**	−0.301**
	(0.078)	(0.079)	(0.078)	(0.079)
Low-education adults:				
Minimum wage	0.075	0.021	0.112*	−0.160*
	(0.052)	(0.059)	(0.053)	(0.065)
Minimum wage* age	0.001	0.001	0.001	0.003*
	(0.001)	(0.001)	(0.001)	(0.001)
Minimum wage* no high school	−0.040	−0.074*	−0.118**	−0.152**
	(0.029)	(0.029)	(0.029)	(0.030)

†$p < 0.1$; *$p < .05$; **$p < 0.01$

Note: Shown are estimated derivatives of coefficients on the natural log of the real minimum wage from probit regressions; the dependent variable equals 1 if an individual is employed and 0 otherwise. All regressions include age and age ^{2} (dummy variables for age 16, age 17, and age 18 in the teenage regressions), sex, a dummy variable for no high school (8 years of education or less), business cycle controls, and state and survey month/year fixed effects. Separate regressions were estimated for teens and low-education adults. Less-educated adults are ages 20–54 and do not have a high school diploma; teens are ages 16–19. Robust, clustered standard errors are in parentheses. Observations are weighted using the outgoing rotation weights.

probit coefficients in Table 9.4. These results indicate the percentage point change in the probability of employment if the minimum wage increases by 1%. The top panel shows results for teens, and the bottom panel for adults who do not have a high school diploma.

The results suggest there is skill substitution among teens in response to a higher minimum wage. Among teenagers, the adverse employment effect of the minimum wage decreases monotonically with age for all four groups. In other words, increases in the minimum wage have larger disemployment effects among younger teens, particularly those who are age 16, than among older teens. The education interaction terms for teens similarly indicate that a higher minimum wage typically lowers employment among teens who have at most an 8th-grade education compared with those who have at least some high school (or more) education. Interestingly, the education result does not hold for foreign-born Latino teens (row 5, column 1), who have the lowest average levels of education among teenagers.

Some of the results for adults also suggest skill substitution. First, the "main effect" of higher minimum wages is to boost employment among low-education white adults and reduce employment among low-education black adults (row 6). Looking at the interaction terms for the minimum wage and age among adults who have not completed high school, we generally do not find that the employment effect of the minimum wage differs by age (row 7). Only among blacks does the effect of the minimum wage depend on age, with older low-education blacks experiencing relative employment gains when the minimum wage rises. That effect is consistent with skill substitution if older workers are more skilled than younger workers.

The education interaction terms for low-education adults are generally consistent with skill substitution. The results indicate that any disemployment effect of higher minimum wages is larger (more negative) among adults who have not gone to high school than among high school dropouts for native-born Latinos, whites, and blacks.

The employment effect does not differ by education among foreign-born Latinos, however (row 8, column 1). This suggests that education may be less of a signal of skill among Latino immigrants than among other groups. This result is also consistent with the results for foreign-born Latino workers in Table 9.3: minimum wages have a smaller positive effect on earnings among foreign-born Latino workers than among other low-education adults, and higher minimum wages appear to boost employment among foreign-born Latinos. This occurs despite the fact that foreign-born Latinos have considerably less education, on average, than the other workers in our sample. This suggests that, among the pool of low-education workers, immigrants may be the most productive workers. A positive selection process on unobservable characteristics, such as motivation and willingness to work hard, may underlie this finding, although other factors, such as undocumented status, may also play a role.

Legal Status and Years of US Residence

Our main results indicate that the positive relationship between the minimum wage and average hourly earnings is smaller among adult Latino immigrants than among other workers and that higher minimum wages are associated with an *increase* in employment among adult Latino immigrants. Employers may substitute adult Latino immigrants for other workers when the minimum wage rises if adult Latino immigrants are perceived as more productive than other low-skilled workers. Another possibility is that many adult Latino immigrants are paid less than the legal minimum wage because they are undocumented immigrants, causing increases in the minimum wage to have less effect among this group and causing employers to substitute toward them when the minimum wage increases. Indeed, in our sample of adult low-education hourly-paid workers, 4.8% of immigrant workers report earning less than the legal minimum, compared with 3.8% of native-born workers.[19]

Theoretically, the effect of minimum wages could be smaller or larger among undocumented immigrants than among those who are legally present in the US.[20]

Employers may be more likely to pay undocumented workers less than the legal minimum, particularly if they are aware that the workers lack legal status and, therefore, are unlikely to complain to authorities for fear of being deported. An employer who is already breaking the law in knowingly hiring undocumented workers may also disregard minimum wage laws. If so, then undocumented workers are less likely to be affected by changes in minimum wage laws than legal immigrants.

However, undocumented workers tend to be less skilled than legal immigrants. They have less education, are younger, and have fewer years of US experience, on average (11, 12). Hence undocumented workers may be more likely to earn low wages than legal immigrants and, therefore, be more affected by changes in minimum wages. On the other hand, despite lower education levels, it could be that illegal immigrants work harder under tougher conditions, making them more productive in spite of their low education levels. On a theoretical level, it is simply not clear whether undocumented immigrants are more or less affected by minimum wage laws than other workers.

Undocumented immigrants appear to compose a large and growing fraction of the low-wage foreign-born labor force. Estimates suggest that up to one-half of all low-skilled immigrant workers—or about 3.1 million people—were undocumented in 2005 (13). Many of these undocumented workers are Latinos, as Latin American countries accounted for at least 80% of undocumented immigrants present in the US in 2000 (14, 15).

The CPS does not ask about visa type or other direct indicators of legal status. However, years of US residence, country of origin, and US citizenship––variables that are included in the CPS—should be associated with whether an immigrant is undocumented.[21] Most undocumented immigrants have been present in the US for less time than legal immigrants, and the majority of undocumented immigrants are from Mexico.[22] We investigate whether years of US residence, being from Mexico, and being a naturalized US citizen influence the impact of minimum wages on earnings and employment among immigrants from Latin America.[23]

Within the sample of Latin American immigrants, we interacted the minimum wage variable with a linear variable measuring years of US residence and with dummy variables indicating whether an immigrant was from Mexico and whether an immigrant reported being a naturalized US citizen. We estimated the following regression model:

$$\text{Labor Market Outcome}_{ist} = \alpha + \beta_1 \ln \text{MW}_{st} + \beta_2 \ln \text{MW}_{st}*\text{Years in U S}_i$$

$$+\beta_3 \ln \text{MW}_{st}* \text{Mexico}_i + \beta_4 \ln \text{MW}_{st}* \text{ naturalized U.S. citizen}_i \qquad (9.4)$$

$$+\beta_5 \text{Demographics}_i + \beta_6 \text{Business Cycle}_{st} + \beta_7 S_s + \beta_8 T_t + \varepsilon_{ist},$$

where the dependent variable is the natural log of hourly earnings (and the regression is estimated using OLS) or a dummy variable that equals 1 if an individual is employed (and a probit model is estimated). The set of demographic controls includes the number of years that an individual has lived in the US, the Mexico and naturalized US citizen dummy variables (the "main effects"), as well as age, age squared, and sex. As before, we report estimated OLS coefficients for the earnings regressions and marginal probit coefficients for the employment regressions.

If undocumented immigrants tend to have fewer years of US residence and minimum wage laws affect undocumented immigrants less because employers pay them less than the minimum wage, then we expect to find that the impact of the minimum wage on earnings and employment grows with years of US residence. A similar result should hold for US citizenship—individuals who report being US citizens should be more affected by minimum wage laws if employers violate these laws when paying undocumented immigrants. If immigrants from Mexico are more likely to be undocumented and undocumented workers are more likely to be paid less than the minimum wage, then the minimum wage should have less of an impact on earnings and employment among Mexicans.

Table 9.5 shows the results. Few of the estimated coefficients are significant for teenagers. This is not surprising since the teenage samples are relatively small because most immigrants come as adults. The results for teens indicate that years of

Table 9.5 Effect of the minimum wage among Latin American immigrants

	Teens		Low-education adults	
	Earnings (1)	Employment (2)	Earnings (3)	Employment (4)
Minimum wage	0.120	−0.002	0.091	0.081
	(0.155)	(0.161)	(0.058)	(0.068)
Years of US residence	−0.037†	−0.010	0.009*	0.007†
	(0.019)	(0.019)	(0.004)	(0.004)
From Mexico	0.089	0.316	−0.058	0.206*
	(0.247)	(0.196)	(0.076)	(0.093)
Naturalized US citizen	0.105	−0.248	−0.306**	−0.379**
	(0.363)	(0.241)	(0.100)	(0.108)
Minimum wage* years of US residence	0.021†	0.002	−0.001	−0.004†
	(0.011)	(0.011)	(0.002)	(0.002)
Minimum wage* from Mexico	−0.054	−0.134	0.017	−0.134**
	(0.142)	(0.143)	(0.043)	(0.047)
Minimum wage* naturalized US citizen	−0.041	0.195	0.216**	0.220**
	(0.203)	(0.219)	(0.056)	(0.054)

$^{\dagger}p < 0.1$; $^{*}p < 0.05$; $^{**}p < 0.01$

Note: The sample includes only immigrants from Latin America, Cuba, and the Dominican Republic. Columns 1 and 3 show estimated coefficients on the natural log of the real minimum wage from OLS regressions; the dependent variable is the natural log of the real hourly earnings. Columns 2 and 4 show estimated derivatives of coefficients on the natural log of the real minimum wage from probit regressions; the dependent variable equals 1 if an individual is employed and 0 otherwise. All regressions include age, age^2, sex, US citizenship status, state and survey month/year fixed effects, and business cycle controls. Less-educated adults are ages 20–54 and do not have a high school diploma; teens are ages 16–19. Robust, clustered standard errors are in parentheses. Observations are weighted using the outgoing rotation weights.

US residence is negatively associated with earnings for foreign-born teens—a surprising result—and that higher minimum wages boost wages more among teens the longer they have lived in the US.

In the adult low-education sample, both earnings and employment increase with years of US residence (row 2) and are lower among naturalized US citizens (row 4). Immigrants from Mexico are more likely to be working than other Latino immigrants (row 3, column 4). Any adverse impact of higher minimum wages on employment increases with years of US residence, which is consistent with the hypothesis that legal immigrants are more affected by minimum wage increases than the undocumented (row 5, column 4). The positive wage effect of higher minimum wages is also larger among naturalized US citizens (row 7, column 3). Any adverse employment effect is larger among immigrants from Mexico, who are more likely to be undocumented (row 6, column 4). In addition, the employment effect of higher minimum wages is positive (or less negative) among naturalized US citizens (row 7, column 4).

These results provide mixed support for our hypothesis that undocumented immigrants are less likely to be affected by changes in the minimum wage, which could account for the somewhat anomalous results for Latin American immigrants. We caution that we are not able to identify which immigrants in the CPS data are undocumented and use only crude indicators of undocumented status. Other researchers have noted, for example, that the citizenship variable overstates naturalization among recent immigrants—many of whom are likely undocumented (16). Correcting the citizenship variable and combining CPS data with better data on undocumented immigrants, such as data from the Mexican Migration Project and the Latin American Migration Project, might shed more light on non-compliance and the effect of minimum wages among undocumented immigrants.

Conclusion

This chapter examined whether the impact of minimum wages differs between foreign- and native-born Latinos and their non-Hispanic counterparts in the US. Data from 1994 to 2007 indicate that higher minimum wages are associated with an increase in teens' hourly earnings that is similar across race/ethnicity/nativity groups. However, the disemployment effect is smaller among foreign-born Latino teenagers than among their black and native-born Latino counterparts and non-existent among white teens. This, combined with other results here, suggests substitution across skill groups as the minimum wage increases. Among adults who do not have a high school diploma (or equivalent), our results indicate that the wage-boosting effect of higher minimum wages is smallest among foreign-born Latinos. Employment among low-education adult Latino foreign- and native-born workers (and among whites) is positively associated with the minimum wage.

Our results suggest more non-compliance with minimum wage laws among low-education Latino immigrants, many of whom are undocumented, but these findings are not conclusive. Even though minimum wage laws apply equally to citizens, legal immigrants, and the undocumented, workers who lack legal status might not know about their worker rights or might be reluctant to confront employers for fear of reprisal.

Acknowledgement   We thank participants of the Latinos and Public Policy sessions at the Inter-University Program on Latino Research conference "SIGLO XXI: Economies of Class, Economies of Culture" (Austin, Texas, April 2007) for comments on this chapter. The views expressed here are those of the authors and do not necessarily reflect those of the Federal Reserve Bank of Dallas or Federal Reserve System.

Notes

1. Most US data sets (including the ones we use here) ask individuals whether they are Hispanic, not Latino. We treat the two as equivalent here. Individuals of Spanish ancestry might identify themselves as Hispanic but usually would not be considered Latinos, while individuals of Brazilian ancestry might not identify themselves as Hispanic but usually would be considered Latinos.
2. Authors' calculations based on education statistics from Bureau of the Census data available at http://www.census.gov/population/www/socdemo/education/cps2006.html [accessed April 4, 2008].
3. Authors' calculations based on summary tables from the Census 2000 Summary File (SF 3).
4. For a survey, see Neumark and Wascher (2006).
5. For formal models of the effects across skill levels of minimum wage increases, see, for example, Connolly (17) and Lang and Kahn (18).
6. Another potential explanation is imperfectly competitive labor markets (monopsony). For an overview, see Zavodny (19).
7. The tip credit specifies a lower minimum wage (currently $2.13 per hour) for employees who earn tips. When tips are included, the tipped workers must earn at least the legal minimum wage (currently $7.25 at the federal level). We also do not control for changes in the Earned Income Tax Credit (EITC) or for welfare reform, which might affect the incentive to work among low-skilled workers. The year fixed effects capture any national-level effects of changes in such factors. Neumark and Wascher (1) examine the effects of minimum wages and the EITC among teens and young adults.
8. Because the July 2007 increase went into effect on the 24th of that month, its direct effects would show up in the August 2007 survey (since the survey asks about the week that includes the 12th of the month).
9. The table, like all of the earnings analyses presented here, is based only on workers paid an hourly wage. The results are qualitatively similar if workers paid at other frequencies are included, although the workers then tend to be older and have more education. Unlike the other tables shown here, Table 9.1 includes all Latinos, regardless of place of birth. The samples we use later on restrict native-born Latinos to Hispanics born in the US (and not in outlying areas such a Puerto Rico) and foreign-born Latinos to Hispanics born in Latin America, Cuba, or the Dominican Republic.
10. The share of workers who lack a high school degree or its equivalent is overstated in the table as some people may yet go on to complete such a degree in the future.

11. People born in outlying areas (e.g., Puerto Rico and Guam) are US citizens at birth. These people are not included in the sample used here.
12. The small shares of immigrants among non-Hispanic whites and blacks are due to the fact that our sample is limited to adults who lack a high school degree and teens.
13. For a discussion of measurement error in earnings variables in the CPS, see Lemieux (20).
14. This restriction drops 0.04% of the teenage sample and 0.07% of the low-education adult sample.
15. The personal income data are deflated using the personal consumption expenditures index. Both are published quarterly by the Bureau of Economic Analysis. Real personal income is linearly interpolated throughout quarters. The population data are data for July of each year from the Bureau of the Census and are linearly interpolated. The initial claims and permits data are from BLS and Census, respectively, and are seasonally adjusted. The unemployment rate data are published monthly by the Bureau of Labor Statistics and are seasonally adjusted.
16. Only the estimated elasticities for white and black teenagers are statistically significantly different from each other. Nonetheless, the difference is small in economic terms.
17. Another way to examine substitution across workers is to look for differences across groups in transitions into and out of employment using panel data. This approach would involve matching individual records across two consecutive years in the CPS. The CPS is a survey of housing units (residences), not household or individuals. It does not track individuals or households over time, so movers disappear from the sample. We do not pursue this approach because young adults and immigrants tend to have relatively high mobility rates and therefore are not likely to reappear in the CPS.
18. Because the minimum wage variable is interacted with dummy variables for all four age groups for teens, those regressions do not include a "main effect" variable for the minimum wage. In other words, $\beta_1 = 0$ in the regressions for teenagers.
19. The literature on immigrant-native differentials in non-compliance with minimum wage laws generally finds no significant difference between immigrants and natives in the fraction earning less than the federal minimum wage (21–23).
20. Winegarden and Khor (24) make a similar argument in modeling the effect of undocumented immigration on unemployment rates among US-born youth and minority workers when wages are sticky.
21. The CPS reports year of entry in intervals, and we used the midpoint of those intervals to calculate the numbers of years of US residence. Our approach obviously assumes that the CPS includes some undocumented immigrants. Bean et al. (25) and Hanson (26) both explicitly state that the CPS includes undocumented immigrants. Previous studies have used the CPS to examine undocumented immigrants (e.g., 15, 27–31).
22. In 2004, over half of Mexican immigrants present in the US were undocumented, including at least 80% of those who entered during the 1990s and early 2000s (29, 30). Because of the 1997 Nicaraguan Adjustment and Central American Relief Act (NACARA) as well as greater distance from the US border, immigrants from other Latin American countries are more likely than Mexicans to be legally present in the US. See Kaushal (27) for a discussion of the effect of NACARA on earnings and employment.
23. We caution that the quality of self-reported variables on immigration status is an issue in this type of exercise. While it seems unlikely that undocumented immigrants would report being naturalized US citizens, misreporting of citizenship status is a well-known problem in the literature that relies on CPS and decennial Census data (16, 32).

Appendix

Table A1 States that exceeded the federal minimum wage

	1994	1995	1996	1997	1998	1999	2000	2001	2002	2003	2004	2005	2006	2007
Alaska	X	X	X	X	X	X	X	X	X	X	X	X	X	X
Arizona														X
Arkansas													X	X
California				X	X	X	X	X	X	X	X	X	X	X
Colorado														X
Connecticut	X	X	X	X	X	X	X	X	X	X	X	X	X	X
Delaware			X	X		X	X	X	X	X	X	X	X	X
D.C.	X	X	X	X	X	X	X	X	X	X	X	X	X	X
Florida													X	X
Hawaii	X	X	X	X	X	X	X	X	X	X	X	X	X	X
Illinois											X	X	X	X
Iowa	X	X	X											X
Kentucky														X
Maine								X	X	X	X		X	X
Maryland													X	X
Massachusetts			X	X	X	X	X	X	X	X	X	X	X	X
Michigan													X	X
Minnesota												X	X	X
Missouri														X
Montana														X
Nevada														X
New Hampshire														X
New Jersey	X	X	X	X								X	X	X
New York												X	X	X
North Carolina														X
Ohio														X
Oregon	X	X	X	X	X	X	X	X	X	X	X	X	X	X
Pennsylvania														X
Rhode Island	X	X	X	X		X	X	X	X	X	X	X	X	X
Vermont		X	X	X	X	X	X	X	X	X	X	X	X	X
Washington	X	X	X	X	X	X	X	X	X	X	X	X	X	X
West Virginia													X	X
Wisconsin												X	X	X

Note: The federal minimum wage rose from $4.25 an hour to $4.75 an hour in October 1996, to $5.15 an hour in September 1997, and to $5.85 in July 2007. Shown are states that exceeded the federal minimum wage at any time during the year(s) indicated.

References

1. Neumark, David, and William Wascher. 2007. "Does a Higher Minimum Wages Enhance the Effectiveness of the Earned Income Tax Credit?" NBER Working Paper No. 12915, February.
2. Neumark, David, and William Wascher. 1996. "The Effects of Minimum Wages on Teenage Employment and Enrollment: Evidence from Matched CPS Surveys." In *Research in Labor Economics, Volume 15*, ed. Solomon W. Polachek, 25–63. Greenwich, CT: JAI Press.
3. Turner, Mark D., and Berna Demiralp. 2001. "Do Higher Minimum Wages Harm Minority and Inner-City Teens?" *Review of Black Political Economy*, 28(4): 95–121.
4. Card, David. 1992a. "Using Regional Variation in Wages to Measure the Effects of the Federal Minimum Wage." *Industrial and Labor Relations Review*, 46(1): 22–37.
5. Card, David. 1992b. "Do Minimum Wages Reduce Employment? A Case Study of California, 1987–89." *Industrial and Labor Relations Review*, 46(1): 38–54.
6. Card, David, Lawrence F. Katz, and Alan B. Krueger. 1994. "Employment Effects of Minimum and Subminimum Wages: Panel Data on State Minimum Wage Laws: Comment." *Industrial and Labor Relations Review*, 47(3): 487–497.
7. Card, David, and Alan B. Krueger. 1994. "Minimum Wages and Employment: A Case Study of the Fast-Food Industry in New Jersey and Pennsylvania." *American Economic Review*, 84(4): 772–793.
8. Katz, Lawrence F., and Alan B. Krueger. 1992. "The Effect of the Minimum Wage on the Fast-Food Industry." *Industrial and Labor Relations Review*, 46(1): 6–21.
9. Mehta, Chirag, Nik Theodore, Iliana Mora, and Jennifer Wade. 2002. "Chicago's Undocumented Immigrants: An Analysis of Wages, Working Conditions, and Economic Contributions." Center for Urban Economic Development, University of Illinois at Chicago. http://www.uic.edu/cuppa/uicued/npublications/recent/undoc_full.pdf (accessed March 27, 2007).
10. Orrenius, Pia M., and Madeline Zavodny. 2008. "The Effect of Minimum Wages on Immigrants." *Industrial and Labor Relations Review*, 61(4): 544–563.
11. Jasso, Guillermina, Douglas Massey, Mark Rosenzweig, and James Smith. 2004. *"From Illegal to Legal: Estimating Previous Illegal Experience among New Legal Immigrants to the United States."* Unpublished.
12. Passel, Jeffrey S., Jennifer Van Hook, and Frank D. Bean. 2006. "Narrative Profile with Adjoining Tables of Unauthorized Migrants and other Immigrants, based on Census 2000: Characteristics and Methods." http://www.sabresys.com/whitepapers/EMS_Deliverable_2-3_022706.pdf (accessed March 23, 2007).
13. Capps, Randolph, Karina Fortuny, and Michael Fix. 2007. "Trends in the Low-Wage Immigrant Labor Force, 2000–2005." Urban Institute Report. http://www.urban.org/url.cfm?=411426 (accessed March 23, 2007).
14. Immigration and Naturalization Service (INS). 2003. *"Estimates of the Unauthorized Population Residing in the United States: 1990 to 2003."* Washington, DC: INS.
15. Passel, Jeffrey S., Randolph Capps, and Michael E. Fix. 2004. "Undocumented Immigrants: Facts and Figures." Urban Institute Immigration Studies Program Fact Sheet. http://www.urban.org/url.cfm?=1000587 (accessed March 23, 2007).
16. Passel, Jeffrey S. 2007. "Growing Share of Immigrants Choosing Naturalization." Pew Hispanic Center Report, March. http://pewhispanic.org/files/reports/74.pdf (accessed April 28, 2007).
17. Connolly, Helen. 2003. "Are Low-Educated Workers Disproportionately Affected by a Change in the Minimum Wage?" Working Paper 0301, Northeastern University.
18. Lang, Kevin, and Shulamit Kahn. 1998. "The Effect of Minimum-Wage Laws on the Distribution of Employment: Theory and Evidence." *Journal of Public Economics*, 69(1): 67–82.
19. Zavodny, Madeline. 1998. "Why Minimum Wage Hikes May Not Reduce Employment." Federal Reserve Bank of Atlanta *Economic Review*, 2(Second Quarter): 18–29.

20. Lemieux, Thomas. 2006. "Increasing Residual Wage Inequality: Composition Effects, Noisy Data, or Rising Demand for Skill?" *American Economic Review*, 96(3): 461–498.
21. Cortes, Kalena E. 2004. "Wage Effects on Immigrants from an Increase in the Minimum Wage Rate: An Analysis by Immigrant Industry Concentration." IZA Discussion Paper No. 1064.
22. Fry, Richard, and B. Lindsay Lowell. 1997. "The Incidence of Subminimum Pay among Native and Immigrant Workers." *Population Research and Policy Review*, 16(4): 363–381.
23. Trejo, Stephen J. 1998. *"Immigrant Participation in Low-Wage Labor Markets."* Santa Barbara: Mimeo, Department of Economics, University of California.
24. Winegarden, C.R., and Lay Boon Khor. 1991. "Undocumented Immigration and Unemployment of U.S. Youth and Minority Workers: Econometric Evidence." *Review of Economics and Statistics*, 73(1): 105–112.
25. Bean, Frank D., Rodolfo Corona, Rodolfo Tuiran, and Karen A. Woodrow-Lafield. 1998. "The Quantification of Migration between Mexico and the United States." In *Migration Between Mexico and the United States, Binational Study, Volume 1: Thematic Chapters*, 1–89. Washington, DC: U.S. Commission on Immigration Reform.
26. Hanson, Gordon H. 2006. "Illegal Migration from Mexico to the United States." *Journal of Economic Literature*, 44(4): 869–924.
27. Kaushal, Neeraj. 2006. "Amnesty Programs and the Labor Market Outcomes of Undocumented Workers." *Journal of Human Resources*, 41(3): 631–647.
28. Massey, Douglas S., and Katherine Bartley. 2005. "The Changing Legal Status Distribution of Immigrants: A Caution." *International Migration Review*, 39(2): 469–484
29. Passel, Jeffrey S. 2004. "Mexican Immigration to the US: the Latest Estimates." Washington, DC: Migration Policy Institute. http://www.migrationinformation.org/USfocus/display.cfm?=208 (accessed March 27, 2007).
30. Passel, Jeffrey S.2005a. "Estimates of the Size and Characteristics of the Undocumented Population." Pew Hispanic Center Report. http://pewhispanic.org/files/reports/44.pdf (accessed March 27, 2007).
31. Passel, Jeffrey S. 2005b. "Unauthorized Migrants: Numbers and Characteristics." Pew Hispanic Center Report. http://pewhispanic.org/files/reports/46.pdf (accessed March 27, 2007).
32. Passel, Jeffrey S., and Rebecca L. Clark 1998. "Immigrants in New York: Their Legal Status, Incomes and Taxes." Urban Institute Report. http://www.urban.org/url.cfm?=407432 (accessed March 22, 2007).

Chapter 10
Latino Veterans and Income:
Are There Gains from Military Service?

David L. Leal, Curt Nichols, and Jeremy M. Teigen

"We don't ask for experience, we give it!"
(Late 1970s US military recruiting slogan)

Abstract Using national cross-sectional data from 2006 through 2009, we test hypotheses concerning the effects of military service on later-life earnings for men. The results suggest that serving in the armed forces augments or penalizes civilian income later in the life cycle depending on race and ethnicity when controlling for formal educational attainment. Although some of the results for race and ethnicity vary according to model specification, we conclude that Latino veterans earn more money than nonveteran Latinos. Further, our data imply that age does not substantially condition the influence of military service on earnings after discharge. Past research has conceptualized the military experience in various ways vis-à-vis income: negatively, as a "tax" or "disruption," or positively, as an enhancement of "social capital," serving as a "bridging environment," or as a "screening device" to signal employability. Our results suggest that these perspectives should be seen as context dependent related to the individuals' race and ethnicity.

Introduction

Since the military's shift away from what Moskos termed an "institutional" to an "occupational" orientation (1–3),[1] the armed forces have, to one degree or another, openly sold themselves as a "great place to start." Implicit in such recruiting pitches is the idea that military service provides young recruits with training and life skills that will be valuable to them later in life. Social scientists have long been interested in evaluating the validity of this claim. One way this has commonly been done is

D.L. Leal (✉)
University of Texas at Austin, Austin, TX, USA
e-mail: dleal@austin.utexas.edu

D.L. Leal, S.J. Trejo (eds.), *Latinos and the Economy*, Immigrants and Minorities,
Politics and Policy, DOI 10.1007/978-1-4419-6682-7_10,
© Springer Science+Business Media, LLC 2011

through comparison of the subsequent earnings of veterans and non-veterans. Past research has revealed findings that vary not only according to the race of the veteran, but also by the era the veteran served in the military. Additionally, there is some evidence that findings can vary across the life course of veterans.

This chapter extends this line of research by using recent Bureau of Labor Statistics Current Population Survey (CPS) datasets and OLS regression analysis to test these varying hypotheses. Although some of the results for race and ethnicity vary according to model specification, we conclude that military service has a statistically significant and positive effect on the subsequent earning potential of male Latinos, which has not been found previously. Lastly, the results are inconclusive about whether military service affects subsequent earnings differently over the life-course of veterans.

Literature Review

Within social science research, there is an established body of work that has examined the individual-level relationship between military service and subsequent civilian earnings (see Teachman 2004 for an excellent summary of theory and findings, to which the first two sections of this chapter are indebted). The findings on this relationship have tended to vary by era, with a positive relationship generally found by analyses that examine the post-World War II era (4–10, 54). Furthermore, research on this era generally concludes that African-American and less well-educated Anglo non-Hispanic white men most benefit from military service (11, 12, 60). Several "status-attainment" explanations have been offered to account for this positive effect, including the indirect "social capital theory" (6, 7), the sociological "bridging environment" theory (8, 54), and the employer focused "screening device" theory (4, 7).

The positive trend in these findings became decidedly mixed in studies of the Vietnam era. While some research continued to indicate that earnings were positively affected by military service, other studies suggested a negative relationship (13–19, 61). For the latter, it is argued that military service either interrupts an individual's civilian career path or reduces the years available for accumulating wealth. Implicit in this argument is the idea that military service imposes a "tax" (57). One possibility is that this penalty is higher for those veterans who were drafted during Vietnam (15, 20). However, even during this time period, the effect was somewhat mitigated for African Americans and the less well educated, who were not as strongly "taxed" (8, 13, 16, 21).

An additional, and well-recognized difficulty, is that effects tend not to be consistent across time as the "life course" of a veteran fully develops. Indeed, some research suggests that the effect of military service on subsequent economic performance varies depending on how long the veteran has been out of uniform (19, 21–23, 59). In almost all cases, initial differences between vets and non-vets changed over time, as each had "earning curves" with different slopes and subsequently differing overall trajectories. Thus, what is most important for this kind of research is often not the initial difference but rather the lifetime difference in earning potential.

This chapter also examines a population that has received surprisingly little attention from social scientists interested in the effect of military service on potential earnings: Latinos.[2] The most important demographic change in the United States is the growing Latino share of the population. Latinos currently constitute over 15% of the population, and by some estimates, they will reach one quarter by the year 2050. As a result, the traditional black-white racial paradigm in American politics and society is gradually but steadily transforming into a more complex black-white-Latino perspective. While migration is now declining because of the recession—migration from Mexico is at three-quarters of pre-recession figures— there is little evidence of substantial returns. In addition, Latinos have relatively high birthrates in comparison to other population groups in the United States, which will also contribute to demographic change. As a consequence, the armed services are increasingly interested in Latinos as a potential source of recruits. If the future of the armed forces is a Latino future (see 24), evidence that this minority group's earning potential significantly benefits from or is reduced by military service would constitute a substantively significant finding with important implications for individuals and institutions.

Theoretical Accountings

Military Service as a Positive Start—Status-Attainment and Social Capital Theories

Sociological research has tended to account for the positive effect of military service on subsequent earnings in terms of "status-attainment" and "social capital" theories. Both are interested in how individual achievement and social mobility are secured (25). Within the status-attainment perspective, military service is viewed as an experience that intersects the normal processes of attainment like an intervening variable, and thereby alters outcomes in some (usually positive) way. In this formulation, military service serves as an opportunity for individuals to remove themselves from resource-poor surroundings and receive access to resources not otherwise available. This "new path taken" explanation tends to be stressed in research that has found military service particularly beneficial to minorities and the less educated (4, 8–10, 19, 21, 26, 27, 60).

Social capital theorists have provided an additional extension of the status-attainment perspective by stressing how military service provides individuals with additional resources to use in attainment processes (28, 29). Essentially, these scholars argue that veterans obtain more technical skills (6) and education in the military (or afterwards Mason 1970; Fligstein 1976) than do their civilian counterparts. Because the benefits of technical skills and education are well understood, military service may provide an indirect effect on subsequent earnings (10).

Another social capital explanation argues that the military serves as a "bridging environment" that helps to integrate minorities into mainstream society (Browning et al. 1973 5, 8, 19, 30, Poston et al. 1983). According to this sociological explanation, military service "generates lessons about the value of discipline and responsibility" and gives individuals "an ability to understand (how to) operate in a majority, bureaucratic environment" (60, p.711).

An additional possibility is that employers use veteran status as a "screening devise" in the hiring process (4, 7). If employers believe that veterans have the education, discipline, and understanding of organizations necessary to be a productive employee, they will select for veterans. Veteran status may, therefore, serve as a credential that is most beneficial to individuals who might otherwise be disadvantaged in job searches.

Both the status-attainment and social-capital perspectives (in all their variants) have been used to suggest that military service provides a more-or-less permanent advantage to at least some veterans. Accordingly, military service can be seen as an experience that acts as what neo-institutional scholars call a "critical juncture" in the life trajectory of an individual (31, p. 30). Service thus places the individual on a pathway that provides advantages throughout life by initiating "increasing return dynamics" (32, p. 10; see also 33).

Military Service as a Penalty—Human Capital Theory

From the "human-capital" perspective, which is now the most widely used framework for explaining the effects of military service on subsequent attainment (34), the military is seen as providing a tax on those that serve. This tax, or penalty, accrues for two reasons. First, military service reduces the civilian labor market experience of the individual. Second, it cuts the amount of "real world" training that the individual may obtain and transfer to the civilian workplace. These conclusions follow from widely accepted economic research that has found both job experience and transferable training positively affect earnings (35). Because military service tends to reduce these two variables, it is predicted that military service will have a negative effect on the subsequent earning potential of the individual (26, 36).

This theory also suggests that some particular kinds of service can provide skills and experience that substitute for civilian experience (4, 6, 22, 30). However, it bears noting that in a time of war, when service in combat specialties is most needed, such experiences usually do not provide the types of skills or experience that most employers seek. Therefore, even short wartime enlistments are thought to penalize most veterans, as evidenced in the Vietnam era. According to this theory, the negative effect of service should be more substantial early in the "earning curve" when an individual's overall accumulation of market experience is small and the few years spent in uniform represent a high proportion of overall experience. In this case, while the service tax on individuals should actually decrease over time as more civilian experienced is gained, the penalty will never entirely disappear.

Military Service as a Contextually Dependent Setback—The Life-Course Theory

From the "life-course" perspective, military service must be evaluated within the patterns of major life events; it is thought to affect earnings according to the context in which it occurs (37, 38). As such, military service may have the potential to differently influence life-course trajectories within and across cohorts. Central to a life-course theory is the notion that military service "disrupts" normal life patterns (60). The assumption is that the more severely interrupted an individual's life is (in regard to normal civilian pursuits), the greater the negative consequences of military service.

Research has concluded that age plays an important role in many of the life-course decisions of individuals. Institutional opportunities, such as obtaining a college education or entry level job, tend to be more open for younger age groups than just slightly older ones (39, 40). As military service tends to restrict access to these opportunities during peak entry periods, it can act as a penalty and hurt subsequent earnings. Thus, even if veterans were to come out slightly ahead of their peers when they leave the armed forces, they may have suffered life-course disruption penalties that cause their earnings to lag in the long run.

Data and Methods

We estimate the effect of later-life personal earnings using cross-sectional individual-level data provided by the Bureau of Labor Statistics, Current Population Survey (CPS). These data are frequently used to provide employment and earnings information for analysts and policymakers. Using a multistage stratified sample, the survey design produces a nationally representative sample of more than 50,000 households each month (41), though for this analysis the sample is pared down substantially. The nature of the CPS sampling design centers the sampling unit on households, and usually a "reference person" provides information for the remaining members. While there is some evidence that these proxy answers are accurate for some variables in the sample (42), our analyses treat the reference person as the sole respondent and hence all proxy respondents are omitted.

Another facet of the CPS design includes a rotating panel-like structure. Each month's cross-section comprises eight distinct rotation groups, two of which are entering a 4-month process. A given group is measured 4 months in a row, ignored for 8 months, then measured for another 4 months the next year. For example, a group that began in April 2008 would be in the April, May, June, and July samples in 2008 and 2009. Hence, group eight is being measured in its eighth and final month, with an 8-month break between the fourth and fifth iteration.

The relevant aspect of this rotation scheme is that earnings are only asked of "outgoing" groups, those that are in their 4th or 8th month. This pseudo-panel design means that only two of the eight groups are reporting measures of our dependent variable, and hence we lose 75% of the original sample in every month. It is also important to remember that group eight in a given sample comprises the same house-holds as group four from the same month in the prior year. Earnings can, of course, change between these two time points. Because the independent variable of interest, prior military service, cannot vary (one cannot "lose" one's military experience), repeated measurement of the same household unnecessarily complicates the analy-sis. Our data, therefore, do not include any households twice. Because the analyses consider only males,[3] each month's sample includes a remaining sample of approxi-mately 1,300 men.[4] We pool 24 of these cross-sections together and include dummy variables in the models to control for differences between months, including vari-ation stemming from economic fluctuations, unemployment trends, inflation, and other over-time changes. The earliest month we use is September, 2006 and the latest is August, 2009.

Our data are further constrained to include civilian adult men between the ages of 25 and 65, inclusively. Earlier articles that have explored the later-life earnings effect of the military experience included very young respondents. Xie (19) included 18-year-olds in his analysis, but few respondents in our samples under the age of 25 report past military service, which comports with recent general military recruiting practices. Most recruits are at least 18 upon enlistment, and those of 17 years are rare and require parental assent. Further, 4-year enlistments are the norm, so few individuals younger than 23 have military experience. At the top end, we include respondents up to the age of 65. Figures 10.1–10.3 include histograms underneath

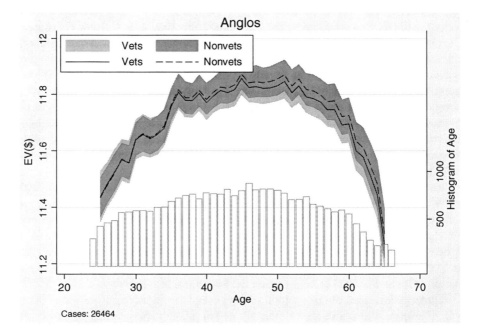

Fig. 10.1 Expected value of logged income across age, Anglos (2006–2009)

the expected value plots to depict the distribution of age for each of the three racial-ethnic groups.

To model the relationship between past military service and earnings, the analyses below rely on ordinary least squares models that regress personal earnings on a military service variable, age (measured in two ways), and other control variables.

The dependent variable is self-reported personal earnings among the employed work force at the time of measurement. The questions used to measure earnings ask respondents about their weekly earnings, but this varies depending on the way respondents report the periodicity of their pay from employers. Respondent data for those that reported hourly or weekly wages are recoded to annual earnings. The mean value for the whole male sample is $54,880 (standard deviation is $33,575), and the measure is topcoded at $150,000.

Veterans, on average, make equivalent earnings to nonveteran males (t-test p-value $= 0.54$) in the 2006–2009 data. When looking at only African-American male respondents, veterans make statistically significantly more money ($3,835 more, $p \leq 0.01$). For Latino veterans, income is remarkably higher on average ($14,315 more, $p \leq 0.001$).

The key independent variable of interest is past military service, measured by a question asking respondents whether or not they had served on active duty in the US armed forces. For clarity's sake, members currently serving in the armed forces are removed from the analysis. Approximately 18% of the sample reported past service. The veteran population has decreased in proportion to the total population over time due to generational replacement and the end of conscription. Prior conflicts, notably Vietnam, Korea, and World War II, involved massive conscription regimes that compelled millions of young men into uniform. The data examined herein sampled the US population between 2006 and 2009. Fewer than 24% of the overall sample was born before 1955—the latest time one could have been born to be 18 years old in the last year of conscription near the end of the Vietnam War.[5]

The male veteran population is older on average than the nonveteran population, 50 and 32, respectively. The mean birth year is 1965 for nonveterans and 1957 for veterans. Age is measured in two ways in the analyses: once as a simple scale-level measure, and subsequently as a series of dummy variables. Both will be used, though in an atypical way. While the linear scale measure of age is intuitively appealing because it will yield a coefficient signifying the amount of effect (increase or decrease in dollars) that corresponds to a one-unit change in years of age, it is difficult to justify the assumption that each year increase in age has an equivalent effect on earnings. The series of 41 dummy variables for each year of age in the sample makes the regression blind to ordering of age, insofar as the regression only sees 32 as different than 31, not older. The implication of this usage, though, is that the model does not impose a linear relationship assumption between age and earnings.

Some of the models include an interaction between age and military service, and herein lies the complication. We contend, at a theoretic level, that the effect of military service on earnings is contingent on a person's age. In other words, we posit a conditional relationship between service and income. Recent scholarship on the use (and abuse) of interactive models in the social sciences (43, 44) has provided

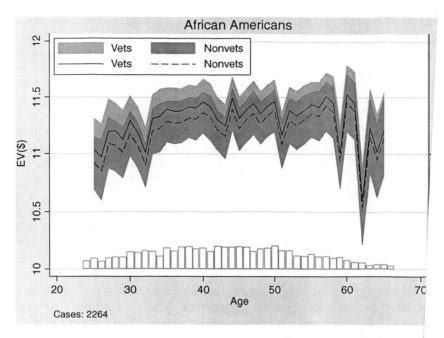

Fig. 10.2 Expected value of logged income across age, African Americans (2006–2009)

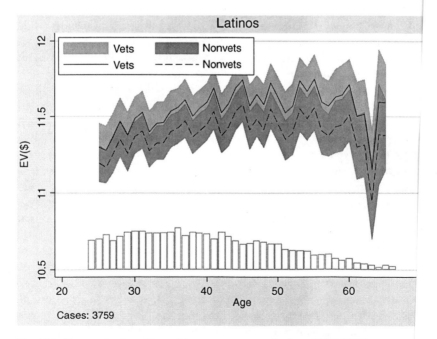

Fig. 10.3 Expected value of logged income across age, Latinos (2006–2009)

reminders that interaction terms themselves are nearly useless for interpreting conditional effects, and that models that interact two variables (age × veteran) need to include the interaction term as well as the constitutive terms (age and veteran). To include the constitutive terms when modeling age as a linear scale is simple; one multiplicative term along with age and veteran are all that is required. When measuring age as a series of 41 dummy variables, the model would need to multiply veteran by every one of these dummies, hence resulting in an untenable and difficult to interpret array of 41 age dummies, the veteran dummy, and 41 different interaction terms, as well as all the remaining control variables. Our solution is intended to clarify interpretation by including the age dummies and the veteran dummy as the constitutive terms and include a linear age × veteran variable for the interaction.

Education is an obvious and important control variable for modeling personal-level income or earnings. The CPS asks respondents about formal education levels via a precise instrument, which is left as is. Approximately 92% of male respondents report at least a high school education or equivalency, and 37% have a bachelor's degree or higher. Veterans enjoy slightly higher levels of formal education on average among the US male population in 2006–2009. On the 16-point CPS education scale, a 10 is "some college but no degree" and 11 is an occupational or vocational associate degree. The nonveteran male mean is 10.19 and the veteran male mean is 10.94 (t-test p-value ≤ 0.001).

Race and ethnicity are important correlates of personal earnings in the US. Akin to the Census Bureau's practice of measuring ethnicity (Latino versus non-Latino) apart from race (white, black, Asian, etc.), the CPS instrument allows respondents to self-report both ethnicity and race. While questionnaire options allow for respondents to select multiple races (e.g., reporting both white and black), we omit such cases and make racial categories mutually exclusive. Almost 8% of the sample described themselves as African American and 13% as Latino. Research finds that African Americans are over-represented in the military[6] while Latinos are under-represented when looking simply at their population percentages versus their shares in the military (45); although see (46).[7] More generally, there is also a growing and related literature on the political implications of veteran status in minority communities (47–49), which finds that military service is often associated with higher levels of political participation.

Results

Table 10.1 conveys the results of the regression analyses. Model 1 is the most straightforward estimation of the effect of military service in later life. Making the debatable assumption that the effect of age is linear across the lifespan and ignoring any conditional effects between age and military service, veterans make $3,425 less than nonveterans, ceteris paribus, controlling for education level, race, ethnicity, and age. Note that this model, as well as all the remaining models, includes a dummy variable (less one) for each of the months of the sample, but those coefficients and their standard errors are omitted from the table due to their substantive irrelevance.

Table 10.1 Reported personal income among men, 2006–2009

	Whole sample 1	Whole sample 2	Anglos 3	Blacks 4	Latinos 5	Anglos interaction 6	Blacks interaction 7	Latinos interaction 8
Veteran	-3425**	-1843**	-2191**	1952	6205**	-109.9	13834*	-669.2
	(546.1)	(540.4)	(586.9)	(1365)	(1875)	(2610)	(6743)	(7269)
Formal education	5275**	5259**	5300**	4987**	3106**	5300**	4984**	3105**
	(83.73)	(83.19)	(87.48)	(293.9)	(137.4)	(87.47)	(293.6)	(137.3)
Black	-13463**	-13842**			-6852**			-6856**
	(577.5)	(574.3)			(2448)			(2452)
Latino	-4660**	-4407**	-4491**	1972		-4482**	1970	
	(535.8)	(536.4)	(558.1)	(2652)		(558.4)	(2656)	
Age scale	335.1**							
	(18.82)							
Veteran × age scale						-42.97	-256.6	152.8
						(54.44)	(141.7)	(152.5)
Constant	-15312**	-20476**	-21633**	-27236**	-1319	-21655**	-27302**	-1329
	(1485)	(1655)	(1739)	(5640)	(2373)	(1740)	(5645)	(2374)
Observations	28887	28887	26464	2264	3759	26464	2264	3759
R-squared	0.227	0.249	0.237	0.245	0.217	0.237	0.247	0.218

Ordinary least squares regression, robust standard errors in parentheses (**$p \leq 0.01$, *$p \leq 0.05$).

Model 2 reports the results of an otherwise identical model that includes age dummies instead of linear age. The military service penalty halves when estimating the model in this fashion. However, the coefficient representing the effect of prior military service in both models 1 and 2 represent an estimate of the effect irrespective of age. This result, while easy to report, assumes that the effect of military service is identical for all age groups. A more substantively meaningful depiction of the results should demonstrate how the service experience influences earnings for younger versus older veterans.

Three more columns (3–5) run the same model with the age dummies among racial and ethnic subsets of the data. For Anglos, the earnings penalty is evident. Among African Americans, the effect of military service on earnings is positive but statistically insignificant. Latino veterans, however, enjoy over $6,000 more in earnings per year than their nonveteran peers when controlling for the other independent variables.

Because sociologists and economists who have studied earnings have taken the natural log (typically $ln(1 + y)$ because $ln(0)$ is undefined), Table 10.2 includes the same models as Table 10.1 but with a logged dependent variable. The magnitude of the coefficients changes, of course, befitting the considerable difference between the two dependent variables, but the differences are substantively uninteresting. [8]

However, these results do not incorporate the conditional relationship that we theorize: the effect of military service varies according to age. Columns 6–8 include the results of models similar to 3–5, but they also include the interaction term (age × veteran) discussed above.

The coefficients and their standard errors do not reveal substantively interesting information in the same fashion as purely additive models. In order to convey the conditional relationship, Figs. 10.1–10.3 plot the post-estimation expected values of logged earnings for veterans and non-veterans for each age. Each figure is a post-estimation plot using Tomz, Wittenberg, and King's (50) Clarify software within Stata, which runs a Monte Carlo simulation on the results of the regression model for the purposes of garnering substantively meaningful quantities of interest along with quantifications of the surrounding uncertainty. Each of the figures also includes a simple histogram of age along the x-axis to characterize the distribution.

The solid lines track the expected value for logged earnings for veterans across age, and the lighter shade displays the 90% confidence intervals around the estimates. The dashed lines and darker shade denote the expected value for nonveteran earnings across age values. Beneath the plots conveying the expected values, each figure also includes a histogram for each value of age to convey the distribution of age and demonstrate the approximate number of cases for that age value.

Figure 10.1 demonstrates that Anglo veterans and nonveterans do not differ in terms of their earnings later in life. The difference between veterans and nonveterans are not statistically different, although it appears to show a gap developing as age increases whereby veterans earn less.

In examining minority income, we see that veterans can earn more than nonveterans as they become older. In Fig. 10.2, which includes the African-American respondents in our sample, veterans earn slightly more than nonveterans when

Table 10.2 Reported personal logged income among men, 2006–2009

	Whole sample 1	Whole sample 2	Anglos 3	Blacks 4	Latinos 5	Anglos interaction 6	Blacks interaction 7	Latinos interaction 8
Veteran	−0.0415**	−0.00133	−0.0140	0.111*	0.153**	0.0647	0.139	0.0624
	(0.0116)	(0.0115)	(0.0118)	(0.0432)	(0.0419)	(0.0573)	(0.245)	(0.179)
Formal education	0.0963**	0.0958**	0.0944**	0.115**	0.0709**	0.0944**	0.115**	0.0709**
	(0.00170)	(0.00168)	(0.00169)	(0.00867)	(0.00287)	(0.00169)	(0.00868)	(0.00287)
Black	−0.300**	−0.308**			−0.143*			−0.144*
	(0.0169)	(0.0167)			(0.0643)			(0.0644)
Latino	−0.130**	−0.123**	−0.131**	0.0985		−0.130**	0.0985	
	(0.0119)	(0.0118)	(0.0120)	(0.0755)		(0.0120)	(0.0755)	
Age scale	0.00440**							
	(0.000437)							
Veteran × age scale						−0.00162	−0.000626	0.00201
						(0.00121)	(0.00574)	(0.00385)
Constant	10.52**	10.25**	10.28**	9.646**	10.47**	10.28**	9.646**	10.47**
	(0.0323)	(0.0430)	(0.0430)	(0.209)	(0.0680)	(0.0430)	(0.209)	(0.0680)
Observations	28887	28887	26464	2264	3759	26464	2264	3759
R−squared	0.187	0.218	0.213	0.178	0.205	0.214	0.178	0.205

Ordinary least squares regression, robust standard errors in parentheses ($**p \leq 0.01$, $*p \leq 0.05$).

controlling for education levels. This small gap between African-American veterans and non-veterans is relatively stable across age values, although it is not statistically significant. In Fig. 10.3, for Latino respondents, military service provides a larger improvement in later-life earnings. This improvement is substantively larger than the gap between veterans and non-veterans in the African-American and Anglo subgroups, and it is statistically significant.

Conclusions

The overall results demonstrate that the earnings of veterans and non-veterans can differ even after controlling for important influences on income. In addition, the legacy of military service plays out differently for different racial and ethnic groups, both overall and across age groups.

The basic models show that military service has a small but negative effect on earnings among the employed in the civilian economy for the entire sample and specifically for Anglos. Among Latinos, however, there is an earnings benefit that comes with service in the armed forces, even after controlling for education levels. There were no earnings differences between African-American veterans and non-veterans.

The theory that age conditions the effect of military service on later life earnings did not find general support. For the three racial/ethnic groups, we do not generally see stark differences in the veteran/nonveteran gap between younger and older age groups. Inferring age-related trends regarding the influence of military service on income would require larger changes than what is seen in the figures.

Given the limitations of the cross-sectional data, it is important to be cautious about these results at this stage. The samples include months in 2006 through 2009, and due to the amount of time elapsed and actuarial realities, these data do not include many men who served in the mid-20th century (WWII and Korea). Further, the samples were drawn within 3 years of each other, and the implication of this narrow band of sampling is that all the 60-year-olds in our sample were born around 1948. This means that our age measures are unintentionally incorporating cohort as well as age effects. In other words, if there is something special about having served at a particular time that influences later-life earnings that is not already controlled for by the other independent variables, the effect of that unmeasured special event will register through the age variable. Subsequent analysis could include older samples to mitigate the conflation of age effects and cohort effects.

Another caveat involves the issue of self-selection when analyzing the differences between veterans and nonveterans. Under a male conscription regime that selects some to serve, the government is imposing what is almost a natural experiment by choosing some males while others remain civilians who comprise a "control group."[9] Given that our data do not include measures of voluntarism or conscription, nor do they measure variables that could serve as instrumental variables thereof in a two-stage model, our analysis does not contend with self-selection effects, ie., forces that might drive later-life income as well as recruitment propensity.[10]

Notes

1. See also Segal (51).
2. Also known as Hispanics. These are individuals with heritage from the Spanish-speaking nations of the American hemisphere, including Mexico and most nations in Central America, South America, and the Caribbean.
3. Women are omitted because of their relative scarcity in the veteran population. Future analyses of the veteran population should consider women. The numbers of females in the service has grown in recent years, but they constitute a small percent of our sample.
4. The March samples are not included in our dataset because of a difference in the way income and earnings are measured for that month.
5. See Teigen (52) for discussion of cohort delineation for veterans.
6. One explanation for African-American representation is that the institution is a racially tolerant meritocracy (53).
7. Although a Pew (46, p. 1) report found that "In sum, Latino enlisted personnel are underrepresented when compared to the size of the civilian labor force of the appropriate age. They are on par when compared to civilian labor force of the appropriate age that possesses the necessary educational credentials. And, they are overrepresented when compared to the civilian labor force of the appropriate age that possesses both the necessary educational credentials and immigration status."
8. However, there are four substantive changes when modeling earnings as logged earnings. The veteran variable in models two and three change from negative and statistically significant effects to negative and statistically insignificant effects. The veteran variable in model four changes from positive and insignificant to positive and significant. These differences are probably not important given that we ultimately plot the effect of service across all ages rather than rely on single coefficients.
9. Although some are not drafted for reasons that may have economic implications.
10. Angrist (14, 26) uses military entrance standardized test scores and draft lottery numbers, neither of which is available in the CPS.

References

1. Moskos, Charles. 1986. "Institutional/Occupational Trends in Armed Forces: An Update." *Armed Forces and Society*, 12(3): 377–382.
2. Moskos, Charles. 1978. "The Emergent Military: Calling, Profession, or Occupation?" In *The Changing World of the American Military*, ed. Franklin Margiotta, 199–206. Boulder, CO: Westview Press.
3. Moskos, Charles. 1977a. "From Institution to Occupation: Trends in Military Organization." *Armed Forces and Society*, 4(1): 41–50.
4. DeTray, Dennis. 1982. "Veteran Status as a Screening Device." *American Economic Review*, 72(1): 133–142.
5. Fredland, John, and Roger Little. 1985. "Socioeconomic Status of World War II Veterans by Race: An Empirical Test of the Bridging Hypothesis." *Social Science Quarterly*, 66(3): 533–551.
6. Goldberg, Matthew, and John Warner. 1987. "Military Experience, Civilian Experience, and the Earnings of Veterans." *Journal of Human Resources*, 22(1): 62–81.
7. Little, Roger, and J. Eric Fredland. 1979. "Veteran Status, Earnings, and Race: Some Long Term Results." *Armed Forces and Society*, 5(2): 244–260.
8. Martindale, Melanie, and Dudley Poston. 1979. "Variations in Veteran /Nonveteran Earnings Patterns among WWI, Korea, and Vietnam War Cohorts." *Armed Forces and Society*, 5(2): 219–243.

9. Sampson, Robert, and John Laub. 1996. "Socioeconomic Achievement in the Life Course of Disadvantaged Men: Military Service as a Turning Point, circa 1940–1965." *American Sociological Review*, 61(3): 347–367.
10. Villemez, Wayne, and John Kasarda. 1976. "Veteran Status and Socioeconomic Attainment." *Armed Forces and Society*, 2(3): 407–420.
11. Elder, Glen. 1987. "War Mobilization and the Life Course: A Cohort of World War II Veterans." *Sociological Forum*, 2(3): 449–472.
12. Elder, Glen, and Avshalom Caspi. 1990. "Studying Lives in a Changing Society." In *Studying Persons and Lives*, ed. Albert Rabin, Robert Zucker, Susan Frank, and Robert Emmons, 204–247. Springer.
13. Angrist, Joshua. 1989. "Using the Draft Lottery to Measure the Effect of Military Service on Civilian Labor Market Outcomes." In *Research in Labor Economics*, Vol. 10, ed. Ron Ehrenberg, 265–310. Greenwich, CT: JAI Press.
14. Angrist, Joshua. 1990. "Lifetime Earnings and the Vietnam Era Draft Lottery: Evidence from Social Security Administrative Records." *American Economic Review*, 80(3): 313–336.
15. Card, Josephina. 1983. *Lives after Vietnam*. Lanham, MD: Lexington Books.
16. Rosen, Sherwin, and Paul Taubman. 1982. "Changes in Life-Cycle Earnings: What Do Social Security Data Show?" *Journal of Human Resources*, 27(3): 321–338.
17. Schwartz, Saul. 1986. "The Relative Earnings of Vietnam and Korean-Era Veterans." *Industrial and Labor Relations Review*, 39(4):564–572.
18. Teachman, Jay, and Vaughn Call. 1996. "The Effect of Military Service on Educational, Occupational, and Income Attainment." *Social Science Research*, 25(1): 1–31.
19. Xie, Yu. 1992. "The Socioeconomic Status of Young Male Veterans, 1964–1984." *Social Science Quarterly*, 73(2):379–396.
20. Hirsch, Barry, and Stephan Mehay. 2003. "Evaluating the Labor Market Performance of Veterans Using a Matched Comparison Group Design." *Journal of Human Resources*, 38(3): 673–700.
21. Berger, Mark, and Barry Hirsch. 1983. "The Civilian Earnings Experience of Vietnam-Era Veterans." *Journal of Human Resources*, 128(3): 455–479.
22. Magnum, Stephen, and David Ball. 1989. "The Transferability of Military-Provided Occupational Training in the Post-Draft Era." *Industrial and Labor Relations Review*, 42(2): 230–245.
23. Phillips, Robert, Paul Andrisani, Thomas Daymont, and Curtis Gilroy. 1992. "The Economic Returns to Military Service: Race-Ethnic Differences." *Social Science Quarterly*, 73(2): 340–359.
24. Dempsey, Jason, and Robert Shapiro. 2009. "The Army's Hispanic Future." *Armed Forces & Society*, 35(3): 526–561.
25. Blau, Peter, and Otis Duncan. 1967. *The American Occupational Structure*. New York: Wiley.
26. Angrist, Joshua. 1998. "Estimating the Labor Market Impact of Voluntary Military Service Using Social Security Data on Military Applicants." *Econometrica*, 66(2): 249–288.
27. Bryant, Richard, V.A. Samaranayake, and Allen Wilhite. 1993. "The Effect of Military Service on the Subsequent Civilian Wage of the Post-Vietnam Veteran." *Quarterly Review of Economics and Finance*, 33(1): 15–31.
28. Coleman, James. 1988. "Social Capital in the Creation of Human Capital." *American Journal of Sociology*, 94(1): 95–120.
29. Lin, Nam. 1999. "Social Networks and Status Attainment." *Annual Review of Sociology*, 25: 467–487.
30. Fredland, John, and Roger Little. 1980. "Long-term Returns to Vocational Training: Evidence from Military Sources." *Journal of Human Resources*, 15(1): 49–66.
31. Collier, Ruth, and David Collier. 1991. *Shaping the Political Arena: Critical Junctures, the Labor Movement, and Regime Dynamics in Latin America*. Princeton, NJ: Princeton University Press.

32. Pierson, Paul. 2004. *Politics in Time: History, Institutions, and Social Analysis*. Princeton, NJ: Princeton University Press.
33. North, Douglass. 1990. *Institutions, Institutional Change, and Economic Performance*. Cambridge: Cambridge University Press.
34. Becker, G. 1993. *Human Capital: A Theoretical and Empirical Analysis, with Special Reference to Education*. Chicago: University of Chicago Press.
35. Willis, Robert. 1986. "Wage Determinants: A Survey and Reinterpretation of Human Capital Earnings Functions." In *The Handbook of Labor Economics*, ed. Orley Ashenfelter and Richard Layard, 525–602. Amsterdam: North-Holland.
36. Bryant, Richard, and Al Wilhite. 1990. "Military Experience and Training Effects on Civilian Wages." *Applied Economics*, 22(1): 69–81.
37. Elder, Glen. 1996. "The Life Course Paradigm." In *Examining Lives in Context: Perspectives on the Ecology of Human Development*, ed. Phillis Moen, Glen Elder, and Kurt Luescher, 101–139. Washington, DC: Americans Psychological Association.
38. Settersten, Richard, and Karl Mayer. 1997. "The Measurement of Age, Age Structure, and the Life Course." *Annual Review of Sociology*, 23(1): 233–261.
39. Foner, Anne, and David Kertzer. 1978. "Transitions over the Life Course: Lessons from Age-Set Societies." *American Journal of Sociology*, 83(5): 1081–1104.
40. Hogan, Dennis, and Nan Astone. 1986. "The Transition to Adulthood." *Annual Review of Sociology*, 12(1): 109–130.
41. Current Population Survey (CPS). 2002. "Technical Paper 63RV (Design and Methodology)." http://www.census.gov/prod/2002pubs/tp63rv.pdf   (accessed April 17, 2010).
42. Highton, Benjamin. 2005. "Self-Reported versus Proxy-Reported Voter Turnout in the Current Population Survey." *Public Opinion Quarterly*, 69(1): 113–123.
43. Braumoeller, Bear. 2004. "Hypothesis Testing and Multiplicative Interaction Terms." *International Organization* 58(4): 807–820.
44. Kam, Cindy, and Rob Franzese, Jr. 2007. *Modeling and Interpreting Interactive Hypotheses in Regression Analysis: A Refresher and Some Practical Advice*. Ann Arbor: University of Michigan Press.
45. Kleykamp, Meredith. 2006. "College, Jobs, or the Military? Enlistment during a Time of War." *Social Science Quarterly*, 87(2): 272–290.
46. Pew Hispanic Center. 2003. *"Hispanics in the Military."* Washington, DC: Pew Hispanic Center.
47. Ellison, Christopher. 1992. "Military Background, Racial Orientations, and Political Participation among Black Adult Males." *Social Science Quarterly*, 73(2): 361–378.
48. Leal, David L. 1999. "It's Not Just a Job: Military Service and Latino Political Participation." *Political Behavior*, 21(2): 153–174.
49. Parker, Christopher. 2009. "When Politics Becomes Protest: Black Veterans and Political Activism in the Postwar South." *Journal of Politics*, 71(1): 113–131.
50. Tomz, Michael, Jason Wittenberg, and Gary King. 2003. CLARIFY: Software for Interpreting and Presenting Statistical Results. Version 2.1. Stanford University, University of Wisconsin, and Harvard University. http://gking.harvard.edu/   (accessed April 17, 2010).
51. Segal, David R. 1986. "Measuring the Institutional/Occupational Change Thesis." *Armed Forces and Society*, 12(3): 351–376.
52. Teigen, Jeremy. 2006. "Enduring Effects of the Uniform: Previous Military Experience and Voting Turnout." *Political Research Quarterly*, 59(4): 601–607.
53. Moskos, Charles, and John Butler. 1996. *All That We Can Be: Black Leadership and Racial Integration the Army Way*. New York: Basic Books.
54. Browning, Harvey. L., Sally. C. Lopreato, and Dudley. L. Poston. 1973. "Income and Veteran Status: Variations Among Mexicans, Blacks, and Anglos." *American Sociological Review*, 38: 74–85.
55. Fligstein, Neil. 1976. "The G.I. Bill: Its Effects on the Education and Occupational Attainment of U.S. Males" 1940–1973. Unpublished master's thesis: University of Wisconsin, Madison WI.

56. Mason, W.M. 1970. "On the Socioeconomic effects of Military Service." Unpublished doctoral dissertation, University of Chicago, Chicago, IL.
57. Miller, James C., and Robert D. Tollison. 1971. "The Implicit Tax on Reluctant Military Recruits" *Social Science Quarterly*, 51: 924–931.
58. Poston, Dudley L. Jr., Mady W. Segal, and John S. Butler. 1984. "The Influence of Military Service on the Civilian Earning Patterns of Female Veterans: Evidence From The 1980 Census," In *Women In the United States Armed Forces*, ed. Nancy Goldman. Chicago: Inter-University Seminar on Armed Forces and Society.
59. Rosen, Sherwin and Paul Taubman. 1982. "Changes in Life-Cycle Earnings: What Do Social Security Data Show?" *Journal of Human Resources*, 17(3):321–338.
60. Teachman, Jay. 2004. "Military Service during the Vietnam Era: Were There Consequences for Subsequent CivilianEarnings?" *Social Forces*, 83(2): 709–730.
61. Teachman, Jay and Lucky Tedrow. 2007. "Did Military Service in the Early All Volunteer Era Affect Subsequent Civilian Income?" *Social Science Research*, 36(4): 1447–1474.

Part V
Economic Impacts of Latinos

Chapter 11
Do Recent Latino Immigrants Compete for Jobs with Native Hispanics and Earlier Latino Immigrants?[1]

Adriana Kugler and Mutlu Yuksel

Abstract The perception that immigrants take jobs away and push down the wages of native workers is longstanding. Given that the recent wave of Latin American immigration in the 1980s and 1990s coincided with the fall in earnings and employment of the less skilled, it is not surprising that, like previous immigration waves, recent Latin American immigration is sometimes blamed for the misfortunes of less skilled Americans. There is, however, little evidence showing that immigration reduces native employment and earnings. Some believe that this is because immigrants are employed in jobs that natives are not willing to do in any case. In this chapter, we examine whether recent Latino immigrants are hurting the chances of earlier Latino immigrants and native Hispanics who are more likely to do the same jobs as recent Latin American migrants. We find little evidence showing that the recent influx of Latin Americans hurts Latinos and Hispanics. If anything, once we control for ongoing trends in regions receiving immigrants, we find that the recent Latin American immigration helped native Hispanics but had no effect on previous Latin American immigrants. The earnings of native Hispanics increased with the most recent wave of Latin American immigration, probably because immigrants help the productivity of native Hispanics by providing cheap services and doing jobs that free up the time of natives for more specialized tasks.

Introduction

Since World War II, the United States experienced two waves of immigration from Latin America. Largely motivated by political turmoil, one wave took place from the 1960s to the 1980s. Since the end of the Cold War, a second wave has been driven mainly by economic factors.

A. Kugler (✉)
Georgetown University, Washington, DC, USA; National Bureau of Economic Research (NBER), Cambridge, MA, USA
e-mail: ak659@georgetown.edu

D.L. Leal, S.J. Trejo (eds.), *Latinos and the Economy*, Immigrants and Minorities, Politics and Policy, DOI 10.1007/978-1-4419-6682-7_11,
© Springer Science+Business Media, LLC 2011

Latin American migration during the 1960s and 1970s was mostly driven by political instability in some of these countries (e.g., Cuba, Argentina, and Chile). Even in 1970, we find that, according to Census figures, the fraction of Latin American immigrants in the population was only 0.005. After the 1970s, the increase in Latin American immigration due to political factors is more noticeable. By 1980, we find that the share of Latin American immigrants in the population had risen to 0.009. A much larger migration started to arrive after the 1980s. While civil wars in Central America served to push many migrants to the United States, a growing number—especially after the end of the Cold War—were motivated by poor economic conditions in most Latin American countries. The debt crisis in the 1980s and the structural reforms during the 1990s followed by the Mexican and the Brazilian crises and the contagion effect of the Asian Crisis in the region generated a large flow of immigration from the rest of Latin America into the US. The increase in the share of Latin American immigrants in the population is most noticeable after the 1980s. We find that the share of Latino immigrants in the population rose to 0.015 in 1990 and 0.031 in 2000.

The first and second waves of Latin American immigrants differ in terms of their educational attainment, however. In contrast to previous waves of immigrants, recent immigrants are less educated and are generally less skilled than earlier immigrants from the region (see, e.g., (1, 2)). The lower skill of the more recent Latin American immigrants would suggest that they are likely to compete for jobs with less skilled natives or other equally unskilled immigrants who came before them. Moreover, they are likely to compete with others with similar language skills, who may either be serving the same Spanish-speaking market or who do similar jobs that do not require English fluency. On the other hand, more skilled natives and previous immigrants would not likely be affected by the competition from these immigrants and may actually benefit from having less-skilled workers either work for them or work with them.

This chapter analyzes the impact of the recent wave of unskilled Latin American immigrants on native Hispanics and previous Latin American immigrants, who are likely to have similar language skills. Moreover, we focus on the impact of recent Latin Americans on the earnings and employment of Hispanics with various levels of educational attainment (i.e., dropouts, high-school graduates, and college-educated workers).

We take advantage of the fact that the recent Latin American immigration varied widely across regions and states. Because many immigrants come to the US for economic reasons and to seek a better life, a usual problem when estimating the impact of immigration on the earnings and employment of natives in different states is that immigrants may move precisely to states with good economic opportunities. This means that one may be unlikely to find any adverse effects of immigration on natives, since natives will also be doing particularly well in the states that attract immigrants.

We use two strategies to control for this possibility. First, we study Latin American immigration patterns that are driven by the presence of previous Latin American migrants from the same countries. The former likely arrived at a state because of the benefits provided by their social networks rather than by economic conditions (see 3 for a discussion of this strategy). The idea is that social networks make immigration less costly by providing initial housing and may increase the benefits of locating in a specific place by providing job information and opportunities. Second, we study Latin American immigration that came to the border-states in the US following Hurricane Mitch. The idea is that those who came after the Hurricane were forced to migrate due to the natural disaster and could not be as picky in terms of their destination choice. Consequently, these immigrants went to the closest states rather than to states with better economic conditions (4).

We find no evidence that the recent wave of unskilled Latin Americans displaced native Hispanics or even previous Latin Americans from their jobs. Neither do we find that they competed with them in any way by reducing the earnings of low skilled native Hispanics or previous Latin Americans. Instead, we find that unskilled Latin Americans who came to the US in the past few decades raised the earnings of the more skilled Hispanic men.

Why would unskilled Latin American immigrants have a positive impact on the earnings of skilled Hispanics? There are two possible channels through which this may occur. On the one hand, unskilled Latin American workers may work directly with skilled Hispanics and they may complement each other at work, making skilled Hispanics more productive. A good example would be unskilled or semi-skilled Latin Americans who speak Spanish well and can serve the Spanish-speaking market.[2] On the other hand, the price of goods and especially of services bought by skilled Hispanics, like child-care and gardening, may have declined with the arrival of unskilled Latin Americans, thus, increasing the real earnings of skilled Hispanic workers.

In the next section we summarize the existing literature on the impact of immigration on US natives and explain the importance of focusing on recent unskilled immigration from Latin America and its impact on Hispanics. The following section describes the demographic and labor market characteristics of native Hispanics and previous and recent Latin American immigrants, and compares them with immigrants from other parts of the world. Finally, we present evidence on the impact of the recent wave of Latin American immigration on Hispanics in the US and discuss some policy implications of our analysis.

Why Focus on the Impact of Immigration on Hispanics?

An extensive literature focuses on the effect of immigration on the labor market conditions of all natives in the US. Like this chapter, one strand of this literature focuses on immigration settlement patterns to different states to analyze the impact of immigration on natives. For the most part, analyses of US data following this approach find little or no effect of immigration on American workers (e.g., 3, 5, 6).[3] Another strand of the literature analyzes the impact of immigration by exploiting the drastic change in the shares of immigrants in the labor force over time. For the most part, studies in this tradition find larger negative effects of immigrants on US workers (e.g., 7, 8).

Studies in both traditions tend to focus on the impact of immigrants on the earnings and employment of natives of different skill levels. Studies focus on different skill groups because immigrants have been relatively less skilled than the rest of the population during the past few decades, so that immigrant workers may be expected to generate more competition for less-skilled native workers. Previous studies indeed tend to find negative effects on less-skilled Americans. On the other hand, our recent study (4) and a study by Ottaviano and Peri (9) find evidence of the positive effects of immigration on more-skilled Americans.[4]

While distinguishing the impact of immigrants on natives with different educational attainment and experience is informative, worker skills may also differ along other dimensions. For instance, individuals may differ in terms of other observable skills, such as language and social skills. As an attempt to deal with this, some studies have examined the effect of immigration on different ethnic and racial groups. For example, the well-known Mariel boatlift analysis examines the impact of the Marielitos not only on all US natives, but in particular on African Americans and previous Cuban immigrants. Card (2001) distinguished natives by income deciles as an attempt to distinguish the impact on natives with different observable and unobservable skills. Similarly, a recent study by Borjas et al. (10) looks at the impact of immigration on African Americans.

In this study, we focus on the impact of recent Latin American immigration to the US, which has been composed of relatively unskilled workers compared to previous waves of immigration. Moreover, here we focus on the impact of these recent Latino immigrants on US Hispanics and on previous Latino immigrants.

Why would we be interested in focusing on the impact on Hispanics? First, as discussed in more detail in the next section, native Hispanics are relatively less educated than the population at large and, thus, most likely to be affected by the recent immigration wave from Latin America. The percentage of Latin Americans among those with less than a high-school education has been steadily increasing since the 1980s. In 1980, Latin American immigrants accounted for 4.44% of those with less than a high school education, while this increased to 10.15% in 1990, 19.03% in 2000, and 19.25% in 2005. By contrast, non-Latin American immigrants account for less of the less-educated population today than they did back in the 1990s. Non-Latin American immigrants accounted for 4.37% and 6.9% of those with less than a high school degree in 1980 and 1990, respectively. However, they only accounted for 6.67% and 6.38% of those with less than a high school education in 2000 and 2005.

Similarly, while non-Hispanic natives account for less and less of the less educated workforce, native Hispanics are now a larger share of the less educated. Native Hispanics accounted for 6.34% of the less educated population in the US in 1980, but for 6.25% in 1990, 7.85% in 2000, and 8.64% in 2005. By contrast, the share of non-Hispanic natives among the less educated has been decreasing over time. In 1980, African-American natives and other natives accounted for 15.71% and 69.34% of those with less than a high school degree, but by 2005 they accounted for 12.27% and 53.6% of those without a high school degree, respectively.[5]

Second, recent Latino immigrants are not only more similar to previous Latin American immigrants and Hispanics in terms of educational attainment but they also share similar language skills and other less tangible skills (e.g., in terms of serving a Spanish-speaking market and providing certain services). For this reason, it would seem like recent Latino immigrants may be particularly substitutable with native Hispanics and previous Latin American immigrants. Finally, given the slow assimilation of second generation Hispanics, it is important to understand why newer generations of native Hispanics are not catching up as quickly as older generations of native Hispanics in terms of earnings with other Americans.[6] Competition from new immigrants may be one factor that affects their earnings but not those of white natives.

Demographic and Labor Market Characteristics of Native Hispanics, and Latino and Non-Latino Immigrants

Our analysis uses data from the 1970, 1980, 1990, and 2000 Censuses. In particular, we focus on US-born workers who report to be Hispanic and on foreign-born workers who were born in Central America, Mexico, South America, and the Caribbean. We begin by presenting comparisons of native Hispanics with other natives and comparisons of recent Latin American immigrants to veteran Latin American immigrants and immigrants from the rest of the world.

Table 11.1 reports descriptive statistics for native Hispanic men and women (i.e., US-born workers who identify as Hispanic) as well as descriptive statistics for native white and native black men and women. This table reports labor market and demographic characteristics of Hispanic, white, and black men and women in 2000 between 16 and 65 years of age. The table shows that Hispanic men and women earn lower hourly wages than both whites and blacks and work less than whites in terms of employment, number of weeks in a year, and number of hours per week. On the other hand, the employment rate and weeks and hours worked of Hispanic men are slightly higher than those of black men. On average, Hispanic men drop out of high school, while Hispanic women have completed 12 years of high school on average. The educational attainment of Hispanics contrasts with that of white men and women and black women who have, on average, attained some education beyond high school; black men differ from Hispanic men in that they have, on average, completed about 12 years of high school. Native Hispanic men and women are also more likely to work in blue-collar occupations and in the agriculture and construction sectors than both whites and blacks. Finally, Hispanic men and women are somewhat younger on average than native whites and blacks.

Table 11.2 presents similar statistics for immigrants from Latin America and all other countries who arrived more than 10 years ago ("veteran" immigrants) and less than 10 years ago ("recent" immigrants). Comparing this table with Table 11.1, while the earnings of veteran Latin American immigrants are closer to the earnings of native Hispanics, the earnings of recent Latin Americans are lower than those of the veteran Latin American immigrants and native Hispanics, and substantially lower than those of native whites and blacks. By contrast, the earnings of

Table 11.1 Descriptive statistics

Variable	Native Hispanics		Native whites		Native blacks	
	Men	Women	Men	Women	Men	Women
Hourly wage	14.91	12.68	19.31	14.31	15.57	13.75
	(32.75)	(22.83)	(45.01)	(39.65)	(39.79)	(42.65)
Employed	64.27	57.44	77.76	66.76	55.15	57.89
Weeks worked	43.14	41.34	46.09	43.76	42.75	42.29
	(14.21)	(15.14)	(12.12)	(13.60)	(14.74)	(14.77)
Hours worked week	40.57	36.22	42.59	36.27	40.25	37.34
	(11.51)	(11.01)	(11.55)	(11.54)	(11.46)	(10.54)
Education	11.85	12.11	13.06	13.22	12.07	12.53
	(2.77)	(2.72)	(2.37)	(2.23)	(2.52)	(2.35)
Age	32.80	33.43	39.91	40.19	37.22	38.01
	(12.76)	(12.79)	(13.41)	(13.25)	(13.37)	(13.26)
Married	43.42	46.14	59.33	61.09	40.07	32.07
Agriculture	3.35	0.89	3.90	0.91	1.64	0.26
Construction	11.82	1.06	12.39	1.51	8.25	0.59
Manufacturing	13.77	7.22	18.62	8.51	16.36	9.85
Services	57.71	71.11	57.06	73.59	54.98	70.41
White-collar	28.41	37.51	36.11	44.96	27.33	41.13
Blue-collar	58.24	42.77	55.86	39.55	53.90	39.97
N	199,266	208,339	3,110,768	3,194,741	389,674	452,073

Notes: All statistics are for men and women aged 16–65 in the US 2000 census data. Standard deviations are reported in parentheses.

Table 11.2 Descriptive statistics

Variable	Recent LA		Veteran LA		Recent non-LA		Veteran Non-LA	
	Men	Women	Men	Women	Men	Women	Men	Women
Hourly wage	10.68	10.32	14.92	13.63	18.64	14.49	20.39	17.09
	(22.6)	(37.2)	(33.5)	(78.86)	(47.5)	(28.3)	(57.9)	(101.3)
Employed	68.98	38.93	64.55	45.98	66.29	44.38	75.06	61.11
Education	9.39	9.89	9.71	10.02	13.53	13.24	13.17	12.95
	(4.02)	(4.15)	(4.42)	(4.43)	(3.02)	(3.24)	(3.21)	(3.34)
Age	27.97	30.05	41.21	43.62	32.38	32.78	42.03	43.08
	(9.82)	(10.9)	(14.5)	(15.93)	(11.1)	(11.4)	(12.4)	(12.4)
Married	40.96	55.01	66.30	57.96	51.70	61.82	65.90	65.42
Agriculture	7.25	2.71	6.00	1.93	0.85	0.38	1.06	0.41
Construction	20.62	0.76	13.87	0.67	5.10	0.60	7.16	0.84
Manufacturing	15.69	11.71	17.08	11.41	14.76	8.41	17.31	10.21
Services	47.08	50.83	51.34	55.43	64.46	59.73	66.33	68.22
White-collar	27.40	30.33	26.99	34.01	47.19	39.66	45.07	43.73
Blue-collar	63.24	35.69	61.30	35.43	37.97	29.45	46.80	35.95
Black	4.65	6.72	8.83	11.43	7.14	6.47	4.07	3.13
Asian	0.55	0.68	0.71	0.82	43.91	47.22	39.26	40.42
N	86,211	65,231	234,610	225,028	62,527	66,578	205,148	229,952

Notes: All statistics are for immigrant men and women aged 16–65 in the US 2000 census data. Recent (non) Latin American immigrants' statistics are of those (non) Latin Americans who came after 1995. Veteran immigrants are those who came before 1990. LA represents Latin American immigrants. Average hourly wages are reported for wages and salary workers. Standard deviations are reported in parentheses.

both recent and veteran non-Latin American immigrants are much closer to those of native whites.

This partly reflects differences in the educational attainment and experience of recent Latin Americans compared to veteran Latin Americans and other immigrants. While recent Latin American men and women have on average 9.39 and 9.89 years of education, veteran Latin Americans have on average 9.71 and 10.02 years of education.[7] More striking is the fact that the education of non-Latin American immigrants is much higher. Recent non-Latin American men and women have on average 13.5 and 13.2 years of schooling and veteran non-Latin American immigrant men and women have, respectively, 13.2 and 13 years of schooling on average—very close to the educational attainment of native whites. At an average of about 29 years of age, recent Latin American immigrants are also younger than previous Latin American immigrants and immigrants from other regions. This suggests they have less experience compared to previous immigrants, who are closer to 40 years old on average. Recent Latin Americans are also more likely than other immigrants to be blue-collar workers. These differences in skills and labor market outcomes between Latino and non-Latin American immigrants highlight how distinct this recent wave of immigrants from Latin America is and helps to explain why we are interested in focusing on this group of workers for our study. At the same time, recent Latin American immigrants, though less educated and experienced and more likely to work in blue-collar occupations, are most similar in their characteristics to veteran Latin Americans and native Hispanics. Thus, we may expect recent Latin Americans to be more substitutable with other Latinos in the US economy.

The Impact of Recent Latino Immigrants on Native Hispanics and Earlier Latino Immigrants

Our analysis begins by establishing simple relationships between the share of recent Latin American immigrants in a state and the wages and employment of native Hispanic and earlier Latino immigrants. The analysis controls for the following: (1) individual characteristics of the native Hispanics and veteran Latinos; (2) fixed differences across states; (3) aggregate shocks that affect all states, and (4) differential ongoing factors that affect different regions differently. Thus, the regression we run here is as follows:

$$Y_{ijt} = \mu_j + \tau_t + \beta' X_{ijt} + \gamma S_{LAjt} + \varepsilon_{ijt},$$

where Y_{ijt} is the log of earnings or an indicator of whether the person is employed, μ_j are state effects, and τ_t are time effects. X_{ijt} are individual-level controls including the following: years of schooling; potential experience and a quadratic term of experience; a marital status indicator; black, Asian, and Hispanic indicators; and industry and occupation indicators. S_{LAjt} is the share of Latin American immigration in a given state at a point in time.

Tables 11.3 and 11.4 show the relationship between immigrant shares, wages, and employment by educational attainment. The results in Table 11.3 show that

Table 11.3 Effects of immigration on the hourly wages of native Hispanics and Latin American veteran immigrants

Outcome	Men			Women		
	Dropouts	HS	College	Dropouts	HS	College
A. Native Hispanics						
Hourly Wage No Trend	0.046*	0.051*	0.051*	0.048*	0.060*	0.041*
	(0.012)	(0.009)	(0.004)	(0.008)	(0.007)	(0.003)
Hourly Wage Region-specific Trend	0.045*	0.064*	0.060*	0.048*	0.066*	0.063*
	(0.006)	(0.012)	(0.007)	(0.005)	(0.003)	(0.008)
N	106,800	120,203	110,586	74,105	108,805	117,652
B. Latin American Veteran Immigrants						
Hourly Wage No Trend	0.043*	0.052*	0.022**	0.047*	0.044*	0.036*
	(0.014)	(0.014)	(0.010)	(0.009)	(0.013)	(0.013)
Hourly Wage Region-specific Trend	0.019	0.032	0.020**	0.011	0.027	0.023
	(0.012)	(0.030)	(0.010)	(0.014)	(0.020)	(0.021)
N	129,743	67,830	64,400	73,298	54,331	64,700

Notes: The table reports OLS estimates of Latin American shares of every state on the hourly wage. Clustered standard errors by state are reported in parentheses. Regressions control for years of education, potential experience and its square, marriage dummy, black, Asian, Hispanic dummies, industry, occupation, state and year fixed effects. We report results with and without region-specific trends. *1%, **5% significance level.

Table 11.4 Effects of immigration on the employment of native Hispanics and Latin American Veteran immigrants

Outcome	Men			Women		
	Dropouts	HS	College	Dropouts	HS	College
A. Native Hispanics						
Employment No Trend	−0.001	0.001	0.007†	−0.006	−0.010†	−0.003
	(0.008)	(0.008)	(0.004)	(0.009)	(0.006)	(0.005)
Employment Region-specific Trend	0.011**	0.009†	0.009*	−0.001	−0.013*	−0.009**
	(0.004)	(0.004)	(0.003)	(0.005)	(0.004)	(0.003)
N	151,408	146,013	130,158	124,319	145,295	141,733
B. Latin American Veteran immigrants						
Employment No Trend	0.011*	0.006	0.001	0.005	0.013**	0.007
	(0.004)	(0.006)	(0.006)	(0.004)	(0.005)	(0.008)
Employment Region-specific Trend	0.012*	0.009	0.001	0.005	0.013**	0.009
	(0.004)	(0.008)	(0.006)	(0.005)	(0.006)	(0.007)
N	163,086	83,449	78,663	125,574	79,216	82,171

Notes: The table reports OLS estimates of Latin American shares on employment. Clustered standard errors by state are reported in parentheses. Regressions control for years of education, potential experience and its square, marriage dummy, black, Asian, Hispanic dummies, industry, occupation, state and year fixed effects. We report results with and without region-specific trends. *1%, **5%, †10% significance level.

immigration is positively associated with the wages of native Hispanic men and women in all educational groups. By contrast, results controlling for regional trends show no association between the immigrant share and the wages of earlier Latino immigrants, except for male college graduates. Similarly, Table 11.4 shows the relation between the immigrant share and the employment of native Hispanics and veteran Latino immigrants. The results with regional trends show that Latin American immigration is associated with higher Hispanic employment and higher employment of less skilled veteran Latino immigrants.

As mentioned above, however, increases in the earnings and employment of Hispanic men and women may not be due to immigrant arrival, but rather due to the fact that immigrants settle in states where native Hispanics and others are already doing well. To address this possibility, we examine Latin American immigration through location choices that may have been driven by other reasons. First, we use the immigration of recent Latinos that was motivated by the presence of social networks of previous waves of immigrants from the same countries. Next, we use the immigration patterns driven by closeness to the countries affected by Hurricane Mitch in the late 1990s (i.e., the Central American countries). Table 11.5 reports the relationship between the share of recent Latin American immigrants and the share of those from the same countries that had already settled in the state during the previous decade.[8] The table also reports how the recent Latino share changed after Hurricane Mitch in the states closer to the affected countries.[9]

The results show that the share of recent Latino immigrants grew more in states where there was already a social network from the same country. Moreover, similar to Kugler and Yuksel (4), we find that the share of recent Latin American immigrants fell in states farther from the Central American countries affected by Hurricane Mitch after the hurricane hit.

We then proceed to use the share of immigrants that came to different states driven by social network and closeness considerations after Mitch, rather than due to economic reasons, to reconsider the impact of immigration on wages and employment. Tables 11.6 and 11.7 show results using the share of immigrants that came because of their social networks, while Tables 11.8 and 11.9 show results using the share of immigrants that came after Mitch to close-by states.[10]

Table 11.5 Recent immigration explained by previous immigration and hurricane Mitch

	Previous Share by Country		Post-Mitch × Distance	
	No trend	Trend	No trend	Trend
Share of recent Latin American immigrants	0.56**	0.55**	−0.0016*	−0.0040*
	(0.26)	(0.22)	(0.0006)	(0.0012)
R^2	0.89	0.91	0.81	0.86

Notes: Robust standard errors are reported in parentheses. All regressions include state and year effects. Trend is region dummies times year. *1%, **5%, +10% significance level.

A. Kugler and M. Yuksel

Table 11.6 Effects of immigration on the hourly wage of native Hispanics and Latin American veteran immigrants, using the share of previous immigrants from each country as IV

Outcome	Men			Women		
	Dropouts	HS	College	Dropouts	HS	College
A. Native Hispanics						
Hourly Wage No Trend	−0.157	0.014	0.061	−0.484	0.278	−0.041
	(0.605)	(0.260)	(0.090)	(1.460)	(0.798)	(0.088)
Hourly Wage Region-specific Trend	0.104**	0.096**	0.080**	0.045†	0.055*	0.050*
	(0.050)	(0.040)	(0.020)	(0.025)	(0.010)	(0.015)
N	106,800	120,203	110,586	74,105	108,805	117,652
B. Latin American Veteran immigrants						
Hourly Wage No Trend	0.083**	0.142**	0.174	0.188*	0.138	0.216
	(0.031)	(0.059)	(0.319)	(0.055)	(0.111)	(0.540)
Hourly Wage Region-specific Trend	0.007	0.038	0.015	0.014	0.019	−0.019
	(0.022)	(0.041)	(0.023)	(0.023)	(0.030)	(0.036)
N	129,743	67,830	64,400	73,298	54,331	64,700

Notes: The Table reports IV estimates of Latin American shares of every state on hourly wages, where the share of immigrants in the previous decade from the same country is the IV. Clustered standard errors by state are reported in parentheses. Regressions control for years of education, potential experience and its square, marriage dummy, black, Asian, Hispanic dummies, industry, occupation, state and year fixed effects. We report results with and without region-specific trends. *1%, **5%, †10% significance level.

Table 11.7 Effects of immigration on the employment of native Hispanics and Latin American veteran immigrants, using the share of previous immigrants from each country as IV

Outcome	Men			Women		
	Dropouts	HS	College	Dropouts	HS	College
A. Native Hispanics						
Employment No Trend	0.267	0.173	0.088	0.171	0.292	0.142
	(1.900)	(0.371)	(0.125)	(0.475)	(0.578)	(0.174)
Employment Region-specific Trend	−0.027	−0.017	−0.007	−0.035	−0.048†	−0.052
	(0.034)	(0.025)	(0.015)	(0.032)	(0.029)	(0.035)
N	151,408	146,013	130,158	124,319	145,295	141,733
B. Latin American Veteran immigrants						
Employment No Trend	−0.002	0.053	0.112	−0.035	0.087	0.180
	(0.025)	(0.074)	(0.273)	(0.045)	(0.127)	(0.520)
Employment Region-specific Trend	−0.001	−0.022	−0.028	−0.002	−0.002	−0.029
	(0.014)	(0.026)	(0.020)	(0.012)	(0.015)	(0.027)
N	163,086	83,449	78,663	125,574	79,216	82,171

Notes: The table reports IV estimates of Latin American shares of every state on employment, where the share of immigrants in the previous decade from the same country is the IV. Clustered standard errors by state are reported in parentheses. Regressions control for years of education, potential experience and its square, marriage dummy, black, Asian, Hispanic dummies, industry, occupation, state and year fixed effects. We report results with and without region-specific trends. * 1%, **5%, †10% significance level.

Table 11.8 Effects of immigration on the hourly wages of native Hispanics and Latin American veteran immigrants, using Post-Mitch x distance as IV

Outcome	Men			Women		
	Dropouts	HS	College	Dropouts	HS	College
A. Native Hispanics						
Hourly Wage No Trend	0.079*	0.050*	0.052*	0.040**	0.041**	0.020*
	(0.017)	(0.010)	(0.010)	(0.022)	(0.016)	(0.009)
Hourly Wage Region-specific Trend	0.053*	0.083**	0.080**	0.044*	0.054*	0.059*
	(0.019)	(0.031)	(0.023)	(0.014)	(0.015)	(0.024)
N	106,800	120,203	110,586	74,105	108,805	117,652
B. Latin American Veteran Immigrants						
Hourly Wage No Trend	0.059**	0.053*	0.021	0.070*	0.055*	0.029
	(0.023)	(0.016)	(0.015)	(0.009)	(0.011)	(0.018)
Hourly Wage Region-specific Trend	0.015	0.041	0.034	0.032	0.051	−0.028
	(0.023)	(0.045)	(0.029)	(0.021)	(0.046)	(0.059)
N	129,743	67,830	64,400	73,298	54,331	64,700

Notes: The table reports IV estimates of Latin American shares of every state on hourly wages, where the interaction between a post-Mitch dummy and distance from Tegucigalpa is the IV. Clustered standard errors by state are reported in parentheses. Regressions control for years of education, potential experience and its square, marriage dummy, black, Asian, Hispanic dummies, industry, occupation, state and year fixed effects. We report results with and without region-specific trends. *1%, **5% significance level.

Table 11.9 Effects of immigration on the employment of natives and Latin American veteran immigrants, using Post-Mitch x distance as IV

	Men			Women		
Outcome	Dropouts	HS	College	Dropouts	HS	College
A. Native Hispanics						
Employment No Trend	−0.031†	−0.014	0.001	−0.024	−0.021	−0.007
	(0.018)	(0.016)	(0.008)	(0.016)	(0.016)	(0.011)
Employment	−0.004	−0.002	0.007	−0.014	−0.038	−0.033
Region-specific Trend	(0.021)	(0.017)	(0.008)	(0.015)	(0.025)	(0.023)
N	151,408	146,013	130,158	124,319	145,295	141,733
B. Latin American Veteran Immigrants						
Employment No Trend	0.012**	0.006	−0.004	0.007	0.009	−0.004
	(0.005)	(0.007)	(0.009)	(0.007)	(0.007)	(0.012)
Employment	0.005	0.002	−0.017	0.010	0.008	−0.009
Region-specific Trend	(0.010)	(0.015)	(0.018)	(0.009)	(0.010)	(0.020)
N	163,086	83,449	78,663	125,574	79,216	82,171

Notes: The table reports IV estimates of Latin American shares of every state on employment, using the interaction between a post-Mitch dummy and distance from Tegucigalpa as IV. Clustered standard errors by state are reported in parentheses. Regressions control for years of education, potential experience and its square, marriage dummy, black, Asian, Hispanic dummies, industry, occupation, state and year fixed effects. We report results with and without region-specific trends. *1%, **5%, †10% significance level

The results in both sets of tables show a similar story. Recent immigrants that did not pick their location for economic reasons increase the wages of native Hispanics, but they have no effect on the wages of veteran Latin American immigrants. On the other hand, recent immigrants seem to have no effect on the employment status of either native Hispanics or veteran Latino immigrants. The results using the Mitch immigrants also suggest that the results are greater for more educated native Hispanic men and women than for the less-educated ones.

These results suggest that an increase in the share of recent Latino immigrants of 10% increases the hourly wages of dropout native Hispanic men by half a percentage point (i.e., multiply 0.53 from Table 11.8 Panel A with region trends by 0.1), while increasing the hourly wages of high school graduates and college educated native Hispanic men by close to one percentage point (i.e., multiply 0.083 and 0.08 from Table 11.8 Panel A with region trends by 0.1). The results for women suggest smaller results of half a percentage point for high school and college educated Hispanic women and less than half a percentage point for dropout Hispanic women (i.e., multiply 0.044, 0.054 and 0.059 from Table 11.8 Panel A with region trends by 0.1).

By contrast, veteran Latino immigrants do not seem to benefit or suffer from the recent immigration from Latin America. This makes sense if one remembers that native Hispanics were more educated and experienced than recent Latino immigrants, so that recent immigrants may complement Hispanic workers rather than compete with them. At the same time, recent and previous Latino immigrants are likely different enough that they do not do the same types of jobs, so that the more recent immigrants are not merely substituting immigrants who came before them, but rather taking up new jobs.

Policy Implications and Conclusions

Immigrants are often perceived as taking away jobs or reducing the earnings of natives by generating competition in the labor market. In this sense, they are viewed as a threat to native workers. However, here we find that less-skilled Latino immigrants increase the earnings of native Hispanics, especially for the most educated. This implies that rather than substituting natives, immigrants tend to complement the work of natives and thus increase their productivity and their earnings.

Borjas (16) points to several benefits of immigration even when native workers suffer wage losses. In particular, there is a welfare gain from the increased employment when wages drop due to the entry of immigrants. In addition, Borjas (16) points to the potential increase in demand for native workers when immigrants arrive to the U.S, which could be due to (1) an increase in consumption by the immigrants themselves or (2) the fact that immigrant workers complement the work of natives and, thus, employers increase the employment of both immigrant and native workers. This last benefit is exactly what we find in our analysis. Consequently, our study suggests that this benefit from immigration is important and should be considered when designing immigration policy. It may be that rather than trying to encourage more skilled immigration, and implicitly discourage unskilled immigration (as is the current focus of US immigration policy), the US may want to attract immigrants who have complementary and different skills from those of the native population. The analysis here suggests that this would generate gains for more educated natives without necessarily hurting the less skilled or even earlier immigrants.

As suggested above, immigrants may be raising the earnings of skilled natives through two channels. First, immigrants may work directly with natives and increase their productivity by complementing their work. Second, immigrants may provide cheap services and goods to natives that lower prices and raise their real earnings. It would be interesting to investigate this further to find out whether it is the first or the second channel that most affects the earnings of natives.[11] While more analysis is needed to clarify which channel is at work, the fact that veteran immigrants do not experience the same gain in real earnings, though presumably they were benefiting from the same drop in prices, suggests that the first channel is probably more important in increasing the real wages of native Hispanics.

Finally, it is important to point out that any deterioration suffered by native Hispanics during the past decades does not appear to be linked to the increased competition by recent immigrants. On the contrary, our analysis suggests that immigration actually improved the fortunes of native Hispanics, so that any deterioration in their labor market conditions needs to be explained by other factors and requires further investigation.

Notes

1. We are grateful to David Leal, Pia Orrenious, Michael Stoll, Steve Trejo, and the participants at the Inter-University Program for Latino Research conference held at the University of Texas at Austin.
2. Saiz and Zoido (11) highlight the returns to speaking another language in the US and make it clear that this is a valuable skill in the US labor market.
3. By contrast, analyses for Europe following this regional approach find larger negative effects on the employment of natives (12–14).
4. Like our previous work, the paper by Ottaviano and Peri (9) also finds positive effects of immigration on other US natives. However, unlike our study, the Ottaviano and Peri (9) analysis finds positive effects on all natives irrespective of skill level. Another major difference between Kugler and Yuksel (4) and Ottaviano and Peri (9) is that our analysis exploits the differences in immigration shares across states, while Ottaviano and Peri mainly exploit changes in immigration shares over time. Finally, in our study, the positive effect of immigration on highly-skilled natives (both Hispanic and non-Hispanic) disappears when we attempt to control for out-migration.
5. These are our own calculations using the 1980, 1990, and 2000 Censuses and the 2003–2004–2005 combined cross-section of the American Community Surveys.
6. Borjas 15 presents evidence showing that the inter-generational transmission coefficient in wages for second generation Americans is 0.6863 compared to 0.42 for third generation Americans.
7. The differences in education between recent and veteran immigrant men and women are both statistically significant.
8. That is, this reports the results from the following regression:

$$S_{LAjt} = \theta_j + \pi_t + \alpha \, S_{SCjt} + v_{jt},$$

where $S_{SCjt} = \left[\sum_c {}_{\varepsilon LA}\left(M_{cjt-1}/M_{ct-1}\right)M_{ct}\right]/\left[\sum_c \left(M_{cjt-1}/M_{ct-1}\right)M_{ct} + N_{jt-1}\right]$ is the predicted share of immigrants from the same country based on previous migration from those countries to the state in the previous past.

9. In this case, the table reports result from the following regression:

$$S_{LAjt} = \theta_j + \pi_t + \alpha\left(\text{Distance}_j \times \text{Post} - \text{Mitch}_t\right) + v_{jt},$$

where Distance$_j$ measures the distance in miles from Tegucigalpa (the capital of Honduras) to the southern-most point in each state and Post-Mitch$_t$ is an indicator of whether the immigrants came before or after the hurricane hit Central America.

10. That is, here we estimate two-stage least squares regressions, where the first stages are those reported in Table 11.5 and the second stages are based on the regression:

$$Y_{ijt} = \mu_j + \tau_t + \beta'X_{ijt} + \gamma\hat{S}_{LAjt} + \varepsilon_{ijt},$$

where $\hat{S}_{LAjt}$ is the predicted share of Latin Americans coming due to social networks and due to Hurricane Mitch, respectively.

11. See Cortes (17) for evidence on the impact of immigration on prices.

References

1. Borjas, George. 1985. "Assimilation, Changes in Cohort Quality and the Earnings of Immigrants." *Journal of Labor Economics*, 3(4): 463–489.
2. Borjas, George. 1995a. "Assimilation and Changes in Cohort Quality Revisited: What Happened to Immigrant Earnings in the 1980s?" *Journal of Labor Economics*, 13(2): 201–245.
3. Card, David. 2001. "Immigrant Inflows, Native Outflows, and the Local Labor Market Impact of Higher Immigration." *Journal of Labor Economics*, 19(1): 22–64.
4. Kugler, Adriana, and Mutlu Yuksel. 2008. "Effects of Low-skilled Immigration on U.S. Natives: Evidence from Hurricane Mitch." NBER Working Paper 14293.
5. Altonji, Joseph, and David Card. 1991. "The Effects of Immigration on the Labor Market Outcomes of Less-Skilled Workers," In *Immigration, Trade and the Labor Market*, ed. John Abowd and Richard Freeman, 201–234. Chicago: University of Chicago Press.
6. Card, David. 1990. "The Impact of the Mariel Boatlift on the Miami Labor Market." *Industrial and Labor Relations Review*, 43(2): 245–257.
7. Borjas, George. 2003. "The Labor Demand Curve Is Downward Sloping: Reexamining the Impact of Immigration on the Labor Market." *Quarterly Journal of Economics*, 118(4): 1335–1374.
8. Borjas, George, Richard Freeman, and Lawrence Katz. 1997. "How Much Do Immigration and Trade Affect Labor Market Outcomes?" Brookings Papers on Economic Activity 1.
9. Ottaviano, Gianmarco, and Giovanni Peri. 2006. "Rethinking the Effects of Immigration on Earnings." NBER Working Paper 12497.
10. Borjas, George, Jeffrey Grogger, and Gordon Hanson. 2010. "Immigration and the Economic Status of African American Men." *Economica*, 77(306): 255–282.
11. Saiz, Albert, and Elena Zoido. 2005. "Listening to What the World Says: Bilingualism and Earnings in the U.S." *Review of Economics and Statistics*, 87(3): 523–538.
12. Angrist, Joshua, and Adriana Kugler. 2003. "Protective or Counter-Productive? Labor Market Institutions and the Effect of Immigration on EU Natives." *Economic Journal*, 113(488): F302–F331.
13. Carrington, William, and Pedro deLima. 1996. "The Impact of the 1970 Repatriates from Africa on the Portuguese Labor Market." *Industrial and Labor Relations Review*, 49(2): 330–347.

14. Hunt, Jennifer. 1992. "The Impact of the 1992 Repatriates from Algeria on the French Labor Market." *Industrial and Labor Relations Review*, 45(3): 556–572.
15. Borjas, George. 1992. "Ethnic Capital and Intergenerational Mobility." *Quarterly Journal of Economics*, 107(1): 123–50.
16. Borjas, George. 1995b. "The Economic Benefits of Immigration." *Journal of Economic Perspectives*, 9(2): 3–22.
17. Cortes, Patricia. 2008. "The Effect of Low-Skilled Immigration on U.S. Prices: Evidence from CPI Data." *Journal of Political Economy*, 116(3): 381–422.

Chapter 12
Immigrants, Hispanics, and the Evolution of Housing Prices in the US

Albert Saiz

Abstract How has immigration and the associated growth in the Hispanic population affected the evolution of housing prices and rents in the United States? The
answer to this question depends on the scale of the local housing demand shock
associated with immigration and the growth in the Hispanic population in a city.
This chapter reviews the existing literature on the issue and introduces a number
of new facts. Cities that received immigrants experienced faster housing price and
rent appreciation during the last two decades of the 20th century. Hispanic-dense
metropolitan areas have more expensive housing. Part of the price differential is
due to the growth in the Hispanic population, and we derive a statistical causal
link between Hispanic growth and average housing price growth. However, within
metropolitan areas it is precisely those neighborhoods with increasing Hispanic
share where relatively slower housing price and rent appreciation took place. The
facts are consistent with immigrant and Hispanic population growth generally driving up the demand for living in a city, but with increasing ethnic segregation within
the city.

Introduction

What is the effect of the growth of immigrant and Hispanic populations on the housing markets of the United States? The relationship between Hispanic and immigrant
population growth and housing price movements is of vital importance in assessing
the impact of immigration on an economy. The housing market itself is of interest
because the evolution of housing prices and rents are key economic indicators of
welfare. Natives and immigrants alike spend about one third of their incomes on
housing in the United States. Individuals in the lower quintile of the income distribution spend an even greater share. Similarly, housing wealth represents about 60%
of total wealth for American homeowners (1).

A. Saiz (✉)
University of Pennsylvania, Philadelphia, PA, USA
e-mail: saiz@wharton.upenn.edu

D.L. Leal, S.J. Trejo (eds.), *Latinos and the Economy*, Immigrants and Minorities,
Politics and Policy, DOI 10.1007/978-1-4419-6682-7_12,
© Springer Science+Business Media, LLC 2011

   Yet much of the previous research in the economic impact of immigration has focused on labor markets. Wages, employment conditions, and unemployment rates are certainly important to understand the social and economic dynamics of the arrival of new immigrants. Labor market conditions are important to understand the interaction of natives and immigrants, and how perceptions among each group about the other are formed. On reflection, however, there are many complementary ways by which the US economy imports foreign labor without immigration. International trade brings the product of foreign workers' efforts to American shores. American firms routinely produce offshore, or outsource parts of their supply chain to foreign producers, always entailing the participation of foreign labor in products that will eventually be purchased by American consumers. More recently, the Internet and improvements in telecommunication technologies have made it possible to hire workers who will deliver their services in the US while working abroad. Customer service representatives, technical support personnel, and salesmen working from a remote office in Bangalore can meet the needs of many American customers.

   Immigration cannot be solely defined by the job market and the fact that immigrants work in the US. economy. Therefore, the study of the impact of immigration on local economics cannot be limited to labor outcomes. Immigrants must dwell into their new destination countries; it is, therefore, important to understand their economic impact on residential markets. Housing markets are important given their weight in the expenditures and wealth of the native and the foreign-born in the US. However, there are at least two other reasons why housing markets should come to the forefront of the study of the economic impact of immigration.

   Firstly, the evolution of housing prices and rents may help us understand the mobility decisions of natives (or non-Hispanics) in cities where immigration or the Hispanic population is growing rapidly. Previous research seems to imply that immigration may not strongly impact wages in the short run, but very high housing prices in California, New York, Miami, or Chicago may account for internal migration of natives.

   Secondly, housing prices at a more micro level may tell us about the existence of segregatory preferences. Cutler et al. (2) demonstrated that immigrant residential segregation has been on the rise for the last 20 years. Similarly, Hispanics are now more segregated than 30 years ago. We can use housing prices as a market measure of the perceived valuation of Hispanic neighborhoods. Keeping physical structural quality constant, if neighborhoods that are becoming denser with immigrants or Hispanics experience relative housing price and rent depreciation, then this implies the existence of ethnic preferences by natives. Why? The easiest way to understand this is to use a simple "financial arbitrage" argument (for a more detailed exposition see 3). If prices are lower in a Hispanic or immigrant neighborhood and the perceived quality is the same as in native areas, then all natives would like to move to the cheaper neighborhood. Keeping other quality attributes constant (which is what the bulk of existing research tries to do empirically) prices should be equalized everywhere. If prices are lower in Hispanic or immigrant neighborhoods relative to the rest of the city, assuming similar location and structural characteristics, this implies different valuations of the neighborhood that are contingent on its ethnic composition.

The research linking immigration to housing prices also informs the debate on the impact of immigration on local prices. Cortés (4) showed that relative prices of services produced with abundant immigrant labor grew more slowly during the 1980s and 1990s. However, it is still possible that absolute prices are growing faster in metropolitan areas where immigrants concentrate. In fact, the cross-sectional correlation between local housing price levels and the American Chamber of Commerce Price Index is a very high 0.8. Clearly, the results on the evolution of rent and housing prices need to be an integral part of future investigations about the evolution of local prices in immigrant areas.

In this chapter, I examine this relationship and the consequences of immigrant and Hispanic population expansion for housing price growth in metropolitan areas of the United States. I first compare the evolution of prices and rents in cities that experienced substantial growth in the Hispanic population with cities in which Hispanic growth has been more muted. I then evaluate the association between "Hispanicization" and local price growth within three metropolitan areas: Houston, Los Angeles, and Chicago. I consider the impact of the growth in the foreign-born population generally, as well as the growth of the Hispanic population. At times I will also focus on the Mexican and Central American communities.

Of course, most Hispanics in the United States are not immigrants, and one should not confuse the two groups. Peoples from Spain were the first European colonizers of North America. About one third of the territories in the United States belonged to Mexico prior to Texas Independence and the Mexican-American War. The Hispanic presence in the United States has always been important and is indeed historic. However, the growth in the Hispanic population has been fueled by recent immigration since 1960. In this sense, I will try empirically to treat Hispanic growth as parallel to the process of international migration from Mexico, Central America, and other Latin American countries, and, therefore, exogenous to the initial conditions of the local economies (more on this below).

Combining the results in this chapter with previous research on the impact of immigration on housing prices and rents yields a number of novel and sometimes unexpected results. Firstly, cities where Hispanics tended to dwell in the 1980s and 1990s were singularly expensive, in terms of both housing rents and prices. Secondly, part of the fact that prices are higher in Hispanic metropolitan areas is due to the demographic pressure exerted by Hispanic growth. In areas where immigrants concentrated in the 1980s and 1990s, housing prices and rents experienced faster inflation. Since the growth of the Hispanic population in the United States is directly linked to recent migratory patterns, it follows that Hispanic population growth has been associated with more expensive housing, on average, in the metropolitan areas where Hispanics clustered. Thirdly, the positive impact on prices was uneven. Within metropolitan areas, neighborhoods with growing Hispanic settlement experienced relatively slower appreciation. The results are consistent with Hispanic growth pushing up demand for a city, but also with increased segregation within the city. Non-Hispanics have been paying price premiums in order to avoid areas of growing Hispanic concentration.

Immigrants and Housing Rents and Prices

This section follows closely the methodology exposited in Saiz (5) and (6), which found that immigration pushes up housing prices in destination metropolitan areas. This earlier work used yearly admissions data (from the former Immigration and Naturalization Service) and yearly rent data from HUD on rents at the median and 45th percentile of each metropolitan statistical area (MSA). The yearly admissions data capture only immigrants who obtained permanent resident status (the green card) in a given year ((6) discusses the advantages and disadvantages of using this data source). That research also examines the evolution of housing prices by MSA using Freddie Mac's repeat sales index. The Freddie Mac index is constructed using repeated observations of separate sales of the same underlying properties, and is relatively robust to structural changes in the composition of the housing stock; this research, therefore, focuses on relative high-frequency changes in rents and housing prices in response to recorded migratory fluxes. Here I will consider lower frequencies, extending the previous results to long differences: 1984–1998. This implies, non-technically, that I will correlate the change in housing prices and rents between the 2 years (1998 and 1984) to the total accumulated immigration inflows during that period. The regressions are, therefore, using a cross section of city[1] changes between two points in time.

Using longer data frequencies has several advantages. More saliently, it avoids problems related to short-term fluctuations in the changes in the variables, which may obscure long-term relationships. Moreover, it reduces issues with measurement error of the variables, which is exacerbated by taking differences of the data at lower frequencies (i.e., annual data).

Table 12.1 shows the results of the exercise. In fact, the results using the change of the log of rents or housing prices on the left-hand side are very similar to those obtained by Saiz (6).

The main explanatory variable of interest is the total number of new permanent immigrant admissions in a metro area (a proxy for recent permanent immigration inflows in a city) between the years 1983 and 1997, divided by the initial level of population in the MSA.[2] The ordinary least squares (OLS) regressions in columns 1 and 3 imply that a "shock" to the immigrant permanent resident population that amounted to 1% of the initial population of an MSA was associated with robust housing inflation: 0.65% for rents and 1.7% for housing prices. Factually, immigrant cities are becoming more expensive cities. All regressions in Table 12.1 control for the change in the log of income between 1983 and 1997. This variable captures the evolution of the local economy during that period, a confounding factor for the evolution of housing prices and rents; previous research has shown that housing prices and rents tend to follow the evolution of local income, other variables being constant (7).

Table 12.1 Impact of new immigrant residents on rents and prices

	Change in log rents 84–98 (FMR)		Change in log prices 84–98 (Freddie Mac)	
	(1)	(2)	(3)	(4)
Immigrant admissions (83–97) per 1983 population	0.654	0.641	1.755	1.796
	(0.212)***	(0.228)***	(0.325)***	(0.341)***
Change in log incomes 83–97	0.418	0.417	0.956	0.960
	(0.091)***	(0.091)***	(0.151)***	(0.151)***
Unemployment rate (1983)	−0.420	−0.416	3.199	3.191
	(0.266)	(0.267)	(0.510)***	(0.511)***
Murders per 100 inhabitants (1983)	0.883	0.903	−14.577	−14.679
	(1.485)	(1.490)	(2.400)***	(2.413)***
Log central city area	−0.017	−0.017	−0.005	−0.004
	(0.008)**	(0.008)**	(0.014)	(0.014)
Log January average temperature (average 1941–1970)	0.007	0.007	−0.049	−0.050
	(0.019)	(0.019)	(0.037)	(0.037)
Log July mean relative humidity (average 1941–1970)	−0.007	−0.007	0.049	0.049
	(0.023)	(0.023)	(0.031)	(0.031)
Percentage with Bachelor's degree 1980	0.004	0.004	0.003	0.003
	(0.002)**	(0.002)**	−0.003	−0.003
Constant	0.209	0.208	−0.301	−0.300
	(0.144)	(0.144)	(0.266)	(0.266)
Observations (MSA)	300	300	155	155
R-squared	0.220	0.220	0.540	0.540

Standard errors in parentheses
*significant at 10%; **significant at 5%; ***significant at 1%

Moreover, a major concern of past studies on the impact of immigration on wages is that immigration could be endogenously capturing the impact of income shocks that attracted immigrants into an area. However, part of the growth in incomes in absolute terms in an area can be attributable to immigration itself. If this is the case, the coefficients in Table 12.1 reflect the effect of immigration that goes above and beyond its impact as mediated by changes in income. In fact, controlling for income does not change the relevant coefficients much. The regressions additionally include other variables that are commonly associated with rent growth in the United States during the relevant period (8).

Columns 2 and 4 in Table 12.2 perform a similar exercise, this time using an instrumental variables (IV) approach. Immigration flows may be endogenous to the growth in housing prices for two reasons. The first is reverse causality: immigrants may be attracted to areas that are experiencing slower price appreciation. In this case, the association between immigration and prices shown in columns 1 and 2

Table 12.2 OLS (MR): Hispanic population "shock" and housing rents/prices

	ΔLog rent (1)	ΔLog median price (2)	ΔLog price index (3)
ΔHispanic population/(population at T-10)	0.458	0.732	0.781
	(0.130)***	(0.241)***	(0.296)***
Log rents/prices at T-10	−0.079	−0.151	−0.052
	(0.026)***	(0.023)***	(0.028)*
ΔLog income	0.859	1.663	1.631
	(0.064)***	(0.134)***	(0.162)***
Unemployment rate at T-10	−0.017	−0.614	0.754
	(0.194)	(0.359)*	(0.518)
Log January average temperature (Average 1941–1970)	0.03	0.006	−0.037
	(0.008)***	(0.017)	(0.021)*
Log July mean relative humidity (average 1941–1970)	−0.02	−0.034	0.005
	(0.014)	(0.025)	(0.030)
Log area	−0.004	−0.014	−0.011
	(0.004)	(0.008)*	(0.010)
Murders per 100 inhabitants	0.518	0.783	−3.041
	(0.827)	(2.001)	(2.624)
Percentage with Bachelor's degree at T-10	0.001	0	0.001
	(0.001)	(0.001)	(0.001)
Year fixed effects	yes	yes	yes
Observations	632	632	442
R-squared	0.74	0.35	0.33

Robust standard errors in parentheses
*significant at 10%; **significant at 5%; ***significant at 1%

would represent a lower bound of the actual causal impact of immigration. The second reason for endogeneity is that relevant variables may be omitted: certain characteristics of a city that attracted immigrants may also be the cause of price/rent growth, independent of immigration, per se. In this case, the sign of the bias in previous estimates is unknown.

To deal with endogeneity issues, a possible approach is to use exogenous sources of variation. Optimally, one would like to have an exogenous immigration shock into a group of metropolitan areas and compare the subsequent price/rent evolution in each. IV techniques try to emulate that ideal experiment. In this case, the approach used in Saiz (6) is implemented. Immigration inflows by year and origin nationality are predicted first using a simple random effects model that fits the US experience with data on immigration by country and other characteristics of the sending country. For instance, immigrant outflows into the US are predicted to decrease in countries with increasing GDP and increase in countries with increasing population. Once I obtain the predictions by country and year, I use the share of immigrants moving to each MSA by nationality in 1983 and subsequent immigrant inflows. For instance, if Mexicans tended to move to Los Angles in 1983 and I predict a substantial inflow of Mexicans into the United States in 1996, we would expect a substantial number of new immigrants in Los Angeles in that year.

Using the predictions as instruments for the actual inflows (details can be found in 6) yields results that are extremely close to the OLS estimates. In fact, just by knowing where immigrants went in 1983 and estimating the size of subsequent inflows by country, one can explain a good deal of the variance of legal immigrant inflows in the period that we study. Therefore, subsequent fluctuations in the economic and social conditions of these cities cannot account for the association between price growth and immigrant intake. The results are clearly consistent with a causal interpretation going from increased housing demand due to immigration to subsequent housing price growth.

The results confirm the previous literature that establishes a link between immigration and housing inflation. First, Gonzalez (9) found a positive association between immigration and housing price levels in California and Texas, which he attributes to a compensating differential in terms of a higher willingness-to-pay of Mexicans and Mexican-Americans for cities with specific amenities that cater to that community. Saiz (10) used the Mariel boatlift in Miami as a natural experiment to show that rents in Miami grew 7–11% faster subsequent to the massive arrival of Cuban immigrants in 1980. Saiz (6) also used all immigrants in the 1970, 1980, 1990, and 2000 censuses and found similar results. Saiz (5, 6, 10), Greulich et al. (11), Ottaviano and Peri (12), and this chapter confirm this link between immigration and price growth at the metropolitan area level using alternative data sources, time periods, geographic coverage, and statistical techniques.

Hispanic Growth and Housing Rents and Prices

Moving beyond immigration, does the growth in the Hispanic population in the US impact US housing markets? As discussed earlier, the phenomenon is linked with the growth in the immigrant Latino population since the late 1960s. However, considerable growth in the native-born Hispanic population has also occurred in that time. What is the impact of overall Hispanic growth in those cities where this phenomenon has been more quantitatively important?

First, however, it is necessary to distinguish Hispanic growth from other components of population growth to show that this question is worth asking. Assessing the impact of Hispanic population growth makes sense if one compares the current scenario to a counterfactual world where the growth of Hispanic population was nonexistent or minuscule. Conventional spatial equilibrium models in economics and geography imply that, in countries with reduced barriers to inter-urban mobility, such as the United States, population flows will equilibrate quality of life across locations. Wages and rents and housing prices tend to adjust until everyone (or at least those individuals who are initially willing to move for realistic changes in local economic and environmental circumstances) is indifferent between locations. For instance, if local productivity increases in a city, with consequently higher wages, then a number of individuals will move to that city, which has now become relatively more attractive. Increased labor supply and higher demand for housing will then tend to depress the initial wage boost and put pressure on housing prices until the new economic conditions cease to make the city more attractive than others.

It is in a context of a hypothetical counterfactual initial spatial equilibrium across locales without Hispanic growth where it makes sense to ask what the impact of this phenomenon was. Clearly, Hispanic growth was disproportionally concentrated in a number of metropolitan areas for reasons other than wages, prices, and other economic factors. New Hispanic immigrants located in areas that corresponded to previous Hispanic population centers, and natural population growth of the Hispanic population has disproportionately concentrated in these areas. Of course, many Hispanic individuals have relocated to other cities searching for higher wages, amenities, and low housing costs.

It therefore makes sense to try to emulate the ideal experiment (comparing a world with exogenous Hispanic growth to a counterfactual without it) by using instrumental variables techniques. In that sense, immigration and the subsequent growth of the Hispanic population in immigrant cities can be considered, conceptually, a "helicopter drop" of people.

Table 12.3 starts by documenting a new stylized fact: Hispanics live in expensive areas. The table consists of an OLS regression where the log of median housing rents (columns 1, and 2) and values (columns 3 and 4) in the 1980, 1990, and 2000 census data by metropolitan area appears on the left-hand side. We include time fixed effects to capture the evolution of inflation in the US and cluster standard errors at the MSA level. On the right-hand side, the main explanatory variable is the Hispanic share (exclusively in columns 1 and 3) and other metropolitan area characteristics, most importantly income.

One can interpret the coefficients as giving us a sense of the strength of the correlation between housing rents and prices and the Hispanic share across cities. Controlling for a number of important variables, from Table 12.3 one can expect cities where the Hispanic share is one percentage point higher to have rents and prices that are from about 0.3% to 0.5% higher. In fact, most of the variation in rents and prices across cities can be explained by a single variable: income. And yet, considering two metropolitan areas with the same income, it is a stylized fact that the one with a higher proportion of Hispanics is more likely to have higher prices.

The regressions in Table 12.3 do not tell us much about the impact of immigration on rents and housing prices. Attributes that made a city more attractive to Hispanics may also be associated with higher prices. In order to know more about this we consider a statistical model that links changes in the size of the Hispanic share to changes in housing prices/rents. Of course, changes in the Hispanic share, per se, should not be associated with increasing prices if Hispanic growth is not associated with growth in the demand for a city. Therefore, the total number of Hispanic population growth in an MSA divided by its initial population level will be considered as a measure of housing demand "shock." For instance, if 200,000 people were Hispanic in a city with 1 million inhabitants in 1990, and their share grew to 300,000 in 2000, this measure would imply a demand "shock" of 10% ($100,000/1,000,000 = 0.1$) of the initial population.

Table 12.3 Hispanics live in expensive metro areas

	Log median rent		Log median house value	
	(1)	(2)	(3)	(4)
Hispanic population/population	0.187 (0.127)	0.285 (0.048)***	0.339 (0.250)	0.482 (0.121)***
Log income		0.725 (0.037)***		1.281 (0.085)***
Unemployment rate		0.575 (0.235)**		1.942 (0.588)***
Log January average temperature (Average 1941–1970)		0.104 (0.016)***		0.137 (0.032)***
Log July mean relative humidity (average 1941–1970)		0.013 (0.019)		−0.031 (0.047)
Log Area		0.006 (0.008)		0.012 (0.017)
Murders per 100 inhabitants		−4.396 (1.047)***		−9.469 (2.455)***
Percentage with Bachelor's degree		0.007 (0.001)***		0.016 (0.002)***
Year fixed effects	Yes	Yes	Yes	Yes
Observations (MSA*time)	954	948	954	948
R-squared	0.79	0.94	0.51	0.82

Clustered standard errors in parentheses
*significant at 10%; **significant at 5%; ***significant at 1%

Following Saiz (6), Table 12.4 provides the relationship between decadal changes in median housing prices and rents from the census and the measure of Hispanic population shocks in each of the decades under consideration (1980–1990 and 1990–2000). The regressions are similar to those in Table 12.1, but the Freddie Mac price index is included along with the Hispanic share, rent, and price measures from the census. In addition, several time observations for each MSA are included, allowing for the variation within cities. The main controls are the change in per capita income in each decade and decade fixed effects, which control for the general evolution of the housing markets in the nation as a whole. As in other specifications, several characteristics of the metropolitan area as measured in the initial year of the decade are also controlled for. Standard errors are clustered at the MSA level.

The results in Table 12.4 suggest very strong associations between Hispanic "demand shocks" and the growth of housing prices and rents. Column 1 suggests that, other things being equal, a Hispanic "demand shock" that amounts to 1% of the initial population is associated with 0.4% rental price inflation. Columns 2 and 3 suggest that the impact on housing prices is slightly higher, 0.5–0.7%, albeit the magnitudes of the price and rent results are not statistically different. It is not only

Table 12.4 OLS: Hispanic population "shock" and housing rents/prices

	ΔLog rent (1)	ΔLog median price (2)	ΔLog price index (3)
ΔHispanic population/(population at T-10)	0.406	0.554	0.686
	(0.098)***	(0.158)***	(0.239)***
ΔLog income	0.889	1.743	1.672
	(0.068)***	(0.146)***	(0.168)***
Unemployment rate at T-10	0.036	−0.627	0.792
	(0.195)	(0.342)*	(0.500)
Log January average temperature (Average 1941–1970)	0.027	−0.002	−0.042
	(0.007)***	−0.015	(0.020)**
Log July mean relative humidity (Average 1941–1970)	−0.028	−0.053	−0.002
	(0.012)**	(0.019)***	−0.026
Log area	−0.006	−0.02	−0.011
	(0.004)	(0.006)***	(0.009)
Murders per 100 inhabitants	0.708	1.701	−2.611
	(0.790)	(1.718)	(2.440)
Percentage with Bachelor's degree at T-10	0	−0.005	−0.001
	(0.001)	(0.001)***	(0.001)
Year fixed effects	yes	yes	yes
Observations	632	632	442
R-squared	0.74	0.31	0.33

Robust standard errors in parentheses
*significant at 10%; **significant at 5%; ***significant at 1%

that Hispanics tend to live in expensive areas; areas with greater Hispanic population shares also happened to experience rapid housing appreciation.

There is an important shortcoming, however, in the results in the previous table. As we saw in Table 12.3, Hispanics tended to live in relatively more expensive areas. This was true in 1980 and all subsequent initial years of the previous estimates (1980 and 1990). Previous literature on the evolution of housing prices and rents has conclusively established mean-reversion as an established empirical fact (13–15).

Prices in expensive areas tend to grow at a slower rate than prices in cheaper areas. The explanations for this fact are many, from data measurement error or the existence of important temporary components in the data generation process to convergence in productivity and amenities across locales. For instance, areas in the South have become more integrated with the national economy and generally have been catching up in most measures of economic and social development. The process of economic convergence within countries (as documented by 16 and 17) implies mean reversion in the distribution of housing prices and rents in a country.

Previous literature on the relationship between demographics and the evolution of housing prices has, to date, tended to ignore this fact. This may generate omitted variable bias insofar as demographic factors are associated with initial housing prices, as is the case in this study. Table 12.2 includes the log of initial housing rents and prices as explanatory variables in order to address this problem.

The results in Table 12.2 point to an even stronger relationship between Hispanic population growth and price and rent appreciation in the housing sector. This makes sense in the presence of mean reversion. Hispanics moved to cities that were initially quite expensive in relative terms: New York, Chicago, Los Angeles, San Diego, and other large metropolitan areas in California and other parts of the country. These are precisely the areas in which, other things being constant, one would have expected housing price growth to be relatively slower, due to the fact that other areas have been catching up. Therefore, Hispanic growth in many of these high-rent areas was a factor slowing convergence of rents and housing prices in the United States.

The previous results can be understood as descriptive statistics. It seems an uncontestable fact that in MSAs with strong Hispanic "demand shocks" (Hispanic growth as a percentage of initial population levels), housing prices and rental contracts experienced faster appreciation. However, two conceptual issues of interpretation remain.

The first conceptual issue pertains to causality. Are the previous estimates the result of Hispanic growth or do they just reflect the fact that Hispanics moved to more expensive areas? Alternatively, initial attributes that attracted Hispanics may have also been associated with economic growth or improving local amenities. In order to make a causal interpretation, an instrumental variable technique is again required. As in the preferred theoretical interpretation for explaining the focus on Hispanic growth (the existence of a hypothetical counterfactual where Hispanic growth would not have happened), the following analysis will try to exploit exogenous shocks to the local populations of cities where an initial market equilibrium was disrupted because Hispanics were attracted to these cities in disproportionate numbers for reasons other than housing prices. As in most of the literature focusing on the economic impact of immigration, I use a "shift-share" of national Hispanic growth as an instrument.

As is well-known from very early literature, the growth of immigrant groups in a city follows a snowball process, where early settlers establish a bridge-head for later comers. The establishment of local ethnic networks is, therefore, very important to explain subsequent growth of ethnic minorities, like Hispanics, which tend to cluster in areas where family, friends, and other co-ethnics settled earlier.

This section makes use of ethnic clustering as an exogenous shock to a population, not related to other factors that generally made the city more attractive to everyone in the country. Consider thus the total growth of the Hispanic population in the United States in a given decade (say 1990–2000). An instrument for Hispanic growth assigns those flows proportionally according to the initial Hispanic share as a proportion of the Hispanic population in the US in 1980. The expected Hispanic inflow in a city will simply be the city's initial "market share" in 1980 (the number of Hispanics in the city divided by the total number of Hispanics in the US) times the total Hispanic growth in the US. The instrument thus produced should be exogenous to the subsequent fortunes of a city after 1980. The instrumental variable technique therefore uses the variation in the data that is related to initial ethnic settlement patterns, as opposed to changes in Hispanic growth after 1980.

Table 12.5 OLS (IV): Hispanic population "shock" and housing rents/prices

	ΔLog rent (1)	ΔLog median price (2)	ΔLog price index (3)
ΔHispanic population/(population at T-10)	0.746	1.255	1.217
	(0.198)***	(0.365)***	(0.404)***
Log rents/prices at T-10	−0.1	−0.168	−0.069
	(0.033)***	(0.029)***	(0.033)**
ΔLog income	0.869	1.687	1.662
	(0.065)***	(0.137)***	(0.163)***
Unemployment rate at T-10	−0.128	−0.791	0.589
	(0.213)	(0.399)**	(0.607)
Log January average temperature (Average 1941–1970)	0.015	−0.022	−0.061
	(0.009)*	(0.021)	(0.024)**
Log July mean relative humidity (average 1941–1970)	−0.003	−0.006	0.026
	(0.018)	(0.031)	(0.033)
Log area	−0.007	−0.019	−0.015
	(0.004)	(0.008)**	(0.010)
Murders per 100 inhabitants	0.588	0.899	−2.899
	(0.839)	(1.978)	(2.640)
Percentage with Bachelor's degree at T-10	0.001	0	0.001
	(0.001)	(0.001)	(0.002)
Year fixed effects	yes	yes	yes
Observations	632	632	442
R-squared			

Robust standard errors in parentheses
*significant at 10%; **significant at 5%; ***significant at 1%

Table 12.5 presents the results of the IV estimation. Yet again, the coefficients of the "Hispanic population shock" on rental and price growth in residential real estate markets show increases in housing prices. The coefficients suggest an impact close to one. The results do not yield a statistical rejection of the hypothesis that a Hispanic shock that amounted to 1% of the initial population in the 1980s and 1990s caused a 1% increase in housing prices and rents, as benchmarked against a counterfactual without growth in the Hispanic population. This suggests that endogeneity bias may have been biasing the OLS coefficients downward. This makes sense, because one could have expected new Hispanic move-ins to avoid metropolitan areas that were becoming inordinately expensive, forcing somewhat of a negative correlation between Hispanic growth and price inflation.

The second conceptual issue that is worth discussion involves the interpretation of the coefficients. IV techniques can help with causal claims, but the impact of immigration and Hispanic population growth on average residential real estate inflation can go through a number of mechanisms. In many senses, the estimated impact is an amalgamation of different channels. When exogenous population growth shocks happen, three responses in the housing market merit attention (see 5, 6, 10 for more extensive discussions). Initially, most of the impact of an unexpected housing demand shock will be translated in higher rents (the first response). If the surge in demand is expected to persist, then housing prices will rise through conventional asset pricing mechanisms. The rise in housing rents, however, will in the long run motivate a surge in construction (the second market response). Depending on the elasticity of housing supply in a metropolitan area, increased supply will some-what mute the initial impact on rents. In areas with quite inelastic housing supply (this is in areas where it is rather difficult to build or where the marginal land has many undesirable features) new construction will not detract much from the initial housing price surge. Finally, the third response to higher housing rents, when pos-sibly slightly more competitive labor market conditions can also exist, may imply the reduced growth in the native population (or reduced internal migration to the city).

Since counterfactual native growth may have been higher in the absence of immi-gration, the final impact on housing prices and rents is also muted. The results should, therefore, be interpreted in the light of this discussion. The parameters on the impact of housing demand shocks (what the IV estimates attempt to ascertain) correspond to the final impact as mediated by housing supply and the response of native populations. In this context, they might very well have been zero or very small. However, they are not, and this supports the validity of measuring the Hispanic population impact as separate from studying population growth as a whole.

One remaining statistical concern must be discussed. The instruments may not be exogenous to the evolution of housing prices. This could happen if, for some rea-son, Hispanics had chosen locations with attributes that happened to predict housing price or rent growth, even in 1980. A way to tackle this issue is to use the other source of variation in the Hispanic growth data: changes in the level of Hispanic growth within a city. Table 12.6 explores this possibility. The table displays a model similar to that in Table 12.2, but now includes MSA fixed effects. Recall that the data contain two decades (1980s and 1990s) and the model's main variables of interest are the change in the log of rents and prices (left-hand side) and the Hispanic demand shock (right-hand side). Due to the two observations by MSA, including the fixed effects is equivalent to taking first-differences of the variables. This associates the acceleration of Hispanic growth to accelerations or decelerations in housing infla-tion. From another perspective, the fixed effects model implies looking at deviations from the previous decade, controlling for a general trend of city growth during both decades. City-specific omitted variables that were generally associated with growth will be included as control variables.

The results in Table 12.6 are, surprisingly, very consistent with the previous ones. The hypothesis that a Hispanic demand shock that amounts to 1% of the initial pop-ulation in a metropolitan area is associated with 1% growth in housing prices and rents cannot be statistically rejected. The results are surprising because the model now uses the absolute opposite source of variation that the IV technique used. In the IV specification the variance was mostly cross-sectional: variation between MSAs in initial Hispanic populations. Now, this specification solely uses longitudinal vari-ation within MSAs to obtain consistent parameters. In all and however one wants to read the evidence, the facts are very clear: the metropolitan areas that experienced

Table 12.6 OLS (FE): Hispanic population "shock" and housing rents/prices

	ΔLog rent (1)	ΔLog median price (2)	ΔLog price index (3)
ΔHispanic population/(population at T-10)	1.019	1.146	0.586
	(0.315)***	(0.383)***	(0.899)
Log rents/prices at T-10	−1.201	−1.52	−1.263
	(0.055)***	(0.047)***	(0.080)***
ΔLog income	0.23	0.263	0.502
	(0.064)***	(0.112)**	(0.189)***
Unemployment rate at T-10	−0.563	−2.656	0.635
	(0.277)**	(0.465)***	(1.382)
Murders per 100 inhabitants	−0.313	2.262	−1.541
	(1.465)	(2.454)	(5.614)
Percentage with Bachelor's degree at T-10	0.008	0.017	0.036
	(0.004)**	(0.007)**	(0.015)**
Year fixed effects	Yes	Yes	Yes
MSA fixed effects	Yes	Yes	Yes
Observations	632	632	442
R-squared	0.97	0.95	0.92

Robust standard errors in parentheses
*significant at 10%; **significant at 5%; ***significant at 1%

fast Hispanic growth also experienced marked appreciation of residential real estate rents and values during the last two decades, on average.

Hispanic Density and Housing Prices: A Neighborhood Analysis Within Cities

While average housing prices and rents are growing faster in metropolitan areas that are becoming more Hispanic, it is not clear a priori whether, within a metropolitan area, prices in the neighborhoods where Hispanics settle should grow at a relatively faster rate.

Previous research has documented increasing segregation for Hispanics. Conventional racial segregation models (18–22) yield a few unambiguous predictions as to the impact of individuals belonging to a minority group moving into a neighborhood. Most models consider three types of neighborhoods: a "white" (non-Hispanic) set of neighborhoods, an entirely "minority" group of neighborhoods, and a number of "mixed" areas (the literature focuses on African Americans as the relevant minority group, although the focus here will be on Hispanic neighborhoods). Mixed neighborhoods are either in long-run equilibrium or on their way to becoming one of the other two types of neighborhoods. If the members of the white group have negative tastes for living with members of the minority group, prices in the mixed neighborhoods must be lower than in the white neighborhoods: this reflects a compensating differential necessary for whites to live in the ethnically mixed place. Similarly, if minority individuals prefer to live with their co-ethnics, there will be a housing premium in minority neighborhoods vis-à-vis the mixed areas. The magnitude of the white versus mixed price differential (or, similarly, the changes in prices in white neighborhoods as minorities move in) can be thought of as a lower bound for the negative amenity as perceived by whites: the marginal white living in mixed neighborhoods is likely to exhibit less of a preference for ethnic segregation.

If a mixed equilibrium is not possible, then the mixed neighborhoods "tip" toward total segregation (as in (21)). In that case, the difference between prices in the white and minority neighborhoods need not reflect the tastes of the marginal white mover. Minority individuals may actually be willing to pay a higher price than whites to live in a minority neighborhood (theoretically, even a premium over the white neighborhood price is possible). However, if prices go down during the transition, then that is a sufficient condition for the existence of racially-based preferences: if whites were indifferent to ethnic composition and prices were going down, that would create an arbitrage opportunity for prospective white movers.

In sum, if prices increase during the transition toward a more minority-dense neighborhood, that does not necessarily say anything about ethnic tastes among non-minorities. However, the decline of prices in a neighborhood where minorities are moving is certainly a signal of racial preferences by whites, and the magnitude of the price decline is a lower bound for the actual valuation of the perceived "negative amenity" to non-minorities.

Saiz and Wachter (3) find that, controlling for the evolution of prices at the metropolitan area level, increases in the share of immigrant population in a neighborhood are associated with lower housing price appreciation. This empirical fact is, indeed, consistent with the idea that natives are, on average, willing to pay a premium for living in predominantly native areas. We focus here on three MSAs from Saiz and Wachter (3). We start by reproducing their results for three areas: Chicago, Los Angeles, and Houston. These three cities have been an important magnet for Latino immigrants, and their Hispanic populations have grown substantially over the last several decades. They are also quite different in terms of geography, land zoning and transportation policies, productive structure, governmental dynamics, and so on. Finding common patterns in three such different cities may point to quite strong and resilient social dynamics.

Table 12.7 focuses on changes in housing prices within each of these metropolitan areas. The basic unit of observation is the census tract. A census tract is a relatively homogenous collection of city blocks that encompasses about 4,000 individuals in the 2000 Census. We use the census-defined geography as a proxy for a neighborhood as previous literature has done. We use a version of the census data compiled by Geolytics™ that keeps the definition of a neighborhood constant in its 2000 boundaries. We focus on the changes in the log average housing values by neighborhood between 1990 and 2000 as the main dependent variable. The main explanatory variable in column 1 is the change in the share of population that is foreign-born between the years 1990 and 2000.

The regressions include a host of neighborhood characteristics that are omitted in Table 12.7 for ease of exposition. The interested reader should consult the

Table 12.7 Intercensal change in log value (census tract)

	(1)	(2)	(3)	(4)
	Chicago			
ΔForeign population/population	**−0.003**	**0.339**		
	(0.043)	(0.145)**		
ΔForeign population/population × share NH white at T-10		**−0.482** (0.207)**		
ΔForeign population/population × house value quartile at T-10		**−0.029** (0.048)		
ΔShare Hispanic			**−0.137** (0.031)***	
ΔShare Mexico				**−0.28** (0.065)***
ΔShare Central America				**−1.109** (0.387)***
	Houston			
ΔForeign population/population	**−0.315** (0.090)***	**−0.192** (0.230)		
ΔForeign population/population × share NH white at T-10		**−0.075** (0.380)		
ΔForeign population/Population × House Value Quartile at T-10		**−0.031**		
		(0.078)		
ΔShare Hispanic			**−0.356** (0.066)***	
ΔShare Mexico				**−0.489** (0.173)***
ΔShare Central America				**−0.199** (0.345)
	Los Angeles			
ΔForeign population/population	**−0.294** (0.040)***	**−0.567** (0.090)***		
ΔForeign population/population × share NH white at T-10		**−2.105** (0.231)***		
ΔForeign population/population × house value quartile at T-10		**0.86** (0.060)***		
ΔShare Hispanic			**−0.318** (0.030)***	
ΔShare Mexico				**−0.132** (0.086)
ΔShare Central America				**−0.763** (0.161)***

*Significant at 10%; **significant at 5%; ***significant at 1%

full specifications in Saiz and Wachter (3). As in that paper, we find now that in all cities, increases in the share of population that is foreign-born in the cities are associated with relative declines in housing prices. These declines are relative, remember, because the general price level in the city is growing everywhere, simply more slowly in areas that are becoming immigrant-dense (as opposed to declining in absolute terms).

For instance, a Houston neighborhood that goes from a 0% immigrant share to a 50% share can expect housing values to be 15% lower than they would have been otherwise. Note that the effect that Saiz and Wachter (3) find as an average for the US is much muted, statistically indifferent from zero, in Chicago. The answer to why is given in column 2 where we interact the change in the immigrant share by neighborhood by its initial non-Hispanic (NH) white share, and by a variable containing the neighborhood's quartile in the MSA price distribution (the first quartile—lowest housing values—is normalized to a value of zero; the other quartiles take value 1, 2, and 3).

Saiz and Wachter (3) also found that the negative association between increases in the immigrant share and price appreciation was much stronger in neighborhoods that used to be more expensive and less dense with minorities initially. In minority neighborhoods with low socioeconomic status (SES as captured by the initial price levels), immigration had a null or even positive impact on prices. We repeat the exercise in Saiz and Wachter (3) here for our three reference cities. While the results on initial housing values are less clear (in these cities, housing values and the share of minorities are extremely related to start with), the results are remarkably consistent for the interaction with the variable capturing minority density. The negative association between increasing immigrant density and lower price appreciation is stronger in neighborhoods that used to be majoritarily non-Hispanic white. This is consistent with a "white-flight" story within these metropolitan areas. In Chicago we also find a negative relative impact of immigration on price growth on white neighborhoods.

In column 3 we go further and repeat a similar exercise, this time with the share of Hispanics as the main explanatory variable. Now all coefficients are clearly negative in the three cities. Whatever the explanation, it is an uncontestable fact that relative prices (within a city) are growing less fast precisely in the areas that are becoming denser with Hispanics in Chicago, Houston, and LA. Again, since changes in structural housing quality do not seem to be at play (Saiz and Wachter 3) this points to social dynamics related to ethnic segregation.

Column 4 focuses on the share of individuals in a neighborhood born in Mexico and Central America. Mexico and the Central American countries are the source of origin of a majority of immigrants in the United States. The social dynamics of neighborhoods in which these groups settle deserve special attention.

As in the previous regressions, neighborhoods where Mexican and Central American populations increased also saw relatively slower growth in housing prices and rents in the three cities. Unfortunately, this seems to point to the fact that many other residents in these cities perceive these new immigrant enclaves as relatively less desirable places to live.

Conclusions

How has immigration and the associated growth in the Hispanic population affected the evolution of housing prices and rents in the United States? The answer to these questions depends on the scale of the local housing demand shocks associated with immigration and the growth in the Hispanic population in a city. This chapter reviews the existing literature on the issue and introduces a number of new facts. Cities where immigrants moved experienced faster housing price and rent appreciation during the two last decades of the 20th century. Hispanic metropolitan areas have more expensive housing. Moreover, part of the price differential is due to the growth in the Hispanic population. In the chapter, we derive a statistical causal link from Hispanic population growth to rising average housing prices at the metropolitan area level. Within metropolitan areas, however, it is precisely those neighborhoods with an increasing Hispanic share that experience relatively slower housing price and rent appreciation. The facts are consistent with immigrant and Hispanic population growth generally drive up the demand for living in a city, but with a simultaneous increase in ethnic segregation within the city and a perception by many that the new Hispanic enclaves are relatively less attractive places to live.

The results indicate that local housing policies have a very important role in immigrant cities. Concretely, policymakers should make concerted efforts to make land available for development in immigrant cities and suburbs in order to avoid overcrowding and prevent housing from becoming too expensive. In fact, Saiz (23) has shown that regulatory real estate development constraints are currently stronger in immigrant metropolitan areas, which compounds the problem.

It is more difficult to provide advice as to how to mute the trend of increasing immigrant-native segregation. Curtailing *snob zoning*, providing immigrants with information about residential choices, and local programs that facilitate resettlement out of immigrant enclaves would seem to be feasible policy alternatives.

Notes

1. I will use the term city and MSA indistinctly throughout the chapter.
2. The measure does not take into account illegal immigration and its growth but focuses on measured permanent inflows. For a discussion of the quantitative interpretation of the coefficients in the presence of omitted illegal inflows, see Saiz (6).

References

1. Tracy, Joseph, Henry Schneider, and Sewin Chan. 1999. "Are Stocks Overtaking Real Estate in Household Portfolios?,." *Current Issues in Economics and Finance*, 5(5). http://papers.ssrn.com/sol3/papers.cfm?abstract_id=996834 (last accessed 8 Nov 2010).
2. Cutler, David, Edward Glaeser, and Jacob Vigdor, 2005. "Is the Melting Pot Still Hot? Explaining the Resurgence of Immigrant Segregation." National Bureau of Economic Research Working Paper 11295.

3. Saiz, Albert, and Susan Wachter. 2006. "Immigration and the Neighborhood." FRB of Philadelphia Working Paper No. 06–22.
4. Cortés, Patricia. 2008. "The Effect of Low-skilled Immigration on U.S. Prices: Evidence from CPI Data." *Journal of Political Economy*, 116(3): 381–422.
5. Saiz, Albert. 2002. "The Impact of Immigration on American Cities." PhD dissertation. Harvard University.
6. Saiz, Albert. 2007. "Immigration and Housing Rents in American Cities." *Journal of Urban Economics*, 61(2): 345–371.
7. Malpezzi, Stephen. 1999. "A Simple Error Correction Model of House Prices." *Journal of Housing Economics*, 8(1): 27–62.
8. Glaeser, Edward, Jed Kolko, and Albert Saiz. 2001. "Consumer City." *Journal of Economic Geography*, 1(1):27–50.
9. Gonzalez, Arturo. "Mexican Enclaves and the Price of Culture." 1998. *Journal of Urban Economics*, 43(2): 273–291.
10. Saiz, Albert. 2003. "Room in the Kitchen for the Melting Pot: Immigration and Rental Prices." *The Review of Economics and Statistics*, 85(3): 502–521.
11. Greulich, Erica, John Quigley, and Steven Raphael. 2004. "The Anatomy of Rent Burdens: Immigration, Growth and Rental Housing." Brookings Papers on Urban Affairs 5.
12. Ottaviano, Gianmarco, and Giovanni Peri. 2006. "The Economic Value of Cultural Diversity: Evidence from U.S. Cities." *Journal of Economic Geography*, 6(1):9–44.
13. Case, Karl, and Robert Shiller. 1989. "The Efficiency of the Market for Single-Family Homes." *American Economic Review*, 79(1): 125–137.
14. Glaeser, Edward and Joseph Gyourko. 2006. "Housing Dynamics." National Bureau of Economic Research Working Paper 12787.
15. Meese, Richard, and Nancy Wallace. 2003. "House Price Dynamics and Market Fundamentals: The Parisian Housing Market." *Urban Studies*, 40(5): 1027–1046.
16. Barro, Robert, and Xavier Sala-i-Martin. 1992. "Convergence." *Journal of Political Economy*, 100(2): 223–251.
17. Sala-i-Martin, Xavier. 1996. "The Classical Approach to Convergence Analysis." *Economic Journal*, 106(437): 1019–1036.
18. Bailey, Martin. 1959. "Note on the Economics of Residential Zoning and Urban Renewal." *Land Economics*, 35(3): 288–292.
19. Courant, Paul, and John Yinger. 1975. "On Models of Racial Prejudice and Urban Residential Structure." *Journal of Urban Economics*, 4(3): 272–291.
20. Kanemoto, Yoshitsugu. 1980. "Externality, Migration, and Urban Crises." *Journal of Urban Economics*, 8(2): 150–164.
21. Schelling, Thomas. 1971. "Dynamic Models of Segregation." *Journal of Mathematical Sociology*, 1(1)143–186.
22. Yinger, John. 1974. "Racial Prejudice and Racial Residential Segregation in an Urban Model." *Journal of Urban Economics*, 3(4): 383–396.
23. Saiz, Albert. 2008. "On Local Housing Supply Elasticity." http://papers.ssrn.com/sol3/papers.cfm?abstract_id=1193422 (last accessed 8 Nov 2010).

Part VI
Inter-Generational Incorporation and Economic Outcomes

Chapter 13
The Effects of English Proficiency Among Childhood Immigrants: Are Hispanics Different?

Mevlude Akbulut-Yuksel, Hoyt Bleakley, and Aimee Chin

Abstract We test whether the effect of English proficiency differs between Hispanic and non-Hispanic immigrants. Using 2000 US Census microdata on immigrants who arrived before age 15, we relate labor market, education, marriage, fertility, and location of residence variables to their age at arrival in the US, and in particular whether that age fell within the "critical period" of language acquisition. We interpret the observed difference in outcomes between childhood immigrants who arrive during the critical period and those who arrive later (adjusted for non-language-related age-at-arrival effects using childhood immigrants from English-speaking countries) as an effect of English-language skills and construct an instrumental variable for English-language skills. We find that both Hispanics and non-Hispanics exhibit lower English proficiency if they arrive after the critical period, but this drop in English proficiency is larger for Hispanics. The effect of English proficiency on earnings and education is nevertheless quite similar across groups, while some differences are seen for marriage, fertility, and location of residence outcomes. In particular, although higher English proficiency reduces (for both groups) the number of children and the propensity to be married, marry someone with the same birthplace or origin, and live in an "ethnic enclave," these effects are smaller for Hispanics.

Introduction

In this chapter, we address two basic questions. First, what is the effect of English-language skills on the labor market, educational, marriage, fertility, and residential location outcomes of US immigrants? Second, does the impact differ between Hispanic and non-Hispanic immigrants?

A. Chin (✉)
University of Houston, Houston, TX, USA; National Bureau of Economic Research (NBER), Cambridge, MA, USA
e-mail: achin@uh.edu

D.L. Leal, S.J. Trejo (eds.), *Latinos and the Economy*, Immigrants and Minorities, Politics and Policy, DOI 10.1007/978-1-4419-6682-7_13,
© Springer Science+Business Media, LLC 2011

The increase in immigration in recent decades has drawn attention to the process of immigrant assimilation in the US. In 1970, just 4.8% of the US population was foreign-born, but by 2005 the figure had risen to 12.4%.[1] Increasingly, immigrants are coming from countries where English is not widely spoken, leading to a rise in the number of US residents who are not fluent in English. In 2005, 23 million US residents aged 5 years and above reported speaking English less than very well, which is 8.6% of this subpopulation. Among foreign-born US residents aged 5 years and above, 52% spoke English less than very well. In this context, it is useful to understand the role of English proficiency in the process of immigrant assimilation. This knowledge may enable us to formulate policies that facilitate adjustment to life in America for immigrants and their descendants. Such policies may be desirable because immigrants tend to be worse off educationally and economically compared to natives, and some of their disadvantages are passed on to their US-born offspring. Immigrants are more likely to be located in the lowest parts of the education and wage distributions. For example, in 2005, 20.3% of immigrants had completed less than 9 years of schooling (compared to 3.7% for natives), and 17.1% of immigrants lived in poverty (compared to 12.8% of natives).

Hispanics accounted for 47% of the foreign-born population and 14.5% of the total population, making them the largest racial/ethnic minority in the US. As a result, Spanish is the second most commonly spoken language in the US, behind only English. Given the large number of Hispanics in the US and their geographic concentration—although the degree of concentration has been decreasing in the past decade, with recent immigrants choosing to settle in "new destination" areas—it is possible that English-language skills may have different effects for Hispanics than non-Hispanics. For example, it may be more feasible for Hispanics to live and work mostly within the ethnic community, in which case English proficiency may have a reduced role in determining their outcomes. In this chapter, we formally analyze whether Hispanic immigrants' outcomes are indeed less sensitive to English proficiency compared to non-Hispanic immigrants' outcomes.

There are considerable challenges to estimating the effect of an individual's English-language skills on his or her socioeconomic outcomes. Since language skills are correlated with many other variables that also affect these outcomes, such as individual ability, family background, and cultural attitudes, it is difficult to separate out what is the causal effect of language skills from the effects of these other correlated variables. This problem is called omitted variable bias, since by omitting relevant variables one is left with an estimated effect that is biased (i.e., it does not give the true effect). Another source of bias is reverse causality. One can imagine high earnings enabling an immigrant to afford better instruction in English, which, in turn, raises his or her English proficiency. Yet another source of bias is measurement error. It is not easy to accurately measure English-language skills, and not having accurate measures would tend to bias the estimated effect. In the Census data we use, individuals are asked to rate their own English-speaking ability, which may lead to some over-reporting or under-reporting relative to some unstated scale. In these situations—with omitted variable bias, reverse causality, or measurement error—ordinary least squares (OLS) regressions of socioeconomic outcomes on language skills are unlikely to give the causal effects of language skills.

In theory, one way to obtain causal effects is to run an experiment in which people are randomly assigned different levels of English proficiency. For example, take a group of people who do not know English and randomly select some to have high levels of English proficiency and the remainder to have low levels of English proficiency. Then the researcher can observe these people's outcomes. In this experimental setting, in which English-language skills are manipulated by the experimenter and not the result of choices made or constraints faced by the individual, then a simple comparison of people who have higher English proficiency and people who have lower English proficiency will provide the causal effect of English proficiency. Of course, for a variety of reasons, such an experiment is not feasible. Additionally, we would have to follow the subjects for many years before some of the outcomes are realized, such as marriage and fertility. Waiting for results is problematic because answers are needed now to guide policymaking, and because sample attrition will worsen over time, which may offset the benefits of the original experimental design.

A more practical approach to obtaining the causal effect of English proficiency is to take advantage of experiments provided by nature. In our work, we use an identification strategy based on the *critical period of language acquisition*. Because younger children learn languages more easily than older children and adults, earlier exposure to English should improve the odds that an immigrant to the US becomes proficient in the language. In other words, it is as if nature assigns each immigrant with a higher or lower cost of acquiring English-language skills based on his or her age at arrival in the US. We apply this identification strategy using 2000 US Census microdata to study the effect of English proficiency on a number of economic and social outcomes.

To preview the results, we find that both Hispanics and non-Hispanics exhibit lower English proficiency if they arrive after the critical period, but this drop in English proficiency is larger for Hispanics. The effect of English proficiency on earnings and education is nevertheless quite similar across groups, while some differences are seen for marriage, fertility, and location of residence outcomes. In particular, although higher English proficiency reduces (for both groups) the number of children and the propensity to be married, marry someone with the same birthplace or origin, and live in an "ethnic enclave," these effects are smaller for Hispanics.

The next section describes the related literature and the data. We document the strong relationship between age at arrival and English proficiency for immigrants from non-English-speaking countries and detail our identification strategy in the following section. We then present our findings on the effect of English proficiency on labor market, education, marriage, fertility, and location of residence variables. Finally, we discuss some policy implications of our findings.

Background and Data

Related Literature

Many studies have examined the correlation between immigrants' English proficiency and their earnings (e.g., 1–4), education (e.g., 5, 6), marital status (e.g., 7–9), and fertility (e.g., 10, 11). Some have focused on Hispanics in particular and others have examined all immigrants. However, English proficiency is likely to be endogenous for reasons mentioned in the introduction (e.g., omitted variable bias, reverse causality, and measurement error); thus OLS estimates of the effect of English proficiency are likely to be biased.

Only a handful of studies have attempted to address the problem of endogeneity in language skills when estimating the effect of destination-country-language proficiency on earnings (e.g., 12–15), education (15), and marital status and fertility (16). Chiswick and Miller (13) and Bleakley and Chin (15, 16) study the US context like we do here, but neither addresses whether the effect of English proficiency differs between Hispanic and non-Hispanic immigrants.

Bleakley and Chin (17) estimate the causal effects of immigrants' English proficiency on various outcomes of their US-born children, and allow the effects to vary by Hispanic origin. We find that children with limited-English-proficient parents have worse English-language skills and are more likely to drop out of high school, be below their age-appropriate grade, and not attend preschool. These intergenerational effects do not differ between Hispanic and non-Hispanics. However, Bleakley and Chin (17) do not examine whether the effects of immigrants' English proficiency on their *own* outcomes vary by Hispanic origin.

The main contribution of this chapter is to test whether the effects of English proficiency on immigrants' own outcomes differ between Hispanic and non-Hispanic immigrants. This study uses the same identification strategy as Bleakley and Chin (15–17). We are not aware of any previous studies that both address the endogeneity of English proficiency and allow the effects of English proficiency to vary by Hispanic origin.

Data

Our empirical analysis uses individual-level data from the 2000 US Census of Population and Housing.[2] The 2000 Census contains a question on English-speaking ability, and we use the responses to this question to construct measures of English-language skills.[3] The main measure of English-speaking ability that we use is coded as follows:

    0 = speaks English not at all,
    1 = speaks English not well,
    2 = speaks English well, and
    3 = speaks English very well or speaks only English.

Thus, a higher value for this measure corresponds to a higher level of English proficiency. We may be concerned, given that this measure is based on individuals' self-reports of English-speaking ability rather than some objective test, whether this measure really captures English proficiency. Kominski (18) finds that measures of English-speaking ability based on the Census question are highly correlated with scores from tests designed to measure English-language skills as well as functional measures of English-language skills.

Our analysis is conducted using childhood immigrants currently aged 25–55.[4] We define a childhood immigrant as an immigrant who was under the age of 15 upon arrival in the US. For these immigrants, age at arrival is not a choice variable since they did not time their own immigration but merely came with their parents to the US.[5] Given these age and age at arrival restrictions, individuals in our sample arrived in the US between 1945 and 1989, with 86% of the sample arriving in 1980 or earlier. These individuals have been in the US for a minimum of 11 years and an average of 30 years. Given the relatively long spans in the US, it is reasonable to believe these individuals would have had the opportunity to learn English if they wished to and could.

The 2000 Census is a general-purpose survey, which enables us to look at a variety of outcomes. For all childhood immigrants, we analyze earnings, employment status, marital status, number of children, and location of residence as outcomes. When we examine the effect on spouse's characteristics, we restrict the sample to those who are currently married with a spouse present in the household.

We divide our sample into three mutually exclusive language categories: (1) individuals from non-English-speaking countries of birth, (2) countries of birth where English is an official language and is the predominant language, and (3) other countries of birth with English as an official language.[6] The first category is our "treatment" group, and is further divided into Hispanic and non-Hispanic.[7] The second category is our "control" group. The last category is omitted from the main analysis since we are not sure how much exposure to the English language immigrants from these countries would have had before immigrating. Appendix Table A1 reports the means and standard deviations of the variables we use in our analysis for Hispanics in the treatment group, non-Hispanics in the treatment group, and the control group.

Age at Arrival and English Proficiency

There is a window of time in which it is easier to learn languages; this window is known in psychology as the "critical period of language acquisition."[8] This appears to be linked to physiological changes in the brain (19)—maturational changes starting just before puberty reduce a child's ability to acquire second languages. If exposure to the language begins during the critical period, acquisition of the language up to native-level proficiency is almost certain. If first exposure commences afterward, the individual's language proficiency is less assured.

US immigrants from non-English-speaking countries generally do not receive their first exposure to English until they enter the US. Given the aforementioned biological constraints to new language acquisition, those who arrive at an early enough age (i.e., during the critical period) can be expected to develop native-level proficiency in English while those who arrive at a later age can be expected to attain a lower level of proficiency. Indeed, this is what we observe in the data. Figure 13.1 plots for each age at arrival the mean English-speaking ability in adulthood.

For immigrants from English-speaking countries (the diamond-marker line), there is no relationship between age at arrival and English proficiency. This makes sense because their age at first exposure to English did not depend on age at

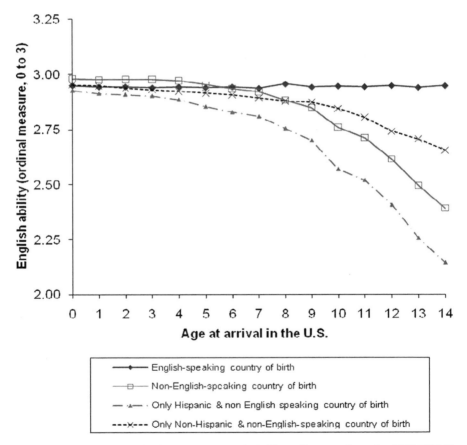

Fig. 13.1 English-speaking ability by age at arrival. Notes: Data are from the 2000 IPUMS. Sample size is 191,534 (composed of people who immigrated to the US before age 15 and are currently aged 25–55, and with nonmissing English variable). Displayed for each age at arrival is the mean English-speaking ability. Means are weighted by IPUMS weights, and regression-adjusted for age, race, Hispanic, and sex dummies. The race categories used were White, Black, Asian & Pacific Islander, Multiracial, and Other. The English ordinal measure is defined as: $0 =$ no English, $1 =$ not well, $2 =$ well and $3 =$ very well

migration—English surrounds them in both their country of birth and the United States. For immigrants from non-English-speaking countries (the square-marker line), however, there is a nonlinear relationship between age at arrival and English proficiency: the English proficiency of earlier arrivers is similar to that of immigrants from English-speaking countries, while the English proficiency of later arrivers declines as a function of age at arrival. This pattern for immigrants from non-English-speaking countries is consistent with the critical period of language acquisition. For childhood immigrants arriving well within the critical period of language acquisition, a slightly later arrival does not depress English proficiency in the long run. On the other hand, those who arrived as their critical period was coming to an end attained significantly worse eventual English skills.

Moreover, among immigrants from non-English-speaking countries, the drop in proficiency is around 2–3 times greater for Hispanics than non-Hispanics. There should be no differences in biological constraints to new language acquisition by age between Hispanics and non-Hispanics, and the probable explanation for the steeper decline for Hispanic older arrivers is due to lower pre-US-entry exposure to English for Hispanics.[9] This seems reasonable since Hispanic immigrants to the US in our sample tend to come from countries that are nearer to the US. The shorter distance facilitates emigration from these countries to the US, and on average emigrants from these countries will be more numerous and less selected. By contrast, on average, emigrants from countries that non-Hispanics tend to come from will be less numerous and more selected. For example, they may be from wealthier households, have attended private schools that teach in English or at least teach English as a subject, or have American expatriate parents.

For the purpose of the statistical analysis in the next section, the relationship between age at arrival and English proficiency shown in Fig. 13.1 can be captured by an interaction between age at arrival and coming from a non-English-speaking country. When we estimate our models, we always control for a full set of dummies for age at arrival and a full set of dummies for country of birth, and are using only the *interaction* as the instrumental variable for English proficiency. This means that we are not attributing the entire difference in outcome between younger and older arrivers from non-English-speaking countries to English proficiency. Instead, we are attributing only the portion that is *over and above* the difference in outcome between younger and older arrivers from English-speaking countries to English proficiency.

A simple example illustrates the intuition behind our instrumental-variables strategy. Consider four immigrants, each brought to the US as a child. Two are from Jamaica (an English-speaking country), one aged five at arrival and the other aged 14. The other two are from Mexico (a non-English-speaking country), with parallel ages of arrival. If we observe a difference in outcome between the two Jamaicans, we could attribute it to non-language age-at-arrival effects (e.g., younger arrivers are able to adjust better to American institutions). But all of these effects are also present in the case of the two Mexicans, in addition to the fact that the Mexicans had substantially less exposure to English before immigrating. As such, the Jamaicans can be used to control for the non-language age-at-arrival effects. Any difference in outcome between the Mexicans in excess of the difference between the Jamaicans can be attributed to language effects, because the Mexican child who immigrated younger has an age of first exposure to English within the critical period while the other Mexican child who immigrated older does not.

We estimate the relationship between English skill and age at arrival in the following equation,

$$\text{ENG}_{ija} = \alpha_1 + \pi_1 k_{ija} + \delta_{1a} + \gamma_{1j} + w_{ija}'\rho_1 + \varepsilon_{1ija}, \qquad (13.1)$$

Table 13.1 First stage regressions

	Endogenous regressor			
	English ability (1)	English ability (2)	English ability × Hispanic (3)	English ability × non-Hispanic (4)
Identifying instruments:				
Max (0, age at arrival—9) × non-English-speaking country of birth	−0.104 *** (0.029)			
Max (0, age at arrival—9) × non-English-speaking country of birth × Hispanic		−0.135*** (0.027)	−0.136 *** (0.027)	0.0010 (0.0010)
Max (0, age at arrival – 9) × non-English-speaking country of birth × non-Hispanic		−0.048*** (0.009)	−0.001 (0.002)	−0.047 *** (0.008)
F-statistic associated with test of joint significance of identifying instruments (p-value)	13.14 0.0004	21.38 <0.0001	13.75 <0.0001	21.59 <0.0001

Notes: The sample is as described in the notes to Appendix Table A1. Each column is from a separate OLS regression that is weighted by IPUMS weights and contains dummies for age at arrival, country of birth, age, sex, race (White, Black, Asian, Multiracial and Other), Hispanic origin and Hispanic × non-English-speaking country of birth. The country-of-birth dummies are based on IPUMS detailed birthplace codes. Standard errors adjusted for country of birth clusters are shown in parentheses. Asterisks denote significance levels (* = 0.10, ** = 0.05, *** = 0.01). English-speaking ability is measured on an ordinal scale as follows: 0 = no English, 1 = not well, 2 = well and 3 = very well.

for individual i born in country j arriving in the US at age a. ENG_{ija} is a measure of English proficiency, k_{ija} is an interaction between age at arrival and coming from a non-English-speaking country[10], δ_{1a} is a set of age-at-arrival dummies, γ_{1j} is a set of country-of-birth dummies and w_{ija} is a vector of exogenous explanatory variables (including age, sex, race, and Hispanic origin). Because there are no endogenous variables on the right-hand side, Eq. (13.1) can be consistently estimated using OLS.

Table 13.1, Column 1 displays the results of estimating Eq. (13.1). There is a significant negative effect of k_{ija} on English skill: for each year past age at arrival 9, English skill declines by a tenth of a unit. In Column 2, we allow the effect of k_{ija} to vary by Hispanic origin. As was seen in Fig. 13.1, the effect of age at arrival is stronger among Hispanic immigrants from non-English-speaking countries: for each year past age 9 at arrival, English skill declines by 0.135 units for Hispanics but 0.048 units for non-Hispanics. But for both groups, the effect is significantly different from zero.

Next, we wish to assess whether the effect of English differs between Hispanics and non-Hispanics. Therefore, our empirical work will divide the English skill measure into two categories: English skill of Hispanic immigrants and English skill of non-Hispanic immigrants. Not surprisingly, based on Column 2 results, $k_{ija} \times Hispanic_{ija}$ and $k_{ija} \times (1\text{-}non\text{-}Hispanic_{ija})$ are jointly significant predictors of English skill of Hispanics (Column 3) and English skill of non-Hispanics (Column 4).[11]

Effects of English Proficiency

In this section, we show the results of estimating the effect of English proficiency on outcome y_{ija} using the following equation:

$$y_{ija} = \alpha + \beta_1 \, ENG_{ija} \times Hispanic_{ija} + \beta_2 \, ENG_{ija}$$
$$\times \left(1 - Hispanic_{ija}\right) + \delta_a + \gamma_j + w_{ija}{}'\rho + \varepsilon_{ija}, \tag{13.2}$$

for individual i born in country j arriving in the US at age a. $Hispanic_{ija}$ is a dummy for being Hispanic, $ENG_{ija} \times Hispanic_{ija}$ is the English proficiency of Hispanics, $ENG_{ija} \times (1\text{-} Hispanic_{ija})$ is the English proficiency of all others, δ_a is a set of age-at-arrival dummies, γ_j is a set of country-of-birth dummies, and w_{ija} is a vector of exogenous explanatory variables (including age, sex, race, and $Hispanic_{ija}$). Because English-language skills are endogenous, OLS estimates of Eq. (13.2) will tend to be biased. To obtain consistent estimates of the parameters in Eq. (13.2), we will use 2SLS estimation with $k_{ija} \times Hispanic_{ija}$ and $k_{ija} \times (1\text{-}Hispanic_{ija})$ as the excluded instruments.[12] We test whether the effect of English skill for Hispanics significantly differs from the effect for non-Hispanics by performing an F-test where the null hypothesis is that $\beta_1 = \beta_2$.

Labor Market Outcomes

Immigrants tend to earn less than natives in the US. Since English is the language used in the American workplace, it is natural to ask the extent to which English proficiency can raise the earnings of immigrants. This is the question we addressed in Bleakley and Chin (15). This chapter introduced the identification strategy described above and applied it to 1990 Census data. In this subsection, we extend this chapter by applying the same empirical methodology to newer data, allowing the effects to vary by Hispanic origin, and examining additional labor market outcomes.

Figure 13.2 shows the mean log annual wages as a function of age at arrival for immigrants from non-English-speaking countries and for those from English-speaking countries.[13] As in Fig. 13.1, the lines corresponding to the means of the two groups are similar at earlier ages at arrival and diverge for later ages. Among the younger arrivers, whether they come from non-English-speaking countries makes no significant difference in their wages. Among the adolescent arrivers, however, wages tend to be lower for the immigrants from non-English-speaking countries. The line for immigrants from English-speaking countries is nearly flat, suggesting that the non-language effects of age at arrival are small.

It is striking how similar the patterns are in Figs. 13.1 and 13.2. This makes it especially convincing that the lower earnings observed for older arrivers from non-English-speaking countries observed in Fig. 13.2 are attributable to English proficiency; why else would there be a relationship between wages and age at arrival that is shaped in a way that is consistent with the critical period of language acquisition? Thus, one estimate of the effect of English proficiency on wages comes from estimating Eq. (13.1) but with wages as the dependent variable—the coefficient for the interaction between age at arrival and coming from a non-English-speaking country gives the effect (where we keep in mind that arriving at a later age means lower English proficiency). Though such reduced-form estimates are interesting in and of themselves, sometimes we want to rescale them in order to obtain the effect of a one-unit increase in English proficiency. But this is exactly what we obtain by estimating Eq. (13.2) using 2SLS using the interaction as the excluded instrument; the identifying assumption is that the interaction affects the outcome only through English proficiency, and Figs. 13.1 and 13.2 provide visual evidence in support of this.

In Table 13.2 (Row A), we present the results of estimating Eq. (13.1) with wages as the outcome. Here and below, we will focus our discussion on the 2SLS estimates in Columns 4–6 since they provide consistent parameter estimates whereas the OLS estimates are not necessarily consistent.[14] English skill raises wages for both Hispanics and non-Hispanics, with the return to English being similar for the two groups. Thus, the value of a unit of English skill (e.g., moving from speaks not well to speaks well, or speaks well to speaks very well) is the same across all immigrants. Specifically, a one-unit increase in English proficiency raises annual wages about 35%. The common effect of English proficiency on wages between the two groups is probably to be expected considering that skill prices are determined by the

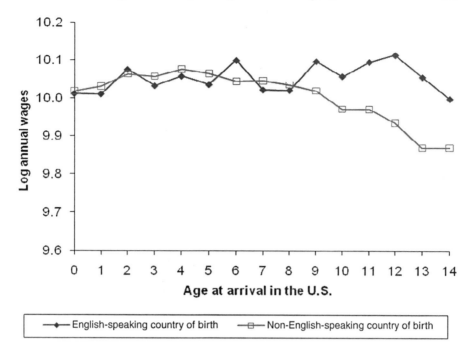

Fig. 13.2 Wages by age at arrival. Notes: Data are from the 2000 IPUMS. Sample size is 127,616 (composed of people who immigrated to the US before age 15 and are currently aged 25–55, and with nonmissing English and wage variables). Displayed for each age at arrival is the mean log wages in 1999. Means are weighted by IPUMS weights, and regression-adjusted for age, race, Hispanic, and sex dummies. The race categories used were White, Black, Asian & Pacific Islander, Multiracial, and Other

broader labor market; if a profit-maximizing firm wishes to have English-proficient workers, why would it be willing to pay a higher price for the same skill (English proficiency) to one group when it can acquire the same skill from another group at a lower price?

However, the effect of English on other labor market outcomes does appear to differ between Hispanics and non-Hispanics. First, Table 13.2 (Row B) indicates that English does raise the probability that a childhood immigrant works, and this effect is significantly stronger for non-Hispanics than Hispanics (the p-value in Column 6 is 0.0391, which means the difference is significant at the 3.91 level of significance). It turns out that all the effects on employment status reported in Row B derive from women (Row C); male employment is not sensitive to English skill (Row D). Hispanic women have both lower levels of employment (see Appendix Table A1) and lower sensitivity to English at the extensive margin of labor supply than non-Hispanic women. Second, the self-employment status of non-Hispanic immigrants is also more sensitive to English proficiency than that of Hispanic immigrants: there is a 10.2 percentage point reduction in being self-employed for non-Hispanics and no effect for Hispanics. Perhaps this lower

Table 13.2 Effect of English proficiency on labor market outcomes

	OLS			2SLS		
	Effect of English for Hispanics (1)	Effect of English for non-Hispanics (2)	p-value of test of equality (3)	Effect of English for Hispanics (4)	Effect of English for non-Hispanics (5)	p-value of test of equality (6)
A. Log annual wages	0.249 *** (0.011)	0.204 *** (0.027)	0.1235	0.377 *** (0.063)	0.354 ** (0.170)	0.8571
B. Worked last year	0.077 *** (0.012)	0.066 *** (0.007)	0.4335	0.070 *** (0.014)	0.152 *** (0.044)	0.0391
C. Worked last year, females only	0.118 *** (0.006)	0.075 *** (0.008)	<0.0001	0.140 *** (0.013)	0.280 *** (0.062)	0.0120
D. Worked last year, males only	0.036 ** (0.015)	0.056 *** (0.009)	0.2712	−0.011 (0.019)	−0.030 (0.050)	0.6260
E. Is self-employed	0.004 *** (0.001)	−0.006 (0.005)	0.0462	−0.008 (0.009)	−0.102 *** (0.037)	0.0057

Notes: The sample is as described in the notes to Appendix Table A1. In each lettered row, Columns 1–3 report the coefficient for English ability for Hispanics, coefficient for English ability for non-Hispanics, and p-value of test of equality of the two aforementioned coefficients, respectively, from an equation estimated using OLS, and Columns 4–6 report the same from an equation estimated using 2SLS. All regressions are weighted by IPUMS weights and contain dummies for age at arrival, country of birth, age, sex, race, Hispanic origin and Hispanic × non-English-speaking country of birth. The identifying instruments when 2SLS is used are max(0, age at arrival − 9) × non-English-speaking country × Hispanic and max(0, age at arrival—9) × non-English-speaking country × (1-Hispanic). Standard errors adjusted for country of birth clusters are shown in parentheses. Asterisks denote significance levels (* = 0.10, ** = 0.05, *** = 0.01).

sensitivity for Hispanics is due to the larger Hispanic community in America (which may make operating an ethnic business more attractive for Hispanics), or due to the smaller improvements in job quality as a result of raising English proficiency for Hispanics (Hispanic immigrants are more likely to be undocumented and not have a college education, both of which may limit access to the attractive jobs outside self-employment).

Educational Attainment

In Bleakley and Chin (15), we found that English proficiency raised wages mainly in an indirect way, through raising educational attainment. In this subsection, we quantify the effect of English proficiency on education and assess the role of education in the observed relationship between English proficiency and wages using 2000 Census data.

Figure 13.3 shows the relationship between years of schooling completed and age at arrival. The pattern of years of schooling completed by age at arrival bears

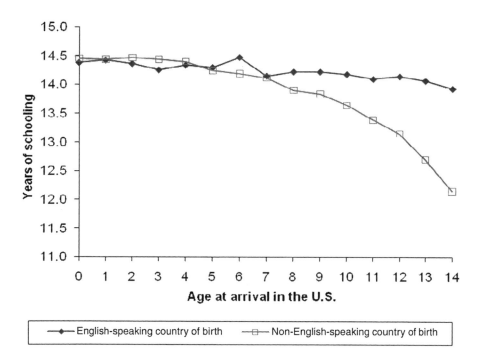

Fig. 13.3 Years of schooling by age at arrival. Notes: Data are from the 2000 IPUMS. Sample size is 188,191 (composed of people who immigrated to the US before age 15 and are currently aged 25–55 and with nonmissing English and educational attainment variables). Displayed for each age at arrival are the mean years of schooling. Means are weighted by IPUMS weights, and regression-adjusted for age, race, Hispanic, and sex dummies. The race categories used were White, Black, Asian & Pacific Islander, Multiracial, and Other

remarkable resemblance to the pattern of English proficiency by age at arrival (in Fig. 13.1), which supports the interpretation of English proficiency playing a causal role in the poorer educational outcomes of older arrivers from non-English-speaking countries. We proceed by estimating Eq. (13.2) by 2SLS to quantify the causal effects of English proficiency on educational outcomes by Hispanic origin. Columns 4–6 of Table 13.3 show that a unit increase in English skill raises years of schooling by about 3 years for both Hispanics and non-Hispanics—there is no significant difference in the effect. However, it is interesting to note that the three extra years of schooling appear to be coming from different parts of the educational distribution for the two groups. In particular, Rows B-D suggest that there is a larger increase at the high school diploma margin for Hispanics compared to non-Hispanics, for whom the largest gain is registered at the college level. Of course the only significant difference is in Row D, for attaining a Bachelor's degree or higher.

Assuming standard returns to a year of schooling (say, 8 %), the educational channel accounts for over two third of the total effect of English proficiency on wages. Thus, other channels—including the direct effect on productivity—play a much smaller role in determining the wages of childhood immigrants. This may sound surprising initially since we may have found the story of direct productivity effects of English proficiency appealing, e.g., since business is conducted in English in the US, English proficiency should facilitate communication with co-workers and customers. However, once we recognize that the return to education in the US has grown dramatically since the 1970s, and that a high school diploma and college education are now prerequisites for most good jobs, then this result is much less surprising.

Family Formation

English proficiency may impact social outcomes as well as economic outcomes for immigrants. For example, when one becomes proficient in English, one's pool of potential spouses may expand since there are more people with whom one can communicate. Alternatively, English proficiency may bring about changes in preferences regarding marriage and family, such as from home-country norms to US norms. Bleakley and Chin (16) estimated the effect of English proficiency on marriage and fertility outcomes, and we extend this chapter by testing whether these effects vary by Hispanic origin.

In Table 13.4 (Panel I), we estimate the impact of English skills on current marital status. We find that English proficiency reduces the probability of being currently married for both Hispanics and non-Hispanics, with the effect being larger for non-Hispanics. This effect derives both from a higher likelihood of being divorced (a one-unit increase in English increases the probability of being divorced by 4.6% for Hispanics and 9% for non-Hispanics) and a lower likelihood of having ever married (a one-unit increase in English increases the probability of having ever married by 4.4% for Hispanics and 23% for non-Hispanics). The differences in the point estimates are large, but it must be pointed out that the estimates in Column 5 are

Table 13.3 Effect of English proficiency on educational attainment

	OLS			2SLS		
	Effect of English for Hispanics (1)	Effect of English for non-Hispanics (2)	p-value of test of equality (3)	Effect of English for Hispanics (4)	Effect of English for non-Hispanics (5)	p-value of test of equality (6)
A. Years of schooling	1.971 *** (0.036)	1.366 *** (0.128)	<0.0001	3.374*** (0.192)	3.089 *** (0.772)	0.6836
B. Has high school diploma	0.234 *** (0.008)	0.127 *** (0.012)	<0.0001	0.400 *** (0.018)	0.306 *** (0.091)	0.2727
C. Has any college or more	0.175 *** (0.016)	0.171 *** (0.020)	0.8663	0.289 *** (0.041)	0.383 *** (0.136)	0.4059
D. Has Bachelor's degree or more	0.052 *** (0.010)	0.146 *** (0.023)	0.0003	0.092 ** (0.042)	0.313 *** (0.111)	0.0087

Notes: See notes for Table 13.2.

Table 13.4 Effect of English proficiency on marriage outcomes

	OLS			2SLS		
	Effect of English for Hispanics (1)	Effect of English for non-Hispanics (2)	p-value of test of equality (3)	Effect of English for Hispanics (4)	Effect of English for non-Hispanics (5)	p-value of test of equality (6)
Panel I: Marital status						
A. Is currently married with spouse present	0.008 (0.012)	0.009 (0.009)	0.9361	−0.070** (0.027)	−0.318*** (0.076)	<0.0001
B. Is currently divorced	0.013*** (0.002)	−0.001 (0.003)	0.0006	0.046*** (0.011)	0.090** (0.037)	0.1137
C. Has never married	−0.001 (0.008)	−0.005 (0.007)	0.7258	−0.044** (0.017)	−0.227*** (0.055)	0.0001
Panel II: Spouse's ethnicity and nativity (conditional on being married with spouse present)						
A. Spouse's English-speaking ability ordinal measure	0.524*** (0.010)	0.463*** (0.039)	0.1354	0.753*** (0.032)	1.198*** (0.099)	<0.0001
B. Spouse is US-born	0.097*** (0.006)	0.138*** (0.014)	0.0172	0.246*** (0.082)	0.800*** (0.263)	0.0073
C. Spouse has the same country of birth	−0.113*** (0.005)	−0.150*** (0.013)	0.0179	−0.272*** (0.080)	−0.846*** (0.264)	0.0048
D. Spouse has the same ancestry	−0.065*** (0.007)	−0.126*** (0.013)	0.0002	−0.095 (0.072)	−0.737*** (0.230)	0.0004

Notes: See notes for Table 13.2.

somewhat imprecise and admit a wide range of values within the 95% confidence interval.

In Table 13.4 (Panel II), we examine the effect on spousal attributes. This analysis is restricted to childhood immigrants who are currently married and living with their spouse. We find that increasing English skill of the childhood immigrant significantly increases his/her spouse's level of English proficiency and the probability that the spouse is US-born. The flip side of being more likely to marry a native is the lower likelihood of marrying someone with the same country of birth; marrying immigrants from other countries seems to have a negligible role. Although childhood immigrants with better English are less likely to marry someone with the same country of birth, there is a less dramatic decline in the propensity to marry someone of the same primary ancestry, at least for Hispanics.[15] Indeed, Hispanic childhood immigrants are not significantly more likely to marry outside their primary ancestry though they are significantly more likely to marry a native, reflecting the fact that some are marrying natives of the same ancestry (e.g., a Mexican immigrant marrying a US-born person of Mexican ancestry).

In addition, the marriage outcomes in Table 13.4 (Panel II) are significantly more sensitive to English proficiency for non-Hispanics than Hispanics. For example, in Row B, a one-unit increase in English raises the probability of marrying a US native by 25% for Hispanics and 80% for non-Hispanics. One possible explanation for the differential effects on marriage outcomes is that, though both Hispanics and non-Hispanics have similar preferences for assortative mating by ethnicity and maintaining "traditional" values at the outset, non-Hispanics may have a reduced opportunity to do so due to their smaller ethnic group size in the US. Due to the larger Hispanic community in America, there is greater potential to find a spouse who not only satisfies the usual criteria for a spouse (e.g., age, educational attainment, personality), but also is of the same cultural heritage. In contrast, non-Hispanic childhood immigrants may have to marry outside their country of birth or ancestry in order to find someone with the usual criteria. Another possible explanation for the differential effects is that Hispanic and non-Hispanic childhood immigrants have different preferences for assortative mating by ethnicity and maintaining "traditional" family values. These two explanations are unlikely to be independent. For example, it is plausible that ethnic group size might itself shape individual preferences. Perhaps growing up in an ethnic enclave causes one to retain more traditional values even as one acquires English-language skills. Although all immigrant groups have their enclaves, enclaves may be more numerous and larger among Hispanics compared to non-Hispanics due to the former's larger population size in the US.

In Table 13.5, we examine fertility outcomes. Our measure of fertility is the number of children currently living in the same household.[16] We find that an increase in English proficiency reduces the number of children, especially for non-Hispanics (Row A). For Hispanics, there is no effect on the extensive margin of having any children (Row B), but there is an effect on the number of children conditional on having at least one. For non-Hispanics, there is a significant reduction both in the probability of having any children and the number of children. The effect on the extensive margin shown in Row B appears to come entirely from the effects of

Table 13.5 Effect of English proficiency on fertility

		OLS			2SLS	
	Effect of English for Hispanics (1)	Effect of English for non-Hispanics (2)	p-value of test of equality (3)	Effect of English for Hispanics (4)	Effect of English for non-Hispanics (5)	p-value of test of equality (6)
A. Number of children living in same household	−0.112*** (0.022)	−0.078** (0.036)	0.4398	−0.374*** (0.070)	−0.814*** (0.201)	0.0129
B. Has a child living in same household	−0.003 (0.005)	−0.013 (0.009)	0.3405	−0.044 (0.027)	−0.236*** (0.083)	0.0022
C. Number of children living in same household, only individuals married with spouse present	−0.178*** (0.011)	−0.173*** (0.051)	0.9288	−0.351*** (0.052)	−0.765*** (0.207)	0.0250
D. Has a child living in same household, only individuals married with spouse present	−0.015*** (0.002)	−0.037*** (0.007)	0.0020	0.008 (0.017)	−0.099 (0.067)	0.0622

Notes: See notes for Table 13.2.

English skill on marital status. Restricting the sample only to married couples, we find that there is no significant effect on having any children for both Hispanics and non-Hispanics (Row D). Thus, it does not appear that couples are foregoing parenthood altogether, but there is a reduction in the number of children conditional on having any children or at least there is a postponement in completing one's family (Row C).

Location of Residence

An additional marker of social integration of immigrants is the extent to which they live in ethnic enclaves. The public-use 2000 Census data used here are not ideal for studying residential choice decisions because to preserve respondent privacy they do not provide detailed information about the neighborhood in which a person resides. The lowest level of geographic aggregation that we can measure is called PUMA (public-use microdata area), which is an area containing at least 100,000 people. A more accurate characterization of one's neighborhood would contain fewer people, but given the data limitations, we form a couple of variables intended to capture the idea of an ethnic enclave. One set of measures is based on the fraction of the population in one's PUMA that shares the same country of birth as the childhood immigrant.[17] Of course there are people of the same background who are born in the US (e.g., US-born Mexicans may have many similarities to Mexicans born in Mexico), so a second set of measures is based on the fraction of one's PUMA that shares the same primary ancestry. A larger fraction from the same country or ancestry may be associated with being in a larger ethnic community and a greater likelihood of living in an ethnic enclave.

In Table 13.6, we find that English proficiency significantly reduces the probability that childhood immigrants live in PUMAs with a high fraction from their own country or with the same ancestry for non-Hispanics, but the extent to which Hispanics live with their own group does not depend on English proficiency. For example, for non-Hispanics but not for Hispanics, Row B shows that a one-unit increase in English proficiency raises the probability of living in a PUMA with above-average fraction of people from the same country of birth. This is consistent with non-Hispanic immigrants moving away from ethnic enclaves and integrating geographically with mainstream America as they gain English proficiency. Hispanic immigrants do not appear to do the same as their English improves.

Why Might the Effect of English Proficiency Differ Between Hispanics and Non-Hispanics?

We have shown that except for wages and years of schooling, English skill tends to have effects of greater magnitude for non-Hispanics than Hispanics. In this subsection, we explore two reasons that we *ex ante* thought could be responsible for the observed difference in effects of English between Hispanics and non-Hispanics.

Table 13.6 Effect of English proficiency on neighborhood of residence

	OLS			2SLS		
	Effect of English for Hispanics (1)	Effect of English for non-Hispanics (2)	p-value of test of equality (3)	Effect of English for Hispanics (4)	Effect of English for non-Hispanics (5)	p-value of test of equality (6)
Panel I: Neighborhood measures based on fraction of population in puma from same country of birth						
A. Fraction from same country of birth	−0.011 *** (0.001)	−0.005 *** (0.001)	0.0004	−0.005 (0.008)	−0.017 ** (0.008)	0.1447
B. Fraction is above mean	−0.044 *** (0.007)	−0.078 *** (0.010)	0.0183	0.014 (0.050)	−0.296 *** (0.091)	<0.0001
Panel II: Neighborhood measures based on fraction of population in puma from same ancestry						
A. Fraction from same ancestry	−0.014 *** (0.001)	−0.007 *** (0.002)	0.0005	−0.010 (0.013)	−0.062 *** (0.018)	0.0005
B. Fraction is above mean	−0.039 *** (0.007)	−0.061 *** (0.009)	0.0910	0.004 (0.050)	−0.214 ** (0.088)	0.0026

Notes: See notes for Table 13.2.

One potential reason for the differential effects on marriage and fertility outcomes is that English proficiency affects the two groups at different parts of the education distribution. As discussed above, an improvement in English proficiency tends to raise the number of years of schooling at the high school level for Hispanics and at the college level for non-Hispanics. Attending college could affect outcomes beyond raising years of schooling. People are more likely to leave their hometown or at least their childhood home in order to attend college. By changing the place of residence, attending college could change the pool of potential spouses and reduce the influence of the family and ethnic community. But to the extent that English skill is only raising schooling at the high school level (e.g., from dropping out at grade 9 or 10 to completing high school), then the three extra years of schooling associated with a unit increase in English proficiency is unlikely to change the potential pool of spouses and relevant community.

To assess this education story for differential effects, we started with Eq. (13.2) and added dummies for each level of educational attainment measured by the 2000 Census.[18] When we do this, we still find similar differences in effects of English proficiency between Hispanics and non-Hispanics as in the base specification. However, as far as the levels of the effects of English skill for Hispanics and non-Hispanics are concerned, it is notable that the effect on wages declines drastically, mirroring the Bleakley and Chin (15) finding that much of the effect of English proficiency on wages is mediated through years of schooling. The effect decreases more for non-Hispanics than Hispanics, which is consistent with mechanisms besides educational attainment mattering more for Hispanics.[19]

A second potential reason for the differential effects on marriage and fertility outcomes is the large size of the Hispanic population in the United States. Hispanic immigrants share a common language, Spanish, and can associate with each other even if they were born in different countries. Even if Hispanic immigrants did not associate with people born in other countries, large ethnic communities based on country of birth would develop due to their relatively large population and geographic concentration. For example, Mexicans (both immigrants and US-born) make up 9% of the US population and are still relatively concentrated in the Southwest, although they are increasingly settling elsewhere. On average then, Hispanic immigrants are more likely to live in ethnic enclaves, and their ethnic-social networks are larger than non-Hispanic immigrants. This may affect the role of English in economic and social assimilation. One can imagine that the existence of a large and diverse ethnic community may create opportunities that are not available to all immigrants, and even an immigrant who becomes proficient in English may desire to continue participating in the ethnic community. For example, an immigrant may participate in the broader society for school and work, but maintain a social life in the ethnic community. Thus, it is plausible that the muted effects of English proficiency on marriage and fertility outcomes for Hispanics could be the result of the larger Hispanic community.

To assess this second reason, we did the following. First, we added super-Public Use Microdata Area (PUMA) of residence fixed effects as an attempt to control for neighborhood characteristics. Some neighborhoods may be heavily concentrated ethnically and others more diverse and adding super-PUMA fixed effects would control for any fixed features (such as ethnic diversity) of the super-PUMA. Considering a super-PUMA contains about 400,000 people, it is a rough measure of one's community, so perhaps not surprisingly results did not change after allowing for super-PUMA fixed effects. Second, we controlled for a variable measuring the fraction of one's PUMA's population with the same country of birth. Adding this fraction as a control did not change any of the results. Finally, we controlled for a variable measuring the fraction of one's PUMA's population with the same primary ancestry. Again, the differential effects between Hispanics and non-Hispanics remained as they were in the base results.

The three empirical tests described above do not provide evidence suggesting that the ethnic enclave is the reason that the effects tend to be lower for Hispanics, but they are rather weak tests. On the one hand, we probably do not have a good measure of each individual's relevant community. PUMAs are still large areas, and two PUMAs with a similar fraction of the same group may, nonetheless, differ in the degree of ethnic segregation across neighborhoods within the PUMA. On the other hand, there may be a nonlinear effect of ethnic community size wherein the ethnic community does not have effects until it reaches a certain size, and currently we do not have precise enough measures of ethnic community size to account for this. Thus, we should not yet dismiss the ethnic enclave story.

It is apparent from this subsection that we do not know why the effects of English on marriage and fertility outcomes differ between Hispanics and non-Hispanics. Undoubtedly there are reasons besides the education and ethnic enclave explanations offered here. In addition, better measures of one's relevant community would enable a better assessment of the ethnic enclave explanation. The role of ethnic enclaves in mediating the effects of English-language skills merits more research, as do other potential explanations for the differential effects between Hispanics and non-Hispanics.

Robustness Checks

Central to our ability to interpret the 2SLS estimates presented in this section as the causal effects of English-language skills is the assumption that non-language age-at-arrival effects are identical for immigrants from English-speaking countries and from non-English-speaking countries. Is this a plausible assumption? One potential concern is that immigrants from non-English-speaking countries are on average from poorer countries than immigrants from English-speaking countries, which may generate stronger age-at-arrival effects for the immigrants from non-English-speaking countries. That is, richer countries may have better education systems and more modern institutions, so the transition to living in the US would be easier for immigrants from richer countries than poorer countries. A second concern is that differences in geographic or cultural distance to the US among English-speaking countries, non-English-speaking countries from which Hispanics tend to come, and non-English-speaking countries from which non-Hispanics tend to come, might cause differential non-language age-at-arrival effects among these three country groups for immigrants.

To address these concerns, we performed a variety of robustness checks with different specifications and subsamples (see 15–17 for details about these robustness checks). It turns out that the estimated effects of English on Hispanics and non-Hispanics, as well as the difference in effects between the two groups, do not change much when we control for these alternative explanations, which supports the assumption and, therefore, the interpretation of the 2SLS estimates as related to English proficiency. Because the findings do not change much in these robustness checks, we do not report their results in tables.

Discussion

In this chapter, we document a strong relationship between age at arrival and English proficiency among childhood immigrants using 2000 US Census microdata. This observed relationship is consistent with the critical period of language acquisition, with young arrivers from non-English-speaking countries developing a high level of proficiency and older arrivers—who entered the US as their critical period was coming to a close—developing lower proficiency. The pattern of our outcomes by age at arrival bears remarkable resemblance to the pattern of English proficiency by age at arrival (to save space, we have only provided graphs for two outcomes, wages, and years of schooling), motivating us to use an instrumental-variables strategy based upon the critical period to identify the causal effects of English-language skills. We allow these causal effects to vary by Hispanic origin, which previous studies have not done. We find for both Hispanics and non-Hispanics that an increase in English proficiency significantly increases wages, educational attainment, intermarriage and divorce, and significantly decreases being currently married, being ever married, fertility and living in an ethnic enclave. The sensitivity of wages and years of schooling to English proficiency was the same for Hispanics and non-Hispanics, but English proficiency tended to have significantly larger-magnitude effects on marriage, fertility, and location of residence outcomes for non-Hispanics than Hispanics.

If policymakers want to close the education and earnings gap between Hispanics and natives, it seems viable to direct resources at raising the English proficiency of Hispanics. Both Hispanic and non-Hispanic immigrants' schooling and earnings exhibit the same responsiveness to a unit change in English proficiency, but Hispanics have, on average, lower levels of English proficiency. It seems logical, then, to raise the level of English proficiency for Hispanics. Had we found that Hispanics' schooling and wages were not sensitive to English proficiency, this would not have been a viable way to achieve the policy objective.

Some advocate English classes for immigrants not so much to help immigrants raise their schooling and wages but to assimilate them into the mainstream culture.

A recent *Washington Post* article reports on the debate over whether the US government should be more pro-active in promoting the assimilation of immigrants into mainstream culture through programs such as English classes.[20] Without taking a position on this debate, this chapter suggests that English-language proficiency does not automatically lead to social assimilation. That the effects of English-proficiency on marriage and fertility outcomes differ between Hispanics and non-Hispanics suggests that ethnicity-specific forces are at least, in part, moderating the role of English proficiency. It is conceivable that the two groups are taking different lengths of time to reach US norms, or that one or both groups will never reach the US norm and instead set their own cultural norm for living in the US.

Acknowledgement We thank Chinhui Juhn, Stephen Trejo, and participants in the IUPLR Conference in April 2007 for helpful comments and discussion. Financial support from the National Institute of Child Health and Human Development (R03HD051562) is gratefully acknowledged. The authors bear sole responsibility for the content of this chapter.

Notes

1. The 1970 figure is from the 1970 US Census and the 2005 figure is from the 2005 American Community Survey. Here and in the rest of this paragraph, we use tabulations of the 2005 American Community Survey done by the Pew Hispanic Center (20).
2. Specifically, we combine the 1% and 5% samples from Integrated Public Use Microsample Series (IPUMS) (21).
3. The Census question based on which the English-ability measure in this chapter is constructed is: "How well does this person speak English?" with the four possible responses "very well," "well," "not well," and "not at all." This question is only asked of individuals responding affirmatively to "Does this person speak a language other than English at home?" We have coded immigrants who do not answer "Yes" to speaking another language as speaking English "very well."
4. For the purposes of the empirical analysis, an immigrant is defined as someone born outside the fifty states and the District of Columbia. This means that a person born in Puerto Rico is considered an immigrant, although legally he/she is a US citizen at birth.
5. According to the US Citizenship and Immigration Services, immigrating parents may bring any unmarried children under age 21. We use a more restricted set of childhood immigrants: immigrants who were under 15 upon arrival (i.e., maximum age at arrival is 14). Using this lower age at arrival cutoff should mitigate the concern that many low-educated young men migrate on their own to the US from Mexico and Central America to look for work, which makes age at arrival a choice variable and may make our identification strategy less plausible.
6. We used *The World Almanac and Book of Facts, 1999* (22) to determine whether English was an official language of each country. Recent adult immigrants from the 1980 Census were used to provide empirical evidence of the prevalence of English in countries with English as an official language. English-speaking countries are defined as those countries from which more than half of the recent adult immigrants did not speak a language other than English at home. The remaining countries with English as an official language are excluded from the main analysis. We made two exceptions to this procedure. First, despite the fact that Great Britain was not listed as having an official language, we included it in the list of English-speaking countries. Second, we classified Puerto Rico as non-English speaking even though English is an official language due to its colonial history.
7. We classify someone as Hispanic if they responded affirmatively to the Hispanic origin question ("Is this person Spanish/Hispanic/Latino?"). In theory, there could be endogeneity in this

measure of Hispanic origin (the most well assimilated people may cease to call themselves Hispanic; see (23). However, this is unlikely to be a concern in our analysis. Our sample consists of the foreign-born, for whom self-reporting to be Hispanic is almost the same as being born in a Spanish-speaking country. When we perform our analysis using being born in a Spanish-speaking country (country of birth is exogenous) to define Hispanic origin, results are basically unchanged.

8. See Newport (24) for an overview of the theory and empirical evidence related to the critical period.

9. This explanation for the weaker relationship between age at arrival and English skill for non-Hispanics compared to Hispanics finds corroboration in two other observations. First, for immigrants born in countries with English as an official but non-dominant language, there is also a weaker relationship than for immigrants born in countries without English as an official language. Second, for non-Mexican Hispanic immigrants from non-English-speaking countries, there is also a weaker relationship compared to Mexican immigrants from non-English-speaking countries.

10. A parsimonious way to parameterize the relationship is as an interaction between a piece-wise linear function of age at arrival and a dummy variable for coming from a non-English-speaking country. The specific piece-wise linear function we use takes on the value zero up through age at arrival nine, and is linear thereafter: $k_{ija} = max(0, a-9) \times I$ (j is a non-English-speaking country). We have used other parameterizations of age at arrival and used full set of dummies for age at arrival to form the interaction and obtained similar results.

11. Columns 3 and 4 are the first stage regressions that underlie the two-stage least squares regressions estimated in the next section.

12. As we documented earlier, these two variables are strong predictors of the endogenous regressors $ENG_{ija} \times Hispanic_{ija}$ and $ENG_{ija} \times (1 - Hispanic_{ija})$. Moreover they are plausible exclusion restrictions since they arise from biological constraints to human language acquisition.

13. Our measure of wages is from the "wage and salary income" item in the IPUMS 2000 Census data, which is money received as an employee for the previous calendar year.

14. As we have found in Bleakley and Chin (15, 16), the 2SLS estimates of the effect of English skill tend to be of greater magnitude than the OLS estimates. Analysis in Bleakley and Chin (15) suggests that while there does appear to be upward bias due to omitted variables-type stories, the downward bias from classical measurement error more than offsets it for an overall downward bias in the OLS estimate.

15. Our measure of primary ancestry is from the "ancestry, first response" item (the 3-digit version) in the IPUMS Census data. Often, the ancestry reflects the country where a person or his ancestors were born, but some countries have more detailed categories. For example, there are several distinct codes for people of Mexican ancestry: Mexican, Mexican American, Chicano/Chicana, Nuevo Mexicano and Californio.

16. The 2000 Census does not contain information on the number of children ever born, a better measure of fertility, but we verified in Bleakley and Chin (16) using 1990 Census data that there are similar estimated effects of English using either fertility measure.

17. Recognizing that an enclave is where there is a large concentration of people from one's own group, we also tried nonlinear functions of the fraction. Here, we show results not only for when the fraction itself is the outcome, but also for when a dummy for whether an individual lives in a PUMA that has a fraction from same country of birth that is above the mean fraction for all immigrants from that same country of birth (this latter measure picks up whether for someone from your country, you tend to live in a neighborhood with an above-average number of fellow countrymen).

18. There are 14 educational categories altogether: no schooling, completing 1st through 4th grade, completing 5th through 8th grade, 9th grade, 10th grade, 11th grade, 12th grade without diploma, high school graduate or GED, some college without degree, associate degree in

occupational program, Bachelor's degree, Master's degree, professional degree, and doctorate degree.

19. Controlling for the education dummies, the effect on wages for non-Hispanics is about one third of the original 2SLS estimate reported in Table 13.2 and is statistically insignificant; for Hispanics, it is about one half of the original estimate and still statistically significant. The difference in effect between the two groups remains insignificant.

20. Brulliard, Karin. 2007. "At Odds over Immigrant Assimilation: Whether the US Government Should Offer Encouragement is Debated." *Washington Post*, August 7, A1.

Appendix

Table A1 Descriptive statistics

	Born in non-English-speaking country		Born in English-speaking country (3)
	Hispanics (1)	Non-Hispanics (2)	
Panel I: Regressors			
English-speaking ability	2.567	2.883	2.980
(ordinal measure, 0–3)	(0.747)	(0.375)	(0.167)
Age	35.871	37.285	38.403
	(7.987)	(8.476)	(8.367)
Female	0.496	0.504	0.528
	(0.500)	(0.500)	(0.499)
White	0.477	0.638	0.666
	(0.499)	(0.481)	(0.472)
Black	0.017	0.045	0.247
	(0.130)	(0.206)	(0.432)
Asian/Pacific Islander	0.003	0.253	0.028
	(0.052)	(0.435)	(0.164)
Other single race	0.455	0.007	0.019
	(0.498)	(0.083)	(0.136)
Multiracial	0.049	0.058	0.040
	(0.215)	(0.233)	(0.196)
Panel II: Labor market outcomes			
Log annual wages	9.993	10.281	10.288
	(0.919)	(0.964)	(0.956)
Worked last year	0.829	0.878	0.891
	(0.376)	(0.327)	(0.312)
Worked last year, females only	0.750	0.823	0.849
	(0.433)	(0.381)	(0.358)
Worked last year, males only	0.908	0.934	0.938
	(0.289)	(0.248)	(0.242)
Is self-employed	0.064	0.099	0.089
	(0.244)	(0.299)	(0.284)

Table A1 (continued)

	Born in non-English-speaking country		Born in English-speaking country (3)
	Hispanics (1)	Non-Hispanics (2)	
Panel III: Schooling outcomes			
Years of schooling	11.882	14.485	14.527
	(3.608)	(2.712)	(2.452)
Has high school diploma	0.640	0.922	0.940
	(0.480)	(0.269)	(0.237)
Has any college or more	0.406	0.730	0.746
	(0.491)	(0.444)	(0.435)
Has Bachelor's degree or more	0.133	0.403	0.375
	(0.340)	(0.491)	(0.484)
Panel IV: Marital status			
Is currently married with spouse present	0.605	0.602	0.561
	(0.489)	(0.489)	(0.496)
Is currently divorced	0.094	0.099	0.120
	(0.292)	(0.299)	(0.325)
Has never married	0.786	0.747	0.736
	(0.410)	(0.435)	(0.441)
Panel V: Spouse's ethnicity and nativity (conditional on being married with spouse present)			
Spouse's English-speaking ability ordinal measure	2.356	2.839	2.979
	(0.908)	(0.456)	(0.170)
Spouse is US-born	0.346	0.654	0.804
	(0.476)	(0.476)	(0.397)
Spouse has the same country of birth	0.536	0.239	0.094
	(0.499)	(0.426)	(0.292)
Spouse has the same ancestry	0.646	0.426	0.245
	(0.478)	(0.494)	(0.430)
Panel VI: Fertility			
Number of children living in same household	1.468	1.005	0.974
	(1.418)	(1.219)	(1.178)
Has a child living in same household	0.645	0.510	0.506
	(0.478)	(0.500)	(0.500)
Number of children living in same household, only individuals married with spouse present	1.997	1.479	1.421
	(1.325)	(1.243)	(1.208)
Has a child living in same household, only individuals married with spouse present present	0.855	0.734	0.715
	(0.352)	(0.442)	(0.451)
Panel VII: Neighborhood of residence			
Fraction of population from PUMA from same country of birth	0.110	0.010	0.008
	(0.122)	(0.026)	(0.019)
Fraction from same country of birth is above mean, within country of birth	0.415	0.333	0.410
	(0.493)	(0.471)	(0.492)

Table A1 (continued)

	Born in non-English-speaking country		Born in English-speaking country (3)
	Hispanics (1)	Non-Hispanics (2)	
Fraction of population from PUMA with same primary ancestry	0.165 (0.184)	0.058 (0.080)	0.044 (0.062)
Fraction with same ancestry is above mean, within ancestry	0.440 (0.496)	0.425 (0.494)	0.470 (0.499)

Notes: The sample consists of individuals from the 2000 1% and 5% PUMS files who are currently aged 25–55, immigrated to the US before age 15 and do not have missing values for the own age, year of immigration, country of birth and English variables. Total number of observations is 191,534 for the English variable, with Columns 1–3 containing 86,387, 79,241, and 25,906 observations, respectively. Statistics are weighted by IPUMS weights. The English-speaking ability ordinal measure is defined as: 0 = no English, 1 = not well, 2 = well, and 3 = very well.

References

1. Chiswick, Barry. 1991. "Speaking, Reading and Earnings among Low-Skilled Immigrants." *Journal of Labor Economics*, 9(2): 149–170.
2. Kossoudji, Sherrie. 1988. "English Language Ability and the Labor Market Opportunities of Hispanic and East Asian Immigrant Men." *Journal of Labor Economics*, 6(2): 205–228.
3. McManus, Walter, William Gould, and Finis Welch. 1983. "Earnings of Hispanic Men: The Role of English Language Proficiency." *Journal of Labor Economics*, 1(2): 101–130.
4. Tanier, Evelina. 1988. "English Language Proficiency and Earnings among Foreign-born Men." *Journal of Human Resources*, 23(1): 108–122.
5. Glick, Jennifer, and Michael White. 2003. "The Academic Trajectories of Immigrant Youths: Analysis Within and Across Cohorts." *Demography*, 40(4): 759–783.
6. Portes, Alejandro, and Dag MacLeod. 1999. "Educating the Second Generation: Determinants of Academic Achievement among Children of Immigrants in the United States." *Journal of Ethnic and Migration Studies*, 25(3): 373–396.
7. Davila, Alberto, and Marie Mora. 2001. "The Marital Status of Recent Immigrants in the United States in 1980 and 1990." *International Migration Review*, 35(2): 506–524.
8. Meng, Xin, and Robert Gregory. 2005. "Intermarriage and the Economic Assimilation of Immigrants." *Journal of Labor Economics*, 23(1): 135–175.
9. Stevens, Gillian, and Gray Swicegood. 1987. "The Linguistic Context of Ethnic Endogamy." *American Sociological Review*, 52(1): 73–82.
10. Sorenson, Ann Marie. 1988. "The Fertility and Language Characteristics of Mexican-American and Non-Hispanic Husbands and Wives." *Sociological Quarterly*, 29(1): 111–130.
11. Swicegood, Gray, Frank Bean, Elizabeth Stephen, and Wolfgang Opitz. 1988. "Language Usage and Fertility in the Mexican-Origin Population of the United States." *Demography*, 25(1): 17–33.
12. Angrist, Joshua, and Victor Lavy. 1997. "The Effect of a Change in Language of Instruction on the Returns to Schooling in Morocco." *Journal of Labor Economics*, 15(1): S48–S76.

13. Chiswick, Barry, and Paul W. Miller. 1995. "The Endogeneity between Language and Earnings: International Analyses." *Journal of Labor Economics*, 13(2): 246–288.
14. Dustmann, Christian, and Arthur van Soest. 2002. "Language and the Earnings of Immigrants." *Industrial and Labor Relations Review*, 55(3): 473–492.
15. Bleakley, Hoyt, and Aimee Chin. 2004. "Language Skills and Earnings: Evidence from Childhood Immigrants." *Review of Economics and Statistics*, 86(2): 481–496.
16. Bleakley, Hoyt, and Aimee Chin. 2010. "Age at Arrival, English Proficiency, and Social Assimilation among U.S. Immigrants." *American Economic Journal: Applied Economics*, 2(1): 165–92.
17. Bleakley, Hoyt, and Aimee Chin. 2008. "What Holds Back the Second Generation? The Intergenerational Transmission of Language Human Capital among Immigrants." *Journal of Human Resources*, 43(2): 267–298.
18. Kominski, Robert. 1989. "How Good Is 'How Well'? An Examination of the Census English-Speaking Ability Question." Paper presented at the 1989 Annual Meeting of the American Statistical Association, Washington, DC.
19. Lenneberg, Eric. 1967. *Biological Foundation of Language*. New York: Wiley and Sons.
20. Fry, Richard, and Shirin Hakimzadeh. 2006a. " *A Statistical Portrait of the Foreign-born Population at Mid-Decade.*" Pew Hispanic Center Report, Washington, DC: Pew Hispanic Center.
21. Ruggles, Steven, Matthew Sobek, Trent Alexander, Catherine Fitch, Ronald Goeken, Patricia Hall, Miriam King, and Chad Ronnander. 2004. *Integrated Public Use Microdata Series: Version 3.0* [Machine-readable database]. Minneapolis, MN: Minnesota Population Center.
22. World Almanac, and Robert Famighetti. 1999. *World Almanac and Book of Facts, 1999*, New York: World Almanac Books.
23. Duncan, Brian, and Stephen Trejo. 2007. "Ethnic Identification, Intermarriage and Unmeasured Progress by Mexican Americans." In *Mexican Immigration to the United States*, ed. George Borjas, 229–268. Chicago: National Bureau of Economic Research and the University of Chicago Press.
24. Newport, Elissa. 2002. "Critical Periods in Language Development." In *Encyclopedia of Cognitive Science*, ed. L. Nadel, 737. London: Macmillan Publishers, Nature Publishing Group.

Chapter 14
Who Remains Mexican? Selective Ethnic Attrition and the Intergenerational Progress of Mexican Americans

Brian Duncan and Stephen J. Trejo

Abstract This chapter argues that selective ethnic attrition creates potentially serious problems for tracking the socioeconomic progress of the US-born descendants of Mexican immigrants. As the descendants of Mexican immigrants assimilate into American society and often intermarry with non-Mexicans, ethnic identification weakens, particularly among the children produced by Mexican intermarriages. This process of ethnic leakage is highly selective, because Mexican Americans who intermarry tend to have much higher education and earnings than Mexican Americans who do not intermarry. Consequently, available data for third- and higher-generation Mexicans, who usually can only be identified by their subjective responses to questions about Hispanic ethnicity, understate the socioeconomic attainment of this population. In effect, through the selective nature of intermarriage and ethnic identification, some of the most successful descendants of Mexican immigrants assimilate to such an extent that they fade from empirical observation. We present several pieces of evidence that are consistent with this story.

Introduction

As a self-styled "nation of immigrants," the United States takes great pride in its historical success as a "melting pot" able to absorb and unify people coming from diverse lands and cultures. At the same time, however, Americans' pride in their immigrant heritage often seems tempered by the nagging fear that the most recent arrivals are somehow different, that the latest wave of foreigners will not integrate into the mainstream of US society. Certainly, this fear was voiced when Italians and other relatively unskilled immigrants arrived in large numbers at the end of the 1800s and the beginning of the 1900s (1). Time has assuaged this particular fear. In terms of outcomes such as educational attainment, occupation, and earnings, the sizeable differences by national origin that initially persisted among earlier

B. Duncan (✉)
University of Colorado, Denver, CO, USA
e-mail: brian.duncan@ucdenver.edu

D.L. Leal, S.J. Trejo (eds.), *Latinos and the Economy*, Immigrants and Minorities, Politics and Policy, DOI 10.1007/978-1-4419-6682-7_14,
© Springer Science+Business Media, LLC 2011

European immigrants have largely disappeared among the modern-day descendants of these immigrants (2–4).

There is considerable skepticism, however, that the processes of assimilation and adaptation will operate similarly for the predominantly non-white immigrants who have entered the United States in increasing numbers over the past several decades (5–7). Of particular concern are Mexican immigrants and their descendants. Mexicans assume a central role in current discussions of immigrant intergenerational progress and the outlook for the so-called "new second generation," not just because Mexicans make up a large share of the immigrant population, but also because most indications of relative socioeconomic disadvantage among the children of US immigrants vanish when Mexicans are excluded from the sample (8, 9). Therefore, to a great extent, concern about the long-term economic trajectory of immigrant families in the United States is concern about Mexican-American families.

Are Mexicans following the same intergenerational trajectory that earlier European immigrants did? Huntington (10), among others, is decidedly pessimistic, and he points to several factors that could slow the pace of assimilation by Mexicans today as compared to Europeans in the past. These factors include the vast scale of current immigration flows from Mexico and other Spanish-speaking countries, the substantial (though lessening) geographic concentration of these flows within the United States, and the fact that such flows have remained sizeable over a much longer period of time than did the influx from any particular European country. In addition, the close proximity of Mexico to the United States facilitates return and repeat migration. These unique features of Mexican immigration foster the growth of ethnic enclaves in the United States where immigrants and their descendants could, if they so choose, live and work without being forced to learn English or to Americanize in other important ways. Another salient factor is that many Mexicans enter the United States as illegal immigrants.

Moreover, today's economy provides fewer opportunities for unskilled workers to advance than did the economy that greeted earlier European immigrants (11, 12). Around 1900, high school completion was uncommon for native-born Americans, so while many European immigrants arrived with relatively meager education, their skill disadvantage was smaller than that faced today by Mexican immigrants, who typically lack the additional years of high school and college that have become the norm for US natives. In addition, recent decades have witnessed a large rise in earnings inequality among American workers, driven by substantial increases in the labor market payoffs to education and other indicators of skill (13, 14). As a result, the skill deficit of Mexican immigrants has become even more of a liability in our modern economy, which places a higher premium on knowledge and cognitive ability.

In contrast to Huntington (10), Perlmann (11) offers a cautiously optimistic assessment of the prospects for assimilation by the descendants of Mexican immigrants. After carefully comparing the intergenerational mobility experienced by low-skill European immigrants arriving in the United States around 1900 with that experienced by modern-day Mexicans, Perlmann (11, p. 124) concludes that

"Mexican economic assimilation may take more time–four or five generations rather than three or four," but that such assimilation is nonetheless occurring. If this is correct, then the long-term integration of Mexican Americans may not turn out all that differently from the success stories often recounted for previous waves of US immigration.[1]

Table 14.1 Average years of education and hourly earnings, men, ages 25–59

	Mexicans			3rd+ Generation Whites	3rd+ Generation Blacks
	1st Generation	2nd Generation	3rd+ Generation		
Years of education	8.78	12.26	12.36	13.64	12.70
	(0.03)	(0.04)	(0.03)	(0.004)	(0.01)
Hourly earnings	12.60	17.79	17.77	22.29	16.84
	(0.07)	(0.18)	(0.15)	(0.03)	(0.06)

Source: 1994–2006 CPS data.
Note: Standard errors are shown in parentheses. The samples include men, ages 25–59. The samples for the hourly earnings data are further limited to men employed at wage and salary jobs during the survey week. Earnings have been converted to $2006 using the Consumer Price Index for All Urban Consumers (CPI-U). For hourly earnings, observations below $1 or above $500 were considered outliers and excluded. First-generation Mexicans are individuals who were born in Mexico. Second-generation Mexicans are US-born individuals who have at least one parent born in Mexico. Third- (and higher-) generation Mexicans are US-born individuals who have US-born parents and who self-identify as Mexican in response to the Hispanic origin question in the CPS. Third- (and higher-) generation whites and blacks are US-born, non-Hispanic individuals who have US-born parents.

Several recent studies have explored this issue by comparing education and earnings across generations of Mexican Americans (15–22). Table 14.1 illustrates the basic patterns that emerge for men.[2] Between the first and second generations, average schooling rises by three and one half years and average hourly earnings grow substantially for Mexicans. The third generation, by contrast, shows little or no additional gains, leaving Mexican-American men with an educational deficit of 1.3 years and a wage disadvantage of 20% relative to whites. Note that, even for individuals in the third generation and beyond, Mexican schooling levels are low not just in comparison with non-Hispanic whites, but also relative to African Americans. Similar patterns emerge for women and when regressions are used to control for other factors such as age and geographic location (15, 16, 19).

The apparent lack of socioeconomic progress between second and later generations of Mexican Americans is surprising. Previous studies have consistently found parental education to be one of the most important determinants of an individual's educational attainment and ultimate labor market success (23, 24). Through this mechanism, the huge educational gain between first- and second-generation Mexican Americans should produce a sizable jump in schooling between the second and third generations, because on average the third generation has parents who are much better educated than those of the second generation. Yet the improvement in schooling we expect to find between the second and third generations is largely absent.

The research summarized in Table 14.1 suggests that intergenerational progress stalls for Mexican Americans after the second generation. As noted by Borjas (25) and Smith (26), however, generational comparisons in a single cross-section of data do a poor job of matching immigrant parents and grandparents in the first generation with their actual descendants in later generations. Indeed, Smith (26) finds evidence of more substantial gains between second- and third-generation Mexicans when he combines cross-sectional data sets from successive time periods in order to compare second-generation Mexicans in some initial period with their third-generation descendants 25 years later. Yet even Smith's (26) analysis shows signs of intergenerational stagnation for Mexican Americans. In his Table 4, for example, five of the six most recent cohorts of Mexicans experience no wage gains between the second and third generations. Moreover, all studies conclude that large education and earnings deficits (relative to whites) remain for third- and higher-generation Mexicans.[3]

These findings–that the economic disadvantage of Mexican Americans persists even among those whose families have lived in the United States for more than two generations, and that the substantial progress observed between the first and second generations seems to stall thereafter–raise doubts whether the descendants of Mexican immigrants are enjoying the same kind of intergenerational advancement that allowed previous groups of unskilled immigrants, such as the Italians and Irish, to eventually enter the economic mainstream of American society. Such conclusions could have far-reaching implications, but the validity of the intergenerational comparisons that underlie these conclusions rests on assumptions about ethnic identification that have received relatively little scrutiny for Mexican Americans. In particular, analyses of intergenerational change typically assume, either explicitly or implicitly, that the ethnic choices made by the descendants of Mexican immigrants do not distort outcome comparisons across generations.

Consider, for example, the Mexican generations defined in Table 14.1. First- and second-generation Mexicans are identified using a more or less "objective" indicator of ethnicity: whether the respondent or either of his parents was born in Mexico. Like virtually all large, national surveys, however, the CPS does not provide information on the countries of birth of an adult respondent's grandparents. As a result, third- and higher-generation Mexicans in these data can be identified only from a "subjective" measure of ethnic self-identification: the Hispanic origin question.[4] Almost without exception, studies of later-generation Mexican Americans rely exclusively on the Hispanic origin question (or something very similar) to identify the population of interest.

Ethnic identification is to some extent endogenous, especially among people at least one or two generations removed from immigration to the United States (27, 28). Consequently, the descendants of Mexican immigrants who continue to identify themselves as Mexican in the third and higher generations may be a select group. For example, if the most successful Mexican Americans are more likely to intermarry or for other reasons cease to identify themselves or their children as Mexican,

then available data may understate human capital and earnings gains between the
second and third generations.[5] In other words, research on intergenerational assimilation among Mexicans may suffer from the potentially serious problem that the
most assimilated members of the group under study eventually fade from empirical observation as they more closely identify with the group they are assimilating
toward.[6]

Recently, we have begun to assess the potential empirical importance of selective
ethnic attrition among Mexican Americans (29–31). Specifically, we have investi-
gated what factors influence whether individuals choose to identify themselves (or
their children) as Mexican origin, and how these ethnic choices may affect inferences about the socioeconomic attainment of later-generation Mexican Americans.
In this chapter, we summarize and synthesize the evidence on this issue.

Ethnic Identification and Ethnic Attrition

For our purposes, the ideal data set would include the family tree of each individual,
enabling us to identify which individuals are descended from Mexican immigrants
and how many generations have elapsed since that immigration took place. It would
then be a simple matter to compare outcomes for this "true" population of Mexican
descendants with the corresponding outcomes for a relevant reference group (e.g.,
non-Hispanic whites) and also with those for the subset of Mexican descendants
who continue to self-identify as Mexican origin.[7] Such an analysis would provide
an unbiased assessment of the relative standing of the descendants of Mexican immigrants in the United States, and it would show the extent to which selective ethnic
identification distorts estimated outcomes for this population when researchers are
forced to rely on standard, self-reported measures of Mexican identity.

Following the 1970 Census, unusually detailed information of this sort was collected for a small sample of individuals with ancestors from a Spanish-speaking
country. After each decennial US Census, selected respondents to the Census long
form are reinterviewed in order to check the accuracy and reliability of the Census
data. The 1970 Census was the first US Census to ask directly about Hispanic
origin or descent, and therefore a primary objective of the 1970 Census Content
Reinterview Study was to evaluate the quality of the responses to this new question.
For this purpose, individuals in the reinterview survey were asked a series of questions regarding any ancestors they might have that were born in a Spanish-speaking
country. Among those identified by the reinterview survey as having Hispanic ancestors, Table 14.2 shows the percent who had previously responded on the 1970
Census long form that they were of Hispanic "origin or descent."[8]

Overall, 76% of reinterview respondents with ancestors from a Spanish-speaking
country had self-identified as Hispanic in the 1970 Census, but the correspondence
between Hispanic ancestry in the reinterview and Hispanic identification in the
Census fades with the number of generations since the respondent's Hispanic ancestors arrived in the United States. Virtually all (99%) first-generation immigrants
born in a Spanish-speaking country identified as Hispanic in the Census, but the

Table 14.2 Hispanic identification of individuals with ancestors from a Spanish-speaking country, as reported in the 1970 census content reinterview study

Hispanic ancestry classification in reinterview	Percent who identified as Hispanic in the census	Sample size
Most recent ancestor from a Spanish-speaking country:		
Respondent (i.e., 1st generation)	98.7	77
Parent(s) (i.e., 2nd generation)	83.3	90
Grandparent(s) (i.e., 3rd generation)	73.0	89
Great grandparent(s) (i.e., 4th generation)	44.4	27
Further back (i.e., 5th+ generations)	5.6	18
Hispanic ancestry on both sides of family	97.0	266
Hispanic ancestry on one side of family only	21.4	103
Father's side	20.5	44
Mother's side	22.0	59
All individuals with Hispanic ancestry	75.9	369

Source: Table C of US Bureau of the Census (32, p. 8).
Note: Information regarding the generation of the most recent ancestor from a Spanish-speaking country was missing for 68 respondents who nonetheless indicated that they had Hispanic ancestry on one or both sides of their family.

rate of Hispanic identification dropped to 83% for the second generation, 73% for the third generation, 44% for the fourth generation, and all the way down to 6% for higher generations of Hispanics. Interestingly, intermarriage seems to play a central role in the loss of Hispanic identification. Almost everyone (97%) with Hispanic ancestors on both sides of their family identified as Hispanic in the Census, whereas the corresponding rate was only 21% for those with Hispanic ancestors on just one side of their family. Given the small number of Hispanics in the reinterview sample (369 individuals reported having at least one ancestor from a Spanish-speaking country), the percentages in Table 14.2 should be regarded with caution, especially those for the very small samples of Hispanics who are fourth generation or higher. Nonetheless, these data do suggest that self-identified samples of US Hispanics might omit a large proportion of later-generation individuals with Hispanic ancestors, and that intermarriage could be a fundamental source of such intergenerational ethnic attrition.

Unfortunately, the microdata underlying Table 14.2 no longer exist, so we cannot use these data to examine in a straightforward manner how selective ethnic attrition affects observed measures of intergenerational progress for Mexican Americans.[9] Out of necessity, we instead adopt the less direct and less comprehensive strategies for trying to shed light on this issue that are described below. Before turning to this description, however, we first discuss some prior research on intermarriage and ethnic identification that is especially relevant for our study.

Frequent intermarriage is one of the strongest signals of social assimilation by an ethnic group (33, 34). After a few generations in the United States, so much intermarriage had taken place among the descendants of earlier European immigrants that most white Americans could choose among multiple ancestries or ethnic identities (27, 28, 35). For such individuals, ethnicity has become subjective, situational, and largely symbolic, and the social boundaries between these ethnic groups have been almost completely erased. In this context, it is interesting to note that exogamy is increasingly common for Mexican Americans. Rosenfeld (36, Table 1) shows that the intermarriage rate of Mexican-American women grew substantially between 1970 and 1980 and even more sharply between 1980 and 1990. As of 2000, more than a third of married, US-born Mexicans have non-Mexican spouses, with the overwhelming majority of these non-Mexican spouses being US-born, non-Hispanic whites (29). Perlmann and Waters (37) argue that the proclivity for intermarriage by second-generation Mexicans today is similar to what was observed for second-generation Italians in the early 1900s. This argument has potentially provocative implications for ethnic attachment among future generations of Mexican Americans, because intermarriage became so commonplace for subsequent generations of Italian Americans that Alba (38) characterized this group as entering the "twilight of ethnicity."

In the US context, analyses of ethnic responses in large national surveys have focused primarily on whites of European descent (3, 39–41), and therefore new insights could be gained from an analysis such as ours that highlights ethnic choices among the Mexican-origin population. For other minority groups, existing research illustrates how selective ethnic identification can distort observed socioeconomic characteristics. American Indians are a particularly apt example because they exhibit very high rates of intermarriage, and fewer than half of the children of such intermarriages are identified as American Indian by the Census race question (42). For these and other reasons, racial identification is relatively fluid for American Indians, and changes in self-identification account for much of the surprisingly large increase in educational attainment observed for American Indians between the 1970 and 1980 US Censuses (43). In addition, Snipp (44) shows that those who report American Indian as their race have considerably lower schooling and earnings, on average, than the much larger group of Americans who report a non-Indian race but claim to have some Indian ancestry.

To cite another example, Waters (45, 46) observes selective ethnic identification among the US-born children of New York City immigrants from the West Indies and Haiti. The teenagers doing well in school tend to come from relatively advantaged, middle-class families, and these kids identify most closely with the ethnic origins of their parents. In contrast, the teenagers doing poorly in school are more likely to identify with African Americans. This pattern suggests that self-identified samples of second-generation Caribbean blacks might overstate the socioeconomic achievement of this population, a finding that potentially calls into question the practice of comparing outcomes for African Americans and Caribbean blacks as a means of distinguishing racial discrimination from other explanations for the disadvantaged status of African Americans (47).

Existing studies (48–53) demonstrate that the process of ethnic identification by Hispanics is fluid, situational, and at least partly voluntary, just as has been observed for non-Hispanic whites and other groups. Most work in this area, however, analyzes Hispanics as an aggregate group, even though available evidence suggests that the ethnic responses of Mexican Americans may differ in fundamental ways from those of other Hispanics (12, 50, 52). More importantly, earlier studies do not directly address the issue that we focus on here: the selective nature of Mexican identification and how it affects our inferences about intergenerational progress for this population. Though previous research has noted the selective nature of intermarriage for Hispanics overall (54, 55) and for Mexican Americans in particular (56, 57), this research has not examined explicitly the links between intermarriage and ethnic identification, nor has previous research considered the biases that these processes might produce in standard intergenerational comparisons of economic status for Mexican Americans. Closer in spirit to our analysis is recent work by Alba and Islam (58) that tracks cohorts of US-born Mexicans across the 1980–2000 Censuses and uncovers evidence of substantial declines in Mexican self-identification as a cohort ages. In contrast with our analysis, however, Alba and Islam (58) are able to provide only limited information about the socioeconomic selectivity of this identity shift, and they focus on the identity shifts that occur within rather than across generations of Mexicans.

Although most research in this area has been conducted by social scientists outside of economics, an emerging literature within economics explicitly recognizes the complexity of ethnic identification and has started to investigate the implications of this complexity for labor market outcomes and policy.[10] In particular, economic models emphasize the potential endogeneity of identity and suggest mechanisms through which ethnic identification could be associated with both observed and unobserved characteristics of individuals. To date, however, most empirical work in the relevant economics literature has focused on immigrants. The analysis presented here demonstrates that some of the same issues can apply to native-born members of minority groups. In addition, we emphasize the complications that intergenerational shifts in ethnic identify can create for measuring the socioeconomic progress of later-generation descendants of immigrants.

Intermarriage and Mexican Identification of Children[11]

The data in Table 14.2 from the 1970 Census Content Reinterview Study not only demonstrate that ethnic attrition could be a serious issue for the later-generation descendants of Mexican immigrants, but these data also suggest that intermarriage plays a leading role in the process. For ethnic attrition to distort significantly the standard measures of intergenerational progress for Mexican Americans, however, it is not enough that such attrition be sizeable; the attrition must also be selective on key indicators of socioeconomic attainment such as education or earnings. In this section, we discuss evidence on the extent and selectivity of Mexican intermarriage and on how intermarriage influences the Mexican identification of children in the subsequent generation.

Extent and Selectivity of Mexican Intermarriage

We start with intermarriage, because intermarriage is probably the predominant source of leakage from the population of self-identified Mexican Americans (through the ethnic choices made by the children and grandchildren of these inter-marriages). Therefore, knowing the extent and selectivity of Mexican intermarriage is important for evaluating the potential bias that such leakage could produce in intergenerational comparisons. More generally, intermarriage is of interest because it is often viewed as the ultimate indicator of assimilation by an ethnic group with immigrant origins (33, 34), and also because it is a key determinant of weakened and/or multiple ethnic attachments for future generations of the group (35, 59).

We employ microdata from the 2000 US Census. The sample includes marriages that meet the following conditions: both spouses are between the ages of 25 and 59, the couple currently lives together, and at least one spouse is a US-born indi-vidual identified as Mexican by the Census question regarding Hispanic origin. Furthermore, we exclude marriages in which the information about Hispanic ori-gin for either spouse has been imputed by the Census Bureau. These restrictions yield a sample of 62,734 marriages.

For the US-born Mexican husbands and wives involved in these marriages, Table 14.3 shows the nativity/ethnicity distributions of their spouses. Intermarriage is widespread in our samples of Mexican-American husbands and wives. The first column indicates that just over half (51%) of US-born husbands of Mexican descent have wives of the same nativity and ethnicity, and another 14% are married to Mexican immigrants. Therefore, the remaining 35% of Mexican-American hus-bands have wives that are neither Mexican nor Mexican American, with the bulk of these wives (27%) being US-born non-Hispanic whites. The nativity/ethnicity distribution of Mexican-American wives is quite similar, except for a somewhat higher rate of marriage to Mexican immigrants and a correspondingly lower rate of marriage to US-born Mexicans.

Table 14.3 suggests that, in terms of nativity and ethnicity, the marital choices of US-born Mexicans can be classified into three main categories of spouses: US-born Mexicans, foreign-born Mexicans, and non-Mexicans. Based on this simplification, Table 14.4 proposes a typology of marriages involving US-born Mexicans that also indicates, for marriages in which only one spouse is a US-born Mexican, whether the other spouse is the husband or the wife. In Table 14.4, the unit of analysis is the mar-riage, rather than the US-born Mexican husband or wife as in Table 14.3. This shift in focus is consistent with our interest in how Mexican intermarriage may impact the ethnic identification and observed socioeconomic characteristics of subsequent gen-erations, because children are a product of the marriage. Table 14.4 demonstrates the potential for ethnic leakage among the children of Mexican Americans. Note that

Table 14.3 Nativity/ethnicity distributions of the spouses of US-born Mexicans

	US-Born Mexican	
Nativity/ethnicity of spouse	Husbands	Wives
US-born:		
Mexican	50.6	45.3
Other Hispanic	2.7	2.3
Non-Hispanic		
White	26.7	28.1
Black	.6	1.5
Asian	.4	.3
Other race	.8	.6
Multiple race	1.0	1.0
Foreign-born:		
Mexican	13.6	17.4
Other Hispanic	1.5	1.8
Non-Hispanic		
White	1.1	1.2
Black	.04	.06
Asian	.7	.3
Other race	.06	.03
Multiple race	.2	.2
	100.0%	100.0%

Source: 2000 Census data.
Note: The sample includes marriages that meet the following conditions: both spouses are between the ages of 25 and 59, the couple
currently lives together, and at least one spouse is a US-born individual identified as Mexican by the Census question regarding Hispanic
origin. For the US-born Mexican husbands and wives involved in
these marriages, the table shows the nativity/ethnicity distributions
of their spouses. There are 62,734 such marriages, and these marriages involve 38,911 US-born Mexican husbands and 43,527 US-born
Mexican wives.

it takes two Mexican-origin spouses to create an endogamous Mexican marriage,
whereas a Mexican intermarriage requires only one Mexican-origin spouse. As a
result, the intermarriage rates for Mexican-American men and women observed
in Table 14.3 imply that, in Table 14.4, almost half (48%) of Mexican-American
marriages involve a non-Mexican spouse.

Next we explore the selectivity of Mexican intermarriage. Using the same typology of Mexican-American marriages as in Table 14.4, Table 14.5 reports two
important indicators of human capital for the husbands and wives in each type
of marriage. The human capital measures are average years of schooling[12] and
percent deficient in English, with standard errors displayed in parentheses. We
define someone to be "deficient" in English if they speak a language other than
English at home and they also report speaking English worse than "very well."[13]
These calculations include *all* husbands or wives in the relevant marriages, not

Table 14.4 Types of marriages involving US-born Mexicans

Type of marriage	Percent of sample
Both spouses US-born Mexican	31.4
Husband foreign-born Mexican (Wife US-born Mexican)	12.0
Wife foreign-born Mexican (Husband US-born Mexican)	8.4
Husband non-Mexican (Wife US-born Mexican)	25.9
Wife non-Mexican (Husband US-born Mexican)	22.2
	100.0%

Source: 2000 Census data.
Note: The sample includes marriages that meet the following conditions: both spouses are between the ages of 25 and 59, the couple
currently lives together, and at least one spouse is a US-born individual identified as Mexican by the Census question regarding Hispanic
origin. There are 62,734 such marriages.

just the Mexican-American husbands or wives. Therefore, we can observe not only
the selectivity of US-born Mexicans who intermarry, but also the characteristics
of their spouses. For example, wife outcomes for the marriage type "Husband
non-Mexican" provide information about Mexican-American women who marry
non-Mexicans, whereas husband outcomes for this same marriage type provide
information about the spouses of these women. For both husbands and wives, outcomes for the marriage type "Both spouses US-born Mexican" provide information
about Mexican Americans involved in endogamous marriages.

Table 14.5 reveals striking differences in human capital between Mexican
Americans married to Mexicans and those married to non-Mexicans. US-born
Mexicans married to non-Mexicans have much higher levels of educational attainment and English proficiency than those with spouses that are also US-born
Mexicans, whereas US-born Mexicans married to Mexican immigrants possess
less human capital than any other group of Mexican Americans. Among Mexican-
American husbands, for example, those with non-Mexican wives average a year
more schooling than those with US-born Mexican wives. Compared to their counterparts in endogamous marriages, intermarried Mexican-American men also have a
nine percentage point lower rate of English deficiency. In addition, Table 14.5 shows
that non-Mexican spouses of Mexican Americans have the highest human capital of
any group considered, and that Mexican immigrant spouses of Mexican Americans
have the lowest. In Duncan and Trejo (29), we find similar patterns for indicators of
labor market performance such as employment rates and hourly earnings, and we
demonstrate that most of these differences in labor market performance derive from
the human capital selectivity of Mexican intermarriage.

Table 14.5 Human capital of husbands and wives, by type of marriage

	Average years of education	Percent deficient English
Husbands		
Type of marriage:		
Both spouses US-born Mexican	12.0	14.1
	(0.02)	(0.25)
Husband foreign-born Mexican	9.6	53.3
	(0.05)	(0.57)
Wife foreign-born Mexican	11.5	24.4
	(0.04)	(0.59)
Husband non-Mexican	13.5	4.0
	(0.02)	(0.15)
Wife non-Mexican	13.1	5.1
	(0.02)	(0.19)
All husbands	12.3	15.0
	(0.01)	(0.14)
Wives		
Type of marriage:		
Both spouses US-born Mexican	12.1	14.2
	(0.02)	(0.25)
Husband foreign-born Mexican	11.4	18.8
	(.03)	(.45)
Wife foreign-born Mexican	10.3	53.5
	(0.05)	(0.69)
Husband non-Mexican	13.1	6.0
	(0.02)	(0.19)
Wife non-Mexican	13.3	4.4
	(0.02)	(0.17)
All wives	12.4	13.7
	(0.01)	(0.14)

Source: 2000 Census data.
Note: Standard errors are shown in parentheses. The samples include husbands and wives in marriages that meet the following conditions: both spouses are between the ages of 25 and 59, the couple currently lives together, and at least one spouse is a US-born individual identified as Mexican by the Census question regarding Hispanic origin. The sample sizes are 62,734 husbands and 62,734 wives.

Our finding of positive human capital selectivity for intermarried Mexican Americans is not unexpected (55). First of all, opportunities for meeting and interacting with people from other racial/ethnic groups are better for more educated Mexican Americans, because highly-educated Mexican Americans tend to live, study, and work in less segregated environments (60, 61). Second, given the sizeable educational deficit of the average Mexican American, better-educated Mexican Americans are likely to be closer in social class to the typical non-Mexican (62). Third, attending college is an eye-opening experience for many students that may work to diminish preferences for marrying within one's own racial/ethnic group.

Finally, the theory of "status exchange" in marriage formulated by Davis (63) and Merton (64) predicts that members of lower-status minority groups (such as Mexican Americans) would tend to need higher levels of socioeconomic attainment to attract spouses who are members of higher-status majority groups.

Mexican Identification of Children

We now investigate the link between intermarriage in one generation and ethnic identification in the next by examining how the children of US-born Mexicans are identified.[14] We start with the same sample of Mexican-American marriages from the 2000 Census used in the preceding intermarriage analysis, but henceforth we further restrict the sample to those marriages that have produced at least one child under age 19 currently residing in the household. We continue to exclude marriages in which the information about Hispanic origin has been imputed for either spouse, and we now impose this condition for the relevant children as well. Finally, to the extent possible with the information available in the Census, we exclude families in which any of the children are suspected of being stepchildren. These restrictions produce a sample of 37,921 families.

Using the same typology of Mexican-American marriages introduced earlier, Table 14.6 reports for each type of marriage the percent in which the youngest child

Table 14.6   Mexican identification of youngest child by type of marriage

	Percent with youngest child identified as Mexican
Type of marriage:	
Both spouses US-born Mexican	98.2 (0.12)
Husband foreign-born Mexican	97.9 (0.20)
Wife foreign-born Mexican	97.8 (0.24)
Husband non-Mexican	63.5 (0.51)
Wife non-Mexican	71.1 (0.51)
All types of marriages	84.4 (0.19)

Source: 2000 Census data.
Note: Standard errors are shown in parentheses. The sample includes marriages that meet the following conditions: both spouses are between the ages of 25 and 59, the couple currently lives together, at least one spouse is a US-born individual identified as Mexican by the Census question regarding Hispanic origin, and the marriage has produced at least one child under age 19 that resides in the household. There are 37,921 such marriages.

is identified as Mexican by the Hispanic origin question in the Census.[15] Of primary interest for our purposes is how this percentage varies with the nativity and ethnicity of the parents. Overall, the youngest child is identified as Mexican in 84% of these families, which raises the possibility of substantial ethnic attrition among the children of Mexican Americans. The crucial determinant of a child's Mexican identification is whether both parents are Mexican origin. In marriages between two US-born Mexicans or between a US-born Mexican and a Mexican immigrant, Mexican identification of the child is virtually assured (i.e., the relevant rates are 98%). In marriages between a US-born Mexican and a non-Mexican, however, the likelihood that the child is identified as Mexican drops to 64–71%, with the precise figure depending on which parent is non-Mexican, the father or the mother.[16]

Table 14.7 shows how the human capital of parents correlates with whether their youngest child is identified as Mexican. In these marriages involving at least one Mexican-American spouse, parents with children not identified as Mexican average about a year more schooling and have approximately a 10 percentage point lower rate of English deficiency than do their counterparts with children designated as Mexican. In Duncan and Trejo (29), we show that parents with children not identified as Mexican also exhibit advantages in employment and earnings. Moreover,

Table 14.7 Parental human capital, by Mexican identification of youngest child

	Average years of education	Percent deficient English
Fathers		
Youngest child identified as:		
Mexican	12.1	18.0
	(0.02)	(0.21)
Not Mexican	13.2	6.2
	(0.03)	(0.31)
All fathers	12.3	16.1
	(0.02)	(0.19)
Mothers		
Youngest child identified as:		
Mexican	12.3	15.8
	(0.02)	(0.20)
Not Mexican	13.1	6.5
	(0.03)	(0.32)
All mothers	12.4	14.4
	(0.01)	(0.18)

Source: 2000 Census data.
Note: Standard errors are shown in parentheses. The samples include fathers and mothers in marriages that meet the following conditions: both spouses are between the ages of 25 and 59, the couple currently lives together, at least one spouse is a US-born individual identified as Mexican by the Census question regarding Hispanic origin, and the marriage has produced at least one child under age 19 that resides in the household. The sample sizes are 37,921 fathers and 37,921 mothers.

within the group of marriages involving a non-Mexican spouse, parents' outcomes do not vary with the Mexican identification of their children. In other words, intermarriage is the crucial link between the ethnic identification of Mexican-American children and the human capital and labor market performance of their parents. The strong correlation observed between parental skills and whether the child is identified as Mexican arises because of the intense selectivity of Mexican-American intermarriage, especially in terms of human capital, and the powerful influence of intermarriage on the ethnic identification of children.

In this section, we have demonstrated that Mexican intermarriage is highly selective on human capital and also that having a non-Mexican parent determines, in large part, whether children of Mexican descent are at risk of losing their Mexican identity. Taken together, these findings provide a mechanism for selective ethnic attrition among Mexican Americans. Those Mexicans who intermarry tend to have higher levels of human capital, and many of the resulting children are not identified as Mexican in Census data. In this way, selective intermarriage interacts with the intergenerational transmission of human capital and ethnic identity to create a situation in which available data for later-generation Mexican Americans may omit an increasingly large share of the most successful descendants of Mexican immigrants.[17]

Despite the apparent strength of intermarriage selectivity and its close link to the Mexican identification of children, one could use our data to argue that these factors ultimately produce little bias in observed outcomes for Mexican Americans. For example, Table 14.7 shows that, in families with at least one Mexican-American parent, fathers average 1.1 years more schooling (and mothers average 0.8 years more schooling) if their youngest child is not identified as Mexican. This pattern reflects the educational selectivity of Mexican intermarriage, but the impact of such selectivity is attenuated by the small overall incidence of non-Mexican affiliation among children with at least one Mexican-American parent (i.e., from the bottom row of Table 14.6, just 16% of these children fail to identify as Mexican). As a result, in Table 14.7, restoring to our samples the potentially "missing" families with children not identified as Mexican only raises the average schooling of fathers from 12.1 to 12.3 years (and of mothers from 12.3 to 12.4 years). Moreover, estimates of intergenerational correlations suggest that less than half of any educational gains for parents get transmitted to their children (24, 65, 66). Therefore, our Census analyses can directly substantiate only a tiny amount of "hidden" progress for these children of Mexican Americans: less than 0.1 years of education, and similarly small amounts for the other outcomes.

We think it premature, however, to conclude that the measurement issues and potential biases which motivated our research can be safely ignored. In our Census samples, for us to know that a child is of Mexican descent, at least one of his US-born parents must continue to self-identify as Mexican. We therefore completely miss any Mexican-origin families in which the relevant Mexican descendants no longer identify as Mexican. Data from the 1970 Census Content Reinterview Study, presented earlier in Table 14.2, indicate that we could be missing a large share of later-generation Mexican-origin families (e.g., well over half of Mexican descendants beyond the third generation). For this reason, we believe that our results show the direction, but not the magnitude, of measurement biases arising from selective intermarriage and ethnic identification by Mexican Americans.

Indirect Evidence of Selective Ethnic Attrition

Do selective intermarriage and selective ethnic identification bias observed measures of socioeconomic progress for later generations of Mexican Americans? In this section, we discuss additional research we have done that provides indirect evidence of such bias and suggests that the direction of the bias is to understate measured attainment for the population of US-born descendants of Mexican immigrants.

Spanish Surname and Hispanic Identification[18]

To acquire the initial piece of indirect evidence concerning ethnic attrition, we exploit the information about Spanish surnames that was made available most recently in the 1980 Census. The microdata file indicates whether an individual's surname appears on a list of almost 12,500 Hispanic surnames constructed by the Census Bureau. This information, however, is provided only for those individuals who reside in the following five southwestern states: California, Texas, Arizona, Colorado, and New Mexico.

Although the surname list constructed for the 1980 Census is more extensive and accurate than those used with previous Censuses, as a tool for identifying Hispanics the list suffers from sins of both omission and commission. Indeed, both types of errors are introduced by the common practice of married women taking the surname of their husbands, as Hispanic women can lose and non-Hispanic women can gain a Spanish surname through intermarriage. The surname list also errs by labeling as Hispanic some individuals of Italian, Filipino, or Native Hawaiian descent who have names that appear on the list (67, 68).

For our purposes, another weakness of the surname list is that it cannot distinguish Mexicans from other Hispanic national origin groups. This weakness is minimized, however, by limiting the sample to the aforementioned five southwestern states. In 1980, the Puerto Rican and Cuban populations in these states were still quite small, and large-scale immigration from Central and South America had not yet begun. As a result, the overwhelming majority of Hispanics in these southwestern states are Mexican origin. Indeed, in the samples of US-born individuals analyzed below, 88% of those who self-report as being of Hispanic origin indicate Mexican as their national origin, and almost all remaining self-reported Hispanics fall into the "Other Hispanic" category. Individuals in this "Other Hispanic" category are especially prevalent in the states of New Mexico and Colorado, where some Hispanics whose families have lived in these regions for many generations prefer to call themselves "Hispanos," emphasizing their roots to the Spaniards who settled the new world over their Mexican and Indian ancestry (67).

The Spanish surname information provided in the 1980 Census is in addition to the race and Hispanic origin questions typically employed to identify racial/ethnic groups. Our hope is that, particularly for men, the presence of a Spanish surname in the five southwestern states provides an objective, albeit imperfect, indicator of Mexican ancestry that allows us to identify some individuals of Mexican descent who fail to self-report as Hispanic and who are, therefore, missed by subjective indicators such as the Hispanic origin question in the Census. If so, then perhaps differences in human capital between Spanish-surnamed individuals who do and do not self-identify as Hispanic can reveal something about the selective nature of ethnic identification for Mexican Americans.

To pursue this idea, we extracted from the 1980 Census 5% microdata sample all US-born individuals between the ages of 25 and 59 who reside in the states of California, Texas, Arizona, Colorado, and New Mexico. We focus on individuals in this age range because they are old enough that virtually all of them will have completed their schooling, yet they are young enough that observed labor market outcomes reflect their prime working years. We focus on persons born in the United States because Hispanic identity is likely to be much more fluid and malleable for US-born Mexican Americans than for Mexican immigrants whose birthplace serves to reinforce their ethnicity.[19] Given our interest in ethnic identification, we exclude from the sample anyone with missing or imputed information about race, Hispanic origin, or country of birth. To increase the accuracy of the Spanish surname indicator, individuals whose race is American Indian or Asian are also excluded.

In our data, there are two different ways for individuals to be identified as Hispanic. They can self-report being Hispanic in response to the Hispanic origin question, and they can possess a Spanish surname. Based on these two Hispanic indicators, we define three mutually exclusive types of Hispanic identification: those identified as Hispanic *both* by self-report and by surname, those identified as Hispanic by self-report *only* (and not by surname), and those identified as Hispanic by surname *only* (and not by self-report). We exclude non-Hispanics (i.e., persons who do not self-report as being of Hispanic origin and also do not possess a Spanish surname).

For our sample of US-born Hispanics, the first column of numbers in Table 14.8 reports the distributions of men and women across the three types of Hispanic identification. For men, self-reported and surname-based indicators of Hispanicity are usually consistent with one another. Just 4% of the men that we label as Hispanic are so identified only by their Spanish surname. A larger share of Hispanic men, 13%, self-identify as Hispanic but do not possess a surname on the Census list of Spanish surnames. The vast majority of these men, 83%, identify as Hispanic through both self-report and surname. For US-born Hispanic women, the corresponding proportions are 13% identify as Hispanic by surname only, 21% by self-report only, and 66% through both indicators. Not surprisingly, women show more inconsistency between self-reported and surname-based indicators of Hispanicity than men do,

Table 14.8 Human capital, by type of Hispanic identification

	Percent of sample	Average years of education	Percent deficient English
Men			
Identified as Hispanic by:			
Self-report and surname	83.1	10.6 (0.02)	28.8 (0.23)
Self-report only	12.9	12.1 (0.05)	14.4 (0.46)
Surname only	4.0	12.2 (0.08)	7.0 (0.61)
All types of Hispanics	100.0%	10.8 (0.02)	26.1 (0.20)
Women			
Identified as Hispanic by:			
Self-report and surname	66.2	9.7 (0.02)	33.3 (0.26)
Self-report only	21.1	11.7 (0.03)	13.0 (0.32)
Surname only	12.7	12.3 (0.03)	3.2 (0.21)
All types of Hispanics	100.0%	10.5 (0.02)	25.1 (0.19)

Source: 1980 Census data.
Note: Standard errors are shown in parentheses. The samples include US-born individuals ages 25–59 who reside in the states of California, Texas, Arizona, Colorado, and New Mexico. Individuals whose race is American Indian or Asian are excluded, as is anyone else with a race other than white or black who neither has a Spanish surname nor self-reports as being of Hispanic origin. The sample sizes are 46,339 men and 53,800 women.

presumably because of errors sometimes introduced when married women take their husband's surname.

The remaining columns of Table 14.8 show how completed years of schooling and English proficiency vary by type of Hispanic identification. On average, those identified as Hispanic by self-report only or by surname only possess much more human capital than those identified as Hispanic by both indicators. For example, men with inconsistent responses to the Hispanic indicators have at least a year and a half more schooling than Hispanic men with consistent responses, and rates of English deficiency are markedly lower for men with inconsistent responses. The bottom panel of Table 14.8 indicates that the patterns for women are qualitatively similar but even stronger. In Duncan and Trejo (29), we report analogous results for labor market outcomes (i.e., employment rates and hourly earnings), and we show that differences in labor market outcomes across the Hispanic identification groups are largely driven by the corresponding differences in human capital (i.e., education and English proficiency).

How should we interpret these patterns? If the group of Hispanic men identified by surname only captures some Hispanics who are choosing to loosen their ethnic attachment, then our evidence suggests that such individuals are positively selected in terms of human capital and labor market outcomes. We also find evidence of positive selection for Hispanic men identified by self-report only. These men may be Hispanics who lost their Spanish surname through intermarriage, as could occur if they have a Hispanic mother or grandmother who married a non-Hispanic man and took his surname. Therefore, the results for the "Hispanic by self-report only" group are consistent with the findings we reported earlier on the selectivity of Mexican intermarriage. Similar patterns emerge for women, though in this case interpretation is clouded by the common practice of married women taking the surname of their husbands. Overall, our findings support the notion that individuals of Mexican descent who no longer self-identify as Hispanic are positively selected in terms of socioeconomic status. Relatively few individuals with Spanish surnames fail to self-identify as Hispanic, however, so it would be unwise to regard these results as anything more than suggestive.

Mexican Ethnicity and Ancestry[20]

Starting in 1980, the US Census has included an open-ended question asking for each person's "ancestry or ethnic origin," and the first two responses are coded in the order that they are reported. This ancestry information is in addition to the race and Hispanic origin questions typically employed to identify racial/ethnic groups. The Hispanic origin and ancestry questions give Mexican Americans multiple ways of expressing ethnic identification in Census data. We consider whether for Mexicans it makes sense to think of different patterns of responses to these questions as indicating varying degrees of ethnic attachment. If so, then the complexity of ethnic responses by Mexican Americans might provide another piece of indirect evidence regarding selective ethnic attrition.

For ease of exposition, throughout this section we will use the term "ethnicity" to refer to an individual's response to the Census question regarding Hispanic origin, and we will use the term "ancestry" to refer to an individual's responses to the Census ancestry question. Employing this terminology, Table 14.9 categorizes individuals based upon their joint responses to the Hispanic origin and ancestry questions. The data are from the 2000 Census, and the samples include US-born men and women ages 25–59 who report Mexican as an ethnicity and/or ancestry.[21] The first column of numbers in Table 14.9 shows the distributions of men and women across ethnicity/ancestry groups, and these distributions illustrate the complexity of ethnic identification for Mexican Americans. In our samples of US-born adults who give some indication that they are of Mexican descent, just over two third of these individuals answer "Mexican" to both the Hispanic origin and the ancestry questions in the Census. About 20% report a Mexican ethnicity but do not list a Mexican ancestry, and the remaining 11–12% identify as Mexican in response to the ancestry question but not the Hispanic origin question.

Table 14.9 Human capital, by Mexican ethnicity/ancestry

	Percent of sample	Average years of education	Percent deficient English
Men			
Ethnicity/Ancestry:			
Ethnicity is Mexican and Ancestry is			
Mexican	67.8	12.3	13.1
		(.01)	(.14)
General Hispanic	7.9	12.1	10.8
		(0.03)	(0.37)
Other ancestry	3.6	12.3	9.7
		(0.05)	(0.53)
Not reported	9.5	10.7	16.5
		(0.04)	(0.40)
Ancestry is Mexican and Ethnicity is			
General or other Hispanic	8.1	11.9	15.0
		(0.03)	(0.42)
Not Hispanic	3.1	12.9	3.8
		(0.05)	(0.37)
All men	100.0%	12.1	13.0
		(0.01)	(0.11)
Women			
Ethnicity/ancestry:			
Ethnicity is Mexican and ancestry is			
Mexican	68.5	12.3	12.4
		(0.01)	(0.13)
General Hispanic	8.8	12.1	9.8
		(0.03)	(0.33)
Other ancestry	3.8	12.3	7.5
		(0.05)	(0.44)
Not reported	6.4	10.9	17.2
		(0.05)	(0.49)
Ancestry is Mexican and Ethnicity is			
General or other Hispanic	9.3	11.9	15.5
		(0.03)	(0.39)
Not Hispanic	3.1	12.9	3.8
		(0.04)	(0.36)
All women	100.0%	12.2	12.3
		(0.01)	(0.11)

Source: 2000 Census data.
Note: Standard errors are shown in parentheses. The samples include US-born men and women ages 25–59 who report Mexican as an ethnicity and/or ancestry. The sample sizes are 88,989 men and 92,644 women.

For our purposes, this last group is of special interest. Because most studies of US-born Mexican Americans identify the target population using only the Hispanic origin question (or something very similar to it), the Mexican-origin samples in these studies typically exclude individuals who report a Mexican ancestry but not a Mexican ethnicity. Table 14.9 shows that most of these excluded Mexicans give a pan-ethnic or "general Hispanic" response to the Hispanic origin question, using labels such as "Hispanic," "Latino," or "Spanish."[22] Note, however, that a significant proportion of these excluded Mexicans instead report their ethnicity as "not Hispanic." US-born adults who identify as "not Hispanic" (in response to the Hispanic origin question that appears near the front of the Census questionnaire) but nonetheless list Mexican as an ancestry (in response to the ancestry question that comes later) may represent a segment of the Mexican-American population with somewhat weaker or more distant ethnic ties. If so, then by studying this segment of the population we might be able to learn something about the selectivity of ethnic identification for Mexican Americans and about the potential for selective ethnic attrition to bias standard measures of socioeconomic status for the US-born descendants of Mexican immigrants.

The second and third columns of numbers in Table 14.9 show how levels of schooling and English proficiency vary across the Mexican ethnicity/ancestry groups. Among persons who report a Mexican ethnicity, the group that stands out is people who do not respond to the Census ancestry question. For both men and women, those who do not report an ancestry have much less human capital than any other group of Mexican Americans. Men with unreported ancestry, for example, average only 10.7 years of schooling, compared to 12.3 years for the majority group of US-born Mexicans who report Mexican as both their ethnicity and their ancestry.[23] Similarly, compared to the majority group, Mexican men with unreported ancestry are three percentage points more likely to be deficient in English. Putting aside the group with unreported ancestry, differences between other groups of men who report a Mexican ethnicity are generally small, except that those with "general Hispanic" or "other" ancestries tend to speak English better than those with a Mexican ancestry. The corresponding patterns for women are similar (see the bottom half of Table 14.9).

Among persons who list a Mexican ancestry but do *not* report a Mexican ethnicity, there are two quite distinct groups. Those who report a "general Hispanic" ethnicity have somewhat lower levels of educational attainment and English proficiency than are observed in the overall samples of US-born Mexican men and women. In contrast, persons who list a Mexican ancestry but simultaneously report their ethnicity as "not Hispanic" have much higher levels of human capital than any other ethnicity/ancestry group of US-born Mexicans. Compared to men who report Mexican as both their ethnicity and their ancestry, for example, men of Mexican ancestry who identify their ethnicity as "not Hispanic" enjoy a schooling advantage of over half a year and a rate of English deficiency that is nine percentage points lower. The patterns are very similar for women. In addition, Duncan and Trejo (30) show that similar patterns emerge for labor market outcomes such as employment rates and hourly earnings.

The two ethnicity/ancestry groups considered in the preceding paragraph represent segments of the Mexican-American population that usually are excluded from empirical research on this population, because most studies use only the Hispanic origin question to identify US-born persons of Mexican descent. As noted by Alba and Islam (58), the very different characteristics of these two groups make it important to distinguish between them whenever possible. Persons of Mexican ancestry who identify their ethnicity as "not Hispanic" possess relatively high levels of human capital. This group seems to provide a prime example of ethnic attrition in which the attrition is "positively" selected, consistent with what we document in the other sections of this chapter. Persons of Mexican ancestry who report a "general Hispanic" ethnicity, on the other hand, possess relatively low levels of human capital, suggesting "negative" selection for the segment of the Mexican-origin population that adopts pan-ethnic Hispanic labels. Much of the selectivity of these two contrasting groups would be hidden if they were combined into a single category consisting of all persons who report a Mexican ancestry but not a Mexican ethnicity.

Direct Evidence of Selective Ethnic Attrition[24]

The empirical patterns reported thus far are suggestive of selective ethnic attrition among Mexican Americans, but this evidence is somewhat indirect. Using data on US-born Mexican-American children from the Current Population Survey (CPS), we now provide more direct evidence on this issue. In particular, we assess the influence of endogenous ethnicity by comparing an "objective" indicator of Mexican descent (based on the countries of birth of the child, his parents, and his grandparents) with the standard "subjective" measure of Mexican self-identification (based on the response to the Hispanic origin question).

A key feature of recent CPS data is their inclusion of the information about parental countries of birth that is currently missing from the Census. For children living with both parents, the CPS data reveal how many parents and grandparents were born in Mexico. By examining how the ethnic identification of these children varies with the numbers of parents and grandparents born in Mexico, we can directly estimate the extent of ethnic attrition among second- and third-generation Mexican children. The analysis sample consists of US-born children ages 17 and below who live in intact families and who have some identifiable Mexican ancestry.[25] We describe as "second-generation Mexicans" those US-born children with at least one parent born in Mexico, and we designate as "third-generation Mexicans" those US-born children with no parents but at least one grandparent born in Mexico.

For comparison purposes, we create one final category of US-born Mexicans, the "fourth-and-higher generation," which denotes US-born children with no parents or grandparents born in Mexico but with at least one parent identified as Mexican by the CPS question regarding Hispanic origin. For expositional convenience, we will refer to this group as the "fourth generation." Note that, whereas second- and third-generation Mexican children can be identified using "objective" criteria (i.e., the countries of birth of their parents and grandparents), fourth-generation Mexican children are revealed only by "subjective" indicators (i.e., whether either parent self-identifies as Mexican). Consequently, for our purposes, the fourth-generation category is flawed, because it misses children descended from Mexican immigrants if neither parent self-identifies as Mexican. Data from the 1970 Census Content Reinterview Study (32), presented earlier in Table 14.2, indicate that we could be missing a large share of later-generation Mexican-origin families. Nonetheless, we think it informative to include statistics for this flawed fourth-generation category in the tables that follow, but interpretation of these statistics should take into account the incomplete and potentially selective nature of this category.

Table 14.10 Generation and Mexican identification of US-born children of Mexican descent

Generation	Percent of all US-born Mexicans	Percent of Generation	Percent identified as Mexican	Sample size
2nd generation Mexicans:				
Both parents born in Mexico	41.9	68.4	97.9	17,235
One parent born in Mexico	19.3	31.6	80.6	7,959
All 2nd generation Mexicans	61.2	100.0	92.4	25,194
3rd generation Mexicans:				
Neither parent born in Mexico and				
Four grandparents born in Mexico	1.3	10.0	96.2	524
Three grandparents born in Mexico	0.9	7.1	95.2	375
Two grandparents born in Mexico	4.4	34.5	78.7	1,815
One grandparent born in Mexico	6.2	48.5	58.4	2,551
All 3rd generation Mexicans	12.8	100.0	71.8	5,265
4th+ generation Mexicans:				
No parents or grandparents born in Mexico and				
Both parents identified as Mexican	11.2	42.9	98.4	4,592
One parent identified as Mexican	14.8	57.1	50.1	6,112
All 4th+ generation Mexicans	26.0	100.0	70.8	10,704
All US-born Mexicans	100.0		84.2	41,163

Source: 1994–2006 CPS data.
Note: The sample includes US-born children, ages 17 and below, who live in intact families and either have at least one parent or grandparent born in Mexico or else have at least one parent identified as Mexican in response to the CPS question regarding Hispanic origin. Suspected stepchildren are excluded. "Identified as Mexican" represents the percentage of these children who are identified as Mexican by the CPS Hispanic origin question.

For the US-born children of Mexican descent in our CPS sample, Table 14.10 shows their distribution by generation and the rates at which these children subjectively identify as Mexican. Given our definitions, the vast majority (61%) of these US-born Mexican-American children are second generation, 13% are third generation, and the remaining 26% are higher generation. The heterogeneity *within* generations of Mexican Americans is striking, however, and perhaps somewhat surprising. Almost a third of second-generation Mexicans have a parent who was *not* born in Mexico, and only 17% of third-generation Mexicans have a majority of their grandparents born in Mexico. Among the so-called fourth-generation Mexicans, 57% have a parent who does *not* self-identify as Mexican.

The generational complexity evident in Table 14.10 has two sources: intermarriage between Mexican ethnics and non-Mexicans, and marriage between Mexican Americans of different generations. The only way that a third-generation Mexican child can have three or four of his grandparents born in Mexico, for example, is if both parents are second-generation Mexicans (i.e., the mother and father are both the US-born children of Mexican immigrants). By contrast, if a second-generation Mexican marries either a non-Mexican or a later-generation Mexican (i.e., a Mexican American from the third generation or beyond), then the children resulting from such a marriage can have at most two Mexican-born grandparents. The generational categories for US-born Mexican-American children listed in Table 14.10, based on how many of a child's parents and/or grandparents were born in Mexico, show in finer detail than usual how far removed each child is from his Mexican immigrant origins.

Moreover, this generational complexity is closely related to children's subjective Mexican identification. Children are virtually certain of identifying as Mexican if both parents or three or more grandparents were born in Mexico, or if both parents self-identify as Mexican. By contrast, rates of Mexican identification fall to 81% for second-generation children with only one Mexican-born parent, 79% for third-generation children with two grandparents born in Mexico, 58% for third-generation children with just one Mexican-born grandparent, and 50% for fourth-generation children with only one parent who identifies as Mexican. Among all US-born children in the CPS with some identifiable Mexican ancestry, 16% do not subjectively identify as Mexican, and this rate of ethnic attrition rises to almost 30% for children in the third generation and beyond.

Table 14.11 begins to explore the selectivity of Mexican identification, in this case by showing how parents' education varies with the Mexican identification of their children. In all generations, children of Mexican descent who fail to identify as Mexican have parents with much higher levels of educational attainment than do the corresponding children who retain a Mexican identification. Consider, for example, the fathers of third-generation Mexican-American children. Compared to their counterparts whose children identify as Mexican, the fathers whose children do not so identify average almost a year more schooling (13.3 vs. 12.4 years), are about half as likely to be high school dropouts (12% vs. 22%), and are over twice as likely to be college graduates (23% vs. 11%). Analogous differences for mothers are similar but slightly less dramatic. The strong correlation between parents' education and children's Mexican identification is not surprising, given previous evidence of the human capital selectivity of Mexican intermarriage and of the powerful influence that intermarriage exerts on the ethnic identification of Mexican-American children.

By examining an indicator of human capital available for a subset of the Mexican-American children analyzed in Tables 14.10 and 14.11. Table 14.12 provides an initial glimpse at the ultimate impact of selective ethnic attrition. For

Table 14.11 Parental education of US-born children of Mexican descent, by child's generation and Mexican Identification

| | Parental education, by Mexican identification of child | | | | | | | | |
| | Average years of education | | | Percent without high school diploma | | | Percent with Bachelor's degree | | |
	Mexican	Not Mexican	All children	Mexican	Not Mexican	All children	Mexican	Not Mexican	All children
Father's outcomes									
Child's generation:									
2nd generation Mexicans	9.00	11.04	9.16	63.61	37.31	61.61	4.22	11.36	4.76
	(.03)	(.08)	(.02)	(.32)	(1.11)	(.31)	(.13)	(.73)	(.13)
3rd generation Mexicans	12.36	13.26	12.61	22.02	11.90	19.16	11.36	23.40	14.76
	(.04)	(.06)	(.03)	(.67)	(.84)	(.54)	(.52)	(1.10)	(.49)
4th+ generation Mexicans	12.31	13.20	12.57	21.09	9.77	17.79	12.17	21.72	14.96
	(.03)	(.04)	(.02)	(.47)	(.53)	(.37)	(.38)	(.74)	(.34)
Mother's outcomes									
Child's generation:									
2nd generation Mexicans	9.24	11.26	9.39	62.28	36.05	60.29	3.84	10.78	4.37
	(.02)	(.08)	(.02)	(.32)	(1.10)	(.31)	(.13)	(.71)	(.13)
3rd generation Mexicans	12.36	13.05	12.55	20.30	11.97	17.95	10.35	18.63	12.69
	(.04)	(.05)	(.03)	(.65)	(.84)	(.53)	(.50)	(1.01)	(.46)
4th+ generation Mexicans	12.21	13.04	12.45	21.52	9.96	18.15	10.56	16.63	12.33
	(.03)	(.03)	(.02)	(.47)	(.53)	(.37)	(.35)	(.67)	(.32)

Source: 1994–2006 CPS data.

Note: Standard errors are shown in parentheses. The sample includes US-born children, ages 17 and below, who live in intact families and either have at least one parent or grandparent born in Mexico or else have at least one parent identified as Mexican in response to the CPS question regarding Hispanic origin. Suspected stepchildren are excluded.

Table 14.12 Dropout rates of US-born youth ages 16–17, by generation and Mexican identification

Generation/ethnicity	Percent identified as Mexican	Dropout rate			Sample size
		Identified as Mexican	Not identified as Mexican	All youth	
2nd generation Mexicans	92.6	5.75	3.30	5.57	1,238
	(0.7)	(0.69)	(1.88)	(0.65)	
3rd generation Mexicans	68.9	3.43	1.09	2.70	296
	(2.7)	(1.28)	(1.09)	(0.94)	
4th+ generation Mexicans	70.6	4.13	2.70	3.71	755
	(1.7)	(0.86)	(1.09)	(0.69)	
No grandparents born in Mexico and					
Both parents US-born, non-Hispanic whites				2.78	25,334
				(0.10)	
Both parents US-born, non-Hispanic blacks				2.70	1,924
				(0.37)	

Source: 1994–2006 CPS data.

Note: Standard errors are shown in parentheses. The sample includes US-born youth, ages 16 and 17, living in intact families. Suspected stepchildren are excluded. "Identified as Mexican" represents the percentage of youth who are identified as Mexican by the CPS question regarding Hispanic origin. The "dropout rate" represents the percentage of youth who are not attending school and have not yet completed high school (either through classes or by exam).

US-born youth, aged 16–17, we investigate the relationship between Mexican identification and high school dropout rates.[26] Information about school enrollment pertains to the CPS survey week, so we exclude observations from the months of June, July, and August when students typically are on summer vacation. Table 14.12 reports how dropout rates vary by generation and Mexican identification. For comparison purposes, the table also displays the corresponding dropout rates for US-born, non-Hispanic white and black youth (with two US-born parents of the same race).

When we do not limit the sample to those who subjectively identify as Mexican, the dropout rate falls sharply from 5.6% for second-generation Mexicans to 2.7% for the third generation. These data thus suggest that by the third generation, Mexican-American youth have converged to the same dropout rate observed for third- and higher-generation non-Hispanic white youth. Moreover, the dropout rate of third-generation Mexican youth is 25% higher (3.4% vs. 2.7%) when the sample is limited to those youth who self-identify as Mexican. Though the sample sizes are small and the estimates are, therefore, imprecise, Table 14.12 provides some direct evidence that selective ethnic attrition could produce sizeable downward bias in standard measures of attainment for later-generation Mexicans which typically rely on ethnic self-identification rather than objective indicators of Mexican descent. Certainly, the apparent extent of such ethnic attrition—in our CPS sample, about 30% of third-generation Mexican youth fail to self-identify as Mexican—creates the potential for endogenous ethnicity to affect our inferences about the progress of Mexican Americans.

Conclusion

This chapter argues that selective ethnic attrition creates potentially serious problems for tracking the socioeconomic progress of the US-born descendants of Mexican immigrants. Almost without exception, studies of later-generation Mexican Americans rely on subjective measures of ethnic self-identification to identify the population of interest. As the descendants of Mexican immigrants assimilate into American society and often intermarry with non-Mexicans, ethnic identification weakens, particularly among the children produced by Mexican intermarriages. Unfolding across generations, this dynamic suggests that an increasingly small fraction of the descendants of Mexican immigrants continue to identify themselves as Mexican. Moreover, this process of ethnic leakage is highly selective, because Mexican Americans who intermarry tend to have much higher education and earnings than Mexican Americans who do not intermarry. Consequently, available data for third- and higher-generation Mexicans, who usually can only be identified by their subjective responses to questions about Hispanic ethnicity, understate the socioeconomic attainment of this population. In effect, through the selective nature of intermarriage and ethnic identification, some of the most successful descendants of Mexican immigrants assimilate to such an extent that they fade from empirical observation.

The evidence presented here is consistent with this story. Data from the 1970 Census Content Reinterview Study (32) suggest that self-identified samples of US Hispanics omit a large proportion of later-generation individuals with Hispanic ancestors, and that intermarriage is a fundamental source of such intergenerational ethnic attrition. Data from the 2000 Census indicate that intermarriage is widespread among Mexican Americans. More than a third of married, US-born Mexicans have non-Mexican spouses; the overwhelming majority of these non-Mexican spouses are US-born, non-Hispanic whites. Because it takes two Mexican-origin spouses to create an endogamous Mexican marriage, whereas a Mexican intermarriage requires only one Mexican-origin spouse, the observed rate of intermarriage implies that almost half of Mexican-American marriages involve a non-Mexican spouse. In addition, Mexican intermarriage is highly selective on human capital and labor market success, and having a non-Mexican parent largely determines whether children of Mexican descent are at risk of losing their Mexican identity. Taken together, these findings provide a mechanism for selective ethnic attrition among Mexican Americans. Those Mexicans who intermarry tend to have higher levels of education and earnings, and many of the resulting children are not identified as Mexican in Census data. In this way, selective intermarriage interacts with the intergenerational transmission of human capital and ethnic identity to create a situation in which available data for later-generation Mexican Americans may omit an increasingly large share of the most successful descendants of Mexican immigrants.

Two pieces of indirect evidence corroborate the direction of the measurement bias generated by this process of selective ethnic attrition. First, in 1980 Census data for five southwestern states where the Hispanic population was overwhelmingly Mexican origin at that time, men with a Spanish surname who nonetheless self-identify as "not Hispanic" are much more educated and English proficient, on average, than their counterparts who are consistently identified as Hispanic by both surname and self-report. Second, in 2000 Census data, human capital advantages are also evident for men and women who list a Mexican ancestry but simultaneously report their ethnicity as "not Hispanic," relative to those who report Mexican as both their ancestry and their ethnicity. In each case, the segment of the Mexican-American population that seems to have weaker or more distant ethnic ties displays significantly higher levels of socioeconomic attainment.

Finally, using data on US-born Mexican-American children from recent years of the Current Population Survey (CPS), we provide some direct evidence of selective ethnic attrition. For children living with both parents, the CPS data reveal how many parents and grandparents were born in Mexico. We assess the influence of endogenous ethnicity by comparing an "objective" indicator of Mexican descent (based on the countries of birth of the child, the child's parents, and the child's grandparents) with the standard "subjective" measure of Mexican self-identification (based on the child's response to the Hispanic origin question). Immigrant generations turn out to be quite complex, and this complexity is closely related to children's subjective Mexican identification. For example, only 17% of third-generation Mexicans have a majority of their grandparents born in Mexico. Moreover, third-generation children are virtually certain of identifying as Mexican if three or more grandparents were born in Mexico, whereas rates of Mexican identification fall to 79% for children with two grandparents born in Mexico and 58% for children with just one Mexican-born grandparent. Overall, about 30% of third-generation Mexican children fail to self-identify as Mexican in our CPS sample. Importantly, this ethnic attrition is highly selective. For example, the high school dropout rate of third-generation Mexican youth is 25% higher when the sample is limited to those youth who self-identify as Mexican. Therefore, these CPS data provide some direct evidence that ethnic attrition is substantial and could produce significant downward bias in standard measures of attainment that rely on ethnic self-identification rather than objective indicators of Mexican descent.

Acknowledgement This research was supported by NICHD grants 5R03HD050574-02 to Stephen Trejo and 5R24HD042849 to the Population Research Center at the University of Texas at Austin.

Notes

1. Also relevant is a study by MacKinnon and Parent (69) that documents the slow but eventual assimilation of the descendants of French Canadian immigrants in the United States. For our purposes, French Canadians are a particularly interesting group because their migration to the United States had several of the same features that Huntington (10) identifies as important obstacles to the past and future assimilation of Mexican Americans.

2. These averages are calculated using outgoing rotation group data from the 1994–2006 Current Population Survey (CPS); the data are described in more detail below. In Table 14.1, standard errors are shown in parentheses. The samples include men, ages 25–59. The samples for the hourly earnings data are further limited to men employed at wage and salary jobs during the survey week. Earnings have been converted to $2006 using the Consumer Price Index for All Urban Consumers (CPI-U). For hourly earnings, observations below $1 or above $500 were considered outliers and excluded. First-generation Mexicans are individuals who were born in Mexico. Second-generation Mexicans are US-born individuals who have at least one parent born in Mexico. Third- (and higher-) generation Mexicans are US-born individuals who have US-born parents and who self-identify as Mexican in response to the Hispanic origin question in the CPS. Third- (and higher-) generation whites and blacks are US-born, non-Hispanic individuals who have US-born parents.

3. Borjas (70) and Card, DiNardo, and Estes (65) investigate patterns of intergenerational progress for many different national origin groups, including Mexicans.

4. Since January 2003, the CPS has collected information about Hispanic origin as follows. Respondents are asked whether they are "Spanish, Hispanic, or Latino," and those who answer affirmatively are then asked to designate a specific Hispanic national origin group (Mexican, Puerto Rican, Cuban, Central/South American, or Other Spanish). The Hispanic origin question in the 2000 US Census is similar. Prior to 2003, the CPS elicited Hispanic origin by asking respondents to choose their "origin or descent" from a list of about 20 possibilities that included responses such as "Italian," "Polish," and "Afro American (Black, Negro)" in addition to the specific Hispanic national origin groups listed above. Responses for the specific Hispanic groups were coded and reported separately in the public use data files, along with a residual category that combines into a single group all of the non-Hispanic responses.

5. For groups such as Mexicans with relatively low levels of average schooling, Furtado (62) shows that assortative matching on education in marriage markets can create a situation whereby individuals who intermarry tend to be the more highly-educated members of these groups.

6. Bean, Swicegood, and Berg (71) raise this possibility in their study of generational patterns of fertility for Mexican-origin women in the United States.

7. Detailed ancestry information of this sort would raise complicated issues about how to define ethnic groups. For example, should calculations for the Mexican-American population differentially weight individuals according to their "intensity" of Mexican ancestry? In other words, among third-generation Mexicans, should those with four Mexican-born grandparents count more than those with just one grandparent born in Mexico? The answer might depend on the question of interest. For the questions of intergenerational assimilation and progress that we study here, our view is that all descendants of Mexican immigrants should count equally, regardless of how many branches of their family tree contain Mexican ancestry. This conceptualization allows intermarriage to play a critical role in the process of intergenerational assimilation for Mexican Americans, as it did previously for European immigrants (3, 34). As we note below, however, some of our analyses can shed light on the direction, but not the ultimate magnitude, of measurement biases arising from selective intermarriage and ethnic identification by Mexican Americans. Our conclusions about the direction of these measurement biases require only that persons of mixed ancestry–i.e., the products of Mexican

     intermarriage–be included with some positive weight in whatever definition is adopted for the Mexican-American population.

8. The information in Table 14.2 is reproduced from Table C of US Bureau of the Census (32, p. 8).

9. Starting in 1980, the Census has included an open-ended question asking for each person's "ancestry" or "ethnicity," with the first two responses coded in the order that they are reported (40). For the purposes of identifying individuals with Mexican or Hispanic ancestors, however, the Census ancestry question is not a good substitute for the detailed battery of questions included in the 1970 Census Content Reinterview Study. Indeed, many 1980–2000 Census respondents who identified as Hispanic in response to the Hispanic origin question failed to list a Hispanic ancestry in response to the ancestry item that comes later on the Census long form questionnaire, perhaps because they thought it redundant and unnecessary to indicate their Hispanic ethnicity a second time. Comparatively few respondents listed a Hispanic ancestry after identifying as non-Hispanic when answering the Hispanic origin question, so the ancestry question actually produces a lower overall count of Hispanics than does the Hispanic origin question (3, 72). See Duncan and Trejo (30), described below, for an analysis of how Mexican Americans respond to the Hispanic origin and ancestry questions in the 2000 Census. The patterns of responses are complex and strongly associated with human capital, labor market outcomes, intermarriage, and the Mexican identification of children. Emeka (73) investigates some of these issues for Hispanics as a whole, rather than specifically for Mexicans.

10. Examples include Akerlof and Kranton (74); Bisin and Verdier (75); Darity et al. (76); Bisin et al. (77); Mason (78); Darity et al. (79); Constant et al. (80); Bodenhorn and Ruebeck (81); Manning and Roy (82); and Nekby and Rodin (83). Constant and Zimmermann (84) and Zimmermann (85) survey some of the relevant literature.

11. Much of this section is based on Duncan and Trejo (29).

12. Beginning in 1990, the Census questions about educational attainment were changed to ask specifically about postsecondary degrees obtained rather than years of schooling. We follow Jaeger's (86) recommendations for how to construct a completed years of schooling variable from the revised education questions.

13. The Census asks individuals whether they "speak a language other than English at home," and those who answer affirmatively then are asked how well they speak English, with possible responses of "very well," "well," "not well," or "not at all."

14. For a wide range of groups, previous research has employed US Census data to investigate the racial/ethnic identification of children in intermarried families. Lieberson and Waters (3, 41), for example, consider the ancestries assigned to children when the mother's ancestry differs from the father's ancestry. Along the same lines, Xie and Goyette (87) study the determinants of Asian identification among children produced by intermarriages between an Asian and a non-Asian. Qian (88) extends this analysis to examine the racial/ethnic identification of children produced by intermarriages between US-born, non-Hispanic whites and several different minority groups: African Americans, Hispanics, Asians, and American Indians.

15. Because Mexican identification varies little across children within a given family, we report results using only information for the *youngest* child. Instead using information for the *oldest* child produces similar results, as does incorporating information from any or all of a family's children. We do not know who filled out the Census form, but parents are likely to be responding for their children. An important question is how these children will respond to survey questions about ethnic identification when they answer or themselves. See Portes and Rumbaut (12), Chapter 8) for a discussion of parental and other influences on the evolving ethnic identities of second-generation adolescents. Eschbach and Gomez (50) analyze changes in the Hispanic identification of adolescents between the first and second waves, 2 years apart, of the High School and Beyond panel, and Brown, Hitlin, and Elder (48) and Perez (52) do similar types of analyses using data from the National Longitudinal Study of Adolescent Health.

16. In analyses not reported here, we find that the impact of intermarriage on the Mexican identification of children does not change when controls are included for the age and gender of the child, the number of additional children in the family, geographic location, and various characteristics of the parents (age, education, and English proficiency).

17. Analyzing 2000 Census data for US-born youth, ages 16–17, who have at least one Mexican-origin parent, Duncan and Trejo (31) show explicitly how ethnic identification and the intermarriage selectivity of human capital gets passed from parents to children. In particular, we find that rates of Mexican identification and high school dropout are much lower, and English proficiency much higher, for Mexican-American youth who are the product of exogamous rather then endogamous marriages.

18. The research discussed in this section comes from Duncan and Trejo (29).

19. Indeed, we show below that the issue of ethnic attrition matters most for Mexican-origin persons whose families have been in the United States for more than two generations.

20. This section is based on Duncan and Trejo (30).

21. We exclude anyone with imputed information about Hispanic origin.

22. The "general Hispanic" ethnicity category also includes individuals who, in response to the Hispanic origin question, check the box for "other Spanish/Hispanic/Latino" (i.e., besides Mexican, Puerto Rican, or Cuban) but do not write anything in the space provided to designate a specific group. Logan (89) and Cresce and Ramirez (90) document and discuss the sharp increase in "general Hispanic" responses to the Hispanic origin question that occurred between the 1990 and 2000 US Censuses.

    A few individuals simultaneously report a Mexican ancestry and an "other Hispanic" ethnicity (i.e., a specific Hispanic national origin group other than Mexican (e.g., Cuban or Salvadoran). In Table 14.9, these individuals are grouped together with the much larger number of individuals who report a Mexican ancestry and a "general Hispanic" ethnicity. Given the relative sizes of its component groups, the combined category representing persons with Mexican ancestry and an ethnicity of "general or other Hispanic" is dominated by individuals who report a "general Hispanic" ethnicity.

23. Farley (40) shows that, in a broad sample of 1980 Census respondents which includes all nativity and racial/ethnic groups, persons with higher educational attainment are much more likely to respond to the ancestry question, and they are also much more likely to list multiple ancestries.

24. The research discussed in this section comes from Duncan and Trejo (31).

25. We exclude children with missing or imputed information about Hispanic origin or country of birth for themselves or either parent. We employ microdata from the CPS for all months from January 1994 through December 2006. The CPS is a monthly survey of about 50,000 households that the US government administers to estimate unemployment rates and other indicators of labor market activity. In addition to the detailed demographic and labor force data reported for all respondents, the CPS collects earnings information each month from one-quarter of the sample, the so-called "outgoing rotation groups." The data we analyze come from these outgoing rotation group samples. The CPS sampling scheme is such that surveys for the same month in adjacent years have about half of their respondents in common (e.g., about half of the respondents in any January survey are re-interviewed the following January). To obtain independent samples, we use only data from the first time a household appears in the outgoing rotation group samples (i.e., we use only data from the 4th month that a household appears in the CPS sample). By pooling together these 13 years of monthly CPS data, we substantially increase sample sizes and improve the precision of our estimates.

26. Note that the CPS sample in Tables 14.10 and 14.11 includes all US-born children ages 17 and below (who live in married, intact families and have some identifiable Mexican ancestry). In order to analyze high school dropout rates, we now further restrict the sample in Table 14.12 to the subset of these children who are ages 16 or 17.

References

1. Higham, John. 1970. *Strangers in the Land: Patterns of American Nativism, 1860–1925*. New York: Atheneum.
2. Farley, Reynolds. 1990. "Blacks, Hispanics, and White Ethnic Groups: Are Blacks Uniquely Disadvantaged?" *American Economic Review*, 80(2): 237–241.
3. Lieberson, Stanley, and Mary Waters. 1988. *From Many Strands: Ethnic and Racial Groups in Contemporary America*. New York: Russell Sage Foundation.
4. Neidert, Lisa, and Reynolds Farley. 1985. "Assimilation in the United States: An Analysis of Ethnic and Generation Differences in Status and Achievement." *American Sociological Review*, 50(6): 840–850.
5. Gans, Herbert. 1992. "Second-Generation Decline: Scenarios for the Economic and Ethnic Futures of the Post-1965 American Immigrants." *Ethnic and Racial Studies*, 15(2): 173–192.
6. Portes, Alejandro, and Min Zhou. 1993. "The New Second Generation: Segmented Assimilation and Its Variants Among Post-1965 Immigrant Youth." *Annals of the American Academy of Political and Social Science*, 530(1): 74–96.
7. Rumbaut, Ruben. 1994. "The Crucible Within: Ethnic Identity, Self-Esteem, and Segmented Assimilation Among Children of Immigrants." *International Migration Review*, 28(4): 748–794.
8. Perlmann, Joel, and Roger Waldinger. 1996. "The Second Generation and the Children of the Native Born: Comparisons and Refinements." Jerome Levy Economics Institute Working Paper 174.
9. Perlmann, Joel, and Roger Waldinger. 1997. "Second Generation Decline? Children of Immigrants, Past and Present – A Reconsideration." *International Migration Review*, 31(4): 893–922.
10. Huntington, Samuel. 2004. *Who Are We?: The Challenges to America's Identity*. New York: Simon and Schuster.
11. Perlmann, Joel. 2005. *Italians Then, Mexicans Now: Immigrant Origins and Second-Generation Progress, 1890–2000*. New York: Russell Sage Foundation.
12. Portes, Alejandro, and Ruben Rumbaut. 2001. *Legacies: The Story of the Immigrant Second Generation*. Berkeley, CA: University of California Press.
13. Autor, David, and Lawrence Katz. 1999. "Changes in the Wage Structure and Earnings Inequality." In *Handbook of Labor Economics*, ed. Orley Ashenfelter and David Card, 1463–1555. Vol. 3A. Amsterdam: North Holland.
14. Levy, Frank, and Richard Murnane. 1992. "U.S. Earnings Levels and Earnings Inequality: A Review of Recent Trends and Proposed Explanations." *Journal of Economic Literature*, 30(3): 1333–1381.
15. Blau, Francine, and Lawrence Kahn. 2007. "Gender and Assimilation among Mexican Americans." In *Mexican Immigration to the United States*, ed. George Borjas, 57–106. Chicago: University of Chicago Press.
16. Duncan, Brian, Joseph Hotz, and Stephen Trejo. 2006. "Hispanics in the U.S. Labor Market." In *Hispanics and the Future of America*, ed. Marta Tienda and Faith Mitchell, 228–290. Washington, DC: National Academies Press.
17. Farley, Reynolds, and Richard Alba. 2002. "The New Second Generation in the United States." *International Migration Review*, 36(3): 669–701.
18. Fry, Richard, and Lindsay Lowell. 2002. *"Work or Study: Different Fortunes of U.S. Latino Generations."* Washington, DC: Pew Hispanic Center.
19. Grogger, Jeffrey, and Stephen Trejo. 2002. *Falling Behind or Moving Up? The Intergenerational Progress of Mexican Americans*. San Francisco: Public Policy Institute of California.
20. Livingston, Gretchen, and Joan Kahn. 2002. "An American Dream Unfulfilled: The Limited Mobility of Mexican Americans." *Social Science Quarterly*, 83(4): 1003–1012.

21. Trejo, Stephen. 1997. "Why Do Mexican Americans Earn Low Wages?" *Journal of Political Economy*, 105(6): 1235–1268.
22. Trejo, Stephen. 2003. "Intergenerational Progress of Mexican-Origin Workers in the U.S. Labor Market." *Journal of Human Resources*, 38(3):467–489.
23. Haveman, Robert, and Barbara Wolfe. 1994. *Succeeding Generations: On the Effects of Investments in Children*. New York: Russell Sage Foundation.
24. Mulligan, Casey. 1997. *Parental Priorities and Economic Inequality*. Chicago: University of Chicago Press.
25. Borjas, George. 1993. "The Intergenerational Mobility of Immigrants." *Journal of Labor Economics*, 11(1): 113–135.
26. Smith, James. 2003. "Assimilation across the Latino Generations." *American Economic Review*, 93(2): 315–319.
27. Alba, Richard. 1990. *Ethnic Identity: The Transformation of White America*. New Haven, CT: Yale University Press.
28. Waters, Mary. 1990. *Ethnic Options: Choosing Identities in America*. Berkeley, CA: University of California Press.
29. Duncan, Brian, and Stephen Trejo. 2007. "Ethnic Identification, Intermarriage, and Unmeasured Progress by Mexican Americans." In *Mexican Immigration to the United States*, ed. George Borjas, 227–269. Chicago: University of Chicago Press.
30. Duncan, Brian, and Stephen Trejo. 2009a. "Ancestry versus Ethnicity: The Complexity and Selectivity of Mexican Identification in the United States." In *Research in Labor Economics*, Vol. 29, *Ethnicity and Labor Market Outcomes*, ed.Amelie Constant, Konstantinos Tatsiramos, and Klaus Zimmerman, 31–66. Bingley, UK: Emerald Group.
31. Duncan, Brian, and Stephen Trejo. 2009b. "Intermarriage and the Intergenerational Transmission of Ethnic Identity and Human Capital for Mexican Americans." Unpublished.
32. U.S. Bureau of the Census. 1974. "1970 Census of Population and Housing, Evaluation and Research Program: Accuracy of Data for Selected Population Characteristics as Measured by Reinterviews." Washington, DC: U.S. Government Printing Office.
33. Alba, Richard, and Victor Nee. *Rethinking the American Mainstream: Assimilation and Contemporary Immigration*. 2003. Cambridge, MA: Harvard University Press.
34. Gordon, Milton. 1964. *Assimilation in American Life: The Role of Race, Religion, and National Origins*. New York: Oxford University Press.
35. Hout, Michael, and Joshua Goldstein. 1994. "How 4.5 Million Irish Immigrants Became 40 Million Irish Americans: Demographic and Subjective Aspects of the Ethnic Composition of White Americans." *American Sociological Review*, 59(1): 64–82.
36. Rosenfeld, Michael. 2002. "Measures of Assimilation in the Marriage Market: Mexican Americans 1970–1990." *Journal of Marriage and Family*, 64(1): 152–162.
37. Perlmann, Joel, and Mary Waters. 2004. "Intermarriage Then and Now: Race, Generation, and the Changing Meaning of Marriage." In *Not Just Black and White: Historical and Contemporary Perspectives on Immigration, Race, and Ethnicity in the United States*, ed. Nancy Foner and George Fredrickson, 262–277. New York: Russell Sage Foundation.
38. Alba, Richard. 1986. *Italian Americans: Into the Twilight of Ethnicity*. Englewood Cliffs, NJ: Prentice-Hall.
39. Alba, Richard, and Mitchell Chamlin. 1983. "A Preliminary Examination of Ethnic Identification among Whites." *American Sociological Review*, 48(2): 240–47.
40. Farley, Reynolds. 1991. "The New Census Question about Ancestry: What Did It Tell Us?" *Demography*, 28(3): 411–429.
41. Lieberson, Stanley, and Mary Waters. 1993. "The Ethnic Responses of Whites: What Causes Their Instability, Simplification, and Inconsistency?" *Social Forces*, 72(2): 421–450.
42. Eschbach, Karl. 1995. "The Enduring and Vanishing American Indian: American Indian Population Growth and Intermarriage in 1990." *Ethnic and Racial Studies*, 18(1): 89–108.

43. Eschbach, Karl, Khalil Supple, and Matthew Snipp. 1998. "Changes in Racial Identification and the Educational Attainment of American Indians, 1970–1990." *Demography*, 35(1): 35–43.
44. Snipp, C. 1989. *American Indians: The First of this Land*. New York: Russell Sage Foundation.
45. Waters, Mary. 1994. "Ethnic and Racial Identities of Second-Generation Black Immigrants in New York City." *International Migration Review*, 28(4):795–820.
46. Waters, Mary. 1999. *Black Identities: West Indian Immigrant Dreams and American Realities*. New York: Russell Sage Foundation.
47. Sowell, Thomas. 1978. "Three Black Histories." In *Essays and Data on American Ethnic Groups*, ed. Thomas Sowell, 7–64. Washington, DC: Urban Institute.
48. Brown J. Scott., Steven Hitlin, and Glen Elder, Jr. 2006. "The Greater Complexity of Lived Race: An Extension of Harris and Sim." *Social Science Quarterly* 87(2): 411–431.
49. Choi, Kate, Arthur Sakamoto, and Daniel Powers. 2008. "Who is Hispanic? Hispanic Identity among African Americans, Asian Americans, Others, and Whites." *Sociological Inquiry*, 78(3): 335–371.
50. Eschbach, Karl, and Christina Gomez. 1998. "Choosing Hispanic Identity: Ethnic Identity Switching among Respondents to High School and Beyond." *Social Science Quarterly*, 79(1): 74–90.
51. Ono, Hiromi. 2002. "Assimilation, Ethnic Competition, and Ethnic Identities of U.S.-Born Persons of Mexican Origin." *International Migration Review*, 36(3): 726–745.
52. Perez, Anthony. 2008. "Who is Hispanic? Shades of Ethnicity among Latino/a Youth." In *Racisn in Post-Race America: New Theories, New Directions,* ed. Charles Gallagher, 17–35. Chapel Hill, NC: Social Forces.
53. Stephan, Cookie, and Walter Stephan. 1989. "After Intermarriage: Ethnic Identity among Mixed-Heritage Japanese-Americans and Hispanics." *Journal of Marriage and the Family*, 51(2): 507–519.
54. Qian, Zhenchao. 1997. "Breaking the Racial Barriers: Variations in Interracial Marriage Between 1980 and 1990." *Demography*, 34(2): 263–276.
55. Qian, Zhenchao. 1999. "Who Intermarries? Education, Nativity, Region, and Interracial Marriage, 1980 and 1990." *Journal of Comparative Family Studies*, 30(4): 579–597.
56. Fu, Vincent Kang. 2001. "Racial Intermarriage Pairings." *Demography*, 38(2): 147–159.
57. Rosenfeld, Michael. 2001. "The Salience of Pan-National Hispanic and Asian Identities in U.S. Marriage Markets." *Demography*, 38(2): 161–175.
58. Alba, Richard, and Tariqul Islam. 2009. "The Case of the Disappearing Mexican Americans: An Ethnic-Identity Mystery." *Population Research and Policy Review*, 28(2): 109–121.
59. Perlmann, Joel, and Mary Waters. 2007. "Intermarriage and Multiple Identities." In *The New Americans: A Guide to Immigration Since 1965*, ed. Mary C. Wagers and Reed Udea, 110–123. Cambridge, MA: Harvard University Press.
60. Alba, Richard, and John Logan. 1993. "Minority Proximity to Whites in Suburbs: An Individual-Level Analysis of Segregation." *American Journal of Sociology*, 98(6): 1388–1427.
61. Massey, Douglas, and Nancy Denton. 1992. "Racial Identity and the Spatial Assimilation of Mexicans in the United States." *Social Science Research*, 21(3): 235–260.
62. Furtado, Delia. 2006. "Human Capital and Interethnic Marriage Decisions." Institute for the Study of Labor (IZA) Discussion Paper 1989.
63. Davis, Kingsley. 1941. "Intermarriage in Caste Societies." *American Anthropologist*, 43(1): 376–395.
64. Merton, Robert. 1941. "Intermarriage and the Social Structure: Fact and Theory." *Psychiatry*, 4: 361–374.
65. Card, David, John DiNardoand Eugena Estes. 2000. "The More Things Change: Immigrants and the Children of Immigrants in the 1940s, the 1970s, and the 1990s." In *Issues in the*

Economics of Immigration, ed. George Borjas, 227–269. Chicago: University of Chicago Press.

66. Couch, Kenneth, and Thomas Dunn. 1997. "Intergenerational Correlations in Labor Market Status: A Comparison of the United States and Germany." *Journal of Human Resources*, 32(1): 210–232.

67. Bean, Frank, and Marta Tienda. 1987. *The Hispanic Population of the United States*. New York: Russell Sage Foundation.

68. Perkins, R. 1993. "Evaluating the Passel-Word Spanish Surname List: 1990 Decennial Census Post Enumeration Survey Results." U.S. Bureau of the Census, Population Division Working Paper 4.

69. MacKinnon, Mary, and Daniel Parent. 2005. "Resisting the Melting Pot: The Long Term Impact of Maintaining Identity for Franco-Americans in New England." Unpublished.

70. Borjas, George. 1994. "Long-Run Convergence of Ethnic Skill Differentials: The Children and Grandchildren of the Great Migration." *Industrial and Labor Relations Review*, 47(4): 553–573.

71. Bean, Frank, Gray Swicegood, and Ruth Berg. 2000. "Mexican-Origin Fertility: New Patterns and Interpretations." *Social Science Quarterly*, 81(1): 404–420.

72. Del Pinal, Jorge. 2004. *Race and Ethnicity in Census 2000*. Census 2000 Testing, Experimentation, and Evaluation Program: Topic Report No. 9. U.S. Census Bureau. Washington, DC: U.S. Government Printing Office.

73. Emeka, Amon. 2008. "Who are the Hispanic Non-Hispanics and Why Do They Matter? Toward a More Inclusive Definition of the Hispanic Population." Unpublished.

74. Akerlof, George, and Rachel Kranton. 2000. "Economics and Identity." *Quarterly Journal of Economics*, 115(3): 715–53.

75. Bisin, Alberto, and Thierry Verdier. 2000. " 'Beyond the Melting Pot': Cultural Transmission, Marriage, and the Evolution of Ethnic and Religious Traits." *Quarterly Journal of Economics*, 115(3): 955–988.

76. Darity, William, Jr., Darrick Hamilton, and Jason Dietrich. 2002. "Passing on Blackness: Latinos, Race, and Earnings in the USA." *Applied Economics Letters*, 9(13): 847–53.

77. Bisin, Alberto, Giorgio Topa and Thierry Verdier. 2004. "Religious Intermarriage and Socialization in the United States." *Journal of Political Economy*, 112(3): 615–664.

78. Mason, Patrick. 2004. "Annual Income, Hourly Wages, and Identity among Mexican-Americans and Other Latinos." *Industrial Relations*, 43(4): 817–834.

79. Darity, William, Jr., Patrick Mason, and James Stewart. 2006. "The Economics of Identity: The Origin and Persistence of Racial Norms." *Journal of Economic Behavior & Organization*, 60(3): 283–305.

80. Constant, Amelie, Liliya Gataullina, and Klaus Zimmermann. 2006. "Gender, Ethnic Identity and Work." Institute for the Study of Labor (IZA) Discussion Paper 2420.

81. Bodenhorn, Howard, and Chistopher Ruebeck. 2007. "Colourism and African-American Wealth: Evidence from the Nineteenth-Century South." *Journal of Population Economics*, 20(3): 599–620.

82. Manning, Alan, and Sanchari Roy. 2007. "Culture Clash or Culture Club? The Identity and Attitudes of Immigrants in Britain." Centre for Economic Performance, London School of Economics and Political Science Discussion Paper 790.

83. Nekby, Lena, and Magnus Rodin. 2007. "Acculturation Identity and Labor Market Outcomes." Institute for the Study of Labor (IZA) Discussion Paper 2826.

84. Constant, Amelie, and Klaus Zimmermann. 2007. "Measuring Ethnic Identity and Its Impact on Economic Behavior." Institute for the Study of Labor (IZA) Discussion Paper 3063.

85. Zimmermann, Klaus. 2007. "Migrant Ethnic Identity: Concept and Policy Implications." Institute for the Study of Labor (IZA) Discussion Paper 3056.

86. Jaeger, David. 1997. "Reconciling the Old and New Census Bureau Education Questions: Recommendations for Researchers." *Journal of Business and Economics Statistics*, 15(3): 300–309.

87. Xie, Yu, and Kimberly Goyette. 1997. "The Racial Identification of Biracial Children with One Asian Parent: Evidence from the 1990 Census." *Social Forces*, 76(2): 547–570.
88. Qian, Zhenchao. 2004. "Options: Racial/Ethnic Identification of Children of Intermarried Couples." *Social Science Quarterly*, 85(3): 746–766.
89. Logan, John. 2002. "Hispanic Populations and Their Residential Patterns in the Metropolis." Lewis Mumford Center Report, State University of New York at Albany.
90. Cresce, Arthur, and Roberto Ramirez. 2003. "Analysis of General Hispanic Responses in Census 2000." U.S. Bureau of the Census Population Division Working Paper 72.

About the Editors

David L. Leal is an Associate Professor of Government and Director of the Irma Rangel Public Policy Institute at the University of Texas at Austin. His primary academic interest is Latino politics, and his work explores a variety of questions involving public policy, public opinion, and political behavior. He has published over 40 journal articles and book chapters on these and other topics. He is also the co-editor of *Beyond the Barrio: Latinos and the 2004 Elections* (2010), *Immigration Policy and Security* (2008), and *Latino Politics: Identity, Mobilization, and Representation* (2007). He is a member of the editorial boards of *American Politics Research*, *Social Science Quarterly*, and *State Politics & Policy Quarterly*. He was an American Political Science Association Congressional Fellow from 1998 to 1999 and a Spencer/National Academy of Education Post-Doctoral Fellow from 2002 to 2004. He received his B.A. from Stanford University and Ph.D. from Harvard University.

Stephen J. Trejo is an Associate Professor of Economics at the University of Texas at Austin. His research focuses on public policy issues involving labor markets, including overtime pay regulation, the experiences of immigrants, and obstacles to the economic progress of minority groups. Much of Dr. Trejo's recent work analyzes patterns of intergenerational improvement among Mexican Americans, and one strand of this work explores how selective intermarriage and ethnic identification might bias standard measures of socioeconomic progress for the US-born descendants of Mexican immigrants. He holds a B.A. from the University of California, Santa Barbara, and a Ph.D. in economics from the University of Chicago.

D.L. Leal, S.J. Trejo (eds.), *Latinos and the Economy*, Immigrants and Minorities, Politics and Policy, DOI 10.1007/978-1-4419-6682-7,
© Springer Science+Business Media, LLC 2011

About the Contributors

Mevlude Akbulut-Yuksel is an Assistant Professor of Economics at Dalhousie University and a Research Affiliate of the Institute for the Study of Labor (IZA). She received her Ph.D. in Economics from the University of Houston and her B.S. in Economics from METU, Turkey. Her main research focuses on labor and development economics. She has been especially interested in educational and health policies, and migration. Her current research explores the impacts of childhood environment on long-run human capital accumulation and health.

Dr. Catalina Amuedo-Dorantes is currently Professor of Economics at San Diego State University and a Research Fellow at CReAM and IZA. She has been a visiting scholar at the Institute for Research and Poverty at the University of Wisconsin, Madison, and at the Public Policy Institute of California. Her areas of interest include labor economics, international migration, and international finance, and she has published on contingent work contracts, the informal work sector, immigrant saving, international remittances, and immigrant health care.

Hoyt Bleakley is an Associate Professor of Economics at the University of Chicago, Booth School of Business. His research focuses on human capital. Recent work considers the role of English-language skill in the assimilation of childhood immigrants to the United States, and the impact of childhood health on lifetime income. He obtained his Ph.D. in Economics from MIT. He has also been a Research Associate at the Federal Reserve Bank of Boston and an Assistant Professor at the University of California at San Diego.

Aimee Chin is an Associate Professor of Economics at the University of Houston. She received her A.B. from Harvard University and her Ph.D. in Economics from MIT. Professor Chin's research is in the fields of labor and development economics, focusing on the effects of human capital investments. Current work has been on language and immigrant assimilation, and educational policy. She is a research fellow of the National Bureau of Economic Research (NBER).

Alberto Dávila is currently Professor of Economics and V.F. "Doc" and Gertrude Neuhaus Chair for Entrepreneurship at the University of Texas–Pan American. Since January 1997, he has also served as Department Chair for the Department of Economics and Finance at UTPA. Before joining UTPA in 1996, Dávila was a tenured faculty member at the University of New Mexico. He earned his Ph.D. degree in economics from Iowa State University in 1982; he also has an M.S. degree in economics from Iowa State and a B.A. degree in economics from UTPA. Dávila's research interests include the economics of the US-Mexico border, the economics of immigration, and Hispanic labor markets.

Brian Duncan is an Associate Professor of Economics at the University of Colorado Denver. His research focuses on the economics of generosity, specifically examining the conflicting motives individuals have for contributing to charitable causes. Professor Duncan has also written on the economic incentives of foster care and adoption, and on the inter-generational progress of the descendants of Mexican immigrants. He holds a Ph.D. in economics from the University of California, Santa Barbara.

Richard Fry is a senior research associate at the Pew Hispanic Center in Washington, DC. A demographic economist, Fry possesses expertise in the analysis of established US education, labor market, and language datasets. He pursues an empirical research agenda on Latino educational, economic, and social outcomes. Fry's research focuses on the value and development of productive skills, particularly among Hispanic youth populations. His research has been published in numerous journals, including the *American Economic Review, Industrial and Labor Relations Review,* and *Contemporary Economic Policy.* At the Pew Hispanic Center, Fry recently authored *The Rapid Growth and Changing Complexion of Suburban Public Schools*, an examination of the implications of minority student enrollment growth in suburban school districts. Fry is currently examining the prevalence of GED certification in minority high school completion, as well as the relationship between educational attainment and marital outcomes. Fry earned his Ph.D. at the University of Michigan.

Arturo Gonzalez is a transfer pricing consultant at Ernst & Young. From 2004 to 2007, he was a research fellow at the Public Policy Institute of California. Prior to 2004, he was an Associate Professor at the University of Arizona and a visiting professor at University Carlos III in Madrid. His research interests include the acquisition of human capital by low-skilled workers and immigrants, including studies on the effect of the Job Corps on earnings of Hispanics and non-Hispanics and the role of ESL classes in the English proficiency of adult immigrants in California. His publications include *Mexican and Americans and the U.S. Economy: Quest for Buenos Días* (2002). He received a Ph.D. in economics from the University of California, Santa Barbara, in 1997 and received an award from that university for the best dissertation in the social sciences from 1996 to 1998.

Chinhui Juhn is the Henry Graham Professor of Economics at the University of Houston. She holds a B.A. from Yale University and a Ph.D. in Economics from the University of Chicago. Professor Juhn's research has focused on US wage inequality and the impact of changing wage structure on employment and unemployment of male workers as well as its impact on the racial wage gap. Her current work examines issues in family labor supply such as the co-movement of couples' employment over the business cycle and over the lifecycle. Her most recent project examines the impact of HIV/AIDS on fertility decisions in Africa. Professor Juhn is a fellow of the National Bureau of Economic Research (NBER) and Institute for the Study of Labor (IZA).

Adriana Kugler is currently a Full Professor of Public Policy at Georgetown University. She previously taught at the University of Houston, University Pompeu Fabra, at the University of Western Ontario, and at the University of the Andes. Adriana earned her Ph.D. from the University of California at Berkeley in 1997 and her B.A. from McGill University in Canada in 1991. In 2007 she received the John T. Dunlop Outstanding Scholar Award from the Labor and Employment Relations Association. Her work on labor and development economics has been published in a variety of professional journals, such as the *Review of Economics and Statistics*, the *Economic Journal*, the *Journal of Labor Economics*, the *Journal of Public Economics*, the *Journal of Development Economics*, the *International Tax and Public Finance* Journal, the *Journal of Policy Reform*, and the *IMF Staff Papers*. Her work has been featured in *The Economist* magazine and in various issues of the World Bank's and Inter-American Development Bank's annual publications and in the OECD's Employment Outlook. Adriana is Associate Editor of the *Economia* Journal, *Labour Economics*, and the *Applied Economics Quarterly Journal,* and she is on the International Advisory Board of the *British Journal of Industrial Relations*. Adriana was a member of the executive committee of the European Association of Labour Economics for 6 years. She is a Research Associate at the NBER, and a Research Fellow of the CEPR, CReAM, IZA and of the Center for the Study of Poverty and Inequality at Stanford University.

Francesca Mazzolari is an Assistant Professor of Economics at the University of California, Irvine. She received her Ph.D. in economics from the University of California, San Diego, in 2005. Her research and teaching interests are in labor economics, public economics, and the economics of immigration. Her work has focused on US wage inequality, the effects of the 1996 US welfare reform on take-up rates for cash transfer programs, and the determinants of immigrant naturalization.

Marie T. Mora is Professor of Economics at The University of Texas–Pan American (UTPA). She is also serving her second term as President of the American Society of Hispanic Economists, and she is on the Editorial Board of *Social Science Quarterly*. Prior to UTPA, Dr. Mora was a tenured faculty member at New Mexico State University. She earned her Ph.D. in economics from Texas A&M University, and B.A. and M.A. degrees (also in economics) from the University of New Mexico in her hometown of Albuquerque. Dr. Mora's research interests are in labor economics, particularly regarding Hispanic labor-market outcomes, the economics of the US-Mexico border, and the economics of language. She has published over 25 refereed journal articles on these topics, and her first book, *Labor Market Issues* *along the U.S.-Mexico Border* (co-authored/co-edited with Alberto Dávila), was published by the University of Arizona Press in 2009.

Max Neiman received his Ph.D. at the University of Wisconsin, Milwaukee, and taught for over three decades at the University of California, Riverside. He is currently Senior Fellow and Associate Director at the Public Policy Institute of California, located in San Francisco. Dr. Neiman has published in a wide variety of political science and interdisciplinary journals on such topics as urban politics, land use and growth controls, energy conservation, and immigration. He is the author of *Defending Government: Why Big Government Works* and together with Paul Lewis has completed a book manuscript entitled *Custodians of Place.* He is currently working on a project examining how concern among non-Hispanic whites about immigrants and immigration affects public support in general for a variety of public services.

Curt Nichols is an Assistant Professor of Political Science at Baylor University. His primary research interests include American political institutions, American political development, and politics and the military. In 2008, he won the APSA Presidency Research Group's Best Paper by a Graduate Student award for his *American Politics Research* article "Exploiting the Reconstructive Opportunity: Presidential Responses to Enervated Regimes" (with Adam Myers). He received his Ph.D. from the University of Texas at Austin in 2009.

Pia Orrenius is Research Officer and Senior Economist at the Federal Reserve Bank of Dallas and Adjunct Professor at the Hankamer School of Business, Baylor University. Her research focuses on the economics of immigration, illegal immigration, and US immigration policy, and her work has been published in the *Journal of Development Economics*, *Labour Economics, Industrial and Labor Relations Review,* and *Economic Theory,* among others. Dr. Orrenius is a Research Fellow at The Tower Center for Political Studies at Southern Methodist University and at the Institute for the Study of Labor in Bonn. She was senior economist on the Council of Economic Advisers in the Executive Office of the President, Washington D.C. in 2004-2005. She received her Ph.D. in economics from the University of California at Los Angeles and B.A. degrees in economics and Spanish from the University of Illinois at Urbana-Champaign.

Belinda I. Reyes is the Director of the César E. Chávez Institute and Assistant Professor of Raza Studies in the College of Ethnic Studies at San Francisco State University. She was formerly a Founding Faculty member at the University of California, Merced, and a Research Fellow at the Public Policy Institute of California. Her research examines policy issues in the areas of immigration, education, social and economic progress, inclusion and the political representation of racial and ethnic groups in the United States. Her publications include *Holding the Line? The Effect of the Recent Border Build-up on Unauthorized Immigration*; *Taking the Oath: An Analysis of Naturalization in California and the United States*; *A Portrait of Race and Ethnicity in California: An Assessment of Social and Economic Well-Being*; and *Preschool Enrollment Among Latino Children in*

California. She has been a senior program associate at PolicyLink; lecturer at the University of California, Berkeley; a research fellow at the University of Michigan; and a visiting scholar at the Federal Reserve Bank of San Francisco. She holds a B.S. in economics from the University of Illinois at Urbana-Champaign and a Ph.D. in economics from the University of California, Berkeley.

Albert Saiz is an Assistant Professor in the Wharton School at the University of Pennsylvania. He received his Ph.D. in economics at Harvard University. Prior to joining the University of Pennsylvania, Saiz worked as an economist at the Federal Reserve Bank of Philadelphia. His research is at the intersection of urban, labor, and population economics, with an emphasis on immigration and immigrant location choices, housing prices, as well as the determinants of city growth and urban revitalization.

Jeremy M. Teigen is Associate Professor of Political Science at Ramapo College in New Jersey. His research and teaching interests include elections, voting behavior, voter turnout, and military service. He has published articles in *Armed Forces & Society*, *Political Research Quarterly*, *Social Science Quarterly*, *Political Communication*, *Political Geography*, and *European Security*, as well as a chapter in Reveron and Stiehm (Eds.), *Inside Defense: Current Controversies in U.S. Civil-Military Relations* (Palgrave-Macmillan, 2008). He received his Ph.D. from the University of Texas at Austin in 2005.

Mutlu Yuksel is currently a Research Associate at IZA in Bonn, Germany. He received his Ph.D. in Economics from the University of Houston in 2007 and a B.S. Degree in Economics from METU in Turkey in 2000. His main research interests include labor and population economics, migration, and ethnicity. He has been mainly working on the effects and integration of immigrants and minorities.

Madeline Zavodny is a Professor in the Department of Economics at Agnes Scott College in Decatur, Georgia, and a Research Fellow of the Institute for the Study of Labor in Bonn, Germany. She received a Ph.D. in economics from the Massachusetts Institute of Technology and a B.A. in economics from Claremont McKenna College. She has been an associate professor of economics at Occidental College, a senior economist and policy advisor with the Federal Reserve Bank of Atlanta, and an economist with the Federal Reserve Bank of Dallas. Her research on the economics of immigration has been published in the *Journal of Labor Economics*, *Journal of Development Economics*, *Demography*, *Research in Labor Economics*, *Georgetown Public Policy Review*, and *Population Research and Policy Review*.

LaVergne, TN USA
16 December 2010
208868LV00001B/48/P